FOR JOBS AND FREEDOM

FOR JOBS AND FREEDOM

Race and Labor in America since 1865

Robert H. Zieger

THE UNIVERSITY PRESS OF KENTUCKY

Publication of this volume was made possible in part by a grant from the National Endowment for the Humanities.

Editorial and Sales Offices: The University Press of Kentucky
663 South Limestone Street, Lexington, Kentucky 40508-4008
www.kentuckypress.com

11 10 09 08 07   5 4 3 2 1

Frontispiece: African American picket captains at Ford's River Rouge plant, 1941. (Walter P. Reuther Library, Wayne State University)

Library of Congress Cataloging-in-Publication Data

Zieger, Robert H.
  For jobs and freedom : race and labor in America since 1865 / Robert H. Zieger.
    p. cm.
  Includes bibliographical references and index.
  ISBN 978-0-8131-2460-5 (hardcover : alk. paper)
  1. African-Americans—Employment—History. 2. Discrimination in employment—United States—History. 3. African American labor union members—United States—History. 4. Labor unions—United States—History. 5. Race discrimination—United States—History. 6. United States—Race relations—History. I. Title. II. Title: Race and labor in America since 1865.
  HD8081.A65Z54 2007
  331.6'396073—dc22
                        2007011032

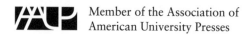

For Robert—
Never for money
Always for love.
　　　　　—The Talking Heads

CONTENTS

Acknowledgments ix

Introduction 1

1. The First Fruits of Freedom 9

2. Into the New Century 43

3. Great War, Great Migration 70

4. Race and Labor in Depression and War 106

5. Race and Labor in the Postwar World 139

6. Affirmative Action and Labor Action 175

7. Back to the Future 208

Notes 235

Bibliographical Essay 255

Index 267

ACKNOWLEDGMENTS

The idea for this book grew out of a project with which I was associated in 1998. That spring, Elsie Allen, president of the North Central Florida Central Labor Council, asked me to work with her and her colleagues to bring the AFL-CIO's A. Philip Randolph Traveling Exhibit to Gainesville. Over several months, with the help of a grant from the Florida Humanities Council, union members from the Gainesville area worked with people at the Matheson Historical Center and with my colleagues at the University of Florida and at the Center for Labor Research and Studies at Florida International University to arrange for and promote the exhibit. We also held a series of forums on themes of race and labor in U.S. history, and I taught a community course in labor history that coincided with the exhibit. In addition, the Florida AFL-CIO held its annual legislative conference in Gainesville that year. As part of the two-month-long series of programs, I had the good fortune to appear on a panel that included Anthony Hill of Jacksonville, then a state representative and leader in the state AFL-CIO.

Although it took me a couple of years to decide to write a book on race and labor in modern America, it was this exhibit and the related activities that provided the initial spark. Thus, first I want to thank the folks with whom I worked on that project. Elsie Allen, state senator Anthony Hill, my graduate assistant Anders Lewis, and members of the wonderful Randolph exhibit coordinating committee are at the top of the list. In 2001, when the American Federation of Teachers and the state National Education Association merged in Florida, I was appointed faculty union delegate to the Labor Council. Serving on it has been a deeply rewarding experience from which I learned much. So thanks to Butch, Zot, Tom, Gunnar, Carol, Brian, Rick, Matthew, Pat, Jean, Emmitt, and all the others who fight the good fight, often in inhospitable circumstances.

Thanks, too, to fellow scholars who provided advice, shared information and materials, and offered needed encouragement. From the beginning of the project, and at several critical junctures along the way, I benefited from discussions with Tim Minchin, drawing on his remarkable fund of knowledge. LeRoy Ashby read large sections of the manuscript with his usual acuity. Joe McCartin was helpful in steering me through the complex issues surrounding public employee unionism. Nancy MacLean kindly let me see the prepublication manuscript of her important book on affirmative action. The University Press of Kentucky's readers, Alex Lichtenstein and Kevin Boyle, provided shrewd and helpful commentary. I thank my colleagues and students at the University of Florida for their support and forbearance.

Steve Wrinn merits special mention. His enthusiasm for this project has been infectious. I'm not sure what I value more, his editorial judgment or his friendship. I am fortunate to have the benefit of both.

I am also much indebted to photographic archivists. Steve Roberts at Georgia State, Tom Featherstone at Wayne State, Erika Gottfried at the Wagner Labor Archives, Adam Watson at the Florida State Archives, Carolyn Marr at the Museum of History and Industry in Seattle, and Barbara Morley at the Kheel Center at Cornell guided me through the complicated processes, both technical and legal, involved in publishing images. John Haynes explained the Library of Congress's mystifying photo identification and ordering system. Joe McCartin and Tim Minchin helped me acquire key photographs. I am also grateful to Leamon Hood for sharing a picture of the 1977 Atlanta sanitation workers' strike and to Richard Copley for granting permission to use his splendid picture of the Memphis sanitation workers' walkout. Anne Dean Watkins and Richard Farkas at the University Press of Kentucky deserve special thanks for their good advice and patience.

In everything that I do, my greatest debt is to my friend, my partner, my good wife, Gay.

INTRODUCTION

Istill have a hard time confessing that I didn't stay for Dr. King's speech. As far as I was concerned, civil rights was a matter of politics and morality, not religion. Anyway, I had parked a long way off, it was getting late, and I had to pick up my wife at the Prince Georges County bank, where she worked. As I threaded my way back through the throng lining the Reflecting Pool, across the Washington Monument grounds, up along Pennsylvania Avenue, the speakers' voices grew fainter. I had parked on one of the side streets off East Capitol Street, behind the Library of Congress (my normal haunt in those dissertation-writing days), so I made my way through the Capitol grounds. It occurred to me that I should find some souvenir of the March on Washington, something to prove to my progeny and to the students to whom I would one day teach U.S. history that I was there. The discarded orange-and-black placard lying behind a low hedge would do the trick, even if it did have a slight tear. "The UAW Says Jobs and Freedom for Every American," it read. Since my ambition was to be a labor historian, it seemed the perfect choice.

But I must admit that I hadn't really thought much about the "jobs" part. Civil rights was about public accommodations, voting rights, and schools.[1] Certainly, demonstrators in southern towns and cities had demanded employment in the stores and shops. But it was the classrooms, the voting booths, and the hotels and restaurants that made the biggest headlines. Of course, an instant's reflection affirmed that the placard was dead right: without jobs, freedom was a coin of limited value. Jobs were the modern equivalent of the Reconstruction era's forty acres and a mule—and we all know what happened when the freedmen were denied title to the land that they and their forebears had worked for generations. Yes, it was true: this was indeed about jobs and freedom.

For Jobs and Freedom rests on two basic assumptions and explores two central themes. The assumptions are (1) that it is appropriate for a study of

1

race and labor in modern America to focus on the experiences of African Americans and to consider other racial and ethnic groups in terms of their relationship to black workers, and (2) that labor unions are legitimate—indeed, necessary—components of a free and democratic society. The two basic themes, both of which flow from these assumptions, are (1) the struggles of African American workers to attain full citizenship, in the workplace as well as in the polity, and (2) the relationship between the labor movement's egalitarian ideology and its racial practices.[2]

Focusing on the experiences of African American workers is appropriate because of their distinctive history and because of the extent to which African Americans have always been regarded—and still are regarded—as "other." It is true that other distinctive ethnic and racial groups have faced discrimination and hardship. Only African Americans, however, were slaves; only African Americans had to endure more than a hundred years of the systematic denigration known as Jim Crow. The special and inferior status of African Americans was established at the beginning of the United States' existence as an independent nation, as asserted in the Constitution and embodied in the Naturalization Act of 1790. The nineteenth-century debate over slavery was a debate about black labor. Questions about the economic, political, and legal status of African Americans dominated the Civil War era. Among discrete ethnic and racial groups, only African Americans have been the specific subject of constitutional amendments.

Over the past decade, labor and race historians have been debating the theme of "whiteness" as it relates to the history of ethnicity in the United States.[3] Discussion has centered on the degree to which various immigrant and minority groups were considered "white" and on the process by which they "became" white. Although this subject has generated sharp exchanges, both sides affirm that blackness was the negativity that defined whiteness. All this work, including the commentary by critics such as Eric Arnesen, accepts as a basic premise that African Americans have been regarded as "other," or nonwhite, throughout American history. Sociologist George Yancey, in *Who Is White? Latinos, Asians, and the New Black/Nonblack Divide*, develops this same theme, projecting it into the next half century.[4]

To be sure, for more than a hundred years, Asians, and especially Chinese, were singled out for particularly harsh and racist treatment. The meager protections available to African Americans by virtue of the Fourteenth and Fifteenth Amendments did not apply to Asians, who were ineligible for citizenship. Clearly, Latinos also suffered degrading treatment, economic exploitation, and political isolation, as ably documented by historical scholarship. In both cases, however, circumstances distinguished Asians and Latinos from African Americans. At any given time between the 1870s and the 1950s, relatively few Asians lived in the United

States, largely because of the draconian immigration laws passed between 1882 and 1924. The Chinese population of the United States, such as it was, was concentrated in a few urban centers, mostly on the West Coast, with smaller communities scattered along the western railroad routes and in mining centers. Once the legal status of Asians had been established, their place in the political and economic order rarely entered into the national political discourse.[5]

From the Mexican War of 1846–1848 to the 1960s, most of the Latino population of the United States had its origins in Mexico. Although it is true that in Texas and elsewhere in the Southwest, Anglo cultural and political authorities erected legal and social barriers against Chicanos reminiscent of Jim Crow, these were usually more sporadically enforced and monitored than was the case in Alabama and Mississippi. Latinos in Texas and California served in economic roles broadly similar to those of their black counterparts in the Southeast, but segregation was less rigid, and the boundaries between claimed ethnic identities were more permeable. Nowhere, even in rural Texas, did the presence of Latino communities evoke the degree of repression and exclusion that virtually all African Americans endured. Far more than African Americans, residents of both Hispanic derivation and Asian origin had representatives of sovereign nations, with which the United States generally sought friendly relations, to monitor and sometimes protest their treatment.[6]

Differences in the status and public regard accorded to African Americans in comparison with other once-despised racial and ethnic groups remain very much in force. According to recent polling data, "black exceptionalism" has retained its potency among whites and is particularly noticeable among Hispanics and Asian Americans. African American economist Glenn Loury, no friend of affirmative action, has stressed the tenacity across the entire nonblack ethnic spectrum of the distinctive "otherness" imputed to blacks. Whites' resentment of affirmative action and preferential hiring policies has focused almost exclusively on black recipients; those polled registered little antagonism toward other beneficiaries, whether Hispanic, Asian, or female. Despite a softening of racial attitudes in the past fifty years, in virtually every area of American life, Americans of all nonblack ethnic identities have singled out African Americans as less worthy than people of other races or ethnicities. White potential home buyers show no concern over the presence of Latinos or Asians in a neighborhood but express significantly negative views when blacks are present. Indeed, John Skrentny, a leading student of the contemporary politics of race, cites one persuasive study that "found that even greater percentages of Latinos and Asians than Euro-Americans wished to live in neighborhoods with no blacks at all." Survey after survey has revealed employers' preference for Asian and Latino workers over African Americans. Blacks have had by far the lowest rates of interracial marriage in comparison with other ethnic groups, and Skrentny notes, "There is the simple but little-noticed fact that only blacks are defined by the one-drop rule that means any black ancestry at all makes a person black," while persons of mixed Latino-white or Asian-white parentage are ordinarily able to select their own racial identity. As novelist Toni Morrison put it in 1973, "the move into mainstream America always means buying into the notion of American blacks as the real aliens. Whatever the ethnicity or nationality of the immigrant, his nemesis is understood to be African American."[7]

The second major assumption of *For Jobs and Freedom*—that a strong and autonomous labor movement is a legitimate and essential component of a democratic society—requires a brief explanation. For much of the century after the end of the Civil War, no domestic issue aroused more passion and public debate than the "labor question." In one sense, the labor question involved a wide range of subissues, such as poverty, immigration, disparities of wealth and power, unemployment, and the health and safety of working people. For most, however, the labor question revolved around workers' efforts to form unions for self-protection and employers' efforts to resist unionization in the name of freedom of contract and industrial efficiency. The slow and sporadic rise of a strong trade union movement, culminating in the emergence of mass unions in the country's central manufacturing, transport, and mining industries in the 1930s and 1940s, brought organized labor into the heart of the nation's economic and political life. In the post–World War II decades, armed with an ideology that the labor movement was intrinsically a force for social justice and with a determination to improve the living standards and reduce the insecurity of industrial workers and their families, newly invigorated unions helped promote the sustained economic expansion and create the social safety net that characterized the postwar period. For a generation, labor leaders such as John L. Lewis, Philip Murray, Walter Reuther, George Meany, and César Chàvez advanced a worker-centered program of political economy that resonated powerfully both in the nation's workplaces and in the voting booths. Over the past twenty-five years, however, the once-potent labor movement has been on the defensive, struggling to come to terms with a rapidly changing economic base, shifting demographic patterns, and a political environment hostile to collective action on the part of workers. Even so, with sixteen million members, the labor movement of the early twenty-first century remains a significant factor in American life, perhaps nowhere more so than in the political arena, where its alliances with women's, civil rights, and even environmental organizations, along with its considerable financial and organizational resources, make it a still-potent force.

Defense of organized labor as a positive factor in American life arouses little argument among most practitioners of labor history. Indeed, for most participants in the boom in labor historiography over the past generation, the problem with the labor movement is that it has been neither strong nor autonomous enough. But in another part of the academic universe, there are many for whom the beneficial presence of labor unions is far from axiomatic. Historians of a free-market orientation, though in the minority in the fields of labor, race, social, and gender history, have produced studies that challenge labor historians' general default in favor of unionism. Of particular note is the work of David Bernstein and Paul Moreno, both of whom see organized labor's often unedifying historical record with respect to workplace racial issues as being rooted in its fundamental illegitimacy as a cartel-seeking and inefficiency-producing special interest.[8]

Most of this critique of unions or the labor movement or organized labor, however, focuses on the activities of the railroad brotherhoods and the building trades' craft unions, particularly as they functioned before the 1950s. Both free-market advocates and civil rights advocates have had no difficulty establishing the role that race played in enabling these unions to restrict the labor supply and create job trusts that excluded blacks, as well as other minorities and women. Critics have amply documented the role played by legislatures and governmental agencies in validating and reinforcing race-based discrimination. They have been less willing, however, to acknowledge that, for the most part, black workers have sought entry *into* the labor movement and, when faced with exclusion by white unions, have sought to create their own unions. Free-market critics likewise find the post–World War II political alliance between organized labor and the civil rights movement, with all its difficulties and internal disagreements, difficult to explain.

By no means are all the critics of labor's racial record doctrinaire free-market advocates, however. Indeed, some of the most stinging criticisms have come from ardent civil rights advocates, many of whom at least initially regarded labor as an ally in the African American freedom struggle. Until his death at age eighty in 2005, Herbert Hill, labor secretary of the National Association for the Advancement of Colored People (NAACP) between 1951 and 1977 and afterward a prominent academic and journalistic commentator, endlessly called attention to the gap between organized labor's egalitarian rhetoric and its actual practices. Committed to the legitimacy of collective action in the achievement of social and racial justice, scholars such as William Gould, Bruce Nelson, Michael Goldfield, and David Roediger have nonetheless emphasized the strains of racism and hypocrisy that they believe have characterized dominant elements in the labor movement—and among the white working class more generally—throughout American history.[9]

For Jobs and Freedom acknowledges these criticisms of organized labor. At the same time, I see it as playing a more complex and, in the end, more edifying role than either free-market or collective-action critics posit. I see organized labor as having a workplace and civic role distinct from its econometric functions. Whereas free-market economists and their historical counterparts see unions exclusively as a means by which workers seek market-distorting wage advantages, *For Jobs and Freedom* is particularly attuned to the role that unions claim in fostering workplace equity and civic engagement. For example, the building trades unions, operating in a notoriously dangerous sector of the economy, negotiated closed-shop agreements in part to ensure that plumbers, ironworkers, electrical workers, and other tradesmen would work with trained fellow craftsmen and thus enjoy a safer workplace. Coal miners sought and gained state regulations restricting entry into the man-killing mines; railroad unions used collective bargaining to attempt to curb the industry's appalling toll of dead and injured. The problem with discriminatory closed-shop agreements and discriminatory municipal licensing laws was not that they regulated the workplace. It was that they discriminated.

Free and potent unions also reflect workers' desire for protection from arbitrary treatment, unfair disciplinary proceedings, and punitive or incoherent personnel policies. Opponents of organized labor and of governmental intervention in labor markets contend that *in the long run,* unfair and ruthless employers suffer from the alienation of their labor force. Even they, however, must acknowledge that the long run can be very long indeed, as Ford Motor Company workers of the 1910s, 1920s, and 1930s could (and did) testify.

Throughout modern American history, black labor activists have combined a critique of "free" labor markets with advocacy of collective action, either in collaboration with whites or, when necessary, apart from them. As A. Philip Randolph and other black labor activists knew, the logic of "free" labor markets leads to competition for jobs, whether along racial lines or on the basis of some other factor. The resulting "rush to the bottom" encourages—indeed, often compels—wage reductions, deteriorating health and safety conditions, and job insecurity. Only by organizing could workers hope to moderate these corrosive features of private enterprise. Black workers no less than their white counterparts knew that "moral capitalism"[10] was too important to be left to the capitalists, especially those whose fixation on short-range profit rendered them heedless of social and human costs. Those who stress the connection between jobs and freedom and who believe that only through principled social activism is progress possible must, in the end, come to terms with the admittedly ambiguous history of the labor movement.[11]

The purely econometric view of the role of unions ignores organized labor's relationship to the broader civic life of the nation. Discussion of politics is restricted to unions' efforts to establish and defend monopoly privileges. Organized labor has consistently supported expansion of the suffrage, expansion of educational opportunities, and, at least since the 1930s, every important initiative in civil rights. The World War II Fair Employment Practice Committee and Titles VI and VII of the Civil Rights Act of 1964—which were supported by organized labor but opposed by most large employers—were thus sensible public policies designed to rectify injustices while leaving untouched the main body of wage, safety, and union recognition legislation that undergirded collective bargaining. Although it is true that labor activists have foregrounded public issues of specific concern to unions, it is also true that the labor movement has led the way in countless voter registration drives, civic education programs, and community forums.

Indeed, the current crisis in health care and pension shortfalls illustrates how organized labor's ability to speak for large numbers of workers and their families can contribute to more rational and enlightened public policies. In the uncertain economic circumstances of the globalized present, the limitations of employer-provided health and pension benefits are becoming increasingly evident. General Motors staggers under the weight of retiree pensions and health care costs as it struggles to compete with foreign firms whose workers can rely on publicly provided benefits. Sixty years ago, Walter Reuther and other labor advocates tried—on the whole, unsuccessfully—to educate their corporate bargaining partners about the dangers of employer-specific benefits and enlist them in the campaign to broaden New Deal pension and health care programs. Failing that, Reuther negotiated the best plans he could, expecting that eventually even the most antigovernment employers would see the logic of public provision. Remarks Malcolm Gladwell, "It has taken half a century, but the world may finally be catching up with Walter Reuther."[12]

In short, although debate over the economic role of trade unions is necessary, the labor movement has never rested its claims for public recognition and worker loyalty on bread-and-butter promises alone. *For Jobs and Freedom* regards the labor movement's relationship to the democratic polity as crucial to its historic mission. Clayton Sinyai captures this critical aspect of organized labor, past and present: "one of the central . . . concerns of the American labor movement [has been] . . . educating working people for democratic citizenship." Unions and laborite political organizations, he continues, have been (and are) "not just engines of economic betterment but of civic education" as well. They have aspired to be "schools of democracy," and continue to do so.[13] Hence, any consideration of the theme of race and labor in modern America must have at its heart the relationship between organized labor's egalitarian civic claims and its complex—and, it must be said, often disappointing—engagement with the country's profound racial dilemmas.

For Jobs and Freedom traces its two central themes—blacks' struggles for equity and inclusion, and organized labor's compromised egalitarianism—through historical narrative. It embraces the period from the abolition of slavery to the present, with a glance back at the antebellum period and a nod toward the future. Its seven chapters are organized chronologically, although chapters 6 and 7, dealing with the very recent past, are somewhat overlapping. Throughout the book, my challenge has been to make use of the energy and aspirations of my personal commitment to both the labor movement and the cause of civil rights while crafting a historical narrative that meets high standards of objective scholarship and intellectual honesty. Since that day in August 1963 when I didn't stay to listen to the greatest public speech of the twentieth century, I have signed a lot of petitions, attended a lot of meetings, voted in a lot of elections, and written some checks. For the most part, however, I have spent my time in libraries and classrooms, pondering, with the help of my colleagues and students, the connections between race and labor in modern America. In the end, it is the story of the struggle that continues to inspire me, both as a student and as a citizen. We still have a long way to go, but there is always the hope that one day we will indeed have jobs and freedom for every American.

1

THE FIRST FRUITS OF FREEDOM

During the last decades of the nineteenth century, the American people embarked on a vast social experiment. Three and a half million former slaves, previously excluded from the civil economy, now joined a free working class, itself undergoing a dramatic transformation. The formal ending of slavery in December 1865 specified no particular political, legal, or social status for the freedmen. Even the great constitutional amendments of 1865–1870 and the Reconstruction-era civil rights laws left key aspects of blacks' status and circumstances unclear. Throughout the first postbellum generation, the role that former slaves would play in the nation's labor force, their relationship to former masters and to fellow workers, and the place of blacks in the labor movement remained ill defined and open to sharp and sometimes violent contestation.

By the end of the nineteenth century, African Americans had become trapped in a subordinative, repressive, and discriminatory economic and racial order, victimized in both North and South by popular attitudes and legal structures. Soon after the Civil War's conclusion, freedmen's dreams of land acquisition died. A regime of agricultural labor characterized by chronic indebtedness and, at best, limited opportunities for self-improvement prevailed. On the land, in the mines, on the building sites, and in the kitchens and laundries, black wage workers toiled in the most hazardous, least desirable, and lowest-paying jobs. The vast majority of black farmers labored as sharecroppers and tenants on land owned by whites. Selective application of harsh penal statutes forced thousands of African Americans into coerced labor in the mines, in construction gangs, and in the pine forests.

Even so, during the bleak postemancipation decades, black workers and farmers continued to struggle for inclusion in the free producing class, and not always fruitlessly. Against the odds, the proportion of black farmers who owned the land they tilled slowly increased. Rising literacy rates and a vigorous black press and civil and religious institutions helped give voice to the aspirations and grievances of African Americans. Agricultural workers, longshoremen, miners, and other African American workers joined together to protect their economic and civil rights. For the most part, the struggles of black farmers and workers to gain recognition as citizen-producers enjoyed little support from their white counterparts and, indeed, often aroused their hostility, but significant episodes of biracial activism provided an intriguing, and some thought hopeful, counterpoint to the otherwise bleak tale of racial victimization.

Visions of Labor

Although contemporary discussion and subsequent historical accounts of the postbellum period often focus on political, legal, and constitutional issues, the labor question lay at the heart of Reconstruction. "'You will find,'" declared one South Carolina planter in late 1865, "'that this question of the control of labor underlies every other question of state interest.'"[1] Northern politicians and reformers, southern whites, and the freedmen themselves advanced sharply divergent views about the role and status of the former slaves and their place in the political economy of work. Southern planters and their political allies grudgingly acknowledged the death of slavery but were determined to maintain tight labor controls. Blacks, they held, would not work except under compulsion; they could not be trusted to work autonomously, nor should they be encouraged to entertain hopes of upward mobility. For most white southern landholders, as well as for many northerners eager to resume the profitable prewar trade in southern cotton, the successful revival of the war-ravaged South's agricultural economy necessitated closely supervised gang labor to ensure faithful and efficient work. For southern planters, effective labor discipline entailed corporal punishment. In the absence of coercion, declared one planter, "The negroes work [only] when they please . . . and rely largely upon hunting and fishing" for sustenance. There was only one conclusion: "Labor must be commanded completely, or the production of the cotton crop must be abandoned." A federal agent summarized the common opinion among Mississippi planters in the summer of 1865: "Every planter . . . premised his statements with the assertion that 'a nigger won't work without whipping.'"[2] This being the case, southern whites moved rapidly at the end of hostilities to impose slavelike conditions that featured corporal punishment, insistence on a deferent and servile demeanor, and closely supervised labor gangs, just as they had before the war.

Northern political and reform leaders rejected this approach even though they shared the desire to rebuild the cotton-based economy of the South. The victory of the North represented not only the victory of the Union; it was the victory of "free labor" as well. The promise of American life lay in the opportunity for men of all stations and races to advance through diligent labor and sober habits. Abraham Lincoln himself had spelled out the formula: "The prudent, penniless beginner in the world labors for wages awhile, saves a surplus with which to buy tools or land . . . ; then labors on his own account," eventually employing others who, in turn, replicate the process.[3] "In ninety-nine cases out of every hundred greatness is achieved by hard, earnest labor and thought," declared the editors of *Harper's Weekly.* Degraded conditions among African Americans, argued free-labor advocates, were the result of slavery; free labor would end them. Far from being congenitally feckless and improvident, freedmen embodied this free-labor doctrine. At a time when increasing numbers of workers in the North were flooding into the factories, southern blacks' overwhelming commitment to agriculture indicated that they would be in a unique position to advance from wage labor to farm ownership, as the free-labor ideal envisaged. Northern white workers joined unions and waged strikes. Lazy southern whites had grown dependent on slave labor. But freedmen, in the view of one representative northern newspaper, were "humble, but self-reliant; teachable . . . anxious to learn. . . . Their ambition," the *Cincinnati Daily Gazette* declared, "is to buy, with their own hard-earned dollars, a little piece of land that they can call their own."[4] Thus, the triumphant North was obliged, in this view, to promote the free-labor ideal by disallowing the restrictive legislation—the "Black Codes"—that southern states adopted in the immediate aftermath of war. Federal troops and civilian authorities occupying the defeated South would curb corporal punishment and insist that landowners pay fair wages.

At the same time, fearful that newly freed slaves would lack the incentive to maximize their cash income, free-labor advocates felt obliged to instruct freedmen about the virtues and obligations of free labor. To this end, in March 1865, Congress created the Bureau of Refugees, Freedmen, and Abandoned Lands—known commonly as the Freedmen's Bureau—to oversee the immediate welfare of former slaves, to promote education, and to put free-labor ideas into practice throughout the former Confederacy. Its director, General O. O. Howard, told a group of expectant blacks in 1865 that the bureau "would promise them nothing but freedom, and freedom means work." Other northern free-labor advocates even more sternly stressed the obligations of freedmen and their families to obey their employers, put aside idle dreams of landownership, and embrace the gospel of hard and disciplined labor.[5]

What of the freedmen themselves? Throughout the postwar years, they advanced distinctive notions of moral economy and asserted the rights due them as victims of slavery and as defenders of the Union. Rejecting both slavelike compulsion and the narrow calculus of profit and loss implicit in the free-labor formulation, most freedmen hoped to gain autonomous access to land so that they could engage primarily in subsistence farming, with at most a modest involvement in the risky cash-producing markets for agricultural goods. Smallholdings, either individually owned or cultivated through self-directed cooperatives, would free them of daily contact with former masters and other whites; provide the social space necessary for the building of schools, churches, and other civil institutions essential for personal and racial advancement; and undergird their exercise of newly gained civil and political rights. And even before the fighting had stopped, former slaves began efforts to realize these goals.

To be sure, some southern blacks, especially younger men, implicitly accepted the free-labor agenda by working for wages on construction projects, in urban trades, and on farms. To an extent, then, these men quickly became part of an emerging multiracial American working class, although for many of them, wage work was a short-term strategy, with landownership or at least farm tenancy the eventual goal. A handful, generally drawn from the lighter-skinned ranks of prewar free Negroes, pursued individual success and mobility through entrepreneurial endeavor, political ambition, professional development, or a combination of these activities. These men became part of the emerging southern black middle class, deemed by free-labor advocates to be the bedrock of a progressive and republican political and social order, and often serving as the articulate voice of the ill-educated black working masses.

The vast majority of former slaves, however, clung to a vision of the future centered around subsistence farming. Former slaves, black newspaper editors, clergymen, and politicians asserted that simple justice dictated some sort of compensation for two centuries of slavery and for African Americans' military contribution to the preservation of the Union. Only widespread black landownership, African Americans believed, could make real the exercise of newly granted civil and personal rights. "This is our home," declared former slaves in South Carolina in a petition to President Andrew Johnson in the fall of 1865; "we have made these lands what they are." Without title to the holdings that they and their ancestors had worked for two centuries, "we cannot feel our rights Safe." Indeed, claimed a Virginia freedman, those who had toiled under slavery and had flocked to the colors during the war had "a divine right to the land."[6]

In fact, freedmen's hope that Reconstruction would include a distribution of land to former slaves quickly died, but they insisted on a sharp departure from the work regimes that had prevailed during slavery. In the wake of war, they had little choice but to enter into individual contracts with landowners, specifying tasks, compensation, and other details. Increasingly, they were successful in compelling planters to agree to arrangements by which each black farmer worked a particular section of the farm, living with his family in separate quarters. They resisted corporal punishment, abandoning landlords who refused to acknowledge their rights and who continued to attempt to control their personal and family lives. Former slaves everywhere strove to keep women and children out of the fields, where, under slavery, they had toiled as a matter of routine. Planters lamented these changes in plantation routine, predicting disastrous declines in production, but freedmen's labor was so crucial to southern agriculture that they were largely successful in limiting landowners' power. Everywhere, freedmen–cum–plantation employees insisted on specific compensation for tasks such as fence mending, equipment repair, and animal tending that were not directly connected with the cultivation of crops.

Farmers, Sharecroppers, and Agricultural Laborers

The exact means by which freedmen pursued an autonomous life differed in the several major agricultural areas of the South. Those who had toiled on cotton farms and plantations—the largest category of former slaves—sought individual farms of their own, free from white supervision and discipline, preferably through landownership (which was rarely achieved). Alternatively, they insisted on various sharecropping and tenant farming arrangements to obtain at least a degree of autonomy, and they refused to work in gangs or endure close scrutiny of their personal lives.

When former slaves in Louisiana's Sugar Belt were thwarted in their desire for individual holdings, they found a source of strength in group labor arrangements to carry out the complex and capital-intensive cultivation and processing of sugarcane. They insisted, however, that they—not their former owners or other planters—be the ones to form up the work gangs, ensuring that these groups would be mutualistic and cohesive. In the distinctive circumstances of southern Louisiana, gang labor encouraged worker solidarity, both in the fields and in the freedmen's communities. For two decades after the end of the war, these cohesive work arrangements encouraged the assertion of labor rights, political activism, and even military mobilization.

On the Sea Islands and lowlands of South Carolina and Georgia, former slaves had cultivated abandoned plantations even during the war, initially with the support of federal authorities. When the government ruled that former owners who took an oath of loyalty were entitled to have their land restored, freedmen fought back, resisting their ouster. The Freedmen's Bureau, which was required to enforce the land restoration, had to call on the U.S. Army—including black regiments—to evict the former slaves. Though thwarted in their attempt to keep the land that they and their ancestors had cultivated for almost two centuries, African Americans in the coastal regions insisted that the special advantages they had gained with respect to relatively unsupervised work routines, access to hunting and fishing land, and cultivation of individual plots be continued, often in violation of the competitive dicta of free labor. Indeed, in some districts along the South Carolina–Georgia border, freedmen were able to force nominal landowners to concede a sort of de facto proprietorship of the land.

In the first three years following the end of the war, former slaves, southern whites, and government officials advanced their competing visions of agricultural labor in the former Confederacy. Military officers and Freedmen's Bureau officials sought to educate both freedmen and their white employers about the meanings and obligations of a free-labor regime. They insisted that planters abandon corporal punishment, which they regarded as incompatible with free labor, and cease efforts to direct the personal lives of their former chattels. At the same time, however, they regarded the prompt revival of staple crop production as critical not only to the rebuilding of the southern economy but also to the economic health of the entire country. For the most part, they were unsympathetic to former slaves' claims for small, individual landholdings, fearing that such arrangements would lead to mere subsistence farming and retard the revival of cash-producing crops such as tobacco, rice, cotton, and sugar. Thus, most northern politicians and reformers upheld the right of former slave owners and other planters to reclaim their land and to employ African Americans to work on it, now as wage earners. They insisted that former slaves sign yearly labor contracts, specifying wages and conditions, on an individual basis. Agents of the Freedmen's Bureau acted as advisers to both planters and freedmen in the drafting of these documents and as arbiters in disputes arising out of their application. To planters, bureau agents counseled restraint and fair dealing; to former slaves, they urged hard and faithful service, frugal habits, and abandonment of hope for a quick redistribution of land. Typical was the advice that the bureau's Virginia representative offered to former slaves there in June 1865. He admonished them not to expect largess from the federal government or to expect former masters "to provide for you in sickness and old age." Freedmen "must be industrious and frugal," he said, and he urged former slaves to avoid agitation and strife. "Be quiet[,] peaceable, law abiding Citizens," he counseled.[7]

Throughout the South, freedmen responded to the realities of free labor with a combination of resentment and resignation. Bitterness over what former slaves believed were broken promises festered. Wrote a newly freed slave to General Howard in 1866, "'we were friends on the march'" and "'brothers on the battlefield, but in the peaceful pursuits of life it seems that we are strangers.'" A lifetime later, another freedman recalled, "'De slaves spected a heap from freedom dey didn't git. . . . Dey promised us a mule and forty acres o' lan','" but delivered only admonitions to work hard and obey former masters.[8] In all, a series of confused and contradictory federal programs that initially seemed to prom▬idespread land redistribution resulted in fewer than 100,000 former slaves gaining title to land, and usually to marginal and isolated holdings that were difficult to farm profitably and difficult to retain in the face of surrounding white hostility to evidence of black advancement.

Bitter disappointment over federal land policies, however, did not preclude an energetic defense of blacks' new civil and political rights. Into the mid-1870s and, in some places, well beyond, former slaves formed the core of an aroused black electorate that sent scores of African Americans to state legislatures and to the U.S. Congress. In most of the former Confederate states, blacks—many of them former slaves and current sharecroppers—held local offices and served as local law enforcement officials. In a few areas, African Americans were able to assert citizenship rights and to resist at least some aspects of mounting oppression and victimization in the political and legislative arenas until the dawn of the twentieth century. Especially during the heyday of Reconstruction, which lasted until 1877 in some states, African Americans, in an alliance with Republicans and reform-minded whites, kept alive the egalitarian legal and political status promised by the Fourteenth and Fifteenth Amendments and by federal civil rights laws.

Although black-supported Reconstruction legislatures were able to enact laws to establish public schools that were open to black children, and local judicial and law enforcement authorities were often able to protect blacks from fraud and violence, it proved nearly impossible to translate political power into direct economic benefit for former slaves. With whites, both former slave owners and those who had the resources to acquire property, holding secure titles to their land, freedmen were powerless to challenge underlying employment relations. Even at the peak of black political power in the early 1870s, African Americans understood the odds against their dream of translating freedom into self-sufficient landholding. "'We've got no chance,'" a freedman mourned in 1871, "'the white people's arms are longer than ours.'"[9]

In effect, throughout the South, black agricultural workers came to an uneasy but enduring set of understandings with their employers. The most common pattern, particularly in the cotton region of the Deep South, was that of sharecropping. In this arrangement, the sharecropper and his family lived on the plantation in a separate domicile. He tilled a plot of around forty acres planted in cotton, typically following the owner's general instructions as to the timing of the crop, fertilization of the soil, and the like, but free to tend the crop without daily intervention. Although freedmen generally resisted planters' efforts to require family members to work in the fields, the truth was that cotton growing under the conditions of tenant farming and sharecropping depended heavily on the toil of women and children. Even young children were assigned the relentless task of weeding the cotton crop, and croppers' families were routinely pressed into service during the harvest season. Wives and daughters raised chickens, sold eggs, tended kitchen gardens, and hired out as domestic servants, laundresses, and child minders.

Legally, the crop belonged to the landowner, who paid the farmer an agreed-upon portion of the proceeds from the sale of the cotton, normally one-third to one-half, depending on what tools or animals the farmer himself provided. Farming on these smallholdings was hard and tedious. Planting, with the aid of a mule and a steel-tipped plow, was backbreaking work. Cotton fields required continual hoeing, or "chopping," to keep the abundant weeds at bay. The equally ubiquitous insect population also required constant vigilance in a day before the common use of insecticides. During the midsummer growing season, there might be time for fishing and hunting, not as leisure sports but as a means of providing for the family, but it was also the time for croppers to repair fencing and equipment, clear new ground, and perform other tasks at the behest of the landowner, often on a cash-per-task basis.

In the fall, given good weather and cooperative insects, the crop would be ready for harvesting and processing. Harvest season, of course, was a critical time, with every family member enlisted in the picking. The trick was to tear the puffy cotton bolls free without taking the stems or leaves as well, and avoiding the cuts and abrasions that the wiry stalks and tough leaves inflicted. Stooped over to reach the thigh-high plants, the men, women, and children trudged slowly down the rows of plants under the hot southern sun and stuffed the bolls into increasingly heavy shoulder sacks, anxious to get the crop in lest killing overnight frosts or torrential downpours reduce the yield.

Under the direction of the planter or his manager, the groaning sacks of cotton were checked for debris and their contents loaded onto farm wagons. At the end of the picking season, a steady stream of farm vehicles made their way to the cotton gins and presses. Hand-operated rakelike machines combed through the raw cotton, pulling out the embedded seeds, which were pulverized to make cottonseed oil, a valuable lubricant and fertilizer. Then the cotton itself was sent to the press, where a screwlike device formed it into bales that were then bound and bundled for market. At the cotton market—held in county seats or crossroads towns throughout the South's Black Belt—factors and merchants inspected the baled cotton and announced the prices they were willing to pay.

Once the cotton was sold, it was time for the planter to settle up with his croppers. Whereas renters paid a flat annual fee for the use of the land, croppers received a prearranged percentage of the final proceeds, minus deductions for goods purchased from the owner's store and other advances. These calculations were crucial and often contested. Many a sharecropper watched helplessly as his employer toted up a mounting column of debts against his share of the crop, only to find that after a year of backbreaking toil he was owed a pittance or even remained mired in debt, which would be carried over to the next year's reckoning. Charges of fraud and chicanery were rife. Croppers typically had little education or knowledge of accounting with which to refute dishonest or inaccurate tabulations. Moreover, in a southland increasingly characterized by racial violence, any display of anger toward an employer or suggestion of his dishonesty risked swift punishment. "'It don't make a speck o' difference'" how many bales he raised, muses an elderly sharecropper in Arna Bontemps's story "A Summer Tragedy": "'If we get much or if we get little, we still gonna be in debt to old man Stevenson when he gets through counting up agin us.'"[10]

The life of a sharecropping family was harsh and impoverished. Throughout the late nineteenth century, cotton prices fell, responding in part to increased worldwide cultivation; they reached a low of 4 cents a pound in 1894 (compared with 28 cents in 1860) before rebounding modestly in the years before World War I. Low prices, of course, meant shrunken incomes and mounting debts, even in a time of general deflation. With annual cash incomes often dropping below $100, croppers typically lived at the margins, eating monotonous and unnourishing food; suffering from chronic diseases such as tuberculosis, hookworm, and pellagra; and having little access to education, public services, or cultural amenities. Early in the twentieth century, a survey of living conditions reported that croppers' houses "are often unspeakable." Typically consisting of only one room and with no sanitary facilities either indoors or out, they were hastily constructed, often from green timber, unpainted, prone to warping and leaking, and presented "a bare and uninviting appearance." "It is in these cabins," noted a government agent, "that families, sometimes large ones, with the added company of several dogs, live."[11]

On some holdings, a small kitchen garden yielded corn, tomatoes, and other vegetables to supplement the family's diet, while a few chickens supplied eggs and meat. The nearby woods and streams might also yield game and fish. Many landowners, however, discouraged garden plots, urging or compelling their croppers and tenants to maximize the acreage and devote their time to cash-producing cotton. On virtually all large-scale farming operations, much of the clothing, food staples, and general work and household items had to be purchased, usually on credit, from a nearby store operated by a merchant or, in many cases, by the planter himself. Indeed, planters sometimes made more profits from selling goods to croppers and tenants than they did from cotton itself. And even when this was not the case, chronic indebtedness kept croppers virtually tethered to the same land year after year and thus increasingly unable to buy their own land or resist their employers' demands and directions.

Despite the hardships and injustices of the sharecropping system, some black farmers were able to realize a version of the free-labor ideal. Ruthless underconsumption, the exploitation of family labor, good luck, and high cotton prices might yield a cash surplus. The ambitious farmer could then pay off his debts, buy a mule, and command more advantageous terms in next year's contract, either with the same landlord or with another. A string of successful crops might enable the cropper or tenant to buy land, and by 1910, about one-quarter of black farmers were landowners, most of them in the upper and coastal South. Rising literacy rates, flourishing churches, successful black business ventures, and a vigorous civic culture within the African American community provided further evidence of the advance of former slaves and their heirs. By certain measures, then, as the new century dawned, the experiment in freedom seemed to be successful.

Even so, the gains that black farmers made were sharply limited. Few blacks achieved landownership in the rich cotton lands of the Black Belt that stretched from Georgia to Arkansas. Most black-owned farms were on more marginal lands in the upper and coastal South, where black farmers often had to supplement the yield from their modest holdings with outside labor or sharecropping on more substantial white-owned spreads. White or black, southern agriculture was notoriously inefficient, lagging both in mechanization and in the application of scientific knowledge. The productivity of southern farms dropped sharply after the Civil War, resulting in poorer nutrition, declining human fertility, rising levels of debilitating disease, and higher infant mortality—afflictions that hit rural blacks particularly hard.

Even modest success brought danger. Black achievement seemed to threaten both white elites and ordinary folks. Successful black farmers provided positive role models for croppers and tenants but also engendered dissatisfaction with their subservient lot. Evidence of black prosperity threatened to disrupt the supply of cheap, tractable labor both on the farms and in the households of white elites. Economic success might fuel blacks' political aspirations, while whites in the South were rapidly disfranchising African Americans, regardless of education or economic standing. Black success threw into sharp relief the poverty and failure that many lower-income whites experienced in the economically troubled South. As one African American teacher noted, when a successful black farmer presumed to build a substantial house for his family, "the whites advised him not to paint it, so he took their advice, which conduced to his personal safety."[12]

Still, as poor and inefficient as southern agriculture was, it provided a living of sorts for millions of farmers—both black and white—and their families. The census of 1910 revealed, for example, that about three-quarters of the South's African Americans toiled in agriculture, about 60 percent of them in sharecropping or tenant arrangements. These men, women, and children occupied an ambivalent place in the overall American working class. In most southern states, the law regarded croppers as wage workers whose compensation happened to be paid in the form of crop shares. However, their mode of life and worldview contrasted with those of typical industrial wage workers. Croppers worked individual holdings and exhibited some of the attributes of proprietorship. They had a positive stake in the success of the crop, since the more it earned, the larger the family's income. Unlike the classic proletariat, whether industrial or agricultural, croppers had a personal connection with the means of production—the land—and typically an individual relationship with the landlord, who often adopted a paternalistic attitude toward his tenants. As late as World War I, the vast majority of southern blacks were rural people whose aspirations for a better life centered on landownership and successful farming—goals that were achieved often enough for them to be a powerful motivational force, even among the impoverished and debt-ridden. In general, the distinctive features of sharecroppers' lives encouraged individual solutions to problems, rather than the collective activism associated with industrial workers.

Nonagricultural Labor in the Postwar South

The presence of several million poor and struggling rural workers had significant implications for all southern workers. The poverty and marginality of croppers and tenants meant that they and their families constituted a sort of reserve labor force that was available for employment in nonagricultural settings. The low income levels of rural southerners, both black and white, translated into a low wage structure in the factories and on the construction sites as well. Although rural life and agricultural hopes kept the great majority of African Americans on the farms, a slow but perceptible drift of folks into southern cities and into nonagricultural occupations was evident. For example, in Georgia, one of the most populated southern states, the urban black population almost doubled between 1890 and 1910, while the proportion of black rural dwellers in the state declined 5.5 percent during the same period.

In 1910, one black Georgian worked in manufacturing, mechanical trades, domestic service, transportation, and other nonagricultural pursuits for every two farmers, croppers, tenants, and farm laborers. African Americans found work on construction gangs, on the railroads as both firemen and maintenance men, as longshoremen in Gulf and Atlantic coast ports, and in a variety of urban trades. In both cities and rural areas, black women and girls were employed as child minders, cooks, washerwomen, and general domestic servants, as well as in food and tobacco processing.

In this work, as was the case in agriculture, African Americans toiled in the hardest, most dangerous, and least well compensated occupations. On the railroads, for example, the elite jobs of conductor and engineer were reserved for whites, while much of the hard work of construction, tracklaying, and track maintenance and repair devolved on blacks. Some blacks worked as firemen, a position that in other parts of the country served as a kind of apprenticeship for those aspiring to the position of engineer. In the South, however, black firemen were rigidly excluded from advancement and were perpetually consigned to the hot, heavy work of keeping the firebox stoked. In fact, southern white engineers regarded their firemen as servants, expecting them to run personal errands, fetch food and drink, and generally tend to the needs of their white superiors. Even so, white railroad workers, seeing the route to advancement in a generally well-paid occupation blocked by blacks working as firemen, waged ongoing campaigns, often involving personal violence, to drive African Americans from the cabs. In the railroad repair shops, black men worked only as helpers and laborers, as whites controlled access to metalworking and other crafts. Even when black workers, in their capacity as helpers or assistants, acquired the requisite skills, their employers, white workers, and white-dominated craft unions kept them from advancement.

In the towns and cities, black craftsmen and artisans faced similar problems. During slavery, some plantation workers and urban slaves had acquired skills such as carpentry, shoemaking, and tailoring, but a variety of forces conspired in the postemancipation era to undermine the development and expansion of the black skilled labor force. Whites' determination to retain a tractable and subordinate labor force on the farms operated in industry and nonfactory work as well. "The slave artisan," as W. E. B. DuBois, a brilliant and pioneering African American scholar and activist, acknowledged in a 1902 study, "was a jack-of-all-trades rather than a mechanic in the modern sense of the term. . . . The average workman was poor, careless and ill-trained, and could not have earned living wages under modern competitive conditions."[13] With vocational education programs, apprenticeships, and a generally nurturing environment, freedmen might have moved steadily into the ranks of skilled labor—a springboard for progressive development. Instead, African American craftsmen could usually ply their trades only within the black community. Employers on major construction projects hired even skilled black workers as only helpers and laborers, and most unions in the building trades barred them from membership.

Some of the new industries of the "New South," promoted by boosters of southern progress, provided employment opportunities of a kind for African Americans. By the 1890s, for example, blacks filled almost 90 percent of the jobs classified as "unskilled" in Birmingham's iron mills. Attracted to the "Pittsburgh of the South" by the lure of high and steady wages, young black men from the rural areas were a crucial element in the iron and steel mills that arose in the 1870s in north-central Alabama. African Americans performed the hot, dirty, dangerous tasks. They toiled, for example, as "top fillers" at the blast furnaces, perched high above the ground amid toxic gases and in extreme heat, shoveling iron ore into the furnace hopper. Blacks did a variety of dangerous jobs, such as regulating the flow of molten iron, using heavy sledges and crowbars to break up encrusted iron, and lifting and hauling iron bars weighing at least a hundred pounds each to railroad cars. Said one iron industry engineer, "the extraordinary muscular exertion required [in iron breaking] bars four-fifths of the laboring class" from these jobs.[14]

But African Americans could not advance into the skilled ranks. Capitalists seeking to exploit Alabama's coal and iron ore deposits had to recruit skilled workers from northern mills. These proud craftsmen bowed to no one in their disdain for blacks. Competition from black workers, declared a labor newspaper, "degraded labor, degraded workmen, [and created] a condition wholly foreign to republican institutions." Convinced that employers would attempt to use black labor to undermine white workers' wages and status, metal trades unions barred African Americans from membership in local lodges. Typical was the announcement of a Birmingham boilermakers' lodge that it would recruit only "white, free-born male citizens of some civilized country."[15]

The new cotton textile mills that began to dot the piedmont regions of the Carolinas were even more discriminatory. Although African Americans could find unskilled jobs in and around the rolling mills and blast furnaces, employer policy, white resistance, and local custom excluded them almost entirely from the textile mills. Textile entrepreneurs advertised mill work as being suitable employment for white women, relatively few of whom had traditionally worked outside the home or the family farm. Gilded Age employers followed the pattern established in the southern textile industry even before the Civil War. Observed an English visitor in 1849, "The masters of these factories hope by excluding colored men . . . [they will] render it a genteel employment for white [female] operatives."[16] The new mills, employers promised, would offer safe and respectable employment in modern surroundings. Late in the century, when union activism among cotton textile workers threatened to disrupt mill operations, employers began to experiment cautiously with black labor. After all, said one manufacturer, the Negro worker "is absolutely loyal to his employer, he is not given to strikes," and an antiunion South Carolina newspaper noted with satisfaction that "the colored man is now knocking at the door of cotton mills asking for work at lower wages than white men would think of."[17] But in a white South increasingly gripped by the fear of miscegenation and "race mixing," some of the most militant and successful job actions on the part of white textile workers were triggered by these tentative efforts to tap into the cheap labor pool that African Americans represented. Thus, African Americans were confined to a small number of ancillary and custodial jobs in the rapidly expanding mills.

Black Workers and the Labor Movement

In the late nineteenth century, the United States developed a multiracial working class, despite the racial antagonisms that divided workers. Its diverse members worked in close and often overlapping proximity. Although there were distinct occupational, spatial, and economic attributes that coexisted with racial and ethnic categories, men of black, Asian, European, and Native American background often toiled at common work sites. On the railroads, in the iron and steel mills, on the docks, and in the mines, blacks and whites often performed similar jobs, although the status and compensation attached to them followed the color line. There were no intrinsic demarcations as to which jobs were "white" and which ones were "black," although at any given moment, white workers might define certain work as being fit only for "inferiors" (i.e., blacks), only to reclaim those jobs during periods of economic downturn. In some cases, white workers drove blacks out of formerly despised occupations, such as the caulking of wooden ships. At the same time, it was all too clear that African Americans constituted a ready supply of replacement workers to take the jobs of dissatisfied or striking white workers. Throughout the late nineteenth century, the American working class's white majority was torn between regarding these racial "others" as deadly competitors for employment and public standing and thinking of them as fellow workers in a common struggle to achieve rising material standards and civic identity.

The historical experiences and political and religious values of white working people pointed simultaneously in both directions. In one sense, white American workers shared fully in the country's long history of racial exclusivism. The American Republic was, in the view of many, a white man's republic. Native Americans were swept aside, and blacks were bound into slavery. In the mid-nineteenth century, immigrants from Ireland and Germany faced contempt and hostility from those born in the United States, while people of Spanish and Mexican descent struggled against even more savage prejudice and disdain. Chinese laborers who drifted into California in the 1840s and 1850s suffered relentless victimization.

Special contempt and dislike were reserved for African Americans, however. "The black man," wrote Chief Justice Roger B. Taney in 1857, in the explosive *Dred Scott* decision, "has no rights that a white man is bound to respect." Indeed, "The American people," declared one antislavery advocate, "are emphatically a *Negro hating* people."[18] The rough and aggressive working-class culture that flourished in antebellum northern cities often defined itself in terms of whiteness. Blacks were the "others"—servile, unmanly, unworthy to associate with real Americans; blacks were the very embodiment of the dependency and subordination that white workers, increasingly vulnerable during the country's lusty but volatile mid-nineteenth-century economic transformation, hated and feared. In 1834, white rioters in one Pennsylvania town beat the community's handful of black residents and drove them from their homes to protest the employment of African Americans in jobs that had formerly been the monopoly of whites. They charged that employers and do-gooders were trying "to break down the distinctive barrier between the colors" and feared that "the poor whites may gradually sink into the degraded condition of the Negroes— that, like them, they may be[come] slaves and tools."[19]

Even working-class opposition to slavery rarely focused on injustice to the bondmen. In general, as workingmen and labor unions became aware of the implications of the expansion of slavery, they grew increasingly vocal in opposing the machinations of the "slave power" that allegedly controlled the federal government and imposed such pro-slavery outrages as the 1854 Kansas-Nebraska Act and the *Dred Scott* decision. But rarely was this hostility toward slavery couched in terms of the brotherhood of all toilers or sympathy for the slaves themselves. Typical was the manifesto adopted by New Jersey labor advocates in protest over the passage of the Kansas-Nebraska Act, a measure that opened up vast swaths of territory in the Midwest to settlement by slave owners. The resolution pointed to "the bold attempts of the Slave Power . . . to degrade the laboring and producing classes . . . by establishing its system of chattel labor in the Free Territories of the West." It said nothing about the moral horror of slavery, nor did it appeal to African Americans to enlist in freedom's common cause. Instead, the aroused laborites pledged to "repel . . . [any] efforts to introduce the black slaves into our workshops."[20]

But more generous and egalitarian notions were also present. Americans proclaimed ideals of equality and celebrated individual achievement. After all, the Declaration of Independence proclaimed that "all men are created equal and are endowed by their Creator with certain inalienable rights." To assert, as Taney had done, that blacks were not included in the Declaration was to start down a slippery slope indeed. As Abraham Lincoln said in 1855, "As a nation we began by declaring '*all men are created equal.*'" Defenders of slavery insisted that "we now practically read it 'all men are created equal, *except negroes.*'" And if the anti-Irish and anti-Catholic bigots had *their* way, it would "read 'all men are created equal, except negroes, *and foreigners, and Catholics.*'" Were the American people to follow that path, Lincoln continued, "I should prefer emigrating to some country where they make no pretence of loving liberty . . . , where despotism can be taken pure, and without the base alloy of hypocrisy."[21]

Although the white working class often expressed hatred of blacks, egalitarian notions of workers' rights sometimes surfaced. For example, antislavery sentiment flourished among the thousands of young women who worked in the New England textile mills. John Greenleaf Whittier's poem "The Yankee Girl," published in 1837, depicts a spirited young woman spurning a southern suitor whose wealth derived from a slave plantation:

> Full low at thy bidding thy Negroes may kneel,
> With the iron of bondage on spirit and heel,
> Yet know that the Yankee girl sooner would be
> In fetters with them than in freedom with thee.

In 1830, Massachusetts trade unionists submitted this "Workingmen's Prayer" to the state legislature: "May the foul stain of slavery be blotted out . . . ; and may our fellow men . . . enjoy that freedom and equality to which they are entitled by nature."[22] Some labor activists groped toward a more inclusive notion of class identity, understanding that failure to reach across the racial barrier would fatally weaken the labor movement. Moreover, in the crisis of the Civil War, northern workers—whatever their mixture of motives—filled the regiments that eventually brought emancipation and laid the basis for racial equality with the passage of unprecedented postwar civil rights measures.

In the immediate aftermath of the Civil War, labor activists paid little attention to the problems of the freedmen. Until 1865, the vast majority of black toilers had been slaves with no direct connection to the trades such as shoemaking, printing, textile work, railroading, and metalworking that formed the heart of the mid-nineteenth-century labor movement. The most consistently expressed sentiment regarding the role of African Americans in the labor force was apprehension over the competition for jobs and wages that an influx of blacks into the North might bring. Though imbued with racialist sentiments, the labor movement did not project a consistently race-based definition of workers' rights and interests. And some prominent labor activists and advocates even reached out to African Americans in the name of worker solidarity. Thus, fabled union organizer Richard Trevellick urged northern unions to repudiate racial exclusion, while abolitionist Wendell Phillips described the postwar struggle for labor rights as an extension of the crusade to end slavery. Abolitionists, he insisted, had fought to free "the *black* laborer, and now we are going to protect the Laborer, North and South, labor everywhere." But despite Trevellick's pleas, many unions did exclude blacks, and fear over possible low-wage competition trumped the social vision of men such as Phillips.[23]

The deliberations and actions of the first national labor federation, the National Labor Union (NLU), founded in 1866–1867, reflected postwar labor's confusion. On the one hand, the organization's founding document, *The Address of the National Labor Union Congress to the Workingmen of the United States,* urged every trade union "to help inculcate the grand ennobling idea that the interests of labor are one; that there should be no distinction of race."[24] Meanwhile, in Massachusetts, labor reformers also reached out to African American workers. "The brotherhood of labor is universal," reformer and activist Ira Steward proclaimed, "and embraces all classes of workingmen of every degree and color." The embryonic socialist movement voiced egalitarian ideals, and American Marxists called for erasure of the color line. In New York City they sought to organize black workers, collaborating with nonsocialists in city and state organizations in that effort. From London, Karl Marx himself hailed the first evidences of biracial unionism, declaring that "Labour cannot emancipate itself in the white skin where in the black it is branded."[25]

On the other hand, even the NLU's founding document admitted that many white workers regarded the new status of Negroes as "unpalatable." The annual conventions of the short-lived NLU refused repeatedly to endorse antidiscrimination resolutions, and individual trade unions often barred blacks from membership. Thus, although their ideology posited the theoretical virtues of inclusiveness, in fact, many laborites in the immediate postwar era practiced exclusion and hostility toward African Americans.

For their part, African American workers in both North and South looked to labor organization as well. In December 1869, Isaac Myers, a freeborn Marylander who had spearheaded a successful cooperative effort to create jobs for black workers in the Baltimore shipbuilding trades, presided over the creation of the National Colored Labor Union (NCLU). From its inception, the NCLU wavered uncertainly between political and trade union strategies and between cooperation with and estrangement from the NLU and other white-only labor bodies. Welcoming unskilled as well as craft workers, and open to women, the NCLU was at least in theory the most inclusive early postbellum American labor organization. As the organization's first leader, Myers stressed the illegitimacy of job discrimination, the expansion of educational opportunities for newly freed slaves, and the need to find common ground with employers, whose success would provide jobs for black workers. In the early 1870s, Myers conducted successful organizing campaigns in Washington, D.C., and Virginia, always holding out hope that the NLU and the NCLU could cooperate in the effort to raise the standards of all workers. Politically, however, the NCLU—

whose most vocal activists included large numbers of ministers, merchants, and politicians—was committed to supporting the Republican Party, which blacks understandably saw as the only plausible instrument for the protection of African American rights in the southern states. NLU leaders, though sometimes giving lip service to the doctrine of equal rights, refused to challenge the discriminatory policies of the affiliated unions. Their often virulent anticapitalist rhetoric and their flirtation with inflationist third-party campaigns alienated both black workers and black elites, making effective cooperation between the two labor organizations problematic at best. Although the NCLU was as much a political organization as a trade union, and the capable Myers rejected the hard-line class consciousness embraced by the NLU trade unionists, this short-lived movement was an example of the appeal of union organization to many black workers.

Neither the National Labor Union nor the National Colored Labor Union survived the devastating depression that began in 1873. Although strikes and demonstrations rumbled through the remainder of the decade, the revival of labor organizations did not begin in earnest until the early 1880s. The most remarkable evidence of renewed activism was the sudden expansion of a once marginal secret society, the Noble Order of the Knights of Labor (KOL), that had been founded in 1869 but had barely clung to life through the depression years. Exploiting widespread worker dissatisfaction with working conditions, wage rates, and high-handed employers, the KOL expanded rapidly through the mid-1880s, winning several spectacular strikes and achieving a membership of three-quarters of a million by 1886. The KOL was less a coherent, agenda-driven labor organization than a repository of the hopes, aspirations, and grievances of large numbers of American workers. The rapid pace and uneven performance of industrial capitalism created a widely shared sense of grievance and resentment and seemed to make a mockery of the promises of upward mobility made by the free-labor ideology. The arbitrary ways that employers tried to change long-standing work practices and to step up the pace of production triggered resistance. During this deflationary period, wage reductions were frequent. And underlying this discontent with specific workplace practices was a smoldering hostility toward the emerging industrial regime, with its increasingly hierarchical methods of management and its growing disparities of wealth and poverty, which seemed to vitiate America's promise of justice and equality.

The KOL tapped into this volatile mixture of grievances, resentments, and mistrust. Although its leadership preached cooperation and moderation, thousands of men and women, using the KOL as a vehicle for their protest, did not hesitate to wield the strike weapon. In important respects, the KOL's vision of an egalitarian producer republic that could somehow redirect the headlong rush to corporate capitalism looked backward to an allegedly simpler and more humane time.

At the same time, however, the KOL's vision of labor activism embraced all workers, regardless of craft, gender, or race. Owing in part to the Christian egalitarianism and abolitionist heritage of some of its early leaders, and in part to a shrewd understanding of the need for worker solidarity in the face of employers' "divide and rule" tactics, the KOL rejected the racial exclusivism of many of the trade unions. "We should be false to every principle of our Order," declared the KOL newspaper in 1880, "should we exclude from membership any man who gains his living by honest toil, on account of his color or creed. Our platform is broad enough to take in all."[26] In fact, the Knights were far from consistent in their egalitarian assertions. In particular, they refused to organize Chinese workers and even sanctioned worker agitation against Asian labor. But with respect to African Americans, the KOL compiled a broadly positive record of organizing black workers and affording some leadership positions.

The star of the KOL fell almost as rapidly as it had risen. After it reached its peak membership in 1886, it began a quick descent. Always more a diverse movement of local unionists and other activists than a cohesive national organization, the KOL fell victim to its own administrative confusion and internal conflicts, savage employer counterattacks, and poorly coordinated strikes. By 1890, this once promising experiment in all-embracing unionism had entered a period of long and eventually terminal decline.

But the fading of the KOL did not mean the demise of an ambitious and energetic labor movement. Unions of workers in particular trades—machinists, iron molders, cigar makers, printers, railroad workers, miners, carpenters—were little affected by the KOL's meteoric rise and fall. These organizations began to gain new life after the depression of the 1870s. Workers in some of these trades joined the KOL, but they never abandoned their primary identification with the unions representing their particular trades. Meanwhile, labor activists sought to create an organization that would serve as a national center of advocacy for workers' interests in public discourse in general and in the political and legislative arenas in particular.

Eventually, in December 1886, the various strands of the labor movement came together in a convention held in Columbus, Ohio, presided over by Samuel Gompers, head of the cigar makers union. Adopting the name the American Federation of Labor (AFL), the delegates created an organization designed to advance the interests of the trade unions and their members, eschewing the broad social vision of the KOL and concentrating on securing higher wages, shorter hours, and improved working conditions. Although the AFL was not explicitly created as a rival of the KOL, its endorsement of the strike as an essential tool, its foregrounding of the narrowly defined economic agendas of the trade unions, and its rejection of broad schemes of workers' cooperatives (which had always been part of the KOL program) soon pitted the two organizations against each other in union meetings around the country. By the early 1890s, the AFL had emerged as the preeminent national labor body.

Like the NLU of the 1860s and 1870s, the AFL faced in two directions on the question of organized labor's relationship to African Americans. Gompers, thirty-six years old at the time of the AFL's founding, had emigrated from Great Britain at age thirteen. Already a tough, seasoned veteran of the labor wars, the doughty Jewish cigar maker was in the process of repudiating his earlier socialist commitments in favor of a narrower—but in his view, more realistic—understanding of labor's mission. Sharing most of the racial prejudices common among Americans of all social classes in the late nineteenth century, Gompers had no particular sentimental or idealistic attitude toward black workers. Indeed, on another contemporary racial matter, Gompers's disdain for Chinese workers, whose presence in California evoked fierce hostility among whites, was clear. He wrote in 1894 to affirm "our policy of protecting our people against the evil effect of Chinese invasion," noting that the Chinese were "a people . . . who allow themselves to be barbarously tyrannized over in their own country, and who menace the progress . . . of the workers of other countries." The Chinese, the AFL leader declared, "cannot be fraternized with."[27]

But African American workers were already *here*. Thus, in Gompers's view, the labor movement had to accommodate that fact. Since the exclusion of black workers from the trade unions would create a hostile and alienated workforce available for use as strikebreakers and as a source of cheap labor, the labor movement would have to reach out to them. The AFL's constitution was silent on racial matters, implicitly including African Americans among the exploited "mechanics and laborers of our country" for whom it claimed to speak. In 1891, the annual convention overwhelmingly adopted a resolution criticizing labor organizations that "exclude from membership persons on account of race or color." Gompers personally reaffirmed this stand, asserting that "organized labor . . . is decidedly in favor of maintaining and encouraging the recognition of the equality between colored and white laborers."[28]

Several of the large trade unions in the AFL, however, either barred blacks from becoming members or permitted their local unions to do so. Most notable was the National Association of Machinists, founded in 1889 in Atlanta to represent skilled workers in the railroad repair shops. For five years, the AFL leadership refused to accept the machinists union as an affiliate so long as its constitution specified a whites-only membership. In the end, however, federation officials' desire to build their organization trumped the principle of racial equality, and in 1895 the union, now called the National Association of Machinists, was admitted to the AFL with only cosmetic changes in its constitution. Before long, the federation had accepted a number of other discriminatory organizations, despite Gompers's periodic warnings that failure to organize black workers would jeopardize the gains made by white workers. Yet even when the AFL leader advanced such views, he conveyed no sense of urgency about reaching out to black workers, much less asserting a leadership role for the AFL in African Americans' struggles against deepening racial oppression, disfranchisement, and segregation. Even in encouraging fellow unionists to accept black members, Gompers was quick to reject the notion that he was a do-gooder or a bleeding heart. "I strip myself absolutely from all sentimental considerations," he declared in 1897, "and base it [a belief in the need to recruit blacks] upon what I am confident will best serve the interests of labor."[29] Nor was the AFL, a struggling and even marginal organization in the 1890s, alone in distancing itself from black workers. Other centers of labor activism were even more discriminatory. The unions that represented workers who operated trains were open and unrepentant in their contempt for African Americans, and even the American Railroad Union, a militant and otherwise progressive effort to create a broad-front organization of railway workers, barred blacks.

By the end of the nineteenth century, the labor movement had laid the groundwork for establishing itself as a significant factor in U.S. economic and political life. Despite some harrowing strike defeats and the devastating effects of the country's first truly industrial depression beginning in 1893, the AFL and the railroad brotherhoods survived and began to build impressive membership numbers. African American leaders, struggling desperately against a tidal wave of repression and legalized discrimination, found little reason to regard this movement, which claimed to speak for all sons and daughters of toil, as an ally in the common fight for human rights. Indeed, leaders such as Booker T. Washington advised black workers to avoid the labor movement and to ingratiate themselves with employers by proving themselves more loyal and productive than militant, strike-prone white unionists. Even African Americans who were sympathetic to the general goals of organized labor grew bitter over its treatment of black workers. As one black editor from Kansas wrote at the end of the century, "They hang the negro in the South, but they are not so bad in the North; they just simply starve him to death by labor unions."[30]

Still, it was important that no matter how discriminatory many labor unions were in practice, the *ideology* of American labor was not racist, at least not vis-à-vis African Americans. Just as the U.S. Constitution proclaimed a vision of equal rights and equal citizenship, even though southern states systematically victimized their black citizens, so the AFL *officially* endorsed racial equality, even though affiliated unions barred blacks. Turn-of-the-century America was deeply racist in practice, but discrimination by both public officials and private parties, such as trade unions, was practiced *in spite of*, not *in accordance with*, the nation's proclamations of equality and democracy. Whether this fact would ever have real meaning or would simply be a legalistic anomaly of no practical importance remained uncertain.

Black Activism

Booker T. Washington and other black leaders continually reassured white employers that African American workers were "not inclined to trade unionism" and that the black worker "is almost a stranger to strife, lockouts and labor wars." Black labor, said Washington, "has never been tempted to follow the red flag of anarchy."[31] But in fact, African Americans in the postbellum period did not conform to Washington's roseate view of their behavior. In actuality, on the farms, in the mines, on the waterfronts, and in some of the urban trades, both on their own and in association with white workers, African Americans were frequent combatants in the labor wars that punctuated Gilded Age America.

Since most African Americans remained in the South and lived in rural areas, it is not surprising that some of the most important instances of black labor activism involved agricultural workers. In the sugar parishes of Louisiana, in the rice-growing low country of South Carolina, and among tenant farmers and farm laborers in Georgia, Arkansas, and the Carolinas, African Americans gave lie to one black editor's reassurance that "the Negro . . . does not join unions and he seldom ever strikes, and if he does, he never uses violence."[32]

Sugar and rice workers were in the forefront of postbellum black labor activism in the South. In Louisiana, the postwar settlement left the sugarcane plantations in the hands of white owners, both small farmers who specialized in producing brown sugar and molasses and a group of ambitious planters eager to modernize sugar production so that they could tap into the burgeoning national market for refined white sugar. The distinctive circumstances of sugar production, along with the ability of African Americans to remain a potent force in Louisiana politics into the 1880s, gave those who planted, cultivated, cut, and processed the cane considerable ability to resist planters' efforts to impose a more regimented and authoritarian work regime. In locally organized job actions, black sugar workers struck in 1874 and again in 1880 to resist pay cuts, compel planters to pay in currency rather than in scrip, and end the practice of withholding substantial portions of workers' earnings until the processing of the cane was complete. Although these job actions were only partially successful, they revealed a pattern of militancy and cohesion among sugar workers, which was also evident at the polls, that impeded planters' efforts to revamp work routines and suppress wages. As one planter complained in 1880, black sugar workers "are becoming more and more unmanageable," and he warned that their militancy threatened "to compel the planter to comply with any request" they might put forth.[33]

Throughout the 1870s and much of the 1880s, violence flickered along the bayous and river courses of the sugar parishes. Farm managers assaulted and even killed recalcitrant workers; outraged workers murdered overseers. Everyone, it seemed, brandished a weapon. Declared one local newspaper, "Our wars are always fought with revolvers." Both labor activism and violence reached a crescendo in 1886–1887. During this heyday of the KOL, white railroaders in Morgan City, a community of two thousand people adjacent to the sugar parishes, formed a KOL assembly and eventually reached out to the nearby sugar plantations, capitalizing on sugar workers' ongoing struggles against large producers. In the summer of 1887, in a remarkable example of biracial labor activism, KOL District Assembly 194 sought negotiations with the Louisiana Sugar Planters Association, which embraced most of the large-scale planters, seeking wage increases and an end to the employers' practice of paying in scrip that was redeemable only at certain local stores. More broadly, however, the KOL sought to resist planters' efforts to institute drastic changes in the prevailing work routines, under which sugar workers enjoyed considerable autonomy and were protected from overwork.

In the 1870s, African American sugar workers had exercised a good deal of political power in southern Louisiana. Under the protection of state and especially local Republican officials—some of them black sugar workers—they had been able to resist planter-directed repression and even to form publicly sanctioned military units that discouraged employers from calling on public authorities during periods of labor conflict. By the late 1880s, however, although African Americans were still able to vote in the Pelican State, "redeemers"—Democrats and their allies who opposed the exercise of black political power and labor activism—had gained power. Thus, when the sugar workers staged a strike in 1887, the planters had a direct pipeline to public authorities, who quickly dispatched battalions of white state militiamen to the troubled region. With internal divisions over strike strategy weakening the KOL's efforts, the troops, aided by unofficial white vigilantes, began arresting KOL leaders and driving sugar strikers from their homes. In two separate episodes on November 5 and November 23, mixed bodies of troops and hastily appointed sheriff's posses murdered dozens of strikers, sympathizers, and bystanders, effectively crushing the strike and all but ending labor activism among the region's sugar workers. Wrote planter-politician Donelson Caffery of the shootings in Patterson, Louisiana, "It was necessary to apply a strong remedy" to the workers' militancy. On November 23, in the nearby town of Thibodaux, Mary Pugh, a planter's wife, witnessed the systematic killing of at least thirty black citizens, some of whom were gunned down after being told to run for their lives. She was horrified, of course, but in the end, she believed that drastic action had been necessary. "I think," she wrote to a friend in the aftermath of the bloodletting, "this will settle the question of who is to rule[,] the nigger or the white man[,] for the next fifty years."[34]

As in Louisiana, African Americans in South Carolina's low country benefited from a relatively long period of black political power in the Palmetto State and successfully resisted planters' efforts to tighten labor discipline on the region's rice plantations. From the first settlements in the seventeenth century, Africans and African Americans had constituted a considerable majority of the people living on the islands and along the creeks and rivers that ran through this coastal region. White rice planters avoided the swampy area, considering it, with good reason, singularly unhealthy; they relied on black hands, directed by plantation managers and overseers, to produce the rice crops that brought them wealth and to maintain the complex system of dikes, sluices, and ditches needed to regulate the water flow. During slavery, the large black majority, along with the relatively loose supervision, had allowed blacks a great deal of self-direction and even autonomy. A distinctive culture, called Gullah, characterized the somewhat insular local black population and undergirded slaves' sense of entitlement to freedom from close supervision of their work and family lives. It was in the low country that the most ambitious and most successful wartime experiments in black landholding were conducted, and freedmen from South Carolina and Georgia were the most resistant to postwar efforts to move them off plantations and reinstall their former masters.

Both the restoration of planter control of the land itself and the planters' subsequent efforts to impose new kinds of discipline and highly regimented work routines met with intense black opposition. Bitter over the government's failure to provide land to those who had worked it for two hundred years, African Americans in the low country struggled for decades after the war to retain possession of, if not legal title to, hundreds of acres of land. Those compelled by necessity to work on white-owned plantations insisted on retaining the unique access they had enjoyed under slavery to woodlots, hunting grounds, fishing places, and the plantation's animals and facilities. They bridled against efforts to turn them into obedient laborers subject to close discipline; they insisted on forming their own work groups, regulating the pace of work, and having time off to attend the many political rallies to which newly freed slaves flocked. Said one returning plantation owner in November 1866, "they cannot get over the notion that they are part proprietors." Disciplining the former slaves was impossible, and "labor is entirely uncontrollable."[35]

Over the next decade, rice plantation freedmen, backed up by state and local government officials (many of them African American), continued to resist their employers. They squatted on remote lands and engaged in sub-sistence farming and hunting and gathering. They moved from plantation to plantation, in effect, boycotting harsh or unscrupulous employers. They insisted on working for shares, and they resisted employers' efforts to break up cohesive work groups and undermine traditions of cooperative labor that the planters believed impeded efficiency. They launched innumerable job actions, many of them conducted through small, cohesive groups of long-term workmates, but some of them escalating into organized actions that had all the earmarks of strikes. "The fact is," complained planter Henry Middleton in 1870, "this is a continuous struggle where the planter is all the time at a great disadvantage."[36] Indeed, some planters abandoned efforts to farm their land and simply rented it to black tenants, who often worked it cooperatively.

These conflicts—some of them confined to individual farms, others in-volving large numbers of workers from several plantations—percolated through the 1860s and into the 1870s. During most of this time, the fact that blacks exercised political power, especially with respect to the local courts and law enforcement agencies, limited employers' ability to call on the government to act in their behalf. The economic depression of the 1870s hit rice growers with particular severity, stiffening their resolve to cut wages and impose stricter work routines. Blacks, whether daily wage laborers or crop-share farmers, fought back, especially in the large planta-tions along the Combahee River, an area notorious for its labor-related violence.

A series of walkouts in the spring of 1876 won a temporary and partial victory for plantation hands. Angry workers not only faced down outnum-bered employers and their farm managers but also assaulted other blacks who failed to honor the strike call. Fearing eviction from his employer-provided home if he joined the strike, one laborer wrote to Governor Daniel H. Chamberlain of his dilemma: A crowd of five hundred strikers, he re-ported, had forced him and his family out of the fields, and now "we can't get nothing. . . . We are a poor people [who] have [no] home nor contry nor money eder. Do tell me how we ar to do for a lively hood."[37] A large major-ity of the plantation workers, however, enthusiastically joined the strike ac-tion, believing that planters' "reforms" threatened not only their livelihoods but also their way of life. The governor, needing black votes to win reelec-tion, helped arrange a settlement that rescinded the wage cut. In the after-math, strikers accused of violence managed to escape punishment, and the Republican governor appointed a man whom planters considered an insti-gator of the violence a local trial judge.

Strikes erupted again in August, and worker unrest rumbled throughout the low country into the fall, amid a tense gubernatorial election campaign in which South Carolina "redeemers" sought (successfully, as it turned out) to oust the black-supported Republicans. Encouraged by the changing political climate, white paramilitary organizations such as the Democratic Green Pond Rifle Club confronted plantation workers engaged in a series of loosely coordinated strikes for higher pay and reforms in wage payment practices. Since blacks dominated the official militia units, full-scale warfare along race-class lines seemed about to erupt on a number of occasions in and around the town of Beaufort and along the Combahee and Cooper Rivers. Once again, strikers won limited concessions, and employers and white Democratic leaders resolved to smash the black political power that prevented them from resisting black workers' demands.

In the gubernatorial election that fall, low-country blacks mobilized to retain the political power that undergirded their effective labor activism. When a prominent black leader appeared in the area to campaign for the Democratic ticket, one observer reported that "the drums of the [black] militia were beaten and he was 'howled down.'"[38] But in the spring of 1877, bitterly contested election returns placed Democrat Wade Hampton in the statehouse. Without a supportive political context, strike activity petered out. Nonetheless, through the late nineteenth century, in response to the declining market for rice, along with the strong cultural and workplace bonds that continued to sustain black resistance to drastic changes in work routines, planters withdrew from large-scale production. In these backwater regions of coastal South Carolina and Georgia, African Americans achieved a degree of cultural autonomy and freedom from direct white control that was rare in the postbellum South, even if the region could no longer provide the economic resources necessary for black advances in education and technological development that would ultimately be necessary for twentieth-century life.

Sugar and rice, of course, were secondary crops in the postbellum South. Insofar as the bulk of agricultural production was concerned, cotton remained king. For a variety of reasons, collective activism on the part of sharecroppers and farm laborers in the Black Belt of the Deep South was more difficult and episodic than that on the sugar and rice plantations of Louisiana and South Carolina. For one thing, southern whites returned to political power in cotton-growing areas earlier than in South Carolina and Louisiana, limiting the possibilities for collective action among those toiling in the heart of the cotton South. Moreover, exploited and indebted though they might be, sharecroppers and tenant farmers tended to have an individualistic perspective on their plight, and their efforts to attain land-ownership were successful often enough to make that goal plausible. Croppers and tenants farmed individual plots of land, in relative isolation from one another, which further impeded collective protest. Farm laborers, who worked for daily or weekly wages, might have been better candidates for collective labor activism, but even so, the particular circumstances of their lives militated against it. Wage-working black laborers tended to be young men hoping to acquire enough cash to buy a mule, with a view to eventually entering into a favorable tenant or cropping agreement with a landowner. Their work was highly seasonal, and farm laborers typically moved from farm to farm, rarely establishing roots in one location that might have encouraged a collective identity and activism.

Even so, the African Americans who produced much of the South's key cash crop were not strangers to collective protest. In the mid-1880s, for example, KOL organizers found ready recruits among rural folks trapped in indebtedness and victimized by the crop lien system of farming. Of perhaps fifty thousand southern workers recruited by the KOL during its heyday, about half were African American; of these, a considerable majority were agricultural workers, some of them members of "mixed assemblies" that also embraced railroad, forest product, and construction workers. African American farmers and agricultural workers found it difficult to formulate agendas for change or protection that fit the template of organized labor. After all, black croppers and tenants hoped to become landowners themselves and sometimes employed other blacks on a wage basis. This divergence of interests between croppers-cum-owners and wage workers was also evident in the Colored Farmers Alliance, an explicitly agrarian movement of the late 1880s and early 1890s that had tenuous links with the more powerful white Farmers Alliances that sought to improve agricultural conditions and challenged the established political parties for power in a number of southern states. In areas where KOL organizers enjoyed success among black workers, the response owed more to the organization's reputation for racial tolerance and its self-proclaimed role as a voice for ordinary people than to any realistic hope for concrete change.

Probably the most dramatic examples of black cotton farmers' activism took place in eastern Arkansas in the early 1890s. During Reconstruction, former slaves in the area centered on Phillips County had organized for better rates and conditions, only to suffer violent repression. Memories of short-lived success lingered, however, and in 1891, another revolt broke out, this time among cotton pickers demanding better wages. Invoking memories of earlier activism and gaining support from local black preachers, organizers of this grassroots movement went from plantation to plantation, calling on workers to withhold their labor until they gained a rate of 75 cents a day. Some planters, desperate to get their crops in, acceded, only to be ostracized or even physically attacked by others who considered any sign of independent black activism a dire threat to a regime based on low wages and black subordination. In the end, quasi-official vigilantes, under the protection if not the direction of planters and public officials, crushed the incipient pickers' revolt, which had remained fragmentary and localized throughout.

Apart from the episodic involvement of the KOL in the bloody sugar strike and, less dramatically, in the sporadic protests of cotton tenants and workers, organized labor played little role in these outbreaks of African American labor activism. Elsewhere, however, African Americans—sometimes in cooperation with white counterparts, and sometimes on their own—often proved stalwart union activists, when given the opportunity. Black workers on the docks, in the mines, and in the urban trades valued union protection, and they often formed their own labor organizations when white unions barred them from membership. In southern cities such as Charleston, Atlanta, New Orleans, Birmingham, and Richmond, black workers compiled an extensive record of union formation and activism; this activity was often linked to vigorous political operations, at least until disfranchisement drove African Americans from the polls. For example, in Richmond in the 1880s, the KOL recruited both black and white workers aggressively, sometimes on an integrated basis, and was a key element in a kind of "movement culture" that offered a sharp alternative to elite control of city politics and institutions. Indeed, black voters were a key element in a KOL-led slate that controlled the Richmond city council for a time. And in Birmingham, vigorous biracial union activism in the nearby coal mines spilled over into the city, encouraging the organization of black barbers, carpenters, and hod carriers in an alliance with white workers, even as state and local authorities imposed increasingly restrictive segregation and disfranchisement measures designed in part to forestall class-based activism that transgressed the color line.

It was in the coal mines and on the wharves of southern port cities, however, that the most impressive examples of biracial unionism emerged. Longshoremen in New Orleans and coal miners in Alabama forged and sustained biracial unions against steep obstacles throughout the late nineteenth century and into the twentieth. The labor activism that flourished in both places owed little to humanitarian sentiments or ideological convictions; rather, it was rooted in practical calculations of mutual benefit. In both cases, substantial numbers of black workers were on site early and were not imported into a previously all-white workforce. In the Alabama coal mines and on the wharves of the Crescent City, white workers who were protesting mistreatment, forming unions, and conducting job actions had no choice but to make common cause with their African American counterparts. Cooperation in labor activism sometimes involved political collaboration as well, as long as blacks retained the franchise. In contrast, even the most fervent advocates of interracial solidarity consistently and vocally disavowed any sympathy for "social equality," a vague but omnipresent term that conjured up lurid images of black intrusion into white people's social lives and perhaps even interracial sexual encounters.

From the onset of modern coal mining in north-central Alabama in the early 1870s, employers recruited both blacks and whites to do the work. Throughout the remainder of the nineteenth century and well into the twentieth, black miners constituted 40 to 60 percent of the labor force. Moreover, the initial dearth of labor in the region and the recruitment practices of mine operators ensured that large numbers of blacks would be skilled laborers and not merely helpers or auxiliary workers, as was the case in the nearby metalworking industry and on the railroads. With African Americans still enjoying the franchise through the 1880s, both black and white miners participated enthusiastically in a series of political campaigns that swept Alabama, challenging the dominance of traditional planter elites in public affairs.

Strikes in 1879 and throughout the 1880s brought both black and white miners out, initially in spontaneous job actions confined to particular mining camps, but increasingly under the auspices of the KOL. Whether black or white, coal miners prized their legendary freedom from direct supervision. Since they were typically paid by the tonnage produced, many miners worked according to their own preferences, determining the amount they produced and the hours they spent in the mines on the basis of the trade-off between their need for cash, on the one hand, and their desire for free time, on the other. Employers regarded the miners' freedom as inefficient and costly. Since the coal deposits in Alabama were difficult to mine, labor costs constituted a high percentage of the total costs of production. This being the case, the large-scale enterprises that increasingly dominated mining constantly sought to reduce tonnage rates and institute changes in work patterns that involved greater centralized direction and discipline. Inevitably, disputes between profit-seeking employers and proud miners led to strikes, many of them short-lived and informal, but some of them lengthy affairs that tested the limits of workers' solidarity.

During the 1880s, the KOL's commitment to interracial labor activism helped bolster workers' cooperation across the color line. Black miners proved no less opposed to wage cuts or changes in work routines than their white counterparts and quickly proved stalwart union men. The Alabama state KOL assembly echoed the national body's stand, urging white workers "to set aside all race prejudices against the colored laborer . . . so that the toilers of both races may be successful in their struggles with trusts, monopoly and organized capital." At a time when segregation, disfranchisement, and rigid racial subordination were becoming commonplace in Alabama and the rest of the South, labor activists often demonstrated a remarkably fluid and egalitarian sensibility. Certain charismatic black organizers were welcomed in white communities and admired for their ability to appeal to workers of both races. In Birmingham, large, racially mixed crowds gathered to hear speeches by both black and white Knights. White workers' fears that blacks would succumb to the paternalistic blandishments or naked threats of employers and abandon the union proved misplaced. "The Knights of Labor in Alabama have had but little cause for complaint against the colored Assemblies," declared a local labor newspaper in 1887.[39]

The sporadic strikes of the 1880s enjoyed mixed success, at best. Miners, in effect, fought a rearguard action against employers and, to some extent, against the uncertain character of the market for Alabama coal. Determined to break the miners' resolve, mine operators experimented with importing Italian immigrants from the northern U.S. ports, a move that served to unite not only native black and white miners but also members of the local press and business community against the interlopers. In a more sustained strategy, operators exploited Alabama's harsh penal system by contracting with state authorities to bring convict laborers, the vast majority of whom were African American, into the mines. In a strike that convulsed the mines in 1890–1891, one large operator brought in masses of black strikebreakers.

Importation of black convicts and strikebreakers tested the limits of interracial unionism. Some white miners responded with violence. According to a local newspaper, at one coal camp, white strikers' wives "got rampant when they saw the colored folks [i.e., strikebreakers, now occupying company-provided houses from which strikers had been forcibly evicted] sandwiched among them" and went after the newcomers with kitchenware "and everything else imaginable." Racial epithets were common, with some white miners using the two pejoratives "nigger" and "scab" interchangeably. Reports of beatings and gunfire circulated.[40]

Yet, despite the provocative introduction of black convicts and strikebreakers, and despite Alabama's intensifying climate of racial subordination, interracial union sentiment remained resilient. In the 1890–1891 strike, and then again in a much larger and more confrontational reprise three years later, the traditions of biracialism endured, even in the face of large-scale recruitment of black scabs. Since the mines had always employed large numbers of black miners, it was obvious that the recruitment of convicts and scabs, whatever their color, threatened black miners as well as whites. Both the Knights of Labor and the new United Mine Workers of America (UMWA) worked hard to deracialize the situation, stressing that the coal companies were seeking to sow racial antagonism and that miners' quarrels were not with their fellow workers, whatever their color or status, but with their employers. "We have no fight to make on the negro," declared a UMWA organizer in December 1890. And for their part, established black miners combined opposition to black strikebreakers with continued adherence to the union. "To the honor of the colored miner," wrote an Alabama labor paper, "he is as a rule devoted to union principles and dreads the stigma of blackleg [i.e., scab] as badly as does his white brother miner."[41]

At no time was the biracialism of Alabama's coal mines fully egalitarian. In most areas, local unions were either all black or all white. When the UMWA brought the various local unions together into a regional district, officers' positions were apportioned along strict racial lines, with whites holding the top positions. Union-sponsored social affairs and community events often excluded blacks or relegated them to subaltern status. When Alabama's new state constitution effectively disfranchised African Americans, no white union leader protested, even though the absence of black miners from the polls deprived working people of an important source of political strength. Even the most enlightened white unionists adopted a somewhat condescending stance toward blacks, regarding even veteran black union activists as requiring white guidance and tutelage.

In the Alabama coal camps, the issues that divided workers from employers were relatively straightforward and clear-cut. They involved the wages, working conditions, and especially work routines of men, both black and white, who toiled in similar circumstances in and around the mines. On the docks of the South's major ports, however, the structure of labor was a good deal more complex, at once offering unique opportunities for interracial collaboration and posing difficult challenges to labor activists. Since much of the heavy work on the docks and in related storage, shipping, and warehousing facilities had been done by slaves before the Civil War, African Americans had always been a major presence in the port cities. During Reconstruction, black goods handlers and longshoremen in Savannah, Charleston, Jacksonville, Pensacola, Mobile, Galveston, and other port cities had created some of the first African American labor unions, which usually functioned as an important part of the emerging civic culture of the newly freed bondmen.

New Orleans, the largest port in the South and the third largest in the entire country, exhibited in rich detail the complex racial situation and division of labor that prevailed on the docks. African Americans, many of them former slaves, performed the rough work of unloading the raw cotton, barrels of molasses, and other products as they arrived in the city from upriver. Other workers, some black and some white, transported the goods to local warehouses and, in the case of cotton, to the presses where it was baled and compressed. As ships arrived to transport these semiprocessed goods to distant ports, teamsters, draymen, and longshoremen loaded them in the holds. Cotton alone, by far the largest export in terms of volume and value, required thousands of workers to handle, compress, bale, transport, and pack it. Screwmen, who wielded heavy jackscrews to accomplish the critical and delicate task of packing baled cotton in the ships in precise, space-saving patterns, stood at the top of the dockside labor hierarchy and commanded the highest wages and the most advantageous work rules.

Over the years, black and white workers developed a division of labor. A variety of dockside unions and workers associations reached complex and unstable agreements as to who would perform what work and what work rules would be followed. Through much of the post-Reconstruction period—which began in the Crescent City with the election of a Democratic-Conservative municipal ticket in 1872—the various unions of teamsters, longshoremen, and screwmen flourished under the protective wing of a corrupt, inefficient local government whose officials depended on working-class votes. New Orleans was known as a labor town, and strong dockside unions spurred the organization of streetcar operators, building tradesmen, and a variety of other workers.

Through much of the 1880s, unions of white and black screwmen and longshoremen collaborated in dividing up the work and achieving both high wages and favorable work rules. Nevertheless, black workers bridled when the dominant white screwmen's union imposed sharp limitations on the number of blacks privileged to hold high-wage jobs. For white unionists, the need to interact with men they regarded as their racial inferiors was a constant source of frustration. Still, at least some of the city's labor activists, both white and black, believed that these carefully negotiated and policed arrangements between white and black workers contained the germ of genuine interracial cooperation and working-class unity. After all, in both the Cotton Men's Executive Council (the dockworkers' umbrella organization) and the New Orleans Central Trades and Labor Assembly, which represented all the Crescent City's unions, white and black delegates worked closely together, and blacks were regularly elected to offices such as vice president and recording secretary. The assembly's annual parade throughout the 1880s featured white and black unionists marching together. In 1887 a visiting northern labor activist hailed the achievements of the Louisianans: "To-day," wrote George McNeill, "the white and colored laborers . . . are as fraternal in their relations as they are in any part of the country." A black newspaper that had frequently criticized organized labor added, "To gaze upon these representatives of every trade and of every shade of colors . . . marshalled by white and colored officers . . . , without discrimination on account of race . . . was very gratifying. . . . God bless the Central Trade [and] Labor Assembly of New Orleans."[42]

Optimism about interracial harmony failed to survive the grim 1890s. A series of bitter strikes, both stemming from and exacerbated by the depression that began in 1893, stretched racial collaboration on the New Orleans waterfront to the breaking point. Black and white screwmen and

longshoremen began a "race to the bottom," each group seeking to under-
bid the other in the hope of claiming scarce jobs for itself. In March 1895,
frustrated by the continued employment of blacks, white screwmen and
longshoremen turned to violence, attacking black dockworkers on several
occasions in organized assaults. On March 12, several hundred white
workers emerged from the morning mist to drive out a black crew loading
an ocean-bound freight. "Bullets sang and whistled round the wharf like
hail," a New Orleans newspaper reported. Fleeing blacks "were given no
quarter and were shot down like dogs . . . blood flowed like water." Six
African American dockworkers were killed in this assault and another that
occurred the same day upriver.[43]

Despite an intensifying climate of racial oppression and violence against
African Americans in turn-of-the-century New Orleans, biracial unionism
on the waterfront proved unexpectedly resilient. Black unions recruited
thousands of new members and even persuaded the AFL to issue a separate
charter for a black city central body, a step made necessary by the increasingly exclusionary policies of the original Central Trades and Labor
Council. On the docks, white screwmen, longshoremen, and goods handlers reluctantly accepted the permanency of black labor and the logic of
cooperation. By 1902, the various waterfront organizations had rebuilt
their earlier alliance. Declared one black longshoreman proudly that year,
"we have been the means of unity of action among the longshoremen of
th[e] . . . port." Added the secretary of the new black central labor body,
soon "we expect to have the color line in [dock] work removed."[44]

In New Orleans, as in Alabama, renewed interracial collaboration was
tenuous and fragile. Nor did it extend outside the workplace. As a New
Orleans Board of Trade report noted, there was no "social equality" among
working people in the South. "The two races will work side by side, but
they will not play together, go to the same schools, or sit together in tram-
way cars." For white miners and waterfront workers, the large-scale presence of blacks in their occupations was a disagreeable fact of life. Clearly,
as the Board of Trade report declared, "The 'color line' is drawn with all
the strictness common in the Southern States."[45]

Yet despite all these caveats, the record of interracial activism in late-
nineteenth-century Alabama and Louisiana was impressive. Nowhere in
the world were there similar examples of this kind of mutuality and collaboration across the color line. In South Africa, in the Caribbean, and in
Asia, there are no contemporary examples of biracial labor activism to rival those that emerged in the American South. Although Alabama miners
and New Orleans dockworkers experienced more defeats than victories,
the traditions of biracial unionism survived the hard times of the 1890s to
emerge anew in the next century, suggesting that however powerful prevailing racialist ideas and customs were, the practical realities of the work-

place had the capacity, under certain circumstances, to loosen, if not to break, their grip.

Even as southern whites imposed an increasingly harsh and restrictive system of racial domination, black workers organized both to resist deteriorating working conditions and to protest disfranchisement. In Florida, for example, through the 1880s and 1890s, black workers—sometimes in cooperation with white fellow workers, and sometimes on their own—tested the emerging Jim Crow system repeatedly. Strikes, mass protests, and other job actions erupted in Pensacola, Fernandina, Jacksonville, Key West, and elsewhere as black workers faced down sheriffs and militia units, sometimes successfully. In January 1890, the small port city of Apalachicola underwent a kind of general strike as African American sawmill, factory, and dockside workers demanded better pay and shorter hours while protesting the growing disfranchisement of black voters. White merchants and city officials were particularly shocked at the behavior of black women, who were, according to one hostile observer, "violent in their denunciation of the action of the whites and are congregating on the streets" in support of their husbands and brothers. Only mass arrests and the dispatch of heavily armed militia units quelled this remarkable outburst of black activism.[46]

Fifty years ago, C. Vann Woodward, in his now-classic *Origins of the New South,* stated clearly the dilemma faced by the labor movement in the Gilded Age South. Given the central role that black workers—whether on farms or in industry—played in the southern economy, how could white workers raise their standards and advance their organizations? "Two possible but contradictory policies could be used," Woodward reflected. One was to "eliminate the Negro as a competitor by excluding him" from the labor force; the other was "to take him in as an organized worker committed to the defense of a common standards of wages."[47] Indeed, black workers faced another version of the same dilemma. Should they, as many members of the emerging black middle class urged, turn their back on union activism and look to the employer, whether white or black, for remunerative work and racial advance? Or should they attempt to expand on the interracial initiatives that had emerged even in an era of mounting racial antagonism? Much of the story of the "first fruits of freedom" involved the efforts of black and white workers to come to grips with these alternatives.

2

INTO THE NEW CENTURY

In the decades before the outbreak of World War I in 1914, race continued to be a major factor in a broad range of labor and workplace contexts. In the South, the disfranchisement of African Americans, the withdrawal of direct federal oversight of race relations, and white elites' determination to maintain blacks' subordination helped launch new forms of racially inflected unfree labor. In the cities of the Northeast and the Midwest, in both established black communities and among the growing number of southern migrants, black workers found both new opportunities and old patterns of discrimination in the emerging industrial and commercial economy. In workplaces and union halls, white workers and their unions, despite official adherence to color-blind values, reflected the larger society's notion's of racial hierarchy, although episodes of interracial activism provided some hope that organized labor might one day align itself more closely with the aspirations of black workers.

Unfree Labor

From their first arrival in North America early in the seventeenth century, African Americans played a central role in creating wealth. Their coerced labor on plantations and farms, especially in the South, was a critical factor in generating the surpluses of food and fiber that underwrote U.S. commercial and industrial expansion. After the Civil War, agriculturalists, publicists, and statesmen in both the North and the South feared that, without compulsion, African Americans would not continue to work in this fashion and thus would no longer generate accustomed levels of production. The resulting decline would reduce the wealth both of those who owned the nation's farms, factories, and places of exchange and of the country overall. As it turned out, the patchwork systems of sharecropping, farm tenancy, and "free" labor that eventually emerged succeeded, however unjustly and inefficiently, in harnessing the freedmen to the southern agricultural system. In addition, white political and economic leaders turned to new forms of unfree labor. Thus, convict leasing, prison labor, the chain gang, and other varieties of forced labor, often reliant on arbitrary and corrupt patterns of law enforcement to supply convict workers, soon became a significant feature of the postwar South. Indeed, in the three-quarters of a century after the war, racially inflected forced labor was crucial to the economic development of the "New South."

Before Emancipation, public authorities in the southern states had had little need to incarcerate or otherwise discipline blacks accused of wrongdoing. Slave owners whipped, chained, yoked, and otherwise punished misbehaving slaves. Violent, incorrigible, and escape-prone bondmen and -women were sold "down the river." Slaves were too valuable for imprisonment. "In slavery times jails was all built for the white folks," mused a former slave. Slaves "had to work; when they done wrong they was whipped and let go."[1] But with freedom, plantation misdeeds became criminal acts that required public adjudication, punishment, and incarceration. And postwar legislatures had to find funds with which to operate a vastly expanded criminal justice system and to build and maintain expensive new jails and prisons.

In part, the enactments of southern legislatures were responding to a very real problem. Inevitably, some former slaves would commit crimes (as, of course, whites would continue to do) that were no longer punishable by slave owners. It was equally true that widespread fear of inherent black criminality, along with the determination to keep blacks subordinate to whites, ensured that black criminality would be expansively defined and severely punished. In addition, the emerging criminal justice system soon provided an answer to another, related problem: an anticipated crisis in manpower. As freedmen withdrew their wives and children from the fields, they often followed agricultural practices that privileged the needs of the family economy over those of the surplus-dependent white planters and bankers. Moreover, whites expected that former slaves would shun the dangerous, demeaning, or arduous work that prewar slave owners had been able to compel. Now free to sell their labor, they would reject such tasks as swamp draining, heavy construction, mining, and work in the remote pine forests. Since large-scale immigration to the South was unlikely, and since few potential employers had the inclination to employ or the authority to compel white men to perform this sort of work, where would entrepreneurs find the manpower to build the New South's infrastructure and exploit its rich, though often inaccessible, resources?

The emerging system of criminal justice supplied a compelling answer. Beginning in the late 1860s, southern states found a number of ingenious ways to address these twin problems of social control and labor supply. Especially after the end of Reconstruction, which in some states came as early as 1868, the needs—both legitimate and merely perceived—of the criminal justice system and the demand for cheap labor meshed. Public authorities found schemes of convict leasing particularly effective in turning a financial liability into a source of revenue. Eager to develop the South's railroads, natural resources, and agricultural potential, legislatures acted to make the newly expanding body of convicts available to entrepreneurs. Imposing stiff penalties for even minor transgressions such as loitering, petty theft, and disorderly conduct, public authorities dramatically increased the number of young black males subject to incarceration. These new "criminals," many of them victims of selective law enforcement or guilty, at worst, of petty crimes, were now available for work in these harsh locales.

Judges and law enforcement officials colluded with would-be employers to expand this supply of cheap, unfree black labor. Legislatures made it a felony to break a work contract, something that was normally regarded as a private legal matter, thus adding to the pool of coerced labor. Arbitrary enforcement of vagrancy and contract violation laws enabled employers to commandeer the labor of thousands of impoverished black men who were unable to the pay the fines and court costs imposed on them by white judges. Legalized duress permitted the exploitation of even ostensibly free workers, especially those toiling in remote locales where employers extended advances on wages and credit at company stores and then legally required that the workers remain under their control until the debts—usually subject to steep interest charges—were paid off. This practice, which amounted to a form of legalized peonage, supplied thousands of workers in the expanding forest products industry of Georgia, South Carolina, and Florida. Indeed, ordinary sharecropping could quickly bleed into de facto debt peonage, as low prices for cotton frequently translated into chronic indebtedness on the part of croppers and bound them to particular planters. In addition, planters and other employers made collusive arrangements with sheriffs, who geared the enforcement of loosely drawn vagrancy and personal conduct laws to the seasonal manpower needs of local farmers and entrepreneurs, often receiving kickbacks for the "legal" provision of these prisoner-workers.

Of course, the various legislative enactments and enforcement mechanisms were ostensibly color-blind, but in fact, African Americans were the targets of the emerging regime of criminalization, incarceration, and labor exploitation. Although some whites labored as convict-workers, debt peons, and members of chain gangs, the vast majority of those who found themselves toiling in these circumstances were black—89 percent in a survey conducted in 1878, and 95 percent in a 1902 survey in Georgia. White prison authorities, judges, police officers, and politicians openly used the criminal justice system to discourage the allegedly lawless propensities and

social irresponsibility they believed to be inherent among the former slaves
and their descendants. At the same time, convict leasing and other forms of
unfree labor exploited African Americans in the service of the dynamic and
progressive New South that elites set out to build. Said one Mississippi
planter in 1866, deploring the end of slavery, "I think the best we can do is
keep 'em as near to a stage of bondage as possible."[2]

As early as 1868, officials in Georgia began entering into convict lease
agreements with railroad builders, mine operators, and forest products entrepreneurs, turning black convicts over to employers in return for a flat fee
and an agreement to feed, clothe, shelter, guard, and see to the medical needs
of the convicts. White officials considered black labor so vital to the postwar
economic development of the state that it mattered little whether neo-
Confederates and "redeemers" or federally appointed military governors
were in charge. Thus, in Georgia's first convict lease agreement, the federal
military governor, under the authority of a law passed by the neo-Confederate
state legislature immediately after the war, entered into an agreement with
William Fort whereby the state would supply "one hundred able bodied and
healthy Negro convicts" for railroad construction in northern Georgia for a
flat fee of $2,500. Fort agreed to provide sustenance and security for the pris-
oners, who would work for one year under his direction.[3]

Other states quickly followed suit. Coal mine operators in Alabama
and Tennessee turned to convicts both as a source of cheap labor and as a
means of keeping union-minded free miners in check. In Mississippi, construction companies leased convicts to drain and clear the malarial swamps
of the rich delta bottomlands. But it was in Georgia that the lease system
reached its apogee. In a survey conducted in 1886, state officials reported
that one of every two hundred black males was a convict, with most of
them leased out to private employers. Over the next forty years, southern
convicts were compelled to toil in agriculture and in brickyards, iron mines,
lumber camps and sawmills, and a wide variety of other manufacturing
and extractive enterprises. Many employers preferred convicts over free
workers, despite their generally lower levels of productivity. Free blacks,
they complained, were unreliable, restlessly moving from job to job, always seeking more favorable wages and conditions. Thus, an Alabama
mine operator extolled the benefits of forced labor, remarking that convicts
were "forced to work steadily [and] their output may be depended upon."
In a convict coal camp, wrote a journalist, if 300 men go to sleep at night,
"300 men get up the next day and are ready for work."[4]

Details of the lease agreements varied, but in general, both the state
treasury and the employers derived substantial—in some cases, spectacular—financial benefits from the arrangements. Leasing prisoners rather
than incarcerating them saved the states enormous sums, as well as bringing in per capita payments from lessees. Thus, the expanding criminal jus-

tice system was often a source of public profit, rather than a drain on the taxpayers.

Moreover, state officials, from the governor through the criminal justice bureaucrats, were able to line their own pockets by entering into collusive agreements with favored lessees. In some cases, businessmen parlayed their successful enterprises into political power for themselves or their families. For example, Georgia governor Joseph M. Brown, who served between 1909 and 1913, was the son of coal and iron magnate Joseph E. Brown, who in the 1870s had used large numbers of leased convict-workers to build the family's substantial holdings in the northwestern part of the state. Nor were large corporate interests shy about tapping into this unfree labor pool. As did individual entrepreneurs, executives of the emerging southern giant Tennessee Coal and Iron Company found convicts cheaper, more easily disciplined, and far more cost-efficient than free labor, as well as a useful means of fighting organized labor. Thus, declared one TC&I executive, "One of the chief reasons which induced the company to take up the system was the great chance it offered for overcoming strikes."[5] Although the southern states' record keeping was far from meticulous, knowledgeable observers believed that in the 1890s, a majority of the region's convicts were working under leasing arrangements.

Some businessmen, rather than directly employing the convicts themselves, subleased them to other employers, brokering substantial profits for themselves while off-loading the costs associated with feeding and guarding the convicts. In Georgia, Florida, and elsewhere, employers and labor brokers created a substantial speculative and futures market in the selling and reselling of convict labor. Subleasing and sub-subleasing arrangements, some of them informal and short term, made oversight by public authorities—which was never very energetic—all but impossible. Thus, it is not surprising that prisoners suffered some of the worst conditions at the hands of sublessees. Indeed, nothing so aptly illustrated the concept of the "commodification of labor" as this increasingly intricate, exploitative, and largely unregulated trade in convict flesh.

Convict leasing was only the most widely known and extensive means by which coerced black labor was made available to build southern infrastructure and further the region's economic development. By the turn of the twentieth century, the South was honeycombed with prisons, labor camps, road-building projects, and work sites of various kinds dependent on convict or debt peon labor. From roughly 1885 to 1920, it is likely that somewhere between ten thousand and twenty thousand debtors, convicts, and prisoners toiled under these circumstances on an average day, the great majority of them African American. In Tennessee and Georgia, they dug coal alongside free miners, both black and white. In Georgia and Florida, hundreds of debt peons harvested resin and processed it to make turpentine. In the Mississippi Delta, prisoners drained the marshlands. In Mississippi, Florida, and elsewhere, prisoners on state-run farms produced agricultural surpluses for state distribution and sale. Convicts worked on the most dangerous and difficult railroad construction projects. Throughout the South, county prisoners toiled on chain gangs, building and maintaining the growing system of hard-topped roads that began crisscrossing the rural areas.

By any standard, the conditions under which these workers toiled were appalling. Governmental regulation and oversight of private lessees were minimal and were often compromised by corruption and malfeasance. On construction sites, employers transported convicts from place to place in great rolling cages, like circus animals. In the pine forests, crudely built stockades, guarded by pistol-toting and whip-wielding guards, served as housing. Inmates, including youngsters barely into their teens, were flogged relentlessly and subjected to other grotesque punishments. At Mississippi's Parchman prison farm, created in 1904 ostensibly to remedy the horrific abuses of the state's convict lease system, the majority of the guards were convict trusties, hard men armed with shotguns and rifles whose substantial privileges depended on their ability to control their fellow prisoners, which they typically did with maximum brutality. There and in the camps and stockades, even minor infractions were met with ingenious physical and psychological punishments, from the "water cure" to hanging by the thumbs to the dreaded "sweat box," an unventilated, coffin-like enclosure into which the miscreant was stuffed and kept for hours at a time.

Death and crippling injury were constant threats. Important elements of the New South's railway system, public roads, and economic development in general were literally built on the corpses of convict-workers. Survivors of construction projects, for example, reported that the bodies of dead fellow workers were simply tossed into excavations, becoming part of embankments and levees. During the building of the Greenville (South Carolina) to Atlanta railroad line between 1877 and 1879, the annual death toll was 45 percent. In Mississippi in the mid-1880s, 11 percent of the state's black prisoners died annually—twice the rate of whites. In 1881, Arkansas authorities reported a death rate of 25 percent.[6]

Since the central purpose of this vast system was to control the black population and exploit its labor, rehabilitation and education played no role in the prison labor regime. Whether on the county chain gangs, in the turpentine camps, at reclamation and construction sites, or on the prison farms, discipline was harsh, food was inadequate in quantity and nutrition, accommodations were crude, and ordinary provisions for hygiene and sanitation were primitive at best and often downright lethal. Indeed, for thousands of African American men in the postbellum South, the harsh conditions and brutality in the camps and on the construction gangs often proved worse than slavery. As one southern employer told a critic of the convict lease system in 1883, "If a man had a good nigger [before the war], he could afford to take care of him. . . . But these convicts: we don't own 'em. One dies, get another."[7]

Profitable employment of convicts was not a given, however. As with any other commodity, convict labor depended on general business conditions for profitability. During a boom period, cheap labor was indeed a boon. But when the economy stalled, lessees were stuck with contracts that obligated them to bear the costs of caring for and guarding the now superfluous workers. Naturally, conditions for prisoners deteriorated during these economic slumps. In general, however, demand for forced labor was strong. State authorities found that they could demand higher rates of compensation to the state treasury (and, in some cases, to their own pockets) as southern economic development required increasingly greater labor inputs. Despite some fabulous profits, by the turn of the twentieth century, southern states began phasing out the convict leasing system, owing in part to declining profitability and in part to growing criticisms of the system's many faults. Moreover, in 1901, prosecutors at the U.S. Department of Justice began at least sporadic efforts to enforce an 1867 antipeonage statute, winning several important cases in the early 1900s.

Attacks on convict leasing and debt peonage, however, by no means ended the South's reliance on unfree black labor. Federal enforcement of the peonage law was sporadic at best, and well into the twentieth century, lurid examples of debt-related forced labor continued to surface. Efforts to replace convict leasing with ostensibly more humane and efficient methods of combining control and profit often yielded equally horrific results. For example, despite an 1893 statute that supposedly ended Mississippi's leasing program, state and local officials, in collusion with planters and other employers, still found ways to make the state's burgeoning convict population available for heavy and profitable labor. In 1904, under the leadership of Governor James K. Vardaman—a sharp critic of leasing, on the grounds that it amounted to a massive state subsidy to wealthy individuals and corporations—the legislature created Parchman, a vast prison farm in Sunflower County. Convicts there—90 percent of them African American— were put to work, under direct state control, producing food and cotton for use by state agencies and generating income for the state. In theory, prisoners would be rehabilitated through healthy, outdoor work and edifying instruction, but in reality, "Parchman" soon became synonymous with the systematic, sadistic mistreatment of inmates.[8]

Although Florida and other southern states also turned to prison farms as a replacement for convict leasing, a more common scheme was to employ prisoners in road-building projects under direct public authority. Indeed, Progressive Era reformers in the South coupled criticism of convict leasing and debt peonage with enthusiasm for the employment of prisoners to construct and maintain the region's much-needed network of automobile-friendly public thoroughfares. Everyone would benefit. Southern states could scuttle the traditional and much-hated practice of requiring all male citizens (or at least those unable to pay for an exemption) to devote several days' labor a year to building and maintaining the roads. Farmers and urban dwellers alike favored road improvements, which facilitated the transport of crops to market and linked cities and rural areas more closely. State officials and civil engineers promoted good roads as the key to the South's modernization. Of course, the construction of a new system of hard-topped roads would be expensive, but that was where convict labor entered the picture. "The value of [convict labor] is not to be underestimated," declared the North Carolina Highway Commission in 1903. The U.S. Department of Agriculture, which enthusiastically encouraged rural road-building projects, noted approvingly that throughout the South "employment [of prisoners] has cheapened the cost of road building."[9]

Nor were farmers, taxpayers, and public officials the only beneficiaries of this scheme of forced labor, at least according to its advocates. Direct employment by responsible and competent public authorities associated with upgrading the states' transport networks would replace the old, corrupt system of leasing, thus eliminating the earlier abuses. Healthy outdoor work performed for the common good would benefit prisoners as well. Use of convict labor in road building, declared one enthusiast, was "identified with the movement to take the prisoner out of the cell, the prison factory, and the mine to work him in the fresh air and sunshine." Thus, everybody gained and, as one academic booster in Georgia declared, "through the employment of convicts on the public roads is offered a rational solution of the road question"—and, he might have added, the "convict question."[10]

In fact, however, these replacements for convict leasing revealed the truth of the adage "the more things change, the more they stay the same." The turn toward public employment of prisoners did nothing to change the basic injustices of the criminal justice system, nor did public authorities prove to be any less obsessed with maximal exploitation of unfree labor than their private entrepreneur counterparts had been. Parchman and similar institutions in Louisiana and Florida quickly developed reputations as hellholes, where prisoners were warehoused in overcrowded and unsanitary conditions and routinely overworked, abused, and degraded. Since most of the responsibility for building and maintaining roads fell to county and local authorities, the airy and high-minded expectations of academics and state and federal officials were less important than the values and attitudes of local politicians and sheriffs. Convict road crews, after all, had to be guarded and had to be convinced that any sign of defiance or lack of effort on their part would be met with swift punishment. In the southeastern states, where the use of convicts on road crews was most common, authorities soon resorted to the chain gang as the preferred method of controlling and disciplining prisoners.

Indeed, by the 1920s, the chain gang had become one of the most widely identified emblems of southern life. Despite the visions of progressive-minded reformers who posited work on road-building crews as a humane alternative to convict leasing, chain gangs largely replicated the pathologies of the earlier system. Heavy steel chains bound the prisoners to one another, forcing inmates to move and work in a synchronized shuffle. Many suffered from "shackle poisoning," as the metal cuffs rubbed their skin raw and invited infection. Local and county officials proved to be as niggardly as private entrepreneurs in providing food and medical attention. Escapees, journalists, and academic observers regularly reported on the horrors of the chain gangs, but southern states expanded their use through the 1920s. As late as the early 1960s, motorists from other parts of the country touring the South were shocked to learn firsthand that the chain gang, long a staple of sensational exposés and the subject of several Hollywood films, was no archaic anachronism. They gaped in amazement at the sight of strings of shackled African American prisoners, clad in gray-and-black stripes, toiling along the roadways as a white horseman brandishing a rifle kept guard.

The South's prison farms, chain gangs, and convict-worked mines and construction projects, with their racism, authoritarianism, and brutal exploitation, were integral elements in the region's quest for modernization and "progress." All these systems of coerced labor shared several common characteristics. They played a significant role in reinforcing the system of general racial control, known as Jim Crow, that characterized the South, especially after Reconstruction. At the same time, they contributed significantly to the South's economic development and to the building of its transportation, industrial, and agricultural infrastructure. They were profitable to entrepreneurs and public officials, both in their legal operations and through the widespread corruption they facilitated. Racially influenced forced labor served to reinforce the South's low-wage, union-unfriendly environment while exacerbating the already great divisions between black and white workers in the region. Along with rigid segregation, low levels of education, and high levels of personal violence, they undergirded the region's reputation as the pathological exception to the national narrative of prosperity and progress.

Race and Labor in the North, 1865–1914

Sharecropping and forced labor were almost exclusively confined to the southern states and were largely associated with rural areas. Increasingly, however, substantial numbers of black workers lived in urban areas, including the growing industrial and commercial centers of the Northeast and Midwest. As the United States entered the twentieth century, about 880,000 African Americans, or 10 percent of the country's African American population, lived outside the former slaveholding South. Dating back to the eighteenth century, small communities of African Americans had developed in Philadelphia, Boston, New York, and other seaboard cities. In the decades immediately after the Civil War, these communities, as well as emerging ones in midwestern cities, grew slowly. Thus, between 1870 and 1890, on average, only about 4,800 African Americans left the South for the North each year. But the pace quickened in the 1890s, and between 1890 and 1910, more than 200,000 made the journey. On the eve of World War I, New York City had a black population exceeding 90,000, Chicago 45,000, and Philadelphia 70,000, and the nonsouthern African American population had surged over the one million mark. Declared a black journalist in 1913, "There are more Southern Negroes in the North and West than original Northern ones, and they are coming all . . . the time."[11]

The vast majority of African Americans who lived in northern cities, whether old-timers or newcomers, were working people. In common with other workers confronting the expanding new industrial and commercial economy, blacks experienced low wages, substandard housing, social disorder, and appalling rates of job-related accidents and illnesses. In addition, however, African American workers faced powerful currents of prejudice and hostility on the part of both employers and fellow workers, along with a political and legal system that relegated them to second-class citizenship and a cultural environment saturated with racist myths and stereotypes. Often adding to the difficulty of black workers attempting to carve out a niche for themselves in this hostile environment were the condescension and misguided advice of black elites.

In 1901, pioneering black scholar W. E. B. DuBois compiled a careful profile of black employment in East Coast cities, all of which were undergoing rapid demographic transformation as southern migrants filtered into them. In Philadelphia, he found that 95 percent of employed African Americans were wage workers, with the great majority concentrated in the "ordinary laborer" and "domestic service" categories, a finding that was broadly repeated in other northern cities with black migrants.[12] Indeed, throughout the half century after the end of the Civil War, the only secure occupational niche for black men and women was in domestic and personal service. To be sure, they struggled to achieve or to preserve tenuous footholds in the expanding industrial and commercial economy of the North, in the face of hostile employers and white workers and indifferent governments. But throughout the northern states in these years, black workers faced chronic job competition from white workers, particularly new immigrants, even in sectors they had dominated before the Civil War.

Overall, the story of African American workers in these cities in the fifty years after the war was a mixture of opportunity and frustration. Migration northward, whatever its injustices and limitations, freed migrants from the unrelenting toil and chronic indebtedness of impoverished southern cotton farms. African American communities in these northern cities developed diverse internal class structures. Ministers, teachers, school administrators, small-business owners, and a handful of public employees typically constituted a sort of middle-class leadership cadre. Although residential segregation was not as pronounced as it became after World War I, black neighborhoods, usually centering on a variety of Protestant churches, supported black professionals and entrepreneurs, who in turn supplied much of the communities' political and cultural leadership. Some ambitious men and women grew wealthy as publishers, caterers, and suppliers of goods and services to African Americans. Thus, Madam C. J. Walker, a St. Louis laundress who eventually settled in New York City, turned a successful hair-straightening process into a substantial fortune, and Mississippi-born Lillian Harris, also known as "Pig Foot Mary," prepared and sold southern food to fellow migrants and parlayed her earnings into lucrative investments in Harlem real estate. William Mack Felton used his ingenuity and mechanical ability to become a pioneering New York auto repair entrepreneur and property owner. Other newcomers built careers as politicians, educators, ministers, and publishers.

What northern cities such as Chicago, New York, Detroit, and Cleveland lacked, however, was a sturdy underpinning of steadily employed, high-wage blue-collar workers. Incoming migrants found themselves relegated to domestic, personal service, and common labor positions. DuBois and other observers noted a disparity in the gender composition of northern black communities, with women outnumbering men by as much as 20 percent. The reason, they found, was that while the demand for unskilled heavy labor was sporadic, the demand for domestic servants almost always remained strong, drawing thousands of young women into the northern cities while their husbands, children, brothers, and sweethearts remained at home.

Moreover, during this period, African American men in the border and northern states found themselves pushed aside by incoming immigrants and other job-hungry white workers. In Baltimore, for example, African Americans had once dominated the relatively skilled and well-paid trade of ship caulking, only to be forcibly replaced in the 1860s and 1870s by white workers. Into the 1890s, black workers had begun to establish footholds in small-town Pennsylvania steelmaking operations and even to advance into lower-level supervisory and skilled occupations. Over the next two decades, however, immigrants from southern and eastern Europe rapidly displaced them, pushing experienced black workers back into the common labor pool or out of the city. Throughout the Midwest, African Americans found themselves losing out in trades as diverse as metalworking, barbering, and building construction. In Detroit, for example, employers replaced blacks with immigrants as soon as the latter became available, despite their lack of skill, experience, or knowledge of the English language. "'First it was de Irish, den it was de Dutch,'" noted a black building tradesman in 1891, "'and now it's de Polacks as grinds us down. I s'pose when dey [the Poles] gets like de Irish and stands up for a fair price, some odder strangers'll come over de sea 'nd jine de faimily and cut us down again.'"[13] In the hotel and restaurant trades, where African Americans had long constituted a large proportion of the waiters and service employees, immigrants made significant inroads. Some African Americans claimed that even in the humblest of occupations, immigrants engaged in "the bitterest competition for the domestic service which the Negro once controlled."[14]

Nor did the expanding economic sectors much benefit African Americans before World War I. In Ohio, at the center of heavy industry, enumerators in 1890 counted only three blacks working in the state's steel mills, and by 1910, the situation had improved only marginally. After the turn of the century, the booming automobile industry of the upper Midwest was almost entirely closed to black workers. In the building trades, the introduction of new materials and methods helped shrink the numbers and marginalize the presence of black craftsmen, who were characteristically barred from vocational and apprenticing programs and excluded from unions and hence from job referrals.

There were, however, some positive sites for black employment. On the coast and at the lake ports, African Americans continued to work as longshoremen. Most whites considered dockside labor rough, uncertain, and dangerous, but for African Americans who lacked other options, these very characteristics provided opportunities in New York, Buffalo, Philadelphia, Detroit, Cleveland, Milwaukee, and other ports. In Ohio's Hocking Valley, black coal miners established a foothold. Although a combination of employer prejudice and union discrimination barred blacks from well-paid and prestigious jobs on the railroads, stereotypes of black servility, on the one hand, and of superhuman physical prowess, on the other, permitted their employment as Pullman car porters and as members of construction and maintenance crews. In northern cities, some African Americans found opportunities in public employment. Cities needed black policemen to patrol black neighborhoods, for example, and the equal-opportunity rules of northern governmental agencies allowed a trickle of African Americans to hold positions as state and municipal government employees. In this respect, it was probably the U.S. Post Office Department that provided the greatest opportunity. In Chicago in the 1910s, for example, as many as five hundred African Americans worked in the city's mail-sorting centers and post offices. In all these enclaves of black employment, however, employer prejudice, the hostility of white workers and managers, and informal rules of racial etiquette almost invariably barred African Americans from attaining—or even aspiring to—leadership or supervisory positions.

Exceptions to the bleak picture of black employment were rare and limited in the security and opportunities they provided. Longshoring and track maintenance work were heavy, dangerous occupations, often associated with rough and transient lifestyles. The handfuls of black salespeople, typists, clerks, and other office workers were overwhelmingly employed in small, vulnerable, black-owned businesses serving the black community. Pullman car porters, often relatively well-educated and cultivated men, enjoyed respect in the black community but were dependent on tips rather than on regular salaries for their livelihoods and constantly faced racial harassment, condescension, and arbitrary disciplinary action.

African American women in the North faced even greater obstacles in the workplace than did their fathers, brothers, and husbands. Poverty and low wages for male workers ensured that a much larger proportion of African American women would work outside the home—and for longer periods—than was the case for even the most impoverished immigrant groups. Yet they were almost completely shut out of the best-paying and most desirable jobs that the emerging industrial and commercial economy had to offer. Thus, before the 1910s, it was virtually impossible for black women to gain factory or clerical jobs. As late as 1920, for example, the Bell Telephone Company counted no African American women among its twenty-five thousand female phone operators. Just about the only employment options, other than domestic work, available to Progressive Era African American women in the North were the heavy and unhealthful work offered in the burgeoning steam laundries and employment as hotel maids or low-paid food service workers. As a result, the vast majority of employed black women worked in private homes as domestic servants, in many cases cut off from their families and subject to arbitrary and exploitative treatment, including sexual harassment, by their employers. In Ohio, for example, the 1910 census reported that fully 87 percent of the state's eighteen thousand black working women were employed as domestics or personal servants.[15]

By no means did African Americans acquiesce in this regime of discrimination and prejudice. Employers often explained their refusal to hire blacks in anything but menial capacities by claiming that domestic and common labor was somehow "natural" to Negroes and that, in the words of one, blacks were "content to remain in that group."[16] But black workers and black leaders angrily rejected such stereotypes and turned to a variety of tactics to protest ill treatment and to demand justice. Since none of the northern state or federal civil rights laws at the time addressed the issue of job discrimination, black workers had no legal recourse to even the most blatant forms of discrimination. Employers were free to reject black applicants out of hand and to include racial preferences or dislikes in their printed advertisements.

Even so, activist editors and organizations, such as the National Association for the Advancement of Colored People (NAACP; founded in 1909), kept up a drumbeat of criticism against employers, restrictive trade unions, and government officials for promoting or tolerating job discrimination. For example, while largely steering clear of racialist formulations, black spokesmen decried the reliance on immigrant labor, charging (with a good deal of justification) that the "whiteness" of even the most exotic new immigrant gave him or her an automatic advantage over black job seekers. There was wide support among blacks for the growing campaign to curtail immigration, which, during the early years of the century, reached massive proportions. Blacks, declared a Norfolk newspaper, had "learned through bitter experiences that foreign labor, though it may be crude, illiterate, and hopelessly unsympathetic with American institutions and ideals, is used to press us further down the economic ladder . . . in spite of our proved loyalty to America."[17] The unfairness of denying to men and women who had contributed so much to the nation's wealth and even to its very survival the same rights and opportunities extended to even the most recent newcomer from Europe was particularly galling to African Americans in every walk of life.

To many actual or would-be race leaders such as Booker T. Washington, black workers' salvation lay in acquiring habits of thrift and diligence. They thought that blacks should perfect skills and abilities in the domestic, service, and agricultural fields and cultivate the goodwill of employers. By proving themselves more diligent, loyal, and productive than strike-prone immigrants and other white workers, black editors, clergymen, and civic leaders advised, African Americans could gain a permanent niche in industry. The Negro, wrote Washington, "has the physical strength to endure hard labor, and he is not ashamed or afraid to work." Educators and race reformers urged black women to improve their domestic skills and thus prove themselves good servants to white employers. In 1897, a speaker at a conference on race relations advised, "One way to establish better relations with the white people will be to give them better cooks, better laundresses, better chambermaids, [and] better housekeepers."[18] African Americans, in the view of Washington and other educators, were best served by learning the humble duties of housekeeping, agriculture, and basic mechanical skills and by proving to white employers that they were worthy of employment. Although there is little evidence that ordinary working people accepted this accommodationist message in its entirety, black workers often concluded that they did, in fact, have to outperform white rivals if they were to have any hope of steady and remunerative employment.

Working people themselves, however, often turned to more activist efforts to improve their employment opportunities and raise their living standards. These efforts included militant union activism, the demonstration of superloyalty and uncommon productivity, and, in some cases, the replacement of striking white workers. Even in the isolating setting of domestic service, African American women sought to gain control over their lives by resisting their employers' intrusive demands for service and deference. They shunned abusive and overbearing employers and formed informal networks for sharing information about working conditions. In some southern cities, where the critical mass of female domestic service was highest, they even formed embryonic labor unions or union-like organizations. Increasingly, black women refused to "live in," that is, to serve as on-demand menial members of a white family's household. Hardworking black women played key roles in the cultural and religious lives of their communities; they both sought out the dance halls and clubs where new forms of African American music and popular entertainment were being forged and formed the backbone of the churches that flourished in the new northern black communities.

For many African Americans, union activism provided a means by which they could achieve and sustain a place in the new economy. Although the turn-of-the-century mainstream labor movement was ambivalent, at best, about the prospects of organizing black workers, the largest affiliate of the American Federation of Labor (AFL), the United Mine Workers of America (UMWA), included large numbers of African Americans, even in its southern locals. Indeed, blacks joined the UMWA at a proportionately higher rate than white miners did and constituted about a quarter of the embattled union's membership at the beginning of the twentieth century. Black railroaders, however, found themselves barred from the main railroad unions, even though they supplied much of the labor in track and roadbed maintenance and other heavy work on the trains and in the yards. Rebuffed by the elitist "brotherhoods" that represented white engineers, firemen, conductors, and trainmen, African Americans began forming their own organizations, several of which gained substantial membership in the 1910s. Black longshoremen, timber and sawmill workers, tobacco workers, oyster shuckers, and washerwomen also formed unions, sometimes under the auspices of radical interracial unions, and sometimes on their own.

The other side of the activist coin, paradoxically, was strikebreaking. In labor union circles, a kind of mythology grew up about the propensity of blacks to engage in strikebreaking. It became an article of faith among white trade unionists that blacks belonged to a "scab race." This blanket condemnation enabled white unionists to ignore or excuse the discriminatory practices of their own unions and to overlook the extent of scabbing among their fellow white workers. In reality, during this period of sustained labor conflict, strikebreaking by workers of all ethnic backgrounds was frequent. One of the sustaining myths of labor activists was that worker solidarity across the lines of skill, ethnicity, race, and gender was the norm and that workers who crossed picket lines were aberrant and morally deformed. But in fact, there was often a thin line between strike supporter and scab, since most workers, like most people everywhere, generally put their own personal and familial obligations and needs first. Wise labor organizers recognized this and realized that today's scab might be tomorrow's picket-line captain. Still, the specter of fellow workers being recruited to take the jobs of other workers trying to protect *their* livelihoods was one that understandably led to passionate rhetoric and sometimes lethal violence.

Although it was true that scabs came in all colors and ethnicities, white union activists, sharing in the pervasive racism of their times, exhibited a visceral hatred for black strikebreakers. In addition to resenting the obvious tactical and economic threat that scabs of any description posed, white workers regarded their replacement by blacks—considered the most inferior and degraded of all people—as profoundly demeaning. Declared one AFL official in 1904, black strikebreakers were invariably "huge, strapping fellows, ignorant and vicious, whose predominating trait was animalism."[19]

In 1913, Booker T. Washington declared bluntly—and proudly—that Negroes were "very willing strikebreakers," but in general, black workers pursued this option for reasons other than those envisioned by accommodationists such as Washington. For African American workers who were denied ordinary opportunities for decent employment, replacing white men whose unions rejected black members was seen as a positive and forward-looking act, and it had little to do with ingratiating themselves with employers. Black strikebreakers sought to provide for their families and to better their prospects. If crossing a picket line opened up opportunities otherwise denied, so be it. "Let them call us scabs if they want to," challenged a defiant black worker who helped break a strike in Washington State in 1891, adding that he and his coworkers were not about to "stand back and suffer while others live."[20]

During the late nineteenth and early twentieth centuries, African American workers in the North battled long odds to gain a secure footing in the emerging industrial-commercial economy. Obviously, discrimination on the part of employers, the hostility of white workers, the competition from waves of new immigrants, and the exclusionary practices of many trade unions severely disadvantaged black workers, whether they were long-term residents of northern cities or newcomers from the South. As DuBois remarked in his classic study *The Philadelphia Negro,* owing to "race prejudice," the exclusion of blacks from unions and from apprenticeship programs, and the unwillingness of employers to hire blacks for any but unskilled positions, "white workmen have not only monopolized the new industrial opportunities . . . , but have also been enabled to take from the Negro workman the opportunities he already enjoyed in certain lines of work."[21]

Black workers had to contend not only with the prejudice of white employers and competition from white workers but also with the condescension and poor advice of their would-be race leaders. Even DuBois, who had not known slavery and was at the beginning of a brilliant academic and activist career, could not always disguise his feelings of shame and even contempt for the habits and pathologies of the southern migrants now arriving in northern cities. He and other commentators repeatedly pointed to the injustice done to long-term northern blacks, who, he complained, were often judged by the behavior and job performance of the new migrants. Newcomers to the cities included too many untrained, rootless young people who were tempted by urban living to join the demimonde of crime and vice. Wrote DuBois of Philadelphia laborers, "we find the ranks of the laborers among Negroes filled to an unusual extent with disappointed men, with men who have lost their incentive to excel, and have become chronic grumblers and complainers, spreading this [unwholesome] spirit."[22]

Other aspiring race reformers were even more scathing in their criticism of the first post-Emancipation generation of southern blacks. Too many young Negroes, critics charged, had lost the incentive to work and used discrimination as an excuse for their lowly status. Declared Oswald Garrison Villard, a white advocate of black advancement and a founding member of the NAACP, too many young blacks "prefer to live in their dilapidated Negro quarters. . . . They are dirty, slovenly, often impudent, habitually lazy and dishonest and unwilling to work steadily."[23] DuBois, at least, saw that the solution to the problem of the disgruntled and underperforming black laborer was the breaking down of barriers to employment and the expansion of educational opportunities, both academic and vocational. In contrast, Villard, along with Washington and other influential reformers and educators, urged young blacks to accept their station, apply themselves diligently, and become the best domestic servants, farmers, or ditchdiggers possible. With mechanical devices beginning to replace servants in the nation's kitchens, the proportion of the population engaged in agriculture dropping sharply, and common labor providing low-wage and sporadic employment at best, advice such as Villard's was a dead end. With friends like these, black workers needed no enemies, though they had many.

In many respects, the America of the post-Reconstruction years was a nation in retreat from the egalitarian ideals of the Civil War era. Although the great constitutional amendments remained on the books, daily practice, lack of enforcement, and damaging Supreme Court decisions virtually nullified their practical application. Doctrines of white supremacy rode high in the pulpits, classrooms, and legislative halls and were acted out daily at work sites and in neighborhoods everywhere. It was in this highly racialized world that the first post-Emancipation generation of African Americans in the northern cities tried to gain a share of the booming economy's bounty. By the outset of the Great War in Europe in 1914, thousands of black workers, old-timers and newcomers alike, had indeed established footholds in the North and Midwest, but it seemed clear that unless the stream of European immigrants slowed, unless employers set aside their refusal to hire black workers, and until white workers began to look to class solidarity rather than racial discrimination to advance their interests, real progress would be slow and difficult.

Organized Labor and African Americans, 1890–1914

In the pre–World War I years, African Americans quickly learned that they could expect little tangible support from the mainstream elements in the American labor movement. Although leaders of the AFL frequently asserted their lack of color prejudice and proclaimed their desire to extend organization to black workers, many of the individual unions affiliated with the federation, as well as the independent railroad brotherhoods, excluded or discriminated against black workers. In many trades, white workers used their unions as exclusionary weapons, employing a variety of devices to ensure that whole categories of jobs in manufacturing, construction, and transport were reserved for white workers. Apprenticeship and training programs barred black applicants. Union constitutions and induction rituals enforced "whites-only" provisions. Unions colluded with employers in negotiating collective bargaining agreements that excluded blacks. In cities and in state legislatures, craft unions secured enactments that, in effect, applied racial criteria for pursuing trades such and plumbing and barbering. And when all else failed, white workers turned to violent attacks to keep their trades lily-white, confident that law enforcement officials would be willing accomplices in maintaining the color line.

The AFL, the umbrella organization with which the separate trade unions were affiliated, did not have a color bar. In fact, Samuel Gompers, its perennial president, initially opposed the racial exclusivism of member unions. Since the AFL's founding document, its 1886 constitution, included no color bar, and since the very ideology of the labor movement posited class solidarity and common struggle against exploitation and injustice, it was natural for black activists to think of organized labor as an actual or at least potential ally in efforts to combat discrimination, subordination, and mistreatment. Repeatedly, Gompers claimed that the labor movement welcomed workers of all races and creeds. At the organization's national convention in 1910, for example, Gompers rejected charges that the AFL was antagonistic to black workers. "We seek to build up the labor move-ment . . . , and we want all the negroes we can possibly get who will join hands with organized labor," he declared.[24]

Encouraged by such statements, black workers and leaders of African American organizations turned to Gompers and the AFL, calling on them to raise their voices against the mounting victimization of blacks. And on occasion, they found nuggets of hope in Gompers's statements and in AFL actions. For example, in 1892, the AFL president celebrated a notable ex-ample of biracial union activism that had recently occurred when white and black longshoremen in New Orleans had supported each other's strikes, sometimes at considerable risk to themselves. In what was probably his most enthusiastic utterance about the virtues of racial solidarity, he de-clared, "Never in the history of the world was such an exhibition, where with all the prejudices existing against the Black man, when the white wage workers of New Orleans would sacrifice their means of livelihood to pro-tect and defend their colored wage workers."[25] Moreover, until near the end of the 1890s, the AFL Executive Council refused to charter several trade unions until they dropped the race bar from their constitutions.

Even so, close attention to Gompers's various statements about race and labor—and to the issues on which the AFL was notably silent—gave little hope that the federation would assume the mantle of racial enlighten-ment in this period of mounting repression. Almost invariably, Gompers's admonitions to white unionists about the need to open their doors to black coworkers were couched in purely utilitarian language. Never did the ver-bose AFL president invoke bedrock principles of human equality and social justice. "You cannot improve your own conditions unless you help the ne-gro move up," he counseled Alabama workers in 1895. "Help him orga-nize. I do not want you to dance with him, or sleep with him, or kiss him, but I do want you to organize with him."[26] In advising the Brotherhood of Locomotive Firemen to drop its color bar, he pointed to the lesson of the abolitionist crusade, which demonstrated, he declared, that "one could de-sire the abolition of slavery without falling absolutely in love with the slaves." Exclusion of blacks, he counseled, played into the hands of employ-ers because it created a pool of workers antagonistic to organized labor and hence available for strikebreaking duty. "If we fail to organize and recognize the colored wage-workers we cannot blame them if they accept our chal-lenge of enmity and do all they can to frustrate our purposes. If we fail to make friends of them, the employing class won't be so shortsighted."[27]

Even before the turn of the century, however, Gompers had all but abandoned any sense of obligation to defend egalitarian principles with re-spect to race. He connived with leaders of several new affiliates in approv-ing de facto discrimination. He resisted suggestions that the AFL actively promote the organization of black workers, establishing instead a kind of pseudo-union apparatus, firmly under the control of white functionaries, for black workers whose low-wage status might jeopardize the standards of nearby white workers. As Jim Crow fastened its grip on the South and the denigration of blacks intensified, the AFL invariably bowed to the sensibilities of white workers, forcing blacks into separate, segregated unions. Gompers reproved African American unionists who insisted on equal and dignified treatment in the hallowed "House of Labor."

Moreover, as organized labor's increasingly influential and prominent public spokesman, Gompers failed to call attention to black disfranchisement, segregation, or the mounting violence against African Americans during this period. Increasingly, he blamed the victim, characterizing black workers as cowardly and opportunistic. He opened the pages of the *American Federationist* to racist diatribes. Thus, in 1898, he printed the fulminations of a southern white AFL organizer who declared that blacks did not have "those peculiarities of temperament such as patriotism, sympathy, etc., which are peculiar to most of the Caucasian race." In 1899, Gompers told federal investigators that black workers had "so conducted themselves as to be a continuous convenient whip placed in the hands of the employers to cow the white men."[28] At times, he was more blunt. Why, asked a reporter, had the AFL been unsuccessful in efforts to organize in the South? It was, Gompers responded, primarily "the fault of the Negroes." "Caucasians," he asserted in 1905, "are not going to let their standard of living be destroyed by negroes, Chinamen, Japs, or any others."[29]

Throughout the AFL and the railroad brotherhoods, discriminatory practices and hostility toward blacks prevailed. In a study of black union activity published in 1902, DuBois counted forty thousand blacks among the AFL's one million members.[30] Forty-three unions, including the large railroad brotherhoods, had no African American members—some because they refused to enroll blacks, and others because they kept them out of training and apprenticeship programs. Most of the rest of the national unions counted few blacks as members, with the UMWA and the International Brotherhood of Teamsters being the two largest exceptions. Some African Americans belonged to the hod carriers and the laborers unions, which represented unskilled construction workers. Others were enrolled in the AFL's "federal" labor unions, small local organizations directly controlled by the AFL leadership. Critics charged, with some justification, that the AFL maintained these usually segregated organizations primarily to control blacks who worked with or near white unionists and who, if left unorganized, might provide employers with a ready supply of cheap labor and strikebreakers.

Nowhere did racial hierarchies prevail more openly and in such thoroughgoing fashion as on the nation's railroads. Native-born and old-immigrant white men dominated the prestigious and well-paid "running" trades, serving as conductors, trainmen, firemen, and engineers. The unions representing these men, among the oldest and most influential in the country, flatly barred blacks from being members. By the turn of the century, these "Big Four" brotherhoods held collective bargaining agreements with most major railroads, so a membership bar amounted to exclusion from these jobs. Among the southern railroads, which were less well organized, a different pattern prevailed. There, African Americans were permitted to work as firemen, performing the heavy labor of shoveling coal into the firebox. On the northern and western lines, where the work was no less arduous, the fireman, who worked closely with the engineer in the locomotive cab, could learn how to drive the train and could aspire to the position of engineer. To be a fireman on a railroad such as the Chicago, Burlington, and Quincy was to be a kind of apprentice engineer. But in the South, the job of fireman was a dead end. White engineers treated their black firemen like their personal lackeys, often dispatching them on errands or demanding tokens of personal service. Other white railroaders resented black firemen, since they believed that every black who served in a locomotive cab was depriving a white worker of the opportunity to train to be an engineer. As a result, black firemen were systematically harassed and driven from the cabs, often violently. By the 1920s, they had largely disappeared from southern locomotives.[31]

The railroads did provide jobs for blacks. It was black men, along with Mexicans in the Southwest and Chinese in the West, who built many of the roadbeds and laid the tracks. Blacks were heavily employed in ongoing construction and the difficult and dangerous work of track maintenance. Black workers also toiled in the repair and maintenance sheds, usually classified as helpers or laborers even if they actually performed skilled work. The chief union in the railroad repair yards, the International Association of Machinists (IAM), had been founded in Atlanta in 1889 in part to protect the jobs of white metalworkers and to prevent employers from replacing white workers with black "helpers" during labor disputes. Indeed, it was the IAM that posed the greatest dilemma for Gompers in his early efforts to keep the explicit color line out of the AFL, since the constitution it submitted when it sought AFL affiliation in 1891 prohibited African American membership. Railroad car builders were no less exclusivist in their attitudes and policies toward blacks. Union organizers of the vast Pullman sleeping car manufacturing and repair facilities in Chicago, for example, ignored black porters and janitors in their sporadic efforts to organize white machinists and car workers. Even the American Railroad Union, a militant, inclusive organization that sought in the mid-1890s to transcend the skill demarcations that often impeded mass action on the railroads, barred black workers from membership. A delegate to the 1905 convention of the Brotherhood of Railway Carmen spoke for a generation of white railroaders when he declared, "God . . . made the Negro but he never made him to be a car worker. I do not believe the time will ever come when he should come into a union along with carmen. . . . When the time does come that I must sit down in social equality with the Negro . . . I want to be carried to the nearest insane asylum."[32]

The skilled building trades were another arena from which white unionists systematically excluded black competition. The AFL Plumbers Union, for example, was highly successful in its efforts to control access to certification. In a number of states, it secured the passage of laws that created a public authority to license plumbers on the basis of standardized tests and review by a board, which invariably (and sometimes by legislative requirement) included union plumbers. Although African Americans had often worked as plumbers and continued to do so within black neighborhoods, these laws were applied in such a way as to drive blacks out of general construction work, the most desirable and highest-paid sector (which, as some white plumbers boasted, was the intent). Although city ordinances and state enactments did not explicitly invoke race, their promoters were often quite frank in acknowledging the purpose of these measures. Thus, in 1905, one Virginia plumber extolled the virtues of a proposed licensing ordinance in his town because it would "entirely eliminate" blacks from the trade. Another plumber decried the large number of black plumbers in Danville, Virginia, complaining that "owing to the fact of not having an examining board it is impossible to stop them."[33] One of the most damaging effects of craft union discrimination, whether enforced through legislative, organizational, or physical means, was to discourage young black men from pursuing careers in the skilled trades, where, until the late nineteenth century, African Americans had established promising footholds. As one journalist noted in 1898, "wherever the union develops effective strength the black workmen must put down the trowel and take up the tray"—in other words, leave a skilled trade such as bricklaying and settle for being a waiter or a servant.[34]

Actually, the AFL leadership's negative response to the problems of African American workers—to say nothing of the even more negative attitudes and policies of key affiliates and white workers more generally—was a manifestation of the labor movement's broader turn-of-the-century race problem. White American-born and old-immigrant workers, and the unions to which many of them belonged, looked with growing distaste and apprehension at the increasing ethnic and racial diversity in industrializing America. Before the Civil War, immigrant Irish and German workers had often clashed with American-born workers, white and black, in competition over jobs, housing, and urban space. On the West Coast, an influx of Chinese workers had triggered widespread racial antagonism that mounted in intensity throughout the century, even after Congress effectively barred the immigration of Chinese workers in an act passed in 1882. Even the Knights of Labor, notable for its inclusive and egalitarian approach to organizing, usually drew the line at admitting Chinese.

With respect to European immigration, laborites faced a dilemma. On the one hand, many of them came from immigrant backgrounds themselves and had an instinctive sympathy for those who hoped to build a better life in America. In supporting a bill to curtail the importation of *contract* laborers in 1870, for example, one union official affirmed that "we at the same time, heartily welcome all *voluntary* emigrants from every clime, and pledge them our sympathy and encouragement."[35] Indeed, many labor activists—at least rhetorically—included even Asians among those to be welcomed, as long as they came as individuals and were not brought to the country in conditions of debt servitude.

On the other hand, as immigration from southern and eastern Europe increased at the end of the nineteenth century and became a tidal wave in the new century, hostility mounted. Anglo-American workers saw their country changing before their very eyes. The dramatic expansion of corporate power, the restructuring of the workplace and the introduction of new technologies and new managerial methods, and the sudden emergence of vast conurbations posed enormous challenges not only in the workplace but also in the realm of culture and values. What did impoverished Slavic, Greek, Italian, and Chinese workers know of Americans' high standards with regard to wages and living conditions? As refugees from corrupt monarchies and authoritarian governments, what could they possibly know about free political institutions? Gompers, an immigrant himself, declared that the newcomers pouring into the country represented "a heterogeneous stew of divergent and discordant customs, languages, [and] institutions" and were "impossible to organize."[36] For native-born and old-immigrant white workers, employers' encouragement of this flood of new immigrants was just another example of how they were subverting American republican values in the service of corporate greed. Thus, in 1897, the AFL convention for the first time urged the adoption of a strict literacy test as a means of regulating the number of aliens.

At the same time, notions of the United States as a beacon of liberty and a land of opportunity died hard. The AFL did not make the literacy test a priority item on its political agenda, and its spokesmen generally refrained from egregious public utterances about European immigrants, even when the 1906 convention revived the literacy test demand. And although the AFL remained the bailiwick of established, mostly native-born workers, its affiliates sometimes successfully organized immigrant workers, who often proved to be sturdy and loyal union recruits. Whatever their private misgivings, Gompers and his colleagues drew back from racist characterizations of the European newcomers, increasingly casting the call for restriction in practical terms. The country, they argued, needed time to assimilate the hundreds of thousands of newcomers who were already here before it welcomed millions more. Italians, Greeks, Poles, Russians, and other new European immigrants, they acknowledged, might well be worthy human beings, but for now, their low-wage expectations played into the hands of employers and undermined the standards that American-born workers had struggled so long and hard to achieve.

The Chinese presented a different problem altogether, according to most laborites. Although working people and the labor movement had not been prime movers behind the Exclusion Act of 1882, animosity toward the Chinese mounted through the late nineteenth century and into the twentieth. Indeed, at times, it seemed as if the hapless Chinese had become the lightning rod that attracted the most vicious and violent laborite hostility. In the late nineteenth century, for example, anti-Chinese riots and massacres, mostly in California and other western states and territories, left scores of Chinese workers dead.[37] Labor newspapers and convention speeches bristled with attacks on the Chinese, who were depicted as heathen, unclean, and utterly alien to American standards and values. With the Chinese, according to the 1892 AFL convention, came "nothing but filth, vice and disease." In 1902, Gompers published a pamphlet whose title carried its message: "Meat vs. Rice—American Manhood vs. Asiatic Coolieism."[38]

Throughout the late nineteenth and early twentieth centuries, politicians of both major parties, concerned about labor unrest yet unwilling to antagonize corporate employers, launched repeated attacks on the minuscule number of Chinese workers in the country as a means of courting the support of white workers. Prominent union officials were appointed to key posts in the U.S. Bureau of Immigration, which enforced the Exclusion Act, and they used their offices to heighten anti-Chinese sentiment. Thus, Terence V. Powderly, erstwhile grand master workman of the egalitarian Knights of Labor, served as U.S. commissioner of immigration from 1898 to 1902 and was replaced by Frank Sargent, former president of the Brotherhood of Locomotive Engineers, who served until 1908. Both men applied the law rigorously with respect to the handful of Chinese who did seek entry into the country, and each used his office as a bully pulpit from which to warn of the ongoing threat posed by the Chinese. Powderly, for example, pledged his determination to "check the advancing hordes and whores who seek our shores," while insisting, "I am no bigot." Sargent, if anything, outdid Powderly in his excoriation of the Chinese and his efforts to keep them out of the country.[39]

The mainstream labor movement's pervasive racism did not set it apart from other contemporary American institutions. The early twentieth century was the heyday of "scientific" racism. Whether from the pulpit, the university lectern, or the Oval Office, the ruling orthodoxy was that a powerful and natural racial hierarchy existed, with Africans and African Americans at the bottom. Organized labor's discrimination against and neglect of black workers drew little public criticism. Indeed, in some respects, even Gompers's flawed and inconsistent opposition to the color line in the AFL put him ahead of most contemporary business, religious, political, and academic leaders. Even labor's often vicious hostility toward Asians only mirrored widespread beliefs and attitudes, tempered in political circles only by certain diplomatic necessities.

Within the world of organized labor, hostility toward the racial "other" was often expressed in the context of upholding cherished American values. At a time of violent labor conflict, the mass importation of impoverished European, Asian, or African American workers seemed to many white laborites to be only another cynical example of corporations' ruthless quest for profit and control. Greedy employers, one unionist declared in 1898, would "willingly take up with a nigger for the purpose of enslaving a white wage earner."[40] In San Francisco, a hotbed of anti-Asian sentiment, articulate trade unionists combined a kind of American republicanism —committed to the idea that, through unions, workers could exercise real power and that ill-gotten corporate wealth and power should be curbed through direct, energetic political and union action—with a root-and-branch denigration of Chinese and Japanese workers. The occasional labor or socialist visionary might argue that American labor must expand its definition of republican virtue to embrace the "other" and pursue the logic of class solidarity rather than continue down the dead end of racial division, but few such voices were heard in turn-of-the-century America.

Surprisingly, despite the ubiquity of racialist beliefs and practices, there were significant examples of interracial labor cooperation. Yet, when forced by circumstances to join in common cause with their black coworkers, rarely did white workers or their leaders explain their actions in terms of human rights or racial equality. Indeed, white organizers and union leaders almost invariably explained collaboration with black workers in terms of necessity and almost never by adherence to socialist, Christian, or republican values. With the exception of a few socialists and radical union activists, white trade unionists would go only so far as to acknowledge black workers' rights to fair treatment on the job, despite their general inferiority. Thus, in 1898, a UMWA official explained his union's attitude toward its black members, who may have numbered twenty thousand at the time: "As far as we are concerned as miners, the colored men are with us in the mines. . . . They are members of our organization; [and] can receive as much consideration from the officials of the organization as any other members. . . . We treat them that way."[41]

Throughout the turn-of-the-century period, the UMWA—one of the largest AFL affiliates—included the greatest number of African Americans.

Even in the southern mines, African Americans often participated in union deliberations and sometimes held positions as officers and organizers. One particularly notable black UMWA organizer, Richard Davis, became a legendary figure among miners, both black and white, for his oratorical and organizing skills.

Other unions with substantial numbers of black workers were the International Brotherhood of Teamsters and a variety of longshoremen's organizations, especially in the Gulf ports. In both cases, segregation of work sites was virtually impossible. Both wagon and truck driving and longshoring often involved either casual or unskilled labor. On the docks and in urban areas, black workers performed much of the heavy lifting associated with the handling and transporting of goods. In the Gulf ports, it was common for black longshoremen to have their own local unions, with which white longshoremen often found it necessary to cooperate, lest employers adopt a divide-and-conquer strategy. Urban teamster locals were usually racially integrated, at least in northern cities such as Chicago, with black drivers and laborers sometimes holding local offices.

These uncharacteristic, though not completely marginal, cases of interracial unionism gave hope to some black leaders that organized labor might one day shed its racial provincialism. The logic of an increasingly interconnected industrial society, a few visionary activists believed, would force working people of all ethnic and racial backgrounds to recognize their common plight and the need for mutual support. No one carried this logic further in the early decades of the twentieth century than the radicals and activists who marched under the banner of the Industrial Workers of the World (IWW). Founded in 1905, the IWW proclaimed its root-and-branch antagonism toward capitalism and toward labor organizations, such as the AFL, that were willing to work within its purview. Appealing particularly to workers in remote mining, timbering, and agricultural work sites and to the unskilled masses that the AFL largely ignored, the IWW preached a doctrine of revolutionary anarcho-syndicalism that was based on the fundamental equality of all workers, regardless of gender, skill, or race. Although the IWW never made the extensive (if rather shallow) inroads into the agricultural South that the Knights of Labor had made in the 1880s, in the early 1910s, in the pine forests of Louisiana and Texas, it did build interracial unions that fought fierce battles with unscrupulous employers. And in Philadelphia, African Americans led in the building of a durable longshoremen's local under the "Wobbly" banner.

On the whole, though, hopes for some sort of black-labor rapprochement were disappointed. Courageous and farsighted as the IWW was, it was constantly under attack from local vigilantes, state and federal government authorities, and the mainstream labor movement. Even the UMWA's relative racial enlightenment was hardly consistent or universal. At times, for example, its journal printed both Davis's eloquent accounts of organizing efforts and insulting racial "jokes" and stereotypes in the same issue. In the violent world of coal mining unionism, employers frequently resorted to the importation of strikebreakers, and even though the majority of these strikebreakers were not African Americans, it was for those men that white miners reserved their most vehement hatred. They referred to imported whites as merely misguided or ignorant dupes of cynical employers; in contrast, blacks who appeared in the mining towns of Illinois and Indiana during strikes were depicted as alien invaders threatening to destroy miners' homes and families. Typical was the bitter complaint of an Illinois journalist in 1896: black strikebreakers, he declared, were a "horde of barbarian niggers."[42]

The mainstream labor movement paid a steep price for its intolerance. Confined largely to skilled trades, the AFL made little headway in its few halfhearted efforts to extend organization into the emerging mass production industries. Increasingly, its leaders concentrated on protecting the jobs and standards of current members, and a central tactic for accomplishing this goal was to keep the labor pool in a given trade small. Thus, racial tirades against new immigrants, Asians, and blacks were not mere exercises in verbal bigotry. More important, they served to protect white workers' standards by eliminating possible competition and thus compelling employers to pay union wage rates. Moreover, the virulence of labor's hatred of the Chinese—who constituted only a minute portion of the labor force, even in California—legitimated the politics of race and easily spilled over into attitudes toward blacks and immigrants generally. Although Gompers and his colleagues largely held back from violent verbal assaults against European immigrants, and although they never explicitly made the AFL into a whites-only organization, their ready embrace of the racist assumptions and politics of their generation cut them off from their own best traditions and played directly into the hands of their corporate adversaries, as Gompers sometimes reminded himself.

3

GREAT WAR, GREAT MIGRATION

B etween 1914 and 1932, the ethnic and racial composition and the geographic distribution of the American working class changed dramatically. These were years of war, vast economic reconfiguration and expansion, and bewildering social and cultural change. The migration of over a million rural southern blacks to northern industrial centers and to expanding southern cities, along with the imposition of ethnically defined restrictions on immigration, triggered a complex reshuffling of the demographics of work. During and after World War I, episodes of savage racial violence and intriguing examples of biracial activism punctuated the massive labor turmoil of these years. Throughout the 1910s and 1920s, African American leaders bitterly assailed the mainstream labor movement's failure to repudiate racialist practices and attitudes, even as black workers sought entry into the House of Labor or, finding the doors closed, sought to build their own unions. Wartime federal actions initially raised hopes that enlightened public policies might at last challenge racial injustice in the workplace, but key congressional enactments in 1926 and 1931 served to validate railroad and construction unions' discriminatory policies and practices. During the prosperous 1920s, African American workers began to benefit modestly from their increased involvement in the expanding industrial and service economy, but the onset of the Great Depression quickly demonstrated that the rubric "last hired, first fired" still applied to black workers.

The Great Migration

In the 1910s and 1920s, the movement of hundreds of thousands of African Americans from the rural South to urban and industrial centers was one of the great events of the twentieth century. The numbers were staggering. Between 1914 and 1920, somewhere between 450,000 and 700,000 southern African Americans relocated to the North. After the recession of 1920–

1921, this exodus resumed, with more than half a million additional migrants by 1930. Between 1910 and 1930, South Carolina lost 280,000 black citizens, Georgia 335,000, Alabama 150,000, and Mississippi 200,000. In these same decades, New York gained 335,000, Pennsylvania 185,000, Michigan 125,000, and Illinois 190,000.[1] By 1930, more than 1.3 million African Americans born in the South were living elsewhere, primarily in the northeastern and midwestern industrial states.

The movement of African Americans northward in pursuit of economic opportunities, political rights, and freedom from the lethal violence and petty indignities of life in the South was not a new phenomenon. Since the end of the Civil War, some blacks, both as individuals and in organized groups, had sought to escape the impoverished and repressive South. In the decades surrounding the turn of the twentieth century, migration northward had quickened. But the scope and dimensions of the World War I–era migration constituted a different order of magnitude. As the outbreak of war in Europe in mid-1914 both dried up sources of cheap labor and stimulated industrial production in the United States, employers looked southward for workers. Companies that had once disdained to hire blacks now eagerly recruited them. In the mid-1910s, advertisements in the *Chicago Defender,* a leading African American newspaper with a wide circulation in the South, encouraged southern blacks to relocate. In the first half of 1916 alone, the Pennsylvania Railroad hired thousands of blacks to work on road maintenance and repair. In Chicago, the great South Side meatpacking firms turned to black labor, with southern newcomers accounting for most of the 10,000-plus blacks who toiled in the stockyards at the end of the war.[2] The number of black steelworkers in the Pittsburgh mills leaped from 800 in 1910 to more than 5,100 ten years later.[3] Burgeoning chemical, munitions, food processing, and metalworking firms throughout the North and Midwest avidly recruited southern black labor as well, and the small prewar urban black communities were now overwhelmed by the influx of job-seeking migrants. For example, in Detroit, the 1910 black population of less than 6,000 had mushroomed by 1918 to around 30,000, and in 1930, it stood at over 120,000; meanwhile, Chicago's black population surged from 44,000 in 1910 to almost a quarter million twenty years later.[4]

Migrants and potential migrants responded eagerly to the war-engendered hope of finding economic gain, personal security, and educational opportunity denied them in the South. This was a people's movement, drawing farmworkers, sharecroppers, domestic servants, and common laborers, especially after the outbreak of war in Europe. It had no central direction. "This migration," observed one prominent northern black clergyman, "differs from all others in that it has no visible leader."[5] Indeed, southern black elites, fearing the loss of congregants, students, customers, clients, and employees, often warned of the dangers and difficulties of life in the North, as did southern employers and editorialists who were fearful of losing their source of cheap labor. But thousands of African Americans, especially those in the Cotton Belt, calculated that the combination of deteriorating economic conditions in the South, the ever-present fear and resentment associated with chronic white-on-black violence, and war-related employment opportunities presented a unique opportunity. As one resident of Memphis wrote in response to a newspaper article depicting job opportunities in the North, "I want a job in a small town some where in the north where I can receive verry good wages and where I can educate my 3 little girls and demand respect of intelegence." Noted a man from New Orleans, "Anywhere north will do us and I suppose the worst place there is better than the best place here."[6]

Some southern whites applauded this exodus. "Many of those young bucks already have criminal records," asserted a North Carolina jurist. "A more equitable distribution of the sons of Ham [i.e., blacks]," predicted a Mississippi editor, "will teach the Caucasians of the North that wherever there is a negro infusion, there will be a race problem." Most cotton growers, however, regarded the migration as a threat rather than an opportunity. As Booker T. Washington observed in 1914, the southern economy was "based on the Negro and the mule." Cotton production depended on the presence of an oversupply of cheap, subservient labor. White families both rural and urban were equally dependent on black women to do the cooking, cleaning, child minding, and other domestic chores. Black workers played crucial roles in the region's forest products, transport, food processing, mining, and heavy construction industries. "The farmers of the Black Belt," admitted the *Montgomery Advertiser*, "cannot get along without Negro labor," a judgment that white housewives, mine owners, and turpentine producers would have readily endorsed.[7]

Some white southerners were confident that, when faced with the realities of cold northern winters and racial prejudice, migrants would return en masse to their native region. And it was true that many southern blacks found living and working conditions in the North harsh and discouraging. Although laws in some northern states barred racial discrimination in public accommodations, refusal of service and contemptuous treatment were commonplace. Housing segregation in the northern cities confined the prewar black population and new migrants alike to constricted enclaves that quickly became overcrowded and run-down. By 1919, according to one report, the African American neighborhood near Chicago's stockyards had become a "festering slum," while in southeastern Pennsylvania, where chemical and munitions plants had drawn thousands of southern migrants, blacks had to live in houses "that had no water and no toilets . . . and whose cellars were flooded." Violent white opposition often met African Americans who sought better housing. In Chicago, for example, where the number of blacks living in South Side neighborhoods tripled in the 1910s, the firebombing of black-occupied residences in "white" streets became commonplace during and immediately after the war.[8]

Black workers faced discrimination and hostility in northern workplaces as well. Although labor-starved employers recruited them aggressively, almost invariably, southern blacks were assigned to the least skilled, most physically demanding, and lowest paid positions in the mills and factories. Even educated migrants or those with mechanical skills found that the only jobs available were as common laborers. In the steel mills of Pittsburgh and Gary, hot, dangerous, and physically punishing work involving the handling of hot metal and close proximity to the superheated blast furnaces was reserved for blacks, whose African origins were thought to make them uniquely able to endure high temperatures. In Chicago's vast packinghouses, African Americans commonly found work on the "kill" floor, notorious for its blood-spattered dispatch and evisceration of terrified animals. The building trades, where craft unions typically barred black membership, employed newcomers almost exclusively as common laborers, regardless of the skills they had brought north with them.

Women usually faced even more restrictive employment opportunities. As in the South, domestic service proved the most common occupation available. The Chicago meatpackers did hire black women, although even there, reported an academic investigator, "they worked at the lowest paid 'blind-alley' jobs in the yards and were excluded openly from the jobs with better work conditions."[9] The other major nondomestic employers of African American women were the huge steam laundries, which were "industrializing" that aspect of housework. According to a U.S. Department of Labor report, "Because of the difficulties and dangers of the work, and because of the traditional linking of Negro women to such tasks, there has been in most places little objection to them or color discrimination against them in laundries."[10]

During the brief period of American belligerency, 1917–1918, some sales and clerical positions became available to black women in northern cities, but the end of the war typically brought an abrupt termination of those occupational experiments. "In the 1920s," recalled one woman, "my mother and five aunts migrated to Cleveland . . . and, in spite of their many talents, they found every door except the kitchen door closed to them."[11] The growing black communities of the northern cities did employ small numbers of black women as secretaries, bookkeepers, and receptionists, and a few women with educational attainments found positions as teachers, nurses, and clerks. Overall, however, migrating black women quickly learned that the same racial and gender discrimination that had relegated them to ill-paid domestic service in Alabama or Mississippi prevailed in New York, Ohio, and Michigan as well.

Despite these difficulties, southern whites who predicted that migrants would find life in the North so harsh and uncongenial that they would flock back to Dixie were wrong. Throughout the entire postwar decade, southern blacks continued to head North, even after the boom in wartime employment had ended. Working men who had left their families to try their luck in the North now sent for their wives and children. Early migrants encouraged friends and neighbors to join them, often providing temporary housing and information about job openings. After reaching a peak in 1917–1918, migration tailed off in the early 1920s, only to spike again in 1924–1925. The burgeoning African American population of Chicago, Detroit, New York, Philadelphia, Pittsburgh, Cleveland, Milwaukee, and a host of smaller cities attested to the determination of southern blacks to claim a share of the nation's rapid economic growth and to exploit the opportunities, however limited, available in the North.

Clearly, the Great Migration represented a great stride forward in education, personal security, and politics. City schools might be overcrowded, insensitive to black children's distinctive needs, and increasingly segregated, but educational opportunities in Illinois and Pennsylvania far outstripped those available in Georgia and Louisiana. Southern blacks "are seeking better education for their children," declared the *Chicago Defender,* "as well as getting away from slavery, Jim Crow [railroad] cars and concubinage."[12] Overcrowded housing and violent resistance to residential mobility added to the tensions of life in the North, but at least in Illinois and Pennsylvania, blacks were not routinely subjected to legally sanctioned humiliation and terror. Nor was there interference with northern blacks' participation in the political process. Indeed, by the late 1920s, African Americans in northern cities were electing aldermen, city councilmen, and school board members. And in 1928, Oscar De Priest of Chicago was elected to the House of Representatives—the first black to serve in Congress since the departure of North Carolina's George White in 1901.

Of course, the achievement and retention of these gains ultimately depended on migrants' ability to find and keep remunerative work. In this key regard, despite black women's relative lack of occupational progress, on the whole, the migration paid off. Especially during the wartime emergency, but generally through the 1920s as well, African American men improved their wages and their occupational status. Government statistics told part of the story. In 1910, before the Great Migration, 30 percent of all black male workers toiled as farm laborers, overwhelmingly in the South. Between then and 1930, the number of such workers fell by 250,000, and in the latter year, they made up only 19 percent of the black labor force. At the same time, the proportion of white-collar, supervisory, and skilled African American workers rose from 6.6 percent to 9.3 percent. Farm labor, especially in the early-twentieth-century South, was notorious for its low wages, insecurity, and repressiveness. Its decline, which was closely associated with black migration northward, was by itself an indication of upward occupational mobility, especially since the number and proportion of black men now classified as semiskilled laborers and service workers grew dramatically during these decades. Although many still toiled as day laborers and in low-wage occupations such as domestic service, large numbers of black men now worked in industrial, urban transport, goods handling, and commercial settings, where wages were often triple those of southern farm laborers. Moreover, even though blacks were more vulnerable to layoffs and earned fewer promotions compared with white workers, urban and industrial work was less likely to involve the kinds of petty wage chiseling, threats of personal violence, and social restriction that was commonplace in the rural South.[13]

Toiling in a Chicago packinghouse or a Gary steel mill might be hard, hot, and unsafe, but migrants overwhelmingly found it preferable to chopping cotton or clearing swampland. For migrants, work in the North was liberation. Industrial jobs were the ticket to dignity, respect, and success. Although employers were initially skeptical about the ability of southern blacks to adjust to the pace and routine of industrial labor, many soon came to value their new hands. Newly recruited black workers, they often found, were eager to prove themselves and were resistant to the appeals of radicals and trade unionists. Declared a Cleveland employer in 1923, "We have [black] molders, core makers, chippers, fitters, locomotive crane operators, melting furnace operators, general foremen, foremen, assistant foremen, clerks, [and] timekeepers[;] in fact, there is no work in our shop that they cannot do and do well."[14] To be sure, northern employers who provided such a wide range of opportunities were few; more common was the relegation of blacks to low-end jobs. Even so, migrants evinced no desire to return to southern conditions. "The Negro," wrote two scholars in a comprehensive analysis of the black worker, "has become an integral part of the labor force in nearly all of the country's basic industries." Writing in 1931, just as the full impact of the Great Depression was beginning to be felt, they also raised the question of "whether the Negro will hold the position in industry he has won since 1916."[15]

Randolph's Way: African American Workers and the Labor Movement, 1917–1930

In 1925, union activists among sleeping-car porters, all of them African American, persuaded radical New York orator and journalist A. Philip Randolph to become president of their fledgling union, the Brotherhood of

Sleeping Car Porters (BSCP). A fiery socialist and antiwar advocate, Randolph had frequently attacked the American Federation of Labor (AFL) for its restrictive racial policies. Yet, having accepted the BSCP presidency, Randolph moved quickly to bring the union into the so-called House of Labor. He believed that, for all its sins, the AFL could become a vehicle for the advance of workers everywhere and that black workers should seek opportunities to transform the federation from within. This belief was based more on his underlying socialist faith in workers as the essential progressive force in modern society than on any direct experience with a labor movement divided by craft, race, and politics. As masses of African American workers abandoned the cotton fields of Dixie and began to play a key role in the industrial centers of the North, they encountered a labor movement that combined occasional bursts of interracial activism with long-established practices of racial exclusion. As two close observers of the American industrial scene declared in a landmark 1931 publication, it was clear that "a labor movement built upon the principle of working-class unity would of course take the Negro into its ranks and fight to raise the general standard." But whether black workers had the patience to await the AFL's racial transformation and white workers had the enlightened self-interest to make common cause with African Americans remained unclear, even as the relative prosperity of the 1920s began to give way to the depression of the 1930s.[16]

The Great Migration brought African American workers into contact with the northern white working class and labor movement as never before. White workers, sharing in the racial prejudice that permeated American life, greeted them with suspicion and often downright hostility. The mainstream labor movement, as embodied in the AFL and the railroad brotherhoods, addressed the sudden influx of black workers with attitudes and policies that ranged from violent antagonism to theoretical (and often condescending) expressions of interracial cooperation. For their part, black workers also exhibited a range of responses to white workers' hostility and to the unions' ambivalence. Many sought entry into the mainstream labor movement, and some gained it; others, keenly conscious of white workers' hostility, looked to employers as providers of opportunity. Still others, excluded from whites-only labor organizations, formed black unions. In the pressurized wartime conditions in the factories, neighborhoods, and other urban spaces, festering racial conflict sometimes exploded into violence. At the same time, however, several remarkable instances of interracial labor activism suggested that, despite the racial tensions that accompanied the Great Migration, elements of the American working class were capable of interracial cooperation even if broader feelings of brotherhood and race-blind solidarity remained elusive.

As early as the 1830s, fear of an influx of racial others into northern workplaces was common. Anti-Irish rioting was a regular feature of ante-bellum urban life as native-born U.S. workers viewed the mass immigration of impoverished people as a threat to their livelihoods and living standards. For their part, the Irish often lashed out against African Americans, whom they regarded as competitors for low-wage jobs, most notably in the bloody Draft Riot of 1863. During the Civil War, schemes to relieve the Union army of the burden of caring for escaped slaves by relocating them in northern states triggered protests from white workers. When the feared mass migration of blacks northward did not occur after Emancipation, northern and western workers turned their attention first to the importation of Chinese workers and then to the mass migration of eastern and southern Europeans. To white workers, the introduction of men and women whom they regarded as racially inferior into their workplaces was a threat to both their living standards and their status as independent and respected worker-citizens. "Between cheap negro labor and cheap foreign labor," lamented one railroader in 1918, "the intelligent American [i.e., white] workingman is threatened in his desire to live and enjoy the benefits of our laws."[17]

The sudden World War I–era appearance of large numbers of blacks in shops and factories created uncertainty and volatility. The novelty of this unprecedented influx spurred a good deal of governmental and journalistic attention. Reporters and investigators toured factories and other workplaces, interviewing managers, workers, and community leaders. They found some employers so fearful of alienating their white workers in tight wartime labor markets that they refused to hire blacks. Thus, a New York telephone company executive told one reporter that although he "personally had no objection to colored employe[e]s, the white operators would leave en masse if they had to work . . . with colored girls." More often, however, observers found that black workers' relegation to the least desirable jobs, along with the general wartime expansion of industrial production, served to mitigate white workers' prejudices and fears. "Negroes do work white men won't do, such as common labor; heavy, hot, and dirty work," reported one factory superintendent. "They are well fitted for this hot work . . . [and] it is hard to get white men to do this kind of work," declared a foreman supervising men who serviced a steel mill's Dantesque coke ovens.[18] Field examiners from the Department of Labor's Division of Negro Economics reported that in scores of workplaces they found blacks and whites toiling alongside each other in apparent harmony.

When white workers believed that employers were recruiting blacks to undermine wage standards or to defeat union organizing, however, violence was always a threat. Thus, in the summer of 1917, rumors circulated that employers in East St. Louis, Illinois, had hatched a scheme to bring in thousands of African Americans to work in the city's booming metalworking, chemical, and munitions plants. The local AFL labor council appealed to city officials to take action to stop the rumored influx, but violence soon erupted. For two weeks in June, mobs of white residents attacked blacks indiscriminately in an orgy of mayhem that left thirty-nine blacks and eight whites dead. So long as employers imported black workers "to destroy organized labor," warned an Illinois union leader, such outbreaks, though regrettable, were predictable. Indeed, declared U.S. Secretary of Labor William B. Wilson, "The situation is serious in many parts of the country," and he believed that "similar outbreaks would occur in Pittsburgh, Newark and a few other points where Southern negroes have been induced to go in larger numbers than can be absorbed."[19]

The unions that represented the vast majority of organized workers during the World War I era either were affiliated with the AFL or represented railroad workers. The largest and most powerful of the railroad unions—called brotherhoods—represented engineers, firemen, trainmen, and conductors and were collectively known as the "Big Four." From their inception in the nineteenth century, these unions had excluded blacks from membership and had colluded with employers to limit the jobs available to blacks. During World War I, the U.S. Railroad Administration (USRA), which operated the country's trains between December 1917 and 1920, gave official sanction to these practices and acquiesced in agreements that forced the replacement of hundreds of black railroad workers with whites. "Colored men," declared a black railroader, "who have been in the service of the railroads for years . . . are forced to stand idly by . . . while young white men with only a few months' service record are given regular jobs." At the insistence of the whites-only Brotherhood of Railroad Trainmen, the USRA issued regulations that "would finally mean complete elimination" of black workers from a wide range of railroad jobs that they had held since before the Civil War.[20]

Unlike the brotherhoods, the AFL did not bar black membership. Indeed, throughout the war and postwar period, AFL president Samuel Gompers reiterated the organization's theoretical commitment to organizing all workers, regardless of race, and invoked the theme of class solidarity. At the same time, however, important affiliates such as the machinists and the boilermakers unions did draw the color line, without rebuke from the AFL. The actions of Gompers and his fellow union leaders indicated that the recruitment of black workers and the achievement of racial justice were well down on their list of priorities. The AFL's fall 1917 convention adopted a resolution endorsing efforts to organize black workers but, fearful of alienating southern white unionists, rejected one that invoked the wartime rhetoric of democracy to denounce the mistreatment of black workers.

During and after the war, Gompers asserted the AFL's official position—namely, that the federation was open to all workers, regardless of race. Although he acknowledged that some unions barred blacks from membership, he stressed that many others did not, and even in those trades with discriminatory unions, blacks were free to form separate unions directly with the AFL. Behind the scenes, and occasionally in public forums, he advised discriminatory affiliates to modify or abandon their exclusivist rules and accept blacks as members. But among many of the AFL's unions, one of their most important functions was controlling the local labor market. Excluding blacks from membership, these men believed, reduced the pool of available labor and permitted the union to demand higher wages and better conditions for its members. The alternative view—that if blacks were not brought into the union they would constitute a ready reserve of strikebreakers—gained little support.

This exclusionary attitude was particularly problematic—to say nothing of its ethical implications—in the huge industrial plants, railroad repair shops, and shipyards in which so many black migrants now toiled. Where local craft unions such as the carpenters or electrical workers controlled a local labor market through collective bargaining agreements that included a closed shop—that is, the stipulation that a given employer would hire only union members—the blanket exclusion of large categories of workers such as African Americans made a kind of practical, if unsavory, sense. But such arrangements were rare in large industrial plants. Thus, throughout the wartime period, black workers flooded into the Pittsburgh steel mills. Union activity, which had been dormant there for many years, began to revive, but the renascent unions often refused to reach out to African Americans. "I will not introduce for membership into this union anyone but a sober, industrious *white* person," read the pledge required of new members of one Steel City union.[21] During the great steel strike of 1919–1920, this discriminatory treatment boomeranged when as many as thirty thousand black workers crossed union picket lines to supply the heavy labor the steel companies needed to resume operations and, in effect, to defeat of the AFL's organizing campaign.

Gompers was not one to issue ringing declarations in behalf of human rights or to point to the immorality of racial exclusion. For him, organizing black workers was a practical matter. He never challenged discriminatory affiliates directly, believing that the principle of trade autonomy—the sacred sovereignty of each separate affiliated union—trumped claims of social or racial justice. Nondiscrimination "is the policy and the principle of the American Federation of Labor," he avowed in 1921, "but it cannot enforce that declaration upon the affiliated international unions if those . . . unions decline or refuse to adopt them."[22]

Within this narrow framework, Gompers and AFL leaders did enlist the support of civil rights and racial reform organizations in an attempt to expand the federation's appeal to black workers. Early in 1918, they met with leaders of the NAACP, the National Urban League, and other black educational and social welfare organizations with a view to hammering out a joint program designed to bring the union message to black workers. This was an awkward process for the unionists, especially when the African American groups asked the AFL to explain publicly "why certain internationals [i.e., affiliated unions] may exclude colored men."[23]

Through much of 1918, drafts of statements were traded back and forth, attempting to arrive at a formula by which the labor organization could simultaneously use the black leaders' endorsement as a recruitment aid and to deflect criticism of the racist practices it tolerated. At the 1918 convention, the AFL's Committee on Organization acknowledged the importance of enlisting the support of black leaders and urged that federation officials "give special attention to organizing the colored wage workers in the future." At the same time, however, it refused to acknowledge that the AFL had a race problem, insisting that "no fault is or can be found with the work done [by the labor movement] in the past" in its relations with black workers.[24] Although some black leaders hailed this AFL gesture as a significant commitment to reach out to African American workers, the federation in fact did little to implement it. "Grudgingly, unwillingly, almost insultingly," observed scholar and activist W. E. B. DuBois early in this black-AFL colloquy, "this Federation yields to us inch by inch the status of half a man, denying and withholding every privilege it dares at all times." Added the *New York Age,* an African American newspaper, "Unionism . . . like that encouraged and fostered by the AFL is a mere sham and a travesty of the term."[25]

When Gompers's low-key recommendation that discriminatory AFL affiliates change their ways met with little success, he resorted to other stratagems. If craft unions would not admit blacks, "federal" charters would be issued, enrolling them directly into the AFL. In a variation of this device, all black workers in a particular plant or locale, regardless of their particular jobs, would be encouraged to join a nonrestrictive union. The Brotherhood of Railway Carmen finally agreed to organize the black workers who cleaned and serviced railroad cars, but only in separate locals that would "be under the jurisdiction of the nearest white local," which would bargain with employers in their behalf.[26] None of these expedients was anything close to satisfactory. Federal locals were the poor stepchildren of the AFL, combining high dues with often ineffectual and remote leadership. The device of enrolling black workers of all kinds in nondiscriminatory affiliates was scuttled by craft unions such as the boilermakers, which asserted their jurisdictional claims even as they barred blacks. The carmen's solution was particularly degrading, relegating dues-paying black members to inferior and dependent status. Did white laborites not understand, asked a Seattle worker-poet in 1919, that "every time They keep ANY WORKER, Man or woman, White, or yellow, or black, OUT of a UNION, They are forcing a worker To be a SCAB, To be used AGAINST THEM." Some black Texans who toiled as helpers in railroad repair shops asked whether "it is the purpose of the Organized Labor Movement to . . . discriminate against them and force them out of jobs . . . , and make scabs of them?"[27]

Despite the brotherhoods' hostility and the AFL's diffidence, many African American workers remained open to the union appeal. Some responded enthusiastically to the egalitarianism of the Industrial Workers of the World (IWW), attracted less, perhaps, by its root-and-branch denunciation of capitalism than by its genuine commitment to interracial organization. In the face of harsh government repression and sometimes lethal vigilante assaults during the war, black longshoremen built a vigorous interracial IWW local on the Philadelphia docks and sustained a strong African American presence there through the 1920s. In places as diverse as Chicago, Little Rock, and rural Louisiana, African American and white workers, through a variety of institutional devices, struggled, albeit with mixed success, to build unions that transcended the color line. Thus, in 1919, white and black lumber workers in Bogalusa, Louisiana, fought to sustain a biracial local of the AFL carpenters union—normally not an outspoken champion of black workers' interests—while battling an employer who resorted to naked physical violence and crude race-baiting in an effort to destroy the union. In Little Rock, Arkansas, during the war, the local white-dominated central labor council took up the cause of black women toiling in the city's steam laundries, which serviced a nearby army base. Thwarted in their efforts to compel the employers to enter into collective bargaining, the labor council helped the women establish a worker cooperative laundry that flourished, at least for a time.

During the World War I era, labor's most significant effort to transcend the color line took place in the stockyards, packinghouses, and neighborhoods of South Side Chicago. Between 1916 and 1922, the AFL's Amalgamated Meat Cutters (AMC), in conjunction with the progressive Chicago Federation of Labor (CFL), conducted a protracted campaign to organize the fifty thousand men and women who toiled in the city's meatpacking plants and stockyards. Since African Americans—some long-term residents of the Windy City, and others new migrants—constituted up to one-third of the labor force in the animal pens, slaughterhouses, disassembly lines, and packing sheds of Packingtown, it was clear to union leaders that the recruitment of blacks was essential. For the fiercely antiunion meatpackers, the large and growing supply of job-seeking blacks from the South, few with any positive experience with organized labor, represented a potentially decisive strikebreaking and antiunion labor force. Thus, both union activists and determined employers worked hard to win the allegiance of the black newcomers.

The campaign to organize meat industry workers was particularly important for the labor movement, since it presented an opportunity for the AFL to expand from its traditional base of craft unions into one of the country's critical mass production industries. In the middle of the campaign, CFL president John Fitzpatrick expressed what was at stake: "the stockyards movement has blazed the way and shown how to organize the basic industries. . . . Everybody is looking to Chicago to take the lead."[28] Well aware of the importance of black workers, the AMC, one of the AFL affiliates that did not bar black workers from membership, stressed its commitment to nondiscrimination. The Stockyards Labor Council (SLC), a consortium of the various craft unions that claimed jurisdiction in the meat industry, echoed this promise. The AMC did create a "black" local, number 651, as a means of bringing workers who were skeptical of the parent union's white leadership into the fold, but in fact, all the AMC locals representing workers at the various facilities on the South Side included African Americans. The SLC called for higher wages and fewer hours of work, especially for the unskilled workers, into which category most of the black workers fell. For their part, employers cultivated black community leaders and journalists, highlighting the AFL's uninspiring record on race and stressing the opportunities that faithful employment offered black workers. More negatively, the meatpackers sought to detach white workers, many of them southern and eastern European immigrants, from the union cause with threats to replace them with African Americans, thus intensifying the racial tension at the work sites and in the nearby neighborhoods.

The campaign to organize the stockyards and packinghouses quickly became embroiled in both the U.S. war effort and the racial turbulence that afflicted Chicago in the late 1910s. Early in 1918, the union initially gained prestige and credibility when government-sponsored mediation and arbitration, designed to forestall a wartime strike in this critical industry, granted substantial improvements in wages and work hours. Membership in Local 651 and other AMC locals spiked, as both long-term residents and new migrants recognized that union pressure had spurred government action. Even so, it soon became clear that the support of black newcomers was fragile. Surveys conducted at the time showed that long-term black residents supported the union effort in about the same proportion as white workers did, but more recent residents were both less likely to join and more prone to drop out if they did join. Although union activists tried to depict the struggle in class terms—oppressed workers of all races versus greedy employers—blacks of southern origin weighed the decision whether to cast their lots with the union or with the employers in racial terms.

Which side, they asked, was more likely to help them secure steady employment and good wages? Which side, in both the long run and the short, was more likely to erase the color line that kept blacks out of the best jobs and relegated them to low wages and uncertain employment?

For their part, many white workers, who represented a mosaic of distinct ethnic and language groups, regarded blacks as members of a "scab race." In the quarter century before World War I, violent strikes in the meatpacking industry and among teamsters had featured the importation of black strikebreakers. "It was the niggers that whipped you in line," South Carolina's race-baiting senator Ben Tillman told white stockyard workers after their union was destroyed in a particularly bitter walkout in 1904. "They were the club with which your brains were beaten out."[29] In reality, no race or ethnic group was immune to antiunion appeals or untainted by episodes of strikebreaking, in Chicago or elsewhere. It was true, however, that in earlier South Side labor disputes, employers had conspicuously recruited African Americans as replacement workers, most recently in the highly publicized strikes in the Pullman Car Company's Chicago maintenance facility and in the city's hotels. Although many black workers had proved to be faithful unionists during the Packingtown strikes, white workers continued to regard African Americans as members of a scab race. Unaware of or ignoring organized labor's discriminatory treatment of blacks, native-born and immigrant white workers alike singled out blacks for hostility and contempt, even as they worked side by side with black fellow union supporters.

Indeed, especially for recent European immigrants, it often seemed that common hostility toward African Americans was a central component of their hope of being considered "American." They learned "American ways" from native-born workers and from earlier immigrants, notably the Irish, and among the most prominent lessons were the fear and hatred of blacks. There was, to be sure, an alternative brand of working-class Americanism, one that promoted equality and solidarity. It was to this tradition that SLC and AMC organizers sought to appeal. At a major rally in July 1919, in a city boiling with racial tension, union orators both black and white called for "a square deal for all," regardless of race or nationality. "It does me good . . . to see such a checkerboard crowd," SLC leader J. W. Johnstone told a biracial mass meeting. "You are standing shoulder to shoulder as men, regardless of whether your face is black or white."[30]

In the summer of 1919, on-the-job racial tension became tangled up in one of the country's most savage and deadly racial outbursts. For months before this bloody eruption, whites had greeted the efforts of African Americans to claim new residential and recreational space with violent assaults. The homes of blacks who dared to move into "white" neighborhoods were bombed, and along the city's racial borderlands, gangs of white youths terrorized blacks. The stoning and drowning of a black youngster who had inadvertently drifted into the "white" section of a Lake Michigan beach on July 25, 1919, triggered several weeks of racial violence, which the Chicago police did nothing to quell. Blacks fought back as whites invaded black neighborhoods in search of victims. By the time the violence sputtered to a halt in late July, twenty-three blacks and fifteen whites were dead, and more than five hundred people had been injured.

This horrific violence coincided with a major effort by the SLC, AMC, and CFL to push a multiethnic organizing drive on the South Side forward. Trying desperately to live down the labor movement's racist practices in an effort to attract blacks, while at the same time trying to persuade white workers of the need for interracial solidarity, organizers attempted to keep the conflict out of Packingtown. Even when black and white workers squared off against each other in the almost daily confrontations that accompanied a series of short wildcat strikes that summer, both black and white union leaders were quick to discount purely racial explanations. "I can get along with these colored fellows . . . that have the [union] buttons on," declared one white local leader, but as for blacks who refused to join the union, "I cannot stand working with them," he said. African American organizers for the AMC and the SLC likewise pointed to southern migrants as the union's Achilles' heel. The "new men," complained black organizer Robert Bedford, were "from one part of the country [i.e., the South] . . . and you cannot do anything with them." Bedford and fellow black activists blamed the meatpacking companies for attempting to foment racial discord by recruiting migrants as strikebreakers and using them "as a big stick" to destroy the union.[31]

In the end, the labor movement could not achieve permanent biracial or interracial unions in the Chicago stockyards and packinghouses. Organized labor and the heavily immigrant white labor force on the South Side simply were not consistently credible to the thousands of southern migrants seeking a foothold in northern industry. At peak moments in the protracted struggle—such as just after government mediation resulted in substantial gains for all workers—hundreds of newcomers surged into Local 651 and other AFL unions. But whereas long-established northern black workers usually remained in the union even after setbacks, new migrants, always aware of the power of the employers and unconvinced that they could find racial justice among white coworkers and even the most forward-looking unions, were quick to defect. "The Negro workman," declared an NAACP observer, "is not at all sure as to the sincerity of the unions."[32] When the AMC and SLC launched a strike in 1921 designed at last to achieve union recognition, few recent migrants remained in the union. Regarding the union cause as both compromised and hopeless, they crossed the picket lines and helped defeat the strike and end Packingtown's flawed experiment in biracial unionism.

By no means did the difficulties of forging biracial unions end the interest of black workers, North or South, in union representation. The hostility and indifference of the railroad brotherhoods and of the AFL steeled the determination of some to build separate unions of black workers, unconnected to the mainstream labor movement. To be sure, some would-be spokesmen for black workers counseled against union activism in any guise, advising them to rely on the benevolence of employers in the quest for economic advance. In 1925, for example, the Improved and Benevolent Order of Elks, a large black fraternity that enjoyed considerable prestige among African Americans, urged workers to "line up with the best element of American citizenship . . . , the large employers of labor," and prominent academician Kelly Miller declared that black workers should always align themselves "on the side of capital" in labor disputes.[33] But other middle-class spokesmen continued to believe that, one way or another, African American workers had to assert their rights to decent wages and decent treatment, and to do this, they had to forge instruments of power—unions— even if that meant organizing outside the confines of the compromised AFL. Thus, although Arnold Hill, director of the Urban League's Department of Industrial Relations, never entirely abandoned the effort to get the AFL to change its racist practices, he encouraged black workers to form their own unions, since, in his view, relying on employers' generosity reinforced black workers' dependency and lowly status.

During the 1920s, Urban League studies estimated that about twelve thousand African American workers belonged to separate black labor organizations.[34] A scattered handful were members of local building trades organizations, established to represent black craftsmen who had been denied membership in AFL affiliates such as the plumbers and electrical workers unions. In places where these local bodies gained demonstrable strength and black craftsmen competed with white union labor, the Jim Crow AFL unions sought in various ways to destroy, marginalize, or co-opt them. Sometimes white unionists encouraged the black unions to accept AFL federal charters and thus put themselves under the "guidance" of federation officials. Knowing little about local conditions, AFL functionaries invariably turned to local white craft unionists to service and "advise" these dependent black unions, which they did in ways that almost always privileged the interests of their white coworkers. In other cases, white unionists boycotted and sometimes even assaulted contractors who employed black labor. In Chicago and other cities, it was commonplace for building inspectors, usually chosen or at least approved by the white unions, to refuse to sign off on work performed by black craftsmen, regardless of its quality. In one city, according to two contemporary scholars, "the Negro plumbers . . . , feeling that their organization could give them no protection, left it and joined the communists."[35]

One of the largest black labor organizations represented workers in the U.S. Post Office Department. By the late 1920s, about 9 percent of all postal employees were African Americans, and in some large cities, the proportion rose to more than 30 percent. The National Alliance of Postal Employees (NAPE) functioned largely as a pressure group, partly within the biracial National Association of Letter Carriers, and promoted the distinct concerns of black postal employees in the union and in dealings with postal authorities. With about twenty-five hundred members, NAPE enjoyed some success in influencing the postmaster general to acknowledge the concerns of African American postal workers. Unlike the AFL postal unions, however, it never gained entrée into the advisory council that the Post Office established for regular consultation with employee organizations.[36]

By far the most vigorous and sustained sector for independent black union activity was the railroads. African American railroad workers, barred from membership in the Big Four brotherhoods and most AFL unions representing maintenance and repair workers, resorted to a variety of devices in their efforts to defend their jobs and advance their interests. By the mid-1920s, those who cleaned the railroad cars, handled freight, maintained the tracks and roadbeds, or performed certain tasks in repair shops were enrolled in AFL unions, but always with second-class status and with little influence over the union's policies and agendas. The AFL also created federal unions for blacks who worked as machinists, sheet metal workers, electricians, carpenters, and other craftsmen but were ineligible for membership in the relevant craft unions. For example, although a black machinist's helper was not technically a member of the International Association of Machinists, he paid dues to a federal labor union that was nominally directed from AFL central headquarters. In reality, however, AFL officials gave the nearest machinists' lodge the actual responsibility for bargaining for and servicing these black workers. Thus, the machinists could be sure that, in case of a strike, the black helpers—who were often highly skilled and experienced—could not serve as replacements for them. Meanwhile, the black helpers had little to say about the contracts under which they worked, contracts that guaranteed their permanent status in a subordinate category.

During the war and immediately after, however, African American railroaders realized that they would have to organize outside the boundaries of the AFL and the brotherhoods if they were to survive in the industry. On the southern roads, where the brotherhoods were weakest, white railroad workers had long sought the elimination of black firemen. Black firemen could never hope to ascend to the elite position of engineer, but elsewhere in the country, white firemen regularly used that job as a stepping-stone for promotion to engineer. Wanting to open up that line of progression for themselves, southern whites pressured employers and, during the war, the U.S. Railroad Administration, to force blacks out of the locomotive cabs. Similarly, miscellaneous yard and train workers, such as brakemen and on-board repairmen, aggressively sought to drive blacks from these jobs, especially on the southern roads.

During and after the war, a variety of black railroad unions emerged to resist these pressures and to represent the grievances and interests of African American brakemen, firemen, trainmen, and others before the USRA and, later, the Railroad Labor Board, which was established in 1920. As early as 1915, black railroad man Robert Mays launched the Railway Men's International Benevolent and Industrial Association (RMIBIA) as an umbrella organization, in the hope of eventually representing all black railroad workers. According to the ambitious Mays, this new organization would protest "against unfair and bad working conditions . . . and against unfair practice[s] of the American Federation of Labor and the railway brotherhoods."[37] For a time, Mays succeeded in persuading federal officials to raise the wages of black railroaders and in building the RMIBIA's membership, which in the early 1920s reached fifteen thousand. Mays, however, could not sustain the momentum. When federal operation of the railroads ended in 1920, it eliminated an important forum for the presentation of black workers' demands. Unrecognized by employers for purposes of collective bargaining and constantly under attack from the brotherhoods, the RMIBIA quickly faded from view, even as Mays's rather grandiose ambitions and pronouncements alienated local black unionists. By the late 1920s, most of the black firemen had been driven from the southern roads, and small organizations of trainmen, switchmen, porters, and other train service employees could do little more than appeal to public sentiment and to employers' sense of fair play. Meanwhile, as two contemporary students of the black working class observed, "They have won some few concessions . . . but they have been powerless to prevent the white unions from steadily forcing the Negro out of all the better railroad jobs."[38]

Among black railroaders, the most successful and enduring attempt to organize was that conducted by the sleeping-car porters. During the heyday of passenger rail travel, sleeping cars that were manufactured, maintained, and staffed by the Pullman Sleeping Car Company were a key feature of long-distance travel. A trip from New York City to Los Angeles, for example, took at least three days and three nights. Sleeping cars accommodated passengers during the long nights, and they were tended by African American porters who made the beds, tidied the cars, stowed passengers' luggage, shined their shoes, and otherwise waited on passengers. Pullman Company regulations required that porters and maids remain on duty throughout the run to meet travelers' demands, however trivial.

From the beginning of sleeping-car service after the Civil War, the Pullman Company recruited black men almost exclusively to serve as car attendants. For white passengers, the presence of a smiling porter, generically named "George" after company founder George Pullman, was a reassuring part of any long-distance train journey. Limited employment opportunities meant that even relatively well-educated African American men could be hired cheaply. The traveling public was used to encountering African Americans in the subservient role of domestic servant, and the company expected its porters to be deferential and accommodating. "It is," counseled the company's employee instruction booklet, "imperative that you be obliging and courteous to passengers, alert to anticipate their wants and diligent and cheerful in executing orders."[39] Porters' and maids' reliance on tips to supplement their low basic wages reinforced these admonitions.

Although the hours were long and the task of remaining pleasant and accommodating in the face of demanding travelers was stressful, the job of sleeping-car attendant had its advantages. The work was relatively clean in comparison with other jobs commonly available to blacks. Although some passengers were contemptuous and overbearing, porters valued the opportunity to interact with the affluent and accomplished men and women they encountered on long-distance journeys. Travel to all parts of the country lent the porter an air of sophistication and importance that gave him prestige in the black community. When critics of the company cited the low wages, long hours, and demeaning treatment of porters and maids, Pullman spokesmen were quick to point out that they had no difficulty recruiting men and women for this work.

But in fact, by the 1920s, the twelve thousand or so Pullman porters were growing increasingly restive. Their basic wage of about $70 a month, even when supplemented with tips that averaged $50 a month, placed them below all other categories of railroad workers. Moreover, porters had to pay for their own uniforms, food, and other personal expenses while on the road, and they even had to buy such items as shoe polish for the passengers' shoes they shined. At a time when economists pegged the annual income needed by an urban American family to attain a modest but adequate standard of living at around $1,800 to $2,000, porters had to survive on less than two-thirds that amount.

The Pullman Company resisted union organization, whether in the shops where the sleeping cars were built and repaired or among the conductors and porters who served the public. In 1920, for example, union activists formed the Pullman Porters and Maids Protective Association. The company responded by creating an in-house "union" controlled and funded by company officials. Porters were compelled to vote for representatives to this organization, which in turn "negotiated" with company representatives. In response to subsequent union agitation, Pullman managers raised wages slightly and proposed changes in porters' long hours. The company presented these improvements in the form of a contract that it would sign with the in-house organization it had created, thus fostering the notion that no outside union was necessary. Union adherents, however, resented and resisted this pseudo-unionism and in 1925 created the Brotherhood of Sleeping Car Porters, an independent labor organization. Long experience had shown that would-be union leaders were vulnerable to company reprisals, so the men who formed the BSCP asked a prominent African American journalist and orator, A. Philip Randolph, to assume presidency of the new union.

Born in Crescent City, Florida, in 1889, Randolph had moved to New York City as a young man with ambitions of becoming an actor. Instead, he quickly became involved in the radical political milieu that flourished in World War I–era Harlem, which was rapidly emerging as the country's largest and most dynamic African American ghetto. A gifted publicist and orator, Randolph forged a distinctive radical perspective, combining socialism, opposition to U.S. participation in World War I, and opposition to the various black nationalist movements that flourished in urban areas during this period. Along with fellow black socialist Chandler Owen, and financed by Randolph's wife, Lucille Green, who operated a successful Harlem beauty shop, Randolph launched the magazine the *Messenger* in 1917. Its antiwar and socialist message brought Randolph and Owen to the attention of government agents, who subjected them to surveillance and threatened to put the magazine out of business. In view of Randolph's oratorical skills and the *Messenger*'s anticapitalist and antiwar stance, U.S. Attorney General A. Mitchell Palmer called Randolph the "most dangerous Negro in America."[40]

Despite Randolph's reputation for system-threatening radicalism, he soon came to the conclusion that black advance could not be achieved through separatist movements. He became convinced that the cause of African American workers was the cause of the working class in general and that, however flawed and disappointing the AFL's record, black workers had no choice but to work through the federation, agitating for change from within while educating white workers that racial division damaged workers of all ethnic backgrounds. Harsh in his criticism of white labor leaders—a 1918 *Messenger* editorial called Samuel Gompers "The Chief Strike Breaker" in the country[41]—Randolph nonetheless encouraged black workers to hammer away at the AFL, demanding entry and forcing the federation to abandon its racist practices. In the long run, he believed, the logic of modern capitalism would force all workers to recognize that their

salvation lay in unity and solidarity; the AFL's antiquated craft union structure and its benighted racial attitudes could not survive the dynamic workplace demographics of the modern age. Moreover, despite his stinging
critiques of American society, Randolph believed that those seeking racial
justice could use the country's very real, if too often compromised, democratic traditions and institutions to promote civil rights. And in this effort,
the labor movement would inevitably play a major role.

Thus, when Randolph accepted the presidency of the BSCP in 1925, he
did so with clear ideas about the fledgling union's agenda and trajectory.
Affiliation with the AFL, he believed, was crucial, despite the federation's
checkered racial record. Black unions were inherently vulnerable, both to
attacks from white workers and to the appeal of black nationalist agitators. Alignment with the AFL would protect the new union from the machinations of other unions, such as the Hotel and Restaurant Workers and the
Order of Railway Conductors. At the same time, an AFL charter would
permit him and other BSCP leaders to agitate for enlightened racial policies
within the AFL. He had no doubt that the cause of labor and the cause of
African Americans were two sides of the same coin and that the sleeping-
car porters could play a key role in pushing the AFL to make its egalitarian
utterances real.

From the start of his leadership of the BSCP, Randolph pressed new
AFL president William Green (succeeding Gompers, who had died in 1924)
to grant the porters an AFL charter. Personally sympathetic to the claims of
the black railroaders, Green was hampered by the same jurisdictional problems that Gompers had always cited. Failing to dissuade the Hotel and
Restaurant Workers, which claimed theoretical jurisdiction over the porters, the AFL Executive Council offered the various BSCP local organizations federal labor union charters in February 1929. Randolph and the
other BSCP leaders were well aware of the limitations of this device, which
tended to subordinate black workers to opportunistic white unionists. But
they believed that the BSCP was strong enough to maintain its own identity. While they continued to press for a separate charter, Randolph and the
others reluctantly accepted the AFL's compromise, since it represented a
kind of recognition and gave them a forum at AFL conventions to articulate the interests and concerns of black workers. Although some regional
BSCP activists opposed this backdoor entry into the House of Labor,
Randolph saw it as an important first step in the effort to build the black-
labor alliance that he believed was crucial in promoting both civil rights
and labor rights.

By the end of the 1920s, there were about sixty-five thousand black
workers enrolled in unions or union-like organizations. This figure represented about 4 percent of African Americans employed in nonagricultural
and nondomestic occupations, a rate about one-third that of white work-

ers. About two-thirds of black union members were enrolled in the AFL, primarily in the United Mine Workers, the Bricklayers, the Laborers, the Longshoremen, and federal unions in the construction trades and among the sleeping-car attendants. The NAPE, less a union than a pressure group, claimed thirty-three hundred members, while various railroad unions, apart from the BSCP and unaffiliated with the AFL, claimed about seventy-five hundred members.

As the relative prosperity of the mid-1920s began to give way to economic uncertainty and eventually to depression, the position of the masses of African American workers remained vulnerable. Important elements in the black communities in the North and South remained adamant that black workers' best hope for progress was the cultivation of white employers. Black clergymen, business leaders, and racial uplift advocates held that it was African Americans' willingness to defy racially restrictive unions by crossing picket lines or accepting lower wages that offered the best opportunities for employment and racial advance. Even spokesmen who harbored no illusions about the good intentions and benevolence of employers wrote off organized labor as a possible partner in black workers' progress. Thus, declared the militant DuBois, "Colored labor has no common ground with white labor. . . . White labor . . . deprives the Negro of his right to vote, denies him education, denies him affiliation with trade unions, expels him from decent houses, and neighborhoods, and heaps upon him the public insults of open color discrimination. . . . [Indeed], the lowest and most fatal degree of [black workers'] suffering comes not from capitalists but from fellow white workers."[42]

Randolph, though sharply critical of organized labor's racial practices and policies, thought that it was possible—indeed, essential—for the labor movement to repudiate its racist traditions and to bring into the House of Labor the hundreds of thousands of black workers now toiling in the country's urban centers and mass production industries. As for black workers themselves, throughout the war and postwar period, they occasionally demonstrated both a capacity for interracial activism, on the one hand, and an acceptance of employers' hegemony, on the other hand. As the economy began to falter in the wake of the October 1929 stock market collapse, key questions about black workers' role in the economy and in relation to a sorely tested labor movement remained unanswered.

Race, Labor, and the Federal Government, 1917–1932

Throughout World War I and its aftermath, the federal government played a larger role in shaping the racial contours of the American working class and in defining the relationship between black and white workers than at any previous time. U.S. entry into the war quickly raised critical questions about the use of manpower and the management of labor relations. With belligerency came the creation of a number of federal agencies, by no means working in harmony with one another, whose job was to sustain maximum production and minimize labor conflict, both of which goals had critical racial dimensions. In the decade and a half after the war, Congress passed key legislation that limited immigration, regulated new machinery for the regulation of labor relations on the railroads, established wage rates for workers on government construction projects, and curbed the issuance of labor injunctions by the courts. Each of these measures involved critical questions of race and labor.

For African American workers especially, the manpower needs of the wartime economy brought a sometimes bewildering mixture of opportunities and setbacks. The need for labor in heavy industry and munitions production encouraged federal authorities to resist the demands of southern planters and northern trade unionists to curb black migration northward. Moreover, the U.S. Department of Labor acknowledged the growing industrial importance of African American workers by creating, for the first time since Reconstruction, an agency whose purpose was to investigate and facilitate the integration of black workers into the nation's economy. The National War Labor Board (NWLB) and the U.S. Railroad Administration (USRA), both charged with ameliorating industrial conflict during the war, issued rulings that implicitly recognized black workers' crucial importance to the war effort by overriding discriminatory practices and imposing egalitarian treatment. Meanwhile, Congress's decision to pay dependents' allowances directly to the wives of conscripted soldiers enabled many black women in the South to demand higher wages for domestic and agricultural work, since soldiers' allotments often brought in more money than did low-wage work in the fields and kitchens.

At the same time, however, the government's wartime intervention in labor markets led to some adverse consequences. For example, while the Department of Labor's newly created and minimally funded Division of Negro Economics worked diligently to ease the transition of southern black migrants into war work, agents of the Department of Agriculture's Extension Service actively colluded with southern white growers to curb the migration of black farm laborers and to discourage them from gaining the higher wages that tight labor markets in the South normally would have required. Moreover, while it was true that some USRA rulings eliminated wage differentials based on race, it was equally—and, in the long run, more significantly—true that USRA officials shared the racist assumptions of white railroaders. After the armistice, but while the trains were still under federal operation, these officials facilitated white workers' efforts to drive blacks out of key job categories. Even the NWLB, probably the most liberal of the labor-related wartime federal agencies, was at best inconsistent and sporadic in its treatment of black workers' claims for equal pay and equal access to jobs.

The most important positive feature of President Woodrow Wilson's wartime race-labor policies was an unwillingness to act forcefully to stanch the flow of black manpower northward. Demands that he do so were many, and they emanated from constituencies, such as organized labor and southern agricultural interests, to which the Democratic Party was normally very responsive. In the early months of the war, declaring that the Great Northern Railroad's recruitment of blacks was creating unrest among whites in the upper Midwest, Minnesota Governor John Lind begged Secretary of Labor William B. Wilson to "stop the movement of Negros [*sic*] into this section at once," because "it is a menace that cannot be over estimated." Southern politicians echoed his plea, citing the devastating effect that the exodus of black farmworkers was having throughout the South.[43]

Southern white employers fought especially hard to retain their entitlement to geographically restricted, low-wage black labor. In the 1910s, southern legislatures passed laws designed to impede or halt outside labor recruitment, and state and local ordinances imposed prohibitive licensing fees on recruiters. Southern mailmen confiscated copies of newspapers such as the *Chicago Defender* that encouraged the exodus. At times, southern state and local officials even sabotaged the federal government's efforts to recruit workers for military construction. In May 1918, for example, the director of the U.S. Employment Service (USES), an arm of the Department of Labor, reported that "Florida . . . has in jail at Gainesville two officers of our Service who have been recruiting common labor for the Army projects at Norfolk." Indeed, state officials told the USES that "Florida absolutely forbids recruiting labor from the state."[44]

Virtually since its inception in 1913, the Wilson administration had pursued a rigidly segregationist and discriminatory course in its dealings with African Americans. And since the U.S. Supreme Court had previously sanctioned certain kinds of restrictions on geographic mobility, there was no guarantee that in the perfervid atmosphere of wartime emergency, the administration would not find ways to curtail black mobility. Indeed, some federal officials endorsed white southerners' efforts to retain the benefits of cheap, captive labor. For example, in the summer of 1918, one southern sawmill operator complained that contractors building the government's great munitions complex at Muscle Shoals, Alabama, were "offering my niggers . . . $3.80 and $4.00 a day, while I am paying them $2." USES director John Densmore expressed sympathy, reflexively endorsing southern employers' sense of entitlement to low-wage black labor. He pledged that "if the $2 fellow in the sawmill down there is satisfied with his $2—and he is or he would not be working there—we, as part of the Government, are not going to . . . lay before him newspapers showing what they do at

Muscle Shoals to get him to move away from there. We will let him alone." Department of Agriculture county agents, always sensitive to local white constituencies in the South, worked with planters to discourage blacks from migrating, demanding higher wages, or even changing jobs.[45]

Overall, however, the secretary of labor resisted pressure to curtail black migration. He acknowledged that "the migration of negroes from the South . . . in larger numbers than can be assimilated in the North has caused a great deal of anxiety to the Department of Labor, both because of the fear of friction in the North and the shortage of labor in the South."[46] And Department of Labor officials sometimes stressed to potential migrants the perils of relocation, even as they counseled southern employers that improved wages and working conditions would help keep blacks on the farms. Nonetheless, Secretary Wilson repeatedly pointed out that no agency of the government, even during wartime, had any authority to impede the free movement of people across state lines. Moreover, the secretary and his aides opposed ordinances adopted by some southern communities designed to compel black women to accept low-wage jobs on farms and as domestic servants. These "work or fight" initiatives, Secretary Wilson believed, introduced a degree of compulsion incompatible with free labor, while sowing bitterness and resentment among those affected. In the end, though politically disfranchised and socially reviled, African Americans simply could not be treated differently from other U.S. citizens when it came to the fundamental right of free transit.

The government's main response to black migration, made through the Department of Labor, was a joint program of detailed study and on-site exhortation and negotiation. Even before U.S. entry into the war, the vast dimensions of the black migration spurred action. In 1916, Secretary Wilson borrowed two black investigators from the Department of Commerce to conduct a preliminary survey of the scope and impact of the migration and then recruited academic and social investigator James H. Dillard to oversee a more ambitious analysis. Spurred in part by concern "expressed over the probable loss . . . of southern crops through the departure . . . of Negro workers in appalling numbers," Dillard's report provided a wealth of information about conditions in both the North and the South but made no specific recommendations for governmental action.[47]

The declaration of war in April 1917 further encouraged blacks' search for industrial opportunities, and the numbers leaving southern plantations and cities swelled. At the urging of black leaders, in May 1918, Secretary Wilson created a new body in the Department of Labor, the Division of Negro Economics (DNE). To head it, he appointed Dr. George Edmund Haynes, a distinguished African American social scientist and a founder of the National Urban League. The DNE had two primary tasks: to monitor and analyze the scope and effects of the migration, and to spur wartime production by easing the so-called labor shortage in the South while promoting amity and accord between white and black workers in newly biracial northern settings.

Throughout its two-year existence, the DNE and its director walked a tightrope. This intrusion into race relations quickly evoked memories of the last time the federal government had concerned itself with black workers. Southern whites and blacks alike recalled Reconstruction and the Freedmen's Bureau—the former with horror and resentment, and the latter with the hope that this federal presence would at last bring justice and opportunity. Haynes carefully explained that his brief was to subordinate all considerations to prosecution of the war effort. Yet southern commercial and agricultural elites were determined to retain their sources of cheap and docile (or so they thought) labor. Although black leaders had pushed for the creation of the new division, militants in the NAACP could be relied on to criticize any concessions it made to southern interests. Moreover, southern blacks themselves were suspicious of any official efforts to discourage migration. Reported one of Dillard's white investigators, "all the advice about staying in the South that we shower on the Negro, he reads backward."[48]

Moreover, Haynes was convinced that migration constituted a magnificent opportunity for members of his race to gain a foothold in industry, improve their living standards, gain access to educational opportunities, and generally promote black betterment. Haynes and his state directors and field agents worked assiduously to ease the economic transitions involved in the migration. Able investigators in Illinois, Michigan, Ohio, and New Jersey conducted illuminating studies of the living, working, religious, and leisure-time activities of new northern workers. At the same time, their southern counterparts worked to blunt the impact of "work or fight" orders, recruit local blacks for war production, and promote the view that the key to the retention of southern labor was higher wages and better working and living conditions on farms, in lumber camps, and at construction sites. Their efforts, given considerable public visibility by Secretary Wilson, helped deflect the call for repressive labor measures and the curtailment of physical mobility.

It was Haynes's great hope that the work of the DNE would continue into the postwar period and that the division would become a permanent agency. The migration, he believed, marked a decisive breakthrough in the struggles of African Americans. "'Mr. Opportunity,'" he advised a Detroit audience, "has taken hold of the Negro worker's right hand and has led him into the place of work." Nor was potential for progress confined to the North, for "one of the striking things is that 'Mr. Opportunity' is concerning himself in the South . . . as well as in the North," since southern whites were being forced to improve conditions if they wanted to retain their labor force. After the armistice, DNE agents continued to file detailed reports of living and working conditions in northern states, as the end of the war failed to stem the flow of African Americans northward. Although Congress quickly cut funding for the USES, into whose budget DNE allocations were folded, Haynes soldiered on into mid-1920, attempting to keep alive what he and his allies in the black community considered the most important federal racial initiative since Reconstruction.[49]

Indeed, if progress was to be steady and secure, blacks and whites needed the support of a benign federal government. In Haynes's view, the racial balance in the North was delicate, with much friction between white and black workers. Militant race-conscious elements were capitalizing on the frustration and anger of migrants, who too often encountered poor housing and hostility on the part of white coworkers. Migrants' "discontent growing out of previous conditions and present maladjustment . . . , their desire for American rights, their resentment against unjust discriminations and other un-American practices . . . make them a very ripe field for unrest, friction and disturbances," he warned. In view of the racial tension that erupted into deadly violence in Washington, Chicago, and elsewhere in the summer of 1919, a federal presence was desperately needed, perhaps more so than during the war itself.[50]

Haynes's appeals, however, were unavailing. By the fall of 1920, this promising experiment in federal manpower and race relations management was a dead letter. Neither the outgoing, southern-dominated Sixty-sixth Congress nor the incoming, Republican Sixty-seventh regarded the federal government's monitoring or amelioration of social conditions a necessary or appropriate function. Stripped of his investigative staff and his office help, Haynes returned to his teaching post at Fisk University. There, he continued to write as a private citizen about the migration, seeking to encourage the efforts of civic and religious bodies to provide moral and practical support to the new black urban communities. Groups such as the Urban League attempted to fill the void left by the federal departure, but for the most part, the Great Migration continued apace into the 1920s with little public oversight or direction.

Other wartime agencies also evidenced some initial concern for the welfare of African American workers, although none specifically targeted the problems of black wage earners. The U.S. Railroad Administration, created in December 1917 to take over operation of the chaotic transport system, promulgated rulings that facilitated the organization of some black workers and even, on occasion, favored the interests of black employees over the demands of the powerful and racist white railroad brotherhoods. Responding to a wave of self-organization on the part of black railroad workers who were ineligible for or ignored by the standard railroad unions, USRA officials sometimes let the logic of efficient wartime production override their racial prejudices. It made no sense, for example, to dismiss experienced black maintenance men or yard workers to provide jobs for covetous but inexperienced whites. The USRA's Board of Railroad Wages and Working Conditions provided a unique forum for organizations representing black workers to air their grievances. And in May 1918, USRA director William G. McAdoo issued General Order No. 27, which contained a sweeping "equal pay for equal work" stipulation, shortened the workday, and provided for overtime wage premiums. The order was particularly welcome among workers at the low end of the industry's pay scale, boosting the wages of unskilled workers by as much as 43 percent. Declared one black union leader, "June 1st 1918," the date on which General Order No. 27 took effect, "will go down upon the pages and annals of history . . . and will as well mark the revolution in the life of the Colored Railway Employees."[51]

Unfortunately, USRA support for black workers was episodic at best, and it ended abruptly with the cessation of the war. Indeed, even General Order No. 27 was a mixed blessing: white railroaders used it as an argument for dismissing blacks and hiring whites in their place, since the chief benefit of employing blacks—their cheapness—no longer prevailed. And once the war had ended, rank-and-file white workers moved aggressively to use the USRA to drive blacks out of a wide range of railroad jobs. Beginning in January 1919 with strike threats and sporadic walkouts in the southern rail center of Memphis, Tennessee, white workers demanded that employment practices reserving certain jobs for blacks be ended and that the railroads dismiss thousands of black yard, maintenance, and baggage handling workers. USRA officials, many of whom had been recruited from the lily-white railroad brotherhoods, proved willing tools of this often militant white activism. After protracted negotiations with leaders of the Brotherhood of Railroad Trainmen and with dissident rank-and-file committees, the USRA eventually approved changes in seniority rules that, though couched in race-blind language, had the effect of ousting black workers from jobs that, in some cases, they had held since the Civil War. With labor unrest dominating the headlines through much of 1919, and with the brotherhoods agitating for permanent federal operation of the railroad system, even those USRA officials who were sympathetic to the black workers readily capitulated. Thus, the USRA's southeastern regional director acknowledged that the new rules were unfair. But, he explained, he "had accepted the less [sic] of two evils,—that is, he had complied with the demands of the white trainmen rather than endure a strike. . . . It was better," he believed, "to inconvenience a few men (colored) than to tie up the entire south" with the inevitable strike that would have resulted from a failure to impose the changes.[52]

During its short life span, the National War Labor Board compiled a somewhat more positive record on racial matters. Established in April

1918, the NWLB played a key role in boosting union membership and extending industrial democracy. Co-chaired by militant progressive Frank Walsh and former president William Howard Taft, it intervened in a number of racially pregnant labor disputes. In cases involving streetcar operators in New Orleans, laundresses in Arkansas, iron- and steelworkers in Alabama, and phosphate miners in Florida, NWLB investigators came down on the side of equal pay for equal work and workers' rights to workplace representation, regardless of race. Walsh was particularly eager to acknowledge the concerns of black workers, whose growing importance in the labor force offered opportunities to forge a vigorous liberal movement. Union growth in the South, he believed, was crucial if the South was to help sustain and expand the progressive impulses that the war had generated. And building union strength necessitated the organization of black as well as white workers.

The situation in Birmingham, Alabama, afforded an opportunity to further Walsh's agenda. In the winter of 1918, thousands of white craftsmen in the city's iron and steel mills walked out, their key demand being the establishment of an eight-hour workday. It quickly became clear, however, that Birmingham's largest producers could withstand the strike and meet production goals, partly because of access to nonunion black labor. Unyielding in their refusal to recruit African Americans into the machinists, pattern makers, and boilermakers unions, strike leaders nonetheless recognized the need to reach out to black workers. AFL leaders turned to one of the federation's biracial affiliates, the International Union of Mine, Mill, and Smelter Workers (IUMMSW), and invited that energetic organization to recruit black workers so that they would be unavailable as replacement labor for the iron and steel companies. IUMMSW organizers made rapid progress, as black workers saw the wartime demand for uninterrupted production as an opportunity to improve their wages and working conditions. The IUMMSW began to make headway among African Americans in the nearby iron mines as well.

The NWLB, which was formally created by President Wilson on April 8, dispatched an agent to Alabama that month to investigate reports of labor and racial turmoil and to advise on whether the board should assume jurisdiction over the strike. Meanwhile, antiunion elements in the Magic City began a campaign of violence and intimidation. In May, the Ku Klux Klan marched through Birmingham, calling for an end to the strike in the name of patriotism. It was commonly known, said one union opponent, that black workers were being influenced by German propaganda, which was "getting a hold on the negroes . . . using the miners' Union as a channel."[53]

Sharing Walsh's sympathies, NWLB representative Raymond Swing sent back vivid accounts of assaults against union activists, particularly the IUMMSW's black organizer Ulysses Hale. Subsequent board hearings and rulings called for wage increases and improvements in iron miners' company-provided housing. "Peonage in Alabama and elsewhere," proclaimed a northern African American newspaper, "has been given a blow by the National War Labor Board."[54]

But in the end, the NWLB did nothing to stem the violence or to improve wages and working conditions in Birmingham's iron and steel mills. Conservative members of the board in effect vetoed direct intervention in the strike, which, they claimed, was not significantly affecting military production. Taft, who sometimes followed Walsh's lead, in this case opposed what he regarded as gratuitous governmental intervention. Indeed, Taft sometimes openly declared that black workers and families neither expected nor merited a "white" standard of living. Although black activists continued to hold out hope that the board might use its federal mandate to protect them from violence and intimidation, they did so in vain, despite Walsh's insistence that since "there is a strike going on" and "it has been repressed by physical violence. . . . we ought to take jurisdiction of it." Without NWLB intervention, the strike, along with the organizing campaign in the iron mines, soon collapsed amid sputtering racial violence.[55]

As soon as the war ended, employers everywhere immediately withdrew their grudging cooperation with the NWLB and refused to implement its judgments, even before its official termination in May 1919. In the actions of both the USRA and the NWLB, African American workers and race spokesmen caught a glimpse of what might be possible from the national government. The brevity of American belligerency and the sharp postwar reaction against virtually all types of war-begotten federal activism, however, quickly ended these seemingly promising experiments in de facto workplace equality and undermined the always difficult project of building a biracial, if not an interracial, union presence in the South.

For thousands of black workers, the limited character of the federal government's involvement in matters of race and labor was a bitter disappointment, especially in view of the fleeting promises held out by such wartime agencies as the DNE, USRA, and NWLB. Warned George Haynes in the summer of 1919, demagogues and Bolshevik-inspired radicals might find fertile ground among disillusioned black workers who would otherwise look gratefully to the federal government for equity and fairness. "They will listen to counsel and guidance from Federal agents as from no others," he informed Secretary Wilson. Federal officials from the Department of Labor, the USES, and the DNE, he found, were widely respected and highly regarded among the volatile new northern black working class. He pleaded for "larger efforts by Federal departments to improve living and working conditions among Negroes," but by the time he issued that appeal, the NWLB had been disbanded, and the DNE had been reduced to a skeleton staff.[56] With the USRA increasingly bowing to the demands of white unionists in the last months of federal operation of the railroads, it was clear that any interest in equity for black workers and their well-being was not due to a change in public policy but rather was the ephemeral artifact of a nation at war.

Throughout the 1920s, the executive branch of the federal government played little role in determining the racial dimensions of labor policy. Although labor problems continued to occupy much governmental attention, it was congressional action that addressed, indirectly, the issues of race and labor. The Republican-controlled Congress of the 1920s dealt with a variety of labor-related issues that carried racial implications, even when race itself was not explicitly invoked. And surprisingly, in view of the overall conservatism of the Republican Party, the main legislative labor initiatives were responsive to and supported by organized labor. In some cases, such as the successful campaign to limit and change the ethnic contours of immigration, African American workers were unintended beneficiaries. In other cases, notably those involving railroad labor, wages in the building trades, and limiting the use of court injunctions in labor disputes, spokesmen for black workers protested that the legislation in question adversely affected African Americans.

In 1921, Congress adopted interim legislation designed to curtail immigration, capping a lengthy struggle by restrictionists to achieve this goal. Then in 1924, this temporary law was replaced by permanent legislation. In both cases, Congress acted not only to sharply limit the overall number of immigrants permitted into the country but also to impose quotas based on the national origin of those seeking entry. The 1924 legislation limited the entrants from a given country to a number equal to 3 percent of those present in the United States as recorded in the census of 1890. The effect of this provision was to grossly underrepresent the countries of eastern and southern Europe. These countries had accounted for the great majority of people coming to the United States in the peak immigration years of the early twentieth century, but these nationalities constituted a far smaller proportion of the U.S. population in 1890 than they did in 1910 or 1920, for example. The 1924 law also affirmed the exclusion of the Chinese and, for the first time, excluded Japanese and other Asians.[57]

Clearly, the Immigration Act of 1924 would have an enormous impact on the composition of the U.S. working class. The great majority of the 13.4 million people who had entered the country between 1900 and 1914 were working people. Immigrants from the Austro-Hungarian and Russian empires, from Greece and Italy, and from Slavic areas of the German empire supplied much of the labor that drove American industry during this period of dramatic economic growth. The curtailment of this influx, first because of the war and then through legislative action, opened up industrial opportunities for African Americans, as the reconstitution of the labor force in meatpacking, steel, munitions, and other heavy industries during the war so graphically demonstrated. Black leaders, who had been criticizing the reliance on immigrant labor and the resultant constriction of opportunities for blacks since the nineteenth century, hailed the passage of the 1924 law, which, they believed, would expand opportunities for black workers. Indeed, A. Philip Randolph deemed the law insufficiently restrictive, since it contained no limit on immigration from the Western Hemisphere. Instead of merely limiting immigration, he declared, "we favor reducing it to nothing . . . shutting out the Germans . . . Italians . . . Hindus . . . Chinese . . . and even the Negroes from the West Indies."[58]

In calling for immigration restriction, African Americans—though victimized themselves by racial stereotyping—joined in the demonization of foreigners that punctuated the debate. Immigrants, declared a southern black newspaper in 1928, were "crude, illiterate, and hopelessly unsympathetic with American institutions and ideals. . . . [They] press us further down the economic ladder . . . in spite of our proved loyalty to America."[59] The BSCP sometimes resorted to racial epithets in protesting the employment of Chinese and Filipino men as attendants, while others deplored the provisions of the Immigration Act that granted free entry to Mexicans and other Latin Americans, whose willingness to work cheap, they charged, threatened black workers' hard-won gains. "If the million Mexicans who have entered the country [in the 1920s] have not displaced Negro workers, whom have they displaced?" asked a black journalist. The prestigious black newspaper the *Pittsburgh Courier* warned of "'little brown men' taking our jobs," just as southern and eastern Europeans had done a generation before.[60] In fact, however, there was little specific evidence of Mexican-born workers replacing African Americans, although it is true that in the 1920s, their availability compensated for the declining number of European immigrants and helped Michigan automakers fill their labor needs without abandoning their policy of discriminating against African Americans.

The changes in immigration policy and the ethnic reconfiguration of the working class in the 1920s were the latest chapter in the ongoing juxtaposition of race and class in American life. African American workers played no role in the passage of the restrictive legislation. Any benefits accruing to them as a result of the curtailment of European and Asian entry were purely fortuitous and unintended. Nor did the AFL's ardent support of the legislation (only marginally important to its passage) refer to the need to protect its African American members from low-wage competition. The rapid onset of the Great Depression made it impossible to draw up a balance sheet of black workers' gains and losses associated with the permanent curtailment of European immigration and the influx of Mexican workers in the 1920s. Owing to developments in the World War I years and their aftermath, black workers now played a more central role in the industrial economy and were part of a working class that, because of the limits on immigration, promised to be ethnically more stable, at least in the industrial heartland of the country.

Other federal labor legislation during this period was less positive from the perspective of African Americans. The Railway Labor Act of 1926, for example, provided federal machinery for the resolution of labor disputes and, in effect, granted the Big Four brotherhoods privileged status as spokesmen for railroad workers. Congressional debate showed no interest in these unions' racial discrimination, nor did federal authorities blink at approving collective bargaining agreements that effectively eliminated the jobs of black workers. The Brotherhood of Locomotive Firemen and Enginemen, in particular, targeted black firemen on the southern roads, since, in the words of one of its leaders, "the Negro is an undesirable in our particular vocation [and] . . . therefore should be supplanted by a white man in all instances." Agreements between the Brotherhood of Locomotive Firemen and Enginemen and various carriers that furthered this goal enjoyed the de facto backing of the U.S. government. "With this legislation," declared Arnold Hill of the National Urban League, "the condition of Negroes engaged in train and yard has grown steadily worse."[61]

Other legislative actions supported by organized labor in this period also had a problematic impact on black workers. The Davis-Bacon Act, which Congress passed on March 3, 1931, provided that contractors doing work for the federal government must pay their employees the "prevailing wage" in the area where the building was taking place. The "prevailing wage," in effect, meant the level of wages achieved by unionized construction workers. Obviously beneficial to AFL members in unions representing the carpenters, electrical workers, sheet metal workers, painters, and other building tradesmen, the law, in combination with these unions' discrimination against black workers, limited opportunities for African Americans. Absent the Davis-Bacon Act, employers might be tempted to hire nonunion labor, including black workers who were banned from the unions and hence forced to compete by accepting lower wages. With no wage advantage, contractors would have less incentive to hire nonunion black workers. In effect, charged contractors and African American commentators, the law endorsed the unions' racial practices and helped prevent black workers from gaining entry into a dynamic and job-rich economic sector.

Similarly, African American spokesmen criticized the Norris-LaGuardia Act of March 23, 1932. This law, long sought by the AFL and other mainstream labor organizations, sharply restricted the courts' ability to issue injunctions in labor disputes. It also outlawed the so-called yellow-dog contract, wherein a worker agreed not to join a trade union during his tenure of work with a given employer. Unionists regarded injunctions as a particularly pernicious form of governmental intervention in labor disputes, since their issuance disrupted strikes and organizing campaigns and often imposed harsh restrictions on what union advocates could do and say in support of their cause. From the 1870s onward, embattled employers had found the issuance of labor injunctions to be a critical weapon in their struggle to resist union demands and discourage union organization. For more than fifty years, labor advocates, led by Gompers, had fought to restrict the issuance of these injunctions, which they regarded as an unfair use of state power by corporate lawyers and their soul mates on the bench.

For many African American workers, however, strikes by white workers and their defeat at the hands of the courts had provided employment opportunities. To the extent that court orders curtailed picketing and otherwise limited strikers' ability to harass or intimidate strikebreakers, African Americans could regard court intervention positively. Outlawing the yellow-dog contract, thus strengthening white unions' ability to gain recognition and bargain for closed-shop provisions, would also limit opportunities for black workers to replace white strikers. Indeed, black workers sometimes regarded strikebreaking as a positive and forward-looking thing to do. Encouraged by editors, clergymen, and other middle-class race spokesmen, they regarded the taking of white strikers' jobs as a sensible exploitation of unique opportunities. "We are not strike breakers," insisted an African American newspaper, "but we are workers," and "necessity forces us to accept work when and where we can get it."[62] In protecting blacks who braved white workers' threats and violent acts, declared an African American attorney, "the Federal courts . . . have been almost their only bulwark against oppression . . . , and the power of injunction has been one of the strongest weapons which those courts have employed" in behalf of black workers.[63]

As a socialist and a trade unionist, Randolph rejected these arguments. He favored passage of the Railway Labor Act, despite its de facto acceptance of discrimination, in part because he believed that its endorsement of collective bargaining and its stipulation that workers be able to choose their own representatives without compulsion would boost the chances of recognition for the struggling BSCP. Moreover, although the trainmen and other railroad brotherhoods barred black membership, Randolph cooperated with these organizations in legal matters and valued their support in the BSCP's protracted struggle against the well-heeled Pullman Car Company. Like any good trade unionist, Randolph decried the labor injunction as a fundamental denial of the rights of free people. Although it was true that these court rulings might occasionally provide jobs for black strikebreakers, and although the absence of prevailing-wage legislation might encourage employers to hire African Americans because they would accept low wages, Randolph believed that there was no future for workers black or white in these desperate devices. The AFL and the railroad brotherhoods were deeply flawed vehicles for the kind of human advancement that Randolph sought, but he believed that justice and dignity for black workers lay in cooperation with their white counterparts, whatever the immediate discouragements, rather than reliance on the largesse and benevolence of corporate employers.

Throughout the 1920s and into the 1930s, African Americans struggled to sustain the employment gains associated with northward migration. This was not an easy task. Periodic recessions, continuing patterns of racial discrimination, and dramatic changes in the character of industrial work combined to undermine the economic positions of black families in both the North and the South. Throughout the mass production industries, blacks were relegated to the low-wage, physically demanding jobs, with little hope of advancement and little job security. In Detroit, a major wartime magnet for black migrants, the booming automobile industry systematically excluded African Americans from all but the most menial occupations. The sole exception was Ford, which offered relatively high-wage work to several thousand black workers but also had a reputation as a particularly harsh and demanding employer. In the words of one resident, "everybody knew Ford was a 'man-killing' place."[64] But black men, especially if they were married and had families, had no other option and clung to even the dirtiest and most unhealthy jobs in the River Rouge foundries, while white workers could choose among the Motor City's many employers.

In Chicago, black workers held their ground in the meatpacking industry, and there was some upward movement into relatively skilled jobs. Even so, the overwhelming proportion of black men and increasing numbers of black women toiled in low-wage jobs, often in unsavory surroundings. In Norfolk, Pittsburgh, Gary, and other industrial centers, the proportion of black men working in manufacturing actually declined in the 1920s, while the proportion of those performing domestic and personal service increased. There were modest gains nationwide in white-collar and skilled employment, but, according to one careful calculation, as of 1930, at least two-thirds of black workers were classified as unskilled, compared with less than one-quarter of white workers.

The rapid onset of the Great Depression posed vast new problems both for the labor movement and for African American workers. Would the dramatic demographic changes brought by the Great Migration and by the immigration legislation of the 1920s reduce interracial tensions and encourage class-based labor activism in common pursuit of security and prosperity?

Or would the ravages of the Great Depression that was descending on the country intensify raw racial conflict in a time of mounting unemployment and diminished opportunities? Would depression-bred calls for governmental action to right the floundering economy reinforce racial barriers in the interests of the white majority? Or would it, as Randolph hoped and expected, provide opportunities for black workers and for interracial activism?

4

RACE AND LABOR IN
DEPRESSION AND WAR

From the onset of the Great Depression to the end of World War II, union membership among African Americans soared from about sixty thousand to around one million. African Americans played key roles in the dramatic expansion of the U.S. labor movement, whose total membership during this period grew by a factor of five to more than fourteen million members. In the 1930s, a combination of favorable federal labor policies, heightened activism among rank-and-file workers, and determined leadership revitalized a hitherto lethargic trade union movement, which now sought to expand into mass production industries. Since the Great Migration had brought thousands of black workers into the heart of the industrial economy, union organizers and left-wing activists quickly realized that they had to offer African American workers more than the AFL's halfhearted and discriminatory gestures. The emergence of a new labor center, the Congress of Industrial Organizations (CIO),[1] in 1935 brought a sense of crusading zeal into the labor movement, along with a distinctively egalitarian approach to organizing drives and workplace protests. CIO competition, in turn, reenergized the AFL, which began to move haltingly toward a more responsive posture with respect to minority workers. During the 1930s and throughout World War II, federal legislation and executive actions played a key role in bolstering interracial union activity and, eventually, advancing African American workers' quest for fairer treatment. For their part, leaders in the African American community began to focus on the economic problems of blacks and, increasingly, to look to the labor movement for allies in the struggle for economic security and social progress. Black workers in the economy's industrial and transport core moved from cautious skepticism of the newly emerging labor regime to ardent embrace of the revitalized labor movement as a powerful instrument of both labor rights and civil rights.

The story of race and labor during this period of dramatic laborite expansion, however, was not one of unalloyed success. Key AFL unions remained bastions of white privilege, as did the major railroad unions. Unions in the rebel CIO, though generally more responsive to the concerns of black workers, often held a narrow view of workplace racial justice and sometimes pursued bargaining strategies that had the effect of locking African Americans into low-wage, insecure jobs. The pro-labor legislation of the 1930s, like the other labor laws passed since 1926, failed to invoke racial equality and on occasion had the effect of limiting black workers' employment opportunities. During the war, a pioneering executive order calling for fair employment practices lacked enforcement and at times functioned as a means of quieting protest rather than as an instrument of racial advance. Even the employment gains that African American workers made during the war were problematic because they were concentrated in war production, the industrial sector most likely to experience postwar cutbacks and layoffs.

Black Workers and the Great Depression

The sudden economic downturn heralded by the stock market crash of October 1929 hit African Americans with particular force. In the South, where a majority still lived, cotton farmers, whether farm owners, tenants, or sharecroppers, watched helplessly as their already marginal incomes plummeted. The wretched housing, inadequate diet, and extreme poverty that characterized much of rural southern black life deteriorated rapidly. Those who left the land in despair to find work in southern cities fared no better; by 1933, over half the South's black urban dwellers were unemployed. Moreover, whites affected by the Depression now claimed jobs that they had formerly disdained as "nigger work." White women replaced black domestics, and white men elbowed blacks aside in bidding for heavy labor and menial work. In Atlanta, whites joined a quasi-fascist organization, the Black Shirts, whose slogan was "No Jobs for Niggers Until Every White Man Has a Job!" The Ku Klux Klan revived, and the number of lynchings spiked. "Dead men," wrote a liberal journalist in 1931, "not only tell no tales but [also] create [job] vacancies."[2]

African Americans in northern cities suffered as well. In the early years of the Depression, unemployment ravaged black communities in Chicago, Detroit, Cleveland, and other urban centers. As white families tightened their belts, thousands of black women working as domestics faced joblessness. Blacks were commonly the first to face layoffs. Moreover, outright discrimination narrowed the range of jobs open to them. Major hotels and department stores in northern cities openly refused to hire African Americans, while urban transit systems, public utilities, insurance companies, and other major employers shunted their few black employees to menial and custodial work. Craft unions barred blacks from membership. Municipal and private relief agencies in the North may have been less overtly discriminatory than their counterparts in the South, but the vast scale of black unemployment and indigence strained even the most generous public and private providers to the limit. Black city dwellers, declared the Urban League in 1931, were "hanging on by the barest thread." Added veteran observer Arnold Hill, "At no time in the history of the Negro since slavery has his economic and social outlook seemed so discouraging."[3]

Leaders of civil rights organizations such as the National Association for the Advancement of Colored People (NAACP) and the National Urban League began to focus on black workers' plight. During the early years of the Depression, the NAACP, which had traditionally stressed the advancement of legal rights and educational opportunities, conducted a sharp internal debate. Younger activists urged that the NAACP make common cause with the labor movement to link the desperate concerns of both white and black workers during the country's economic collapse. Class, rather than race, they argued, was now the dominant fact of American life. In response, in 1934, the civil rights organization established a Committee on the Future Plan and Program, headed by labor expert and sociologist Abram Harris, to make recommendations about the NAACP's response to the Depression.

In their deliberations, Harris and his allies on the committee acknowledged that NAACP leaders had a long record of criticizing the labor movement's racial policies. Obviously, the mainstream labor movement's treatment of black workers would have to change if it was to become a fit ally. Even so, Harris argued, the vast crisis engendered by the country's economic collapse called for a drastic change in the NAACP's direction and for a major effort to make common cause with organized labor. The average black worker, Harris declared, could not secure "his rights as an American citizen under prevailing economic and social conditions"; nor could he do so in isolation from his white coworkers and cosufferers. African Americans, he and his colleagues asserted, had to persuade "white workers and black [workers] to view their lot as embracing a common cause" and to work with the more enlightened elements in the AFL. "White and black masses [had been driven] to a substantially identical economic position," insisted Harris. Clearly, "the plight of . . . black peasants and industrial workers was inextricably tied up with that of white [workers]."[4]

Although the established NAACP leadership, citing the AFL's continuing diffidence, demurred at implementing the Harris Committee's recommendations, rank-and-file workers, black and white, were beginning to demonstrate the progressive possibilities of interracial activism. The most remarkable example occurred in the cotton country of eastern Arkansas and western Tennessee. In the summer of 1934, responding to the effects of the recently passed Agricultural Adjustment Act (AAA), tenant farmers of both races began organizing under the leadership of Clay East and H. L.

Mitchell, two local socialists. In May 1933, in an attempt to inflate disastrously low farm prices, President Franklin Roosevelt's administration had secured passage of the AAA. A key goal of this complex law was to cut the production of cotton and other basic commodities, ultimately through the restriction of acreage, but immediately through the physical destruction of crops that were already planted. Growers would receive a federal subsidy to compensate them for the crop loss and acreage restriction. In theory, farm owners were to redistribute an equitable portion of this payment to sharecroppers and tenants, but in fact, the law resulted in the widespread expulsion of dependent workers from their homes and the slashing of wages for farm laborers, whose ranks were now augmented by recently dispossessed tenants and croppers. Already legendary for their poverty, farmworkers, both black and white, now experienced harsh evictions, complete loss of livelihood, and abject destitution. "Never in America," declared Socialist Party leader Norman Thomas after a visit to Arkansas in the winter of 1934, "have I seen more hopeless poverty."[5]

East and Mitchell saw an opportunity to build a grassroots socialist movement in the South by organizing afflicted cotton farmers of both races. Beginning in the summer of 1934, assisted by the eloquent Thomas and in the face of often violent repression by growers and their allies in state and local governments, farm tenants, sharecroppers, and laborers built an impressive interracial organization, the Southern Tenant Farmers Union (STFU). Combining widely publicized demonstrations at the Agricultural Adjustment Administration's Washington office with strategically timed strikes, the STFU expanded rapidly. Within two years, it claimed thirty-one thousand members in more than two hundred local unions in seven southern states. Moreover, the STFU was a genuinely interracial organization, with more than half of its members African American. East and Mitchell did not insist that each local union be racially integrated, but even where there were separate locals for black and white farmers and farmworkers, important decisions were typically made in integrated mass meetings. Overall, black STFU members were better educated than their white counterparts and tended to be more experienced and skilled in organizational activities, reflecting the important role that congregational black churches often played in rural communities. Still, as one unlettered local black leader observed, "The negros is ready to organize in fact they are the only ones that is willing to strike [of] corse they are afraid to under take to Do any thing By their selves and they cant Do nothing By their selves."[6]

Despite their desperate poverty and the harsh repression that STFU locals faced, the union chalked up some notable achievements. Demonstrations and testimony before federal agencies exposed the greed of the planters and the baleful effects of the AAA on the South's most vulnerable farmers and farmworkers. Harassment of STFU organizers and members was widely publicized, exposing the nakedness of rural class exploitation in the South. Widely publicized outrages spurred additional congressional and journalistic investigations and were featured in newsreel segments seen by millions of moviegoers. STFU leaders and well-connected liberal supporters gained an audience with President Roosevelt, who declared that alleviation of rural poverty and farm tenancy was a priority of his administration. In 1935, FDR, citing information provided by STFU partisans, threw his support behind legislation designed to extend federal assistance to affected tenants and croppers. Over the next two years, however, conservative opposition thwarted FDR's more innovative proposals. Thus, the 1937 passage of the Bankhead-Jones Farm Tenancy Act came as an anticlimax, since this law provided little direct benefit to the poorest classes of farmers and tenants. It did, however, establish the Farm Security Administration, an executive agency that FDR then used to implement limited programs of support for poor farmers and farm tenants. And when Congress repassed the AAA in 1937 (in 1935, the Supreme Court had declared the first AAA unconstitutional), the new version contained stronger—though still inadequate—language designed to protect the interests of tenants and croppers.

From the viewpoint of those who saw the Depression as an opportunity to forge links between black and white workers, however, the disappointing legislative results of STFU agitation were less important than its inspiring record of activism. For three years, an interracial southern labor organization conducted successful strikes, mounted impressive publicity campaigns, and mobilized demonstrations in Washington and in cotton country. Its leaders and supporters gained access to the president and helped shape a national debate over farm tenancy. After his landslide reelection in 1936, FDR named a commission to study the problem of farm tenancy, and STFU supporters lobbied successfully to have one of the union's leaders named to it. The appointment of the Reverend William L. Blackstone, an STFU officer from Arkansas, to this presidential body, claimed a union publication, "is a recognition that the union is a power in the movement to end the condition of tenancy and that its point of view must be heard by the Government."[7] If the ensuing legislation was disappointing and the Farm Security Administration could claim only partial success in alleviating rural southern poverty, the STFU had nonetheless demonstrated that interracial unionism could be a vigorous and effective force in the troubled 1930s.

Union activism in the heavily industrialized area centered on Birmingham, Alabama, during the early New Deal period gave even more convincing evidence to the efficacy of biracial organizing. In May 1933, Congress passed the National Industrial Recovery Act (NIRA), whose Section 7(a) stipulated that workers had the right to organize and to elect leaders of their own choosing. That summer, the United Mine Workers of

America (UMWA), which had suffered disastrous membership losses through the 1920s and the early Depression years, seized on this feature of the NIRA to wage a spectacularly successful effort to rebuild its shattered locals throughout the country's coal mining regions, including those in District 20 in Alabama.

During the late nineteenth and early twentieth centuries, the UMWA had built and sustained vigorous local unions in Alabama. Since about 40 percent of the region's miners were African American, the UMWA had organized them, along with the white majority, on an interracial basis. Indeed, between the 1880s and a disastrous strike in 1921, the Alabama coal mines were an oasis of interracial unionism, with African American miners serving as organizers and officers in a union that was almost alone among AFL affiliates in exhibiting any genuine racial egalitarianism. To be sure, the UMWA's national and regional white leaders were hardly free of racial prejudice. The union's newspaper, the *UMWA Journal,* sometimes printed crude and denigrating racist "humor," occasionally right alongside eloquent reports and speeches by gifted black organizers. Nor did the union's interracialism translate into a broader commitment to civil rights or racial justice. The UMWA in Alabama, for example, insisted that its concern for black workers was limited to matters of wages, hours, and working conditions; it did not extend to "social equality," a term that critics of the union used to imply that interracial activism would necessarily translate into racial mixing and encourage blacks to become "uppity" and sexually aggressive. Nor did UMWA leaders register significant protests when Alabama adopted a new constitution in 1901 that essentially disfranchised African American citizens. Still, for over thirty years, an embattled UMWA had built and sustained an effective interracial presence in a Deep South state that was otherwise notable for the subjugation of its black citizens.

Thus, when UMWA organizers, energized by the apparent sanction given to unionism by Section 7(a), swept into the Alabama coalfields claiming that "the president wants you to join the union," they aimed their appeal at black mine workers as well as white. As early as late summer 1933, a bold and aggressive organizing campaign that employed organizers of both races was yielding impressive results. By the end of 1934, the UMWA claimed that it had established ninety new locals in the district and enrolled twenty-three thousand men, about 60 percent of them African American. The new UMWA locals picked up the threads of the union's earlier interracialism. According to two contemporary observers, these "local unions . . . met almost everywhere in mixed white and Negro meetings. Officers were ordinarily drawn about one-half from each race. . . . Bargaining and other committees usually had people of both races," although it was also true that "the whites . . . [were] given the more important places."[8]

Nor was biracial unionism in Alabama restricted to the coal mines.

Stimulated by UMWA success, another racially progressive AFL affiliate, the International Union of Mine, Mill, and Smelter Workers, began organizing both black and white iron miners and workers in nearby mines, steel mills, and pipe factories. Even the more traditional AFL trade unions in the city reached out to black workers, although some were consigned to separate black locals. In all, reported Horace Cayton and George Mitchell, more than 100,000 Alabama workers were organized during the NIRA period (1933–1935), over half of them African American. Renewed union strength in the coal mines soon translated into the revival of unionism among steel- and other metalworkers in the area. The winning of significant improvements in wages, hours, and methods of compensation demonstrated that biracial unionism could enhance the lives of working people of both races.

The CIO and Black Workers

This early evidence of a new biracial union movement was only the beginning. In the fall of 1935, under the leadership of the dynamic UMWA president John L. Lewis, dissidents within the AFL formed a new body, the CIO, with the goal of encouraging AFL leaders to undertake ambitious organizing campaigns in mass production industries. In particular, CIO activists pointed to the July 1935 signing of the National Labor Relations Act (NLRA), a pathbreaking law that greatly strengthened workers' rights, as providing governmental sanction for mass organizing. Although the AFL and its constituent unions had expanded in the two years since passage of the NIRA, Lewis and his colleagues believed that the federation was failing to take advantage of a unique opportunity to establish itself in the auto, steel, rubber, electrical appliances, farm equipment, meatpacking, food processing, and other basic industries. But AFL officials denounced the CIO initiative as disruptive and divisive. They soon expelled the rebellious unions, thus launching a period of internal conflict and competition within the once monolithic House of Labor.

The emergence of the CIO and the split between it and the AFL had critical implications for African American workers. Lewis's UMWA had a history of reaching out to them. Other unions that supported the CIO initiative included the Ladies' Garment Workers' Union, the Clothing Workers Union, and several smaller unions, all with relatively positive records with respect to black workers. Moreover, from its outset, the CIO attracted younger, politically engaged activists, many from socialist, communist, or radical union backgrounds—men and women who sympathized with the plight of America's black families and who were eager to build on the country's real, though episodic, heritage of biracial labor activism. Meanwhile, those African Americans who had urged the NAACP and other reform organizations to acknowledge the primacy of economic concerns and to seek common cause with organized labor soon embraced the CIO as representing a new and hopeful departure from the racial policies of the AFL and the railroad brotherhoods.

Several of the industries targeted by Lewis and his colleagues for organizing were heavy employers of African American workers. These same industries—notably, steel and meatpacking—had long histories of bitter confrontation both between workers and employers and among the diverse ethnic groups that supplied much of the heavy labor in the mills and packinghouses. Racial issues affected even the Detroit-centered automobile industry, even though most major automakers refused to employ black workers in any but menial capacities. But the exception was a particularly important one: the Ford Motor Company. Partly out of altruism, and partly to build a cadre of faithful workers resistant to any union appeal, Ford had hired substantial numbers of black workers in the 1920s, especially in its vast River Rouge complex just outside Detroit. Any successful effort to organize Ford would have to organize River Rouge, and any successful effort to organize River Rouge would have to embrace the African American men who played a strategic role in the production processes there.

Politics was also part of the racial equation. As the CIO developed from a small group of AFL critics into a coherent and multifaceted organization, its leaders quickly recognized that they must become actively involved in state and national politics. And here too, African Americans found themselves in a strategic position. The Great Migration had brought over a million southern blacks into the northern electorate, and even during the depression-ridden 1930s, another 400,000 joined earlier migrants in the North. In Chicago, Philadelphia, Pittsburgh, New York, Detroit, and other industrial centers, the black vote loomed large, often providing a visible margin of victory for liberal candidates in hotly contested elections. Since the CIO project was dependent in part on the presence of pro-labor officials in Washington and the state capitals, it was natural that the new industrial union adopt a dynamic approach to political action. Clearly, the need to cultivate African American voters in the northern cities—and to reenfranchise black voters in the South—reinforced the CIO's determination to organize black workers.

Yet, whatever its egalitarian rhetoric, the CIO also had a "race problem"—or, rather, a series of interconnected race problems. Despite its dramatic break with the AFL, the CIO was the product of a mainstream labor movement that had for generations marginalized and mistreated black workers. "Negro workers," asserted the president of a new autoworkers union, "have all the benefits and rights of our union. . . . We feel very, very strongly on this matter." But bold proclamations could not offset decades of condescension and abuse. In view of past union failures in the steel, auto, meatpacking, and other key industries, black workers often regarded loyalty to employers and hence resistance to union appeals as the safest course. Early in the CIO's massive campaign launched in 1936 to organize the steel industry, white organizers in Pennsylvania and the Midwest often reported that (in the words of one) "Negroes . . . are the hardest race on earth to organize," an eloquent statement of racial misunderstanding, even if it fell short of capturing the complex realities in America's multiethnic workplaces.[9]

Indeed, the oft-asserted egalitarian principles of CIO leaders could not eliminate the racial and ethnic tensions that fractured the nation's diverse industrial labor force. In heavy industry, the core of CIO strength was often among first- and second-generation immigrants of Italian, Slavic, and Hungarian derivation. Schooled in the dog-eat-dog world of racial job competition, immigrant workers had learned to disdain blacks, just as they were disdained in the nation's schools, churches, courts, and political organs. Competing with blacks for entry-level jobs and viewing them as members of a "scab race," immigrant workers tended to see the new unions they were building as a means of advancing their parochial interests rather than as part of a broad class-conscious movement. For their part, black workers resented the advantages that "whiteness" bestowed on even the most recent European immigrant and were often reluctant to support a union that, they felt, would inevitably bolster white privilege. As an African American journalist reported in 1937 from a strike-torn Pennsylvania steel town, "The Slavs and others of alien extraction . . . are the backbone of the strike." But they "have never helped the local Negroes in their struggle for equal citizenship rights," nor had they ever supported blacks' demands for more equitable treatment on the job. The immigrant workers' "attitude has been almost identical with that of the [other] American whites," who in the past had terrorized black families in the city.[10]

In the South, of course, the CIO faced even more intense racial feelings. There, the racial equation seemed to be the reverse of that characterizing northern industrial centers. Victimized for generations, black workers often responded enthusiastically to the CIO's egalitarianism and became its most ardent supporters. Thus reported an organizer for a new CIO shipyard workers' union from Mississippi in 1938, "All the Negro workers are 100% CIO."[11] But a union built on black support risked alienating the more numerous white workers, steeped as they were in the racist public culture of the Depression-era South. Moreover, local white CIO activists, while acknowledging the need to bring blacks into the new unions, often privileged the concerns of white workers and found it difficult to overcome condescending and dismissive attitudes when dealing with blacks. Even racially progressive national CIO leaders regarded black workers as something of an exotic afterthought rather than as central to the industrial union project. Philip Murray, director of the CIO's massive effort to build a steel-workers union, acknowledged that "the negroes have become an increasingly important factor," but he believed that "the organization of the negro steelworkers will follow, rather than precede, the organization of white mill workers."[12] It was also true that in the collective bargaining contracts the CIO unions managed to negotiate in the 1930s, bargainers were often insensitive to the circumstances of black workers. In the matter of seniority rights—a key demand in virtually all negotiations—black workers started with the disadvantage that they had been relegated to dead-end jobs involving the least desirable work. Early CIO contracts typically called for seniority rights to be exercised on a department-by-department basis, thus confining most African American workers to their inferior positions.

But despite these knotty problems, there was no question that the CIO represented something new in American labor history. To be sure, both the Knights of Labor and the Industrial Workers of the World had built interracial unions, and the UMWA had organized blacks and whites together, often under dire circumstances. But the CIO represented the first large-scale effort to bring workers of all ethnic and racial identities into a sustained, well-resourced, and politically realistic common movement. CIO organizers might occasionally betray their regrettable racial views, and black workers might be skeptical, but by the late 1930s, large numbers of African American workers had joined the new CIO unions in steel, meatpacking, food processing, and other industries. "A new type of union is in the field," declared a veteran black labor activist in 1939. For half a century, I. H. Bratton recalled, "I've fought for full equality for the Negro worker. Today, I've found those things in the CIO."[13] That same year, a writer in the NAACP magazine *Crisis* called the CIO "a lamp of democracy" in the South, which had "not known such a force since the historic Union Leagues in the great Days of the Reconstruction era."[14]

The CIO was a diverse organization, and the role of black workers varied sharply in the different industries in which it operated. For example, the textile industry employed nearly half a million people and was the target of a major CIO organizing campaign launched in 1937, but it had only a handful of African American workers, especially in the crucial southern mills that were the focal point of this effort. Thus, although CIO organizers were often frustrated in their efforts to recruit southern cotton mill workers and made only modest headway in the 1930s and 1940s, job-site racial issues played little role. Nevertheless, the CIO's general commitment to the expansion of civil rights for blacks created problems among white workers in the South. In other industries, local activists and CIO organizers had to confront racial tensions on an almost daily basis and try to convince workers of both races that worker solidarity provided the best hope for improved standards and job security. Developments in the meatpacking and automobile industries illustrate some of the challenges and opportunities facing the industrial union movement in the 1930s.

In meatpacking, African American workers played a leading role in the building of a CIO packinghouse workers union. Constituting between 20 and 30 percent of the labor force in Chicago, the industry's center, black workers occupied particularly strategic positions on the kill floors, where the entire process of turning live animals into roasts, steaks, hamburger, ham, and bacon began. Even before the birth of the CIO in 1935, union activism among the fifty thousand men and women who worked in the stockyards, packinghouses, and meat processing plants had revived. In the earlier efforts to build a meatpackers union during the World War I era, a variety of factors had combined to discourage the participation of most black workers. Recent migrants knew little about the labor movement, and what they did know was often negative. The dominant AFL unions in the stockyards, notably the Amalgamated Meat Cutters, were at best ambivalent about organizing black workers. Clergymen and other middle-class race leaders advised that the best hope for steady employment rested with employers such as Armour, Swift, and Wilson, not with the labor movement. As in other northern-based industries, some meatpackers cultivated the loyalty of black workers by providing rudimentary versions of welfare capitalism, giving financial support to black churches and stressing the benevolence of those who provided jobs for African Americans.

But the Depression changed this equation. Far from being benefactors of black workers, the meatpackers singled out African Americans for layoffs; in the 1930s, the proportion of black stockyard workers declined by one-third. Observed one Armour worker in a 1939 interview, "When they raise a gang . . . you can bet you won't see any Negroes coming in." His employer, he reported, now hired "young [white] boys, raw kids, didn't know a thing, but there was plenty of colored boys waiting for the same chance who never got it."[15]

By now, the raw industrial recruits of 1918 were seasoned veterans of the harsh and demanding work culture of the yards and sheds. Betrayed by the packers' discriminatory hiring and layoff policies, many saw the opportunity to organize, seemingly promised by the NIRA, as a means of gaining job security and equal treatment. "Colored people has woke up to unionism now," one black packinghouse laborer told a researcher; the black worker "won't accept the boss-man's telling him, 'you don't want to be with the white man.' . . . The average Negro makes a good union man."[16] Throughout the 1930s, though still chary of the AFL Meat Cutters Union, black workers responded enthusiastically to efforts to build industrial unionism outside the confining structures of the federation.

The fact that communists were particularly active in the Chicago packinghouses also encouraged black labor activity. In the early 1930s, the

Communist Party's Trade Union Unity League had established unions to compete with the AFL in a variety of industrial sectors, among them meatpacking. Party doctrine insisted on racial equality, and the activists dispatched to organize in Chicago were particularly committed to building egalitarian unions. "Negro and White, Unite and Fight" was their slogan, and they found that black workers were responsive to their efforts, even though few of them ever joined the party. Leaders such as Herbert March and Henry Johnson quickly realized that the key to gaining critical support among African Americans, both in the workplace and in the community, was to downplay the party's ideological formulations and prove its effectiveness in dealing with people's daily struggles at work and in the neighborhoods. The Communist Party's meatpackers union, the Packinghouse Workers Industrial Union, insisted on integrated meetings, the recruitment and advancement of local black leaders, and an energetic response to the workplace concerns of African Americans. Communists were active in the community as well, leading protests against the eviction of impoverished families unable to pay their rent, agitating for more generous public and charitable assistance to the needy, and speaking out against racial violence. Even anticommunists in the black community praised the party's efforts. For example, in July 1933, influential newspaper editor Robert Abbott explained in a *Chicago Defender* column, "Why We Can't Hate the Reds." "Is there any other political, religious, or civic organization in the country," he asked, "that would go to such lengths to prove itself not unfriendly to us?"[17]

The CIO was actually late in tapping into the roiling activism in Chicago's meatpacking industry. Lewis and other CIO officials initially believed that the AFL Meat Cutters Union might be persuaded to throw its lot in with the CIO and adopt a more energetic and egalitarian program. But pressure from union activists in Chicago and other meatpacking centers, along with the meat cutters' continued diffidence, eventually resulted in the creation of the Packinghouse Workers Organizing Committee (PWOC) in October 1937, a CIO organization established to bring together the various strands of union activism that had been rumbling through the stockyards since 1933. By now, the Communist Party had disbanded the unions it had earlier established to rival the AFL, including the Packinghouse Workers Industrial Union, and its local activists enthusiastically embraced the PWOC.

Black workers continued to play key roles in the efforts of this CIO organization to bring the major meatpackers to the bargaining table. Owing to general patterns of job discrimination, even relatively well-educated African Americans often found their best employment prospects in the meatpacking industry. A number of the most effective and eloquent black labor activists were also storefront preachers, who brought both a rough eloquence and a deep commitment to egalitarian Christianity to their union work. Using their strategic positions in the production process, African American workers became adept at timing short job actions to compel employers to meet with union representatives, protect union activists from retaliation, and force foremen and supervisors to redress workers' grievances. Once considered the weak link in efforts to organize the industry, black workers, declared a *Defender* reporter in 1939, had now become "the backbone" of the PWOC. A white PWOC organizer told sociologist Horace Cayton that blacks were "the best union members" in the Chicago stockyards.[18] Indeed, workers in the stockyards, packinghouses, and processing plants built a remarkable "culture of solidarity," as white and black workers were able to put aside, if not transcend, racial differences in common pursuit of union recognition and collective bargaining. Declared one black worker in 1939, reflecting on the decades of racial tension that had divided ethnic whites from African Americans, "with the CIO in, all that's like a bad dream gone."[19] By the time the country entered World War II in December 1941, workers in the meatpacking industry, led by Chicago activists of both races, had laid the foundation for a vigorous and successful national packinghouse workers union under the aegis of the CIO.

If the CIO rode to success on the backs of black workers in Chicago's stockyards in the 1930s, it faced a more problematic racial situation in the automobile industry, centered in southeastern Michigan. For the most part, automakers had refused to hire African Americans to provide the labor for the enormous expansion of automobile production in the 1910s and 1920s, relying instead on immigrant workers, white migrants from the Appalachian South, and young men and women from midwestern farms and small towns. In the 1930s, only about 4 percent of all autoworkers were African American. In Detroit, Flint, and other Michigan production centers, the few black workers employed by auto, auto body, and auto parts companies either were custodians or performed the most dangerous and unhealthy production tasks. At Chrysler and Chevrolet plants in Detroit in the 1920s, for example, an academic observer reported that "certain dangerous emery steel grinding jobs were given only to Negroes." The few African Americans employed by General Motors, Chrysler, and auto body makers in Detroit were overwhelmingly concentrated in the dangerous metal foundries and in the paint-spraying departments, where accidents and work-related illnesses were rife.[20] Hence, when deteriorating economic conditions and the passage of Section 7(a) in 1933 combined to trigger a wave of union activism in the fiercely antiunion auto industry, racial factors played only a minor role in most auto plants.

One Detroit-area employer, however, broke with the virtual exclusion of blacks. Beginning in the early 1920s, Henry Ford, the eccentric and influential developer of modern mass production techniques in the auto industry, had begun to hire black workers. In particular, the opening in 1927 of Ford's huge River Rouge plant, southwest of Detroit, provided unique employment opportunities for black men. In the 1930s, that sprawling facility employed about ten thousand black workers, accounting for approximately 12 percent of the labor force. Nor did Ford relegate blacks to only the most arduous and unpleasant labor. Unlike Detroit's other major employers, Ford provided at least limited opportunities for blacks to gain skilled positions and even to graduate into the ranks of low-level management. There were black foremen at River Rouge, for example, and in some cases, they supervised white workers. A handful of blacks performed white-collar work at Ford, including several whose job it was to recruit and train African Americans.

In the first half of the twentieth century, Henry Ford was a major public figure whose various industrial enterprises, public statements, and social crusades kept him constantly at the center of attention. He was a contradictory figure, at once cherishing a roseate view of the vanishing rural America into which he had been born in 1861 and relentlessly transforming the American landscape by pioneering the mass production and mass marketing of automobiles. In the 1920s, he sponsored outrageous anti-Semitic publications and warned of the insidious plots that Jews were hatching to take over the country. At the same time, however, he adopted a paternalistic and philanthropic attitude toward the expanding black population in the Detroit area. African Americans, he readily conceded, belonged to an inferior, childlike race. He favored segregation in housing and social relations. Yet he also believed that blacks, like the disabled men and the paroled convicts he recruited to work in his factories, deserved a chance to make a living. Indeed, the solution to the "race question," he held, was one that most labor activists could agree with, since it depended on having "enough jobs to go around" and paying the worker, regardless of his race, "a wage which means a secure family life." "The Negro," wrote Ford in the newspaper he sponsored, "needs a job, he needs a sense of industrially 'belonging,' and this it ought to be the desire of our industrial engineers to supply."[21]

This was not just talk. Ford cultivated civic leaders and clergymen in the Detroit area's black community, working with them to identify men worthy of being hired at Ford's plant. And although the majority of African Americans were employed in the foundry and performed other heavy labor or dangerous jobs, only at Ford could black workers gain entry into apprenticeships, hold jobs as skilled electricians and tool-and-die makers, and become foremen. Thus, a job at River Rouge was an emblem of success and respectability, and for many in the African American community, Ford enjoyed a reputation as a friend of the race and as a benefactor to whom loyalty was due. "I'm goin' to get me a job, up there in Mr. Ford's place, / Stop these eatless days from starin' me in the face" went the words to a blues song of the 1920s.[22]

Throughout the 1930s, deteriorating economic conditions, heightened worker militancy, and the union-friendly legal climate fostered by Section 7(a) and the NLRA made the sprawling automobile industry a critical arena in the effort to establish industrial unionism. The United Automobile Workers (UAW), chartered reluctantly in 1934 by the AFL, was among the first of the new unions to cast its lot in with the CIO. The struggle to establish the UAW and to install collective bargaining in the industry soon focused on General Motors (GM), which in the 1920s had surpassed Ford as the largest automaker. It came to a head in late 1936 and early 1937 when unionists in Flint, Michigan, the nerve center of GM's vast empire, occupied key production facilities. In February 1937, with the dramatic assistance of CIO chief John L. Lewis, the UAW wrested a contract from GM. Later that spring, UAW sit-down strikers also brought the third largest automaker, Chrysler Corporation, to the bargaining table. Sit-down strikes and more traditional walkouts also established the UAW in numerous smaller auto parts, auto body, and related metalworking plants in the Detroit area in the mid-1930s.

On the whole, reflecting the racial discrimination that characterized most of the industry, black workers played little role in this activism. On occasion, when black and white workers were employed at common tasks, the two groups united to advance the UAW cause. More often, however, black workers stood on the sidelines or even remained at work in defiance of union picket lines. Michigan's black workers, observed national NAACP officer Roy Wilkins, were "hanging back, asking the usual question: 'Will the union give us a square deal and a chance at some of the good jobs?'"[23] And after the initial wave of union building, both the auto industry and the UAW began to experience troubled times. At the end of 1937, the economy turned sharply downward, resulting in massive layoffs. At the same time, newly empowered workers launched uncoordinated and divisive strikes, often in violation of the contracts the UAW had signed with GM, Chrysler, and other companies. Meanwhile, internal power struggles racked the fledgling union. Dues-paying membership fell off. With the economy in decline and the union in disarray, GM and other employers stymied efforts to improve on the sketchy contracts signed in 1936–1937 and began disciplining union activists and undermining the union, in violation of those contracts.

In addition to uncertain economic conditions and the chaos within the UAW, GM and Chrysler officials pointed to the union's failure to organize Ford as a justification for their unwillingness to bargaining seriously. In 1937, following its victories over GM and Chrysler, the UAW had in fact launched a major organizing drive centering on the River Rouge plant. But

Ford was notorious for the intensity of its antiunion policies. A veritable reign of terror prevailed in Ford plants. A special department manned by former convicts and street brawlers used force and intimidation to crush union activism. When UAW leaders attempted to pass out leaflets at River Rouge's gates in May 1937, Ford employees brutally assaulted them as Dearborn city police stood idly by. Throughout the late 1930s, Ford remained union free. Its defeat of the UAW emboldened GM, Chrysler, and other auto industry employers and gave them a ready excuse to resist the UAW's efforts to improve wages and working conditions in their plants.

By late 1940, however, things had changed. American military rearmament and expansionist federal fiscal policies were beginning to restore employment, including in the auto industry. The UAW resolved its fierce factional conflicts, at least temporarily, and its new leaders were determined to take advantage of tightened labor markets to rebuild the union, improve its existing contracts, and, most important, bring Ford to the bargaining table. To do this, the UAW had to confront the racial dynamics of the River Rouge plant, the heart of the Ford empire.

In the late 1930s, UAW leaders of all factions had at least paid lip service to the union's obligations to black workers. Both main "caucuses," as the factional groups were called, pledged to protect black workers' rights and press employers for antidiscrimination clauses in contracts. Indeed, embattled (and eventually ousted) president Homer Martin established an unofficial "Negro Department" and staffed it with black organizers who were loyal to him. But these gestures were essentially ad hoc efforts that had more to do with gaining an advantage in the union's internal conflict than with waging an aggressive campaign to win the hearts and minds of black workers. To be sure, the union had achieved some success in organizing black workers, and a gifted cadre of young African American organizers and activists had begun to emerge, but overall, black workers were less likely than their white counterparts to join and more likely to default on dues payments or drop out entirely. As one black union activist observed, "The Negro has a long history of discrimination by the AFL, and he is not yet convinced that such discrimination will not be continued by the CIO."[24] Ford's combination of paternalism and repression at River Rouge ensured that many, perhaps most, of his black employees would resist the UAW appeal. Indeed, as the UAW drive gathered force in late 1940 and into 1941, Ford stepped up the hiring of African American workers; by March 1941, as the UAW effort was nearing its climax, no fewer than fourteen thousand African Americans worked at the huge River Rouge complex, accounting for almost 20 percent of the labor force. This strategy seemed to pay off in the black community. As one influential minister declared that spring, "If Henry Ford hires one colored for every ten whites, I am for him first, last, and always."[25]

In the end, the campaign to organize Ford climaxed rather suddenly in April 1941, when UAW-CIO members launched a massive strike at River Rouge. Faced with such strong pro-union sentiment, Ford officials entered into a collusive agreement with a rival AFL union (which also called itself the United Automobile Workers, or UAW-AFL), which they believed could be used to mobilize the anti-CIO sentiments held by some autoworkers. In this, they counted on the loyalty of their black employees, especially those who were recent hires. For ten days, several thousand African American workers remained inside the River Rouge complex, fed and housed in makeshift barracks by the company, even as the UAW-CIO's increasing cadre of black members and organizers sought to persuade them to leave. Clashes between strikers and black workers loyal to Ford erupted; at times, it seemed as if the conflict was about to explode into a full-fledged race war. Since Ford could not resume production with the small remnant of its labor force remaining in the complex, unionists and, increasingly, members of Detroit's black community charged that the company was hoping to foment racial violence as a way of discrediting the strike and perhaps forcing Michigan's Democratic governor Murray D. Van Wagoner to send in the National Guard. Both local and national NAACP leaders, along with an increasing number of other influential citizens, began to denounce the company for promoting a race war whose chief victims would be vulnerable black workers.

Most black River Rouge workers remained hesitant and uncommitted. Even those who advised support for the UAW-CIO did so cautiously. National NAACP secretary Walter White became convinced that the UAW-CIO's victory was inevitable, especially after Ford agreed to hold an election on union representation. White toured the sprawling complex's three-mile picket line, urging blacks to leave the plant and cast their lot with the UAW-CIO. Union leaders, he told them, had pledged to protect black workers' interests and to fight discrimination in hiring and in the workplace. In the end, he told them, they had no alternative. "The Negro worker," he said, "had [only] the grim choice of casting his lot with the union or having its hostility after they organized Ford." In light of the racial dynamics of the River Rouge labor force, whatever their gratitude to Ford for providing employment opportunities, black workers could not afford the bitter enmity they would surely experience if they continued their hopeless resistance.[26]

The UAW-CIO won the representation election conducted by the National Labor Relations Board on May 21, 1941, by an overwhelming margin. Even so, the returns made it clear that a majority of black workers had voted against the UAW-CIO. But remarkably, in view of the bitterness of the strike and company officials' efforts to foment racial discord, most black workers quickly adapted to the new regime. Said one black erstwhile

UAW-CIO opponent, "There wasn't any trouble." Workers on both sides of the issue "all said 'Let's let bygones be bygones.'"[27] Some white workers believed that the behavior of their African American coworkers only confirmed that blacks were inherently a "scab race," but UAW leaders worked hard to build a culture of interracial solidarity. The presence of high-profile black activists, several of whom quickly gained union office, helped reassure the black rank and file of the UAW's good intentions, as did the union's insistence on a clause barring discrimination in hiring in the first contract negotiated with Ford.

The breakthrough at River Rouge helped establish the UAW-CIO as one of the nation's largest and most dynamic labor unions. Although the industry's employment of African Americans was limited, and Ford's black workers were initially diffident about supporting the new union, race played a key role in the struggle for collective bargaining in the automobile industry. The organization of Ford was essential for the building of a strong and effective industrial union; equally important was the commitment of UAW and CIO leaders to workplace equality and the alliance the Ford campaign helped forge between progressive unionists and African American community leaders in the Motor City, then the quintessential locus of both modern industrial production and demographic volatility. Whether African Americans would become an integral part of the UAW and whether the industrial union movement would fulfill its promise of being a "lamp of democracy" remained uncertain as the nation girded for war, but the establishment of a strong basis for biracial unionism in the nation's premier industry was a signal accomplishment.

War

World War II, both before Pearl Harbor and during the period of U.S. belligerency, had an enormous impact on African American workers as well as on the labor movement. Although employers were initially reluctant to hire blacks for war production work, by late 1944, at least 1.25 million African Americans were doing industrial work, a 150 percent increase over their numbers in 1940. Almost a quarter of these workers were women. The great majority of new industrial workers—both men and women—were hired to work in munitions and other war production plants. The sheer need for labor was largely responsible for the opening of doors to black workers, but a pioneering presidential order issued in the spring of 1941 also played a role. Executive Order 8802, issued on June 25, 1941, called for a end to discrimination in hiring and created the Fair Employment Practice Committee (FEPC) which, though only partially effective in advancing black employment rights, represented the first sustained federal intervention in the economy in behalf of African Americans since the end of Reconstruction. Meanwhile, black workers, both new recruits and industrial veterans, asserted their claims to equal rights and job opportunities with a new militancy and sophistication.

The unprecedented demands of wartime production and changes in community life brought both challenges and opportunities for African Americans and for the labor movement. On the whole, industrial jobs paid relatively high wages. During the war, despite its relatively short duration, the movement of blacks from agriculture and low-wage service and domestic work to war work boosted black incomes substantially. Important too was the employment of African Americans in the war-expanded federal government. During the conflict, federal civilian employment among blacks grew from under 60,000 to over 200,000. Although the great majority of these government workers occupied low civil-service positions, federal jobs were free of most of the discriminatory and insecure features of private employment. For all these reasons, during the war, the average wages of black workers grew from about 40 percent of those paid to white workers to over 50 percent. Moreover, at least for black men, employment in the now heavily unionized industrial core of the economy provided significant protection against racially skewed layoffs and firings, although, as the last hired, black workers were still more vulnerable than their white counterparts.

For their part, both the AFL and the CIO grew, partly as a result of the surge of new black members. From 1940 to 1945, the AFL expanded from about 4.2 million to almost 7 million members; the CIO grew from about 2.5 million to 4 million members during the same period. Many of them were, in effect, automatically enrolled owing to special wartime "maintenance of membership" rules promulgated by the National War Labor Board, a presidentially appointed agency charged with maintaining industrial production and price stability. At the end of the war, AFL and CIO unions contained about 750,000 African American members, twelve times the number of organized black workers in 1930 and at least triple the number enrolled in 1940.[28]

African Americans had to fight for opportunities to work in the industrial sector and for equal treatment after being hired. Initially, large-scale military employers flatly rejected the notion of employing blacks, citing stereotyped views of their alleged laziness, lack of mechanical ability, and unreliability. Thus, in September 1941, the country's largest maker of fighter planes reaffirmed its longtime policy of racial exclusion: "The Negro," the California-based company declared, "will be considered only as janitors and in other similar capacities. . . . Regardless of their training, we will not employ them."[29] The railroad unions and the key AFL craft unions that dominated military production were no better. The operating brotherhoods continued their unabashed exclusionary policies, even in the face of sharp legal challenges, and both the International Association of Machinists

(IAM) and the International Brotherhood of Boilermakers (IBB), the dominant AFL unions in aircraft production and shipbuilding, respectively, initially barred black membership.

The IBB's policies were particularly egregious, since, as part of the AFL Metal Trades Department, this union was at the heart of the vast expansion of shipbuilding during the war. At peak production in mid-1944, this industry, which had been all but moribund before the war, employed more than 1.5 million workers in facilities along the East, Gulf, and West coasts. Because it was necessary for shipbuilding companies to employ large numbers of black laborers and helpers, particularly in the southern yards, the IBB grudgingly agreed to admit African Americans to special auxiliary local unions that enjoyed no autonomous standing but were governed in all important respects by the "parent" white IBB local. Black IBB members, however, paid the same dues as their white counterparts. Particularly galling to black workers, however, was the way the IBB came to dominate the shipyards. In several notorious cases, notably on the West Coast, the AFL Metal Trades Department signed closed-shop agreements with employers after plans had been approved for massive expansion, but before the necessary labor force had been recruited. Those contracts were binding on the thousands of new workers hired once increased production began. Caught in this collusive net were thousands of African American workers "represented" by a union not of their choosing and one that, in fact, openly reviled and discriminated against them. In the booming airframe and aircraft sector, the situation was even worse, as the IAM's contracts with compliant employers froze black workers out entirely.

But unlike their World War I counterparts, black workers were no longer patient supplicants for industrial opportunity. African Americans protested discrimination on the railroads, in the shipyards, and elsewhere, using the wartime rhetoric of democracy and the wartime quest for all-out production to dramatize their grievances. Black protest sprang from daily encounters with discriminatory employers and trade unions, and it both stimulated and gained strength from the expansion of such civil rights organizations as the NAACP. African American activism during World War II was far more vigorous than that during the First World War, with black newspapers and organizations promoting a popular, informal "Double V" conception of the war—victory abroad against the fascists and Japanese militarists, and victory at home over the forces of racism and oppression. In their struggles, black workers found important allies in several federal agencies, most notably the FEPC, and in the federal courts.

The FEPC grew out of the efforts of A. Philip Randolph, leader of the Brotherhood of Sleeping Car Porters (BSCP), to dramatize discrimination against blacks in the armed forces and in the defense industry. In 1935, Randolph finally achieved his goal of securing an AFL charter for the BSCP and used the forum provided by the federation's annual convention and the growing challenge posed by the racially progressive CIO to highlight discrimination in the labor movement. Although the BSCP was a small union, Randolph was the nation's best-known black labor activist. His prominence and his considerable oratorical and public-relations skills enabled him to speak with authority in behalf of black wage earners. Moreover, he was well connected with New Deal liberals, men and women who were increasingly sensitive to the devastating impact of the Depression on black Americans and increasingly eager to add racial justice to the reform agenda of the 1930s.

In January 1941, before U.S. entry into the war but as the economy's shift to massive military production was getting into full swing, Randolph challenged the federal government to compel defense contractors to end discrimination in the hiring of new workers. When public appeals proved ineffective, Randolph announced the formation of a March on Washington Movement and began laying plans to bring 10,000 black marchers into the nation's capital to protest employer discrimination and governmental indifference. Randolph's initiative quickly tapped into widespread black resentment. Local NAACP branches around the country, many of which were being energized by an influx of younger and working-class members, responded enthusiastically, and Randolph soon revised his estimates and announced that 100,000 militant protesters would descend on Washington. By June, President Roosevelt had taken notice of the mushrooming movement and, fearing that it would trigger violence and impede military production, brought pressure on Randolph and NAACP leaders to abandon their plans. Eventually, on June 19, Randolph and NAACP secretary Walter White met with FDR and agreed to call off the march in return for an executive order affirming that "the policy of the United States [is] that there shall be no discrimination in the employment of workers in defense industries . . . because of race, creed, color, or national origins." Federal agencies involved with job and vocational training related to defense industries were to provide equal opportunity regardless of race. The order also established the Fair Employment Practice Committee, which was to "receive and investigate complaints of discrimination in violation of . . . this order and take appropriate steps to redress grievances."[30]

Randolph and White hailed Executive Order 8802 as a "Second Emancipation Proclamation," as it was the first time in almost eighty years that the federal government had aligned itself with the aspirations of black workers for fair and equitable treatment. However, more privately, the two leaders shared the doubts of many of their followers about the practical impact of the order and the FEPC. Randolph and White had agreed to remove from their original list of demands the requirement that the U.S. military itself be desegregated—a major concession. Moreover, the FEPC was eventually lodged administratively in the Office of Production Management, a recently created federal agency whose overriding task was to boost military production. Dependent on the Office of Production Management for its funding, the FEPC soon found itself without effective authority and in danger of being a means of deflecting dissent rather than combating racial injustice. Indeed, the FEPC's first chairman, white Kentucky editor Mark Ethridge, privately admitted as much when he left the committee at the end of 1941. Judging his tenure a success, Ethridge told a presidential aide, "we have accomplished what the President wanted. . . . We paralyzed any idea of a march on Washington and we have worked honestly for a better measure of justice for the Negroes."[31]

Indeed, for its first two years, the FEPC was a weak weapon in the fight against job discrimination. An administrative reshuffling in mid-1942 placed it under the newly created War Manpower Commission (WMC). Lacking subpoena powers and kept on a short budgetary leash by WMC director Paul McNutt, committee members were powerless to do more than call attention to the injustice and irrationality of barring black workers from critical but undermanned sectors of the economy, such as the railroads and the shipyards. For example, apparently at the request of the White House, McNutt repeatedly delayed FEPC hearings into the egregiously discriminatory practices of the railroads and the railroad unions. However, mounting protests by black workers, along with a drumbeat of criticism by liberal publications, CIO unionists, and black activists, eventually led to the complete reconstitution of the embattled committee. After meetings with civil rights leaders in the spring of 1943, FDR issued Executive Order 9346 on May 27, 1943, disbanding the original FEPC and replacing it with an identically named body. This time, however, the FEPC was an independent agency that reported directly to the president, and Roosevelt provided the new FEPC with a much bigger budget and authorized a significant expansion in its investigative staff.

Whatever their limitations, FDR's executive orders represented a sharp break with the federal government's largely unresponsive attitude toward minority employment rights. Even the Roosevelt administration's pathbreaking New Deal labor legislation did nothing to challenge workplace segregation and discrimination, and in some respects, it disadvantaged black workers. The 1934 amendments to the Railway Labor Act, for example, reaffirmed the privileged position of the racially retrograde railroad brotherhoods. Neither Section 7(a) of the NIRA nor the provisions of the much more potent NLRA addressed the problem of discrimination in hiring or in union behavior. In hearings held prior to the passage of the NLRA, African American leaders had urged the insertion of provisions that would have denied the services of the National Labor Relations Board (NLRB) to unions that practiced discrimination. Without such a provision, they rightly noted, lily-white unions could enter into contracts with employers that, in effect, provided governmental validation of the exclusion of black workers. The NAACP's White castigated the AFL, which "with ill grace can ask for benefits for white labor while these unions discriminate against black labor." He called on FDR to insist that the proposed labor legislation include a strong antidiscrimination provision "to prevent [the] sacrifice of [the] Negro to Jim Crow unionism."[32] These protests were fruitless, however. In view of the opposition of AFL lobbyists and the likelihood that a solid phalanx of southern Democratic senators and representatives would oppose a bill with this provision, its chief sponsor, New York Democratic senator Robert F. Wagner, shelved his personal sympathy for black workers and dropped the offending provisions from the final version of the bill submitted to Congress.

Another important New Deal labor law, the Fair Labor Standards Act of 1938 (FLSA), also had problematic implications for black workers. Like the Wagner Act, the FLSA exempted precisely those low-wage occupations in which large numbers of African American men and women continued to toil, notably domestic service and agricultural labor. With long-entrenched southern Democrats controlling much of the congressional machinery, proponents of legislation to foster collective bargaining (as in the Wagner Act) and to help low-wage workers feared that inclusion of these categories of workers—hundreds of thousands of whom were southern African Americans—would ensure legislative defeat. Moreover, some black spokespersons believed that passage of the FLSA would result in widespread disemployment for thousands of black workers, especially in the South: faced with the necessity to boost wages in line with FLSA standards, employers would no longer have any incentive to employ low-wage black workers. And in fact, there was some evidence of widespread displacement of black workers in the tobacco industry and other low-wage southern sectors in the immediate aftermath of passage of the FLSA on June 25, 1938.

Despite these negative aspects of New Deal labor legislation, however, black workers and labor spokespersons endorsed the general principles behind them. It was true, perhaps, that the modest minimum wages established under the FLSA might displace some extremely low-wage black workers. But in the view of Randolph and other black labor activists, the dual wage structure that prevailed, especially in the South, offered only a bogus advantage to African Americans—namely, the "opportunity" to work for less. Minimum-wage laws had to be implemented within the context of strong antidiscrimination measures that would prevent the race-based discrimination that had created the low-wage trap for black workers in the first place. As for the NLRA, although its provisions could be used by discriminatory unions, by no means were all labor organizations discriminatory. In particular, the rising CIO unions in mass production industries embraced tens of thousands of black workers who would benefit from provisions of the law that facilitated union recognition and collective bargaining. Moreover, the new law's mechanisms had the unanticipated but salutary result of expanding democratic participation, especially in the South. The NLRB's method of resolving controversies about union recognition was to hold representation elections, administered by the board's staff. Once a union hoping to represent workers in a given factory or shop had demonstrated that it had a certain level of support, workers were permitted to vote via secret ballot whether to accept representation by that union. In scores of southern workplaces—in the pulp mills coming on line along the Atlantic and Gulf coasts; in the mines and smelters of Alabama; in tobacco, food processing, and furniture plants in Tennessee and North Carolina—thousands of black workers had their first taste of genuine democratic participation. Even AFL unions hoping to expand into southern industry were compelled to address black workers' concerns in order to attract their votes. For their part, African American workers did not fail to appreciate the anomaly between the federally enforced right to vote in the workplace and the denial of voting rights in the community.

As the war progressed, various federal agencies, responding to the increased political importance of African Americans and perhaps to the moral imperatives of waging a war for democracy, began to modify or abandon their discriminatory practices. Beginning in the fall of 1942, the U.S. Employment Service announced that it would no longer process racially discriminatory job referrals. The NLRB, despite the failure of its founding legislation to bar discrimination, consistently rejected employers' and unions' efforts to inject racial issues into its decisions with respect to unfair labor practices, the determination of bargaining units, or the holding of representation elections. In a 1943 ruling, the National War Labor Board, established the year before to resolve labor-management disputes, invalidated racially defined pay grades, eloquently declaring that "America needs the Negro; the Negro needs the equal opportunity to work and fight."[33] Even WMC director McNutt earned the praise of some black leaders for his personal efforts to moderate the discriminatory policies of the military, the Selective Service System, and other wartime federal agencies.

During the war, the courts also began to chip away at the structure of employment discrimination. In 1941, a group of southern railroads had signed an agreement with the exclusionary Brotherhood of Locomotive Firemen and Enginemen (BLFE) that had the direct effect of replacing long-term black firemen with whites, regardless of length of service. The National Mediation Board, the federal agency established by the terms of the Railway Labor Act, had helped broker this agreement. African American firemen were continually protesting the BLFE's discriminatory policies and agreements, both individually and through organizations of black railroaders. In

August 1941, one veteran fireman and workers' rights activist, Bester William Steele, brought suit against the BLFE and his employer, the Louisville and Nashville Railroad. Steele hired Charles Houston, a distinguished African American lawyer and former dean of Howard University Law School, to litigate the case. Houston had worked closely with the NAACP on a variety of civil rights issues and eagerly took up Steele's case, as well as a similar one advanced against another southern railroad.

Houston did not legally challenge the BLFE's right to deny membership to blacks. Nor did he stress that, by facilitating the 1941 agreement, the National Mediation Board was in the position of violating the Fourteenth Amendment to the Constitution, which guaranteed equal treatment under the law. He focused instead on the union's obligation to provide "equal representation" for all the workers covered by its contracts, including those who were not union members, which black Louisville and Nashville firemen could not be. After setbacks in the federal circuit and appeals courts, Houston and his clients were spectacularly successful in the Supreme Court, which handed down a landmark decision in December 1944, declaring that the BLFE (and, by extension, all unions using the services of the National Mediation Board and, presumably, the NLRB) had a "duty of fair representation." The Railway Labor Act, the Court held, granted the union—a private party—government-like powers. Although it was not illegal for the BLFE to bar blacks from membership, the law did not "confer . . . power upon the union to sacrifice, for the benefit of its [white] members, rights of the minority." Moreover, since black railroaders had "no means of protecting their interests," being barred from membership in the union whose status as exclusive bargaining agent had been certified and approved by the National Mediation Board, neither the company nor the union could do what the 1941 agreement sought to do—namely, deprive black workers of "equal protection" and, ultimately, of "their right to earn a livelihood."[34]

On the West Coast, African American shipyard workers also won judicial support for their protests against discriminatory hiring, assignment, and compensation practices. Despite being forced to pay union dues under the terms of master agreements signed between the all-white International Brotherhood of Boilermakers (the AFL union with prime jurisdiction in the shipyards) and shipbuilders, black workers were shut out of union affairs, routinely relegated to undesirable work assignments, and prohibited from moving up the job ladder. However, as early as 1941, organized groups of black workers began pressuring both the union and the shipbuilders to rectify these conditions. In a protracted series of hearings and other public forums, the FEPC—prodded by NAACP activists and groups such as the Shipyard Negro Organization for Victory in Portland, Oregon, and the Bay Area Council against Discrimination—ruled repeatedly against both the

IBB and the employers. Although efforts to persuade the federal courts to make these rulings enforceable failed, the California courts were more amenable. Thus, in a key ruling in 1944, *Joseph James, et al. v. Marinship Corporation, et al.*, the California Supreme Court found that it was illegal for unions to practice discrimination in the state, thus invalidating the segregationist and discriminatory practices of both the IBB and shipyard employers. *James v. Marinship* reverberated all along the West Coast, bringing real change to the war-expanded shipbuilding industry.

The *James* decision aside, however, for the most part, the FEPC had to rely on exposure, publicity, and persuasion in its efforts to assist black and other minority workers. The U.S. Employment Service's policy of not making its services available to employers that discriminated, as well as the Department of Labor's efforts to end discrimination in vocational training programs, depended heavily on enforcement by local functionaries, many of whom lacked a commitment to racial equality. In Nashville, Atlanta, and other cities, local project administrators regularly shunted black workers into dead-end training programs designed for, though technically not limited to, African Americans.

Two other Supreme Court decisions—the aforementioned *Steele v. Louisville & Nashville Railroad Company, Brotherhood of Locomotive Firemen and Enginemen, et al.* and *Tunstall v. Brotherhood of Locomotive Firemen and Enginemen, et al.*—though victories for black railroad workers, were limited to the question of "fair representation." They had little immediate impact on the railroads' hiring and promotion practices, nor did either decision outlaw discriminatory union membership requirements or mandate that agencies of the federal government cease lending their authority to discriminatory agreements. Indeed, in the wake of these decisions, both the BLFE and the railroads clung even more fiercely to their traditional practices, assisted, in effect, by the indifference and lethargy of the special committee appointed by FDR to look into employer and union discrimination on the railroads. And although the *James* ruling had immediate effects, with the end of the war, the U.S. shipbuilding industry went into a virtually terminal decline, wiping out thousands of jobs.

What one prominent black CIO leader said in 1943 could well be applied to the whole range of federal involvement in questions of employment discrimination during World War II. The "FEPC," declared Willard Townsend, "was created not out of a keen desire to insure the full participation of negroes in the war employment but rather out of the political necessity on the part of the present administration to placate the growing insistence of the Negro communities for greater opportunities in the field of war employment."[35] To be sure, the FEPC and other federal and judicial gestures marked a bracing contrast to the government's traditional indifference to workplace injustice, but any progress made by African American workers during World War II depended primarily on their own efforts to gain entry and to fight discrimination.

Throughout the wartime economy, black workers challenged employers, the government, and labor unions to implement the promise of the democratic rhetoric of the U.S. war effort. By no means were struggles for racial equity confined to the law courts, the offices of federal agencies, and hearings rooms. Raw racial conflict erupted repeatedly in the factories, shipyards, and transport systems as African Americans' efforts to gain entry into unaccustomed lines of work sparked protest and even violence. For white workers in the North as well as in the South, privileged access to broad categories of industrial jobs was part of the natural order of things. Skilled and semiskilled work was reserved for white men and women; dirty, dangerous, or particularly heavy work was reserved for blacks. In view of the chronic wartime labor shortages, rarely did black workers' movement into new occupational categories jeopardize the actual jobs of white workers. Rather, it was the very idea of African Americans driving streetcars, operating lathes and drill presses, or welding ship bottoms that sparked resistance on the part of white workers. Declared striking white transit workers in 1944, protesting the employment of blacks as streetcar operators in Philadelphia, "we would not accept them as fellow workers. . . . We are not going to work with them. If anybody believes [that we will work with them], let them try it."[36]

Indeed, the employment or upgrading of black workers evoked some of the most militant and even violent job actions of the strike-torn war years. The shipyards of Pinto Island in Mobile, Alabama, were the scene of one of the most dramatic episodes. There, in May 1943, only the arrival of U.S. Army troops put an end to a rampage on the part of white workers, male and female alike, protesting the upgrading of twelve of the yard's seven thousand African American workers to welding jobs. For six months, Alabama Dry Dock had resisted an FEPC directive to open this work to blacks. Company officials had warned that doing so would trigger violence, and its failure to prepare white workers for the change helped make this a self-fulfilling prophecy. Resolving to "get every one of them Niggers off this island," hundreds of workers roamed the huge shipyard assaulting African Americans indiscriminately.[37]

Nor was racial conflict confined to Dixie. In 1942 and 1943, "hate" strikes rippled through northern military production centers. Protests against the employment of blacks in work traditionally reserved for whites erupted in the Baltimore shipyards; the steel mills of Gary, Indiana, Aliquippa, Pennsylvania, and Sparrows Point, Maryland; and even the smelters of remote Butte, Montana. In Detroit, home of the progressive United Automobile Workers, white workers used the organizational apparatus of their local unions to mount strikes in opposition to the promotion of black custodial workers to positions as welders, lathe operators, and as-sembly-line workers. In one well-publicized episode in the summer of 1943, twenty-five thousand workers at a large Packard aircraft plant in the city threw up militant picket lines, defying their own union leaders. "I'd rather see Hitler and Hirohito win than work next to a nigger," one striker was reported as saying.[38] At this plant, as at River Rouge and other Detroit-area defense production facilities, black workers also mounted strikes and dem-onstrations to pressure employers, union officials, and governmental agen-cies to act on their claims to equal opportunity.

Among the most damaging racially inspired job actions was a bitter transit strike in Philadelphia that erupted on August 1, 1944, in which hun-dreds of white workers refused to report to work in protest over a plan to employ eight blacks as motormen trainees. For over a week, this walkout tied up the city's transportation system, causing significant production shortfalls in the area's munitions and war equipment plants. Indeed, the chairman of the FEPC termed it "the most expensive racial dispute of World War II."[39] The Philadelphia Transportation Company seemed to en-courage the dissident white workers, perhaps in the hope of reversing the results of a recent representation election that had installed the CIO's ener-getic Transport Workers Union as the bargaining agent. In this case, the union's vigorous support for the black workers, along with stern federal intervention—ultimately in the form of five thousand U.S. Army troops and Department of Justice threats to prosecute ring leaders under the terms of the recently passed Smith-Connally Act—quashed the walkout, and the recruitment of African Americans proceeded.

Hate strikes and related racial turmoil captured headlines and drama-tized the pressurized atmosphere of wartime production. In reality, how-ever, they afflicted only a small minority of workplaces, and the Philadelphia transit strike notwithstanding, the number and severity of these job actions fell off sharply during the last eighteen months of the war. The actions of both public authorities and organized labor in dealing with these affairs varied according to the local situation. In the case of the Alabama ship-yards, as elsewhere in the South, the CIO's International Union of Marine and Shipbuilding Workers of America (IUMSWA) struggled to win or main-tain bargaining rights by bringing both black and white workers into its local unions. This was no easy task. Organizers reported that although the union's positive position on civil rights attracted black workers, it antago-nized the large majority of whites, many of whom regarded it as "a nigger union."[40] After the violent actions of May 1943, the IUMSWA's Local 18 in Mobile performed a delicate balancing act. It tried to retain the loyalty of black workers while appeasing whites by toning down its vocal support of black workers' rights. Thus, union officials helped craft uneasy compromises in work assignments that permitted the upgrading of some black workers, but only within a strictly segregated setting.

In Detroit, however, the UAW acted quickly and vigorously against racially inspired dissidence. International president R. J. Thomas and other union leaders denounced the hate strikers and threatened ring leaders with suspension from the union and resultant job loss. Working closely with the FEPC and other federal officials, Thomas laid down the law. "I delivered the strongest ultimatum I have ever made in asking those Packard workers to go back," Thomas told fellow unionists. If white workers persisted in their unauthorized strike, he threatened, "large numbers of white workers . . . [will] lose their jobs. . . . We will not retreat."[41] In a city with an outspoken (and fully enfranchised) African American community, and with no threat from rival AFL unions, UAW officials acted on the CIO's antidiscrimination principles in Detroit in ways that their IUMSWA counterparts in Alabama and other southern cities felt they could not.

Throughout the war, CIO leaders called attention to their support of civil rights on and off the job, contrasting the CIO's activism with the AFL's inertia. The CIO itself and many of its affiliated unions established formal antidiscrimination committees and boasted in convention resolutions, union publications, and leaders' speeches about their support for minority rights. In 1943, CIO president Philip Murray appointed a Committee against Racial Discrimination (CARD), which sought to promote racial tolerance on the basis of workers' common economic interests. Its many publications featured earnest appeals for union activists to reject irrational prejudice and "to encourage the friendly association of workers during lunch periods." "Observance of these simple fundamentals," one widely circulated pamphlet declared, "will destroy all fears of race friction." In his capacity as president of the large United Steelworkers, Murray named a veteran black organizer as his special adviser on race matters. The UAW also created an antidiscrimination committee, as did other affiliates and many local unions. The CIO must, UAW vice president Walter Reuther declared, "get this message down to the people in the factories."[42] Throughout the war, the CIO cooperated closely with the FEPC, and its representative on that body consistently supported the committee's efforts to expose both employer and union discrimination.

At the same time, however, even the CIO's commitment to racial equality had some sharp limits. Although CARD urged the inclusion of contract language barring discrimination in hiring, only a handful of CIO affiliates pressed this issue during negotiations with employers. The CIO's view that improved economic conditions would alleviate racial tensions was valid, as far as it went. But it could not account for the naked negrophobia of many of its white members. To veteran civil rights activists who had witnessed firsthand the violence and irrationality of racial confrontations, CARD's vision of lunchroom comradeship as a solution to racial prejudice seemed naive.

Competing views of appropriate action with respect to the role of African Americans clashed at the UAW's 1943 convention in Buffalo, New York. Black activists, supported by the union's vigorous and vocal communist-oriented faction, proposed the creation of a position on the UAW's executive board reserved for an African American. Only such a bold gesture, they argued, could highlight the distinctive problems of the union's growing black membership and provide it with real influence in deliberations. Pious declarations and well-intentioned crisis management, they argued, did not address the festering problems of racial discrimination. Opponents of the creation of an African American seat on the executive board—in the end, a majority—replied that such a move would constitute "racism in reverse." Even Walter and Victor Reuther, who were strong advocates of the union's antidiscrimination efforts, argued that if blacks were granted a separate seat on the board, the UAW would have to grant similar recognition to all ethnic and religious groups with large numbers of members. To some extent, the heated convention battle over this issue was part of an ongoing factional struggle for control of the union, but it highlighted the differing conceptions of the character and significance of racial division in the UAW and, by extension, elsewhere in the labor movement. Proponents of the proposal viewed race as a central issue and the experience of African Americans in the U.S. economy as an exceptional situation that required specific racially defined remedies. The Reuthers and their allies, in contrast, viewed race as incidental and believed that the resolution of racial conflicts required only the consistent pursuit of expanding economic opportunities within the context of democratic and nondiscriminatory policies.

Although the nature and dynamics of racial tensions were contested within the CIO, and its official position was somewhat anodyne, its policies and practices compared favorably with those of the rival AFL, to say nothing of the railroad brotherhoods. Indeed, the older federation refused to acknowledge that it *had* a race problem. President William Green and other AFL spokesmen pointed to convention resolutions that regularly voiced support for civil rights and equal opportunity. They lashed out at those who harped on the discriminatory policies of a few AFL affiliates, noting that most AFL unions did accept black members. Its monthly organ, the *American Federationist,* frequently ran articles, replete with pictures, showing nonsegregated AFL gatherings, even in the South. Green highlighted the appointment of black organizers and the recruitment of thousands of African American workers by the AFL, not neglecting to note that the older federation had more black members than did the upstart CIO.[43] "One only need to attend a party in one of our labor temples," wrote one of the AFL's African American field representatives, "and gaze upon the well-dressed, happy, men, women, and children to realize how much the Negro owes to the AFL and its unions."[44]

The AFL fiercely resisted internal criticism and self-scrutiny. A regular feature at each national convention was a resolution introduced by A. Philip Randolph to force discriminatory affiliates such as the IAM and the building trades unions to end their exclusion of black workers and to reject other affiliates' practice of enrolling blacks in powerless "auxiliary" locals. Thus, in 1943, the BSCP president insisted that "racial discrimination should be abolished by every union affiliated with the AF of L, not only for the benefit of the Negro . . . but for the sake of the AF of L itself." As for the "auxiliary" locals in the shipyards and elsewhere into which the boiler-makers and other unions shunted black workers, Randolph attacked them for creating "colonies of colored people" where black workers were treat-ed as "economic, political, and social serfs" who enjoyed only "the right to be taxed."[45]

Equally predictable were the convention's rejection of Randolph's mo-tions and the defensive rejoinders by AFL national leaders. President Green would declare that of course he personally favored an end to discrimina-tion, but it could not be ended by "forced methods" such as those Randolph urged. Education and tactful persuasion were the only effective means of inducing the recalcitrant affiliates to change their policies. In 1944, he told black workers that "we can only win through patience." Like them, Green said, he had experienced disappointment and injustice in his life; like him, they should not expect instant redress. "I have found in my life's experience that I don't have my way in a good many things, and many times I have to wait a good while before I can have my way," he confided. Indeed, in a con-clusion that could only dishearten black AFL members, he noted, "some-times I never get it." Concluded Swedish sociologist Gunnar Myrdal in 1944, in his classic study of U.S. race relations, "The fact . . . that the American Federation of Labor . . . is officially against racial discrimination does not mean much."[46]

For some black workers, however, the AFL's diffidence was less impor-tant than the opportunities it offered for improved wages and working conditions and individual advancement. For all its lofty principles, the CIO lacked the extensive local infrastructure that the older AFL had developed. The federation's affiliates reached into scores of small cities and into trades and occupations where the CIO had no presence. Even segregated local unions were, in the view of many local black activists, not necessarily a bad thing. In the South Atlantic and Gulf ports, for example, black longshore-men in the AFL's International Longshoremen's Association (ILA) ran their own locals with their own leadership and cooperated from a position of strength with parallel white locals. The AFL's International Brotherhood of

Teamsters, an expanding union just beginning to flex its organizational muscle, boasted dozens of local unions with black members and black officers, even in the South. Strategically located in local economies, the teamsters were a powerful presence in scores of communities that lacked any sort of CIO organization. Randolph might deplore the AFL's foot-dragging and the segregation of black members, but the very decentralization that characterized the older federation redounded to the benefit of some local black labor activists, who in turn parlayed their prominence in the union into leadership roles in the wider black community.

The CIO's International Longshoremen's and Warehousemen's Union (ILWU) found this out in the late 1930s when it sought to move from the successful organization of West Coast docks to the building of progressive interracial unions along the Gulf coast. Although the ILA locals in cities such as New Orleans and Mobile were segregated and often little more than dues-collecting agencies, a number of them were led by African Americans. Moreover, longshoring in the Depression years was one of the few relatively secure jobs still dominated by blacks. Many black dockworkers interpreted the ILWU's idealistic message of interracial and democratic unionism as just another scheme to replace black workers with white. As one black ILA leader in Mobile put it, "anyone voting for the C. I. O. . . . is a traitor to his race." In New Orleans, black community leaders told longshoremen, "It is your duty to your race, your family and your God to vote . . . for the I. L. A."[47] The AFL might not have been a crusading champion of racial justice, but for many black workers, it provided a protected enclave and one of the few opportunities available to talented and ambitious black African Americans living in southern communities.

Despite the suffering and hardship, in certain respects, the Great Depression and World War II brought positive change for African American workers. The continued movement to the North and West brought increased political influence. Indeed, in the border states and upper South, favorable Supreme Court rulings, along with the heightened political consciousness that came with the New Deal and the rise of interracial unionism, substantially expanded the black electorate in parts of the former Confederacy. Although New Deal legislation did not include antidiscrimination provisions, and although some African American workers were disadvantaged by minimum-wage regulations, on the whole, the facilitation of union growth promised by the NIRA and promoted by the NLRA was a positive development for thousands of black workers in both North and South. During World War II, for the first time since Reconstruction, the federal government turned decisively—if with limited immediate impact—against racial discrimination in employment. The dramatic expansion of governmental employment among African Americans, along with their entry in large numbers into the war industry, brought at least 1.5 million black workers into relatively stable, secure, and high-wage employment. During the war years, the average wage or salary income of black workers in comparison with that of whites grew by 13 percentage points.[48]

Finally, these years marked a decisive turn in organized labor's stance toward African American workers. Black union membership expanded by a factor of fifteen between 1930 and 1945, and the proportion of union members who were African American more than tripled. With the emergence of the CIO, for the first time since the short-lived heyday of the Knights of Labor in the 1880s, a significant U.S. labor organization was actively recruiting African American workers and had committed itself unequivocally to the struggle for racial justice in the workplace and in the general culture. The rise of potent forces of interracial union activism helped energize and broaden the base of civil rights organizations, notably the NAACP.

Thus, as the war shuddered to a dramatic close in mid-1945, African American workers had more reason to be optimistic than at any time since the 1860s. Nonetheless, perplexing questions remained for the postwar period. Would the heavy concentration of black workers in the layoff-prone war industry put a halt to their economic gains? Could the progressive impulses of the New Deal era that had helped underwrite black advancement continue in a postwar period fraught with uncertainty? Would the revitalized labor movement continue to be a champion of civil rights, or might the old patterns of discrimination and indifference reassert themselves? Black labor activists such as Randolph, his BSCP colleague Milton Webster, and the vigorous young men and women who fought discrimination through labor activism recognized that many of their gains derived from circumstances unique to the New Deal and to wartime necessity, as well as from their own efforts. Their challenge was to sustain black workers' hard-won progress in the sharply changed circumstances of the dawning postwar era.

5

RACE AND LABOR IN
THE POSTWAR WORLD

In the decades after the end of World War II, African Americans both made significant advances and suffered disappointing setbacks in the nation's workplaces. The general prosperity that characterized this period produced rising levels of real income for most workers, black and white. Black men who had found jobs in the central industrial core during World War II were largely able to retain these positions, taking advantage of the rising wages, enhanced job security, and other benefits that potent industrial unions such as the United Automobile Workers (UAW), the steelworkers, and the packinghouse workers achieved. African Americans also found work in the expanding white-collar sectors of the labor force, particularly in the area of government employment, one of the fastest growing occupational categories. Public policy in the form of antidiscrimination laws, administrative rulings, and court decisions, along with growing public rejection of overtly discriminatory practices, promised to widen the range of employment options open to blacks. The labor movement, as represented by both the AFL and the CIO, emerged in this period as a vocal supporter of the civil rights movement and as one of its key allies in the political and legislative arenas.

At the same time, however, a combination of new economic forces and tenacious patterns of racial discrimination imposed sharp limits on black advance and brought troubling new problems to the fore. For example, after World War II, African American women found that both public officials and private employers expected them to return to the domestic and personal service occupations to which they had traditionally been relegated. For young workers, male and female alike, the entry-level nonskilled jobs that had provided opportunities earlier in the century were disappearing. Employment in manufacturing, mining, and railroading, each with a large contingent of black workers, stagnated or declined as mechanization, foreign competition, and geographic dispersal eliminated thousands of jobs. In the cities, despite rising educational levels, young African Americans

139

were finding it increasingly difficult to secure a place in the changing post-war economy. Unemployment among black youth grew to alarming proportions. State and federal antidiscrimination measures pried open some job categories, but their reliance on individual litigation sharply limited their practical impact on the still flourishing patterns of racial preference among employers and unions. As for organized labor, its vocal public support for civil rights legislation often contrasted sharply with the unions' unwillingness to challenge racial hierarchies in the hiring process and in the workplace itself. Meanwhile, the postwar anticommunist crusade, both within the labor movement and in society at large, targeted those union activists who had often been at the forefront of the struggle for racial justice.

Patterns of Employment

In the post–World War II decades, the migration of African Americans into the urban industrial Northeast and Midwest continued, surpassing in scale and size even the Great Migration of the 1910s and 1920s. Through the first half of the twentieth century, this movement from the impoverished agrarian South to the cities of the North had held out the promise of better jobs, higher wages, and a more capacious life. Increasingly, however, in the rapidly changing economic environment of the 1950s and 1960s, the great northern cities no longer functioned as gateways to a brighter tomorrow; rather, they were becoming a dead end, trapping blacks and other minorities in a self-reinforcing cycle of joblessness, social pathology, and discouragement. The entry-level industrial jobs that had characterized the era of heavy industry were drying up even as major employers chose suburban and greenfield sites for new plant construction. Segregated housing and inferior schools limited blacks' access to jobs in the expanding new economy, while older patterns of outright racial discrimination retained much of their force, despite increasing official disapproval as expressed in antidiscrimination laws and court rulings.

To be sure, many African American workers shared in the benefits of postwar economic expansion and growing prosperity. In the 1940s, the accelerated mechanization of southern agriculture drove 400,000 blacks off the farms and mostly into the cities, where wages and standards of education, medical care, and housing were higher, even if the stable employment opportunities available earlier in the century were disappearing. African American men who had found work in manufacturing in the 1940s were largely able to retain those jobs in the postwar period, protected by union contracts. Thus, in the period 1940 to 1962, the number of African Americans working in manufacturing tripled to over 1.3 million, those working in retail trades grew from 288,000 to almost 1 million, and those engaged in professional and semiprofessional employment increased from

117,000 to over 500,000.[1] Particularly impressive were the gains made in public employment, which generally provided higher levels of job security and more generous benefits packages than did private employment. By 1960, almost 900,000 African Americans, or one in every eight who were employed, worked in local, state, and nonmilitary federal jobs. In Detroit, for example, where African Americans had held barely 1 percent of municipal jobs in 1940, they constituted over 35 percent of a much expanded city payroll in 1963.[2] Immediately after the war, the comparative earnings of black male wage earners continued to improve, and black representation in better-paying and more secure job categories grew substantially.

At the same time, however, other trends were deeply troubling. It soon became clear, for example, that blacks' gains in manufacturing were largely concentrated in older industrial sectors and in aging inner-city plants. Buoyed by the demand for weapons and munitions during both World War II and the Korean War (1950–1953), traditional heavy industry sectors provided thousands of well-paying jobs for the generation of black men who came of age in the 1940s. In some cases, black workers were able to expand on their wartime entry into high-wage industrial sectors. Thus, the proportion of African Americans working in southeastern Michigan's automobile industry expanded from 4 percent in 1940 to 15 percent in 1945, and by the 1970s, blacks constituted more than 20 percent of a larger labor force. Other war-related industries, however, withered in the postwar period. For example, American shipbuilding, which employed over 1.5 million wartime workers, about 12 percent of them African American, collapsed. Moreover, an increasing proportion of cold war–era military production went into sophisticated, electronics-based weaponry that called for a relatively highly skilled and well-educated labor force. Much of the construction of new defense industry plants took place in western and southern states, at sites remote from black population centers.

Income and employment statistics graphically revealed the problems facing black workers in the rapidly changing postwar environment. For a time, blacks continued to advance vis-à-vis their white counterparts, as average black income climbed from less than 40 percent of white workers' income in 1940 to 62 percent in 1951. But in the 1950s, the comparative earnings of black workers began to deteriorate, slipping by 1957 to 55 percent of whites' earnings and remaining below 60 percent for almost the entire 1954–1962 period. Moreover, during this same period of overall prosperity, rates of unemployment among African American men surged. From a postwar low of 4.4 percent in 1953, black joblessness mushroomed to 11 percent nine years later, and it was always at least double that of whites. Particularly alarming was the rapid growth in unemployment and underemployment among young blacks. Thus, even during the Korean War boom, males in the fourteen- to twenty-four-year-old bracket experienced an unemployment rate of 7.1 percent, and in 1964, during a period of economic expansion, around 20 percent were out of work. For women, the figures were even worse, with fully 25 percent of black females aged fourteen to twenty-four jobless in 1964. Indeed, declared one student of labor force patterns in 1965, soaring rates of unemployment among young black people was a "frightful problem," especially in view of the high historical correlation between early-career joblessness and poor long-range prospects in the labor market.[3]

In cities such as Detroit, Pittsburgh, and Chicago, which had earlier provided thousands of entry-level jobs, manufacturers now looked beyond the city limits when expanding their operations. For example, in the immediate postwar period, the "Big Three" automakers—General Motors, Ford, and Chrysler—spent over $6 billion in expansion, building two dozen new plants on the periphery of the Detroit metropolitan area and others in small towns in the Midwest, the South, and California—locations out of reach for most African Americans. In Chicago, reported two students of employment trends, "Between 1957 and 1963 the number of jobs near the Negro ghetto declined by almost 93,000 while the number of jobs in outlying and suburban areas increased by 72,000—generally in the northwestern suburbs farthest away from any sizeable Negro population."[4]

Black Women

The wartime and postwar experience of African American women had its own distinctive patterns of advancement and disappointment. From Emancipation into the 1960s, black women had always been represented in the paid labor force in significantly higher proportions than their white counterparts. Since black men's wages were only a fraction of those of white workers, their wives, daughters, sisters, and mothers had no choice but to work for wages. Higher proportions of black families were headed by women, a consequence of black men's discouraging employment prospects and their necessary reliance on casual, part-time, and seasonal work.

Throughout most of the post–Civil War century, two primary occupations had been available to black girls and women: domestic service and agricultural labor. As late as the eve of World War II, at least 75 percent of all employed black women toiled in these low-wage, low-prestige occupations. In the South in particular, the existence of a large pool of black women needing to work but barred or discouraged from industrial employment and educational opportunities was an integral part of the economic and social structure. The presence of low-wage domestic workers made it possible for white families of even modest means to have the benefit of cleaning, cooking, and child-care labor. Southern planters relied on black women for low-wage seasonal work, just as their wives depended on household help.

Southern politicians worked hard to ensure that federal policies affecting employment and social welfare excluded domestic and agricultural workers, thus keeping black women available as a labor reserve for white employers, both agricultural and domestic. The danger to the "southern way of life" that federal intrusion might bring was illustrated during World War I. In 1917, shortly after the onset of conscription, Congress enacted legislation that provided the wives of drafted soldiers with monthly stipends. Although the amounts were modest by northern and industrial standards, they often amounted to more than the typical domestic worker or field hand earned. For the wives of southern black conscripts, then, the prompt arrival of a government check every month encouraged the rejection of degrading or underpaid domestic or agricultural work and promoted an insistence on higher wages and better conditions. Aghast at this unintended consequence of public policy, southern whites resorted to coercion to force recalcitrant black women back into the fields and kitchens.

In the 1930s, when designing the labor and public welfare legislation that was the hallmark of the New Deal, powerful southern politicians were careful not to repeat this mistake. The key New Deal labor and social welfare legislation, reflecting the powerful influence of southern Democrats in the legislative process, excluded domestic and agricultural workers. In a very real sense, although some black workers benefited from such measures as the Social Security Act (1935), the National Labor Relations Act (1935), and the Fair Labor Standards Act (1938), these measures were designed with the interests of the white majority in mind. "You cannot put the Negro and the white man on the same basis and get away with it," declared a Florida congressman in support of the agricultural and domestic exemptions from the Fair Labor Standards Act.[5]

Although World War II opened up, at least temporarily, new opportunities in industrial, governmental, and clerical work for black women, even at the peak of wartime production, about 60 percent of employed black women still toiled in agricultural and domestic occupations, with another 18 percent working in "personal service" jobs outside the home. Throughout the war, employers were reluctant to hire African American women, even those who had completed industrial training programs. Thus, in August 1943, a personnel manager at a Detroit bomber plant told an unsuccessful black applicant that the hostility of the company's white workers was the reason for her rejection: "When a department is nice and peaceful they don't go around looking for trouble by putting colored people in the department." As late as early 1943, Detroit-area defense plants employed only one hundred of the ninety-six thousand black female workers available. Despite the critical labor shortages in defense plants, black women were still expected to fill jobs in personal and domestic service, their traditional employment. Indeed, government publications advised African

American women to think of ill-paid work in laundries, cafeterias, and white women's homes as "war service," because it freed white women to work in the factories. One investigator for the U.S. Department of Labor's Women's Bureau noted disapprovingly that black women employed as domestics and laundry workers "do not even realize that they are doing war work," and the bureau endorsed the remark of one large military contractor who said, "We think every worker we can place in a laundry is worth three new workers in our own plants."[6]

African American women resented their relegation to low-wage work and constantly sought ways to broaden their occupational options. In the South, some found jobs in food and tobacco processing, laboring as oyster shuckers, cannery workers, and tobacco stemmers. In the North, the meatpacking firms provided one of the few industrial opportunities available to black women. In all cases, they were consigned to the hardest, most unpleasant, and often most dangerous jobs. Oyster shuckers stood at work benches all day, steaming or prying open the oyster shells, their hair and clothing permeated with the fishy smell. The South's cigarette manufacturers employed black women almost exclusively in "stemming," wherein workers removed the tobacco leaf from the hard center stem, a laborious and unhealthy task. Even after the introduction of stemming machines in the mid-1930s, tobacco required a warm and humid environment, making conditions in the stemming rooms physically and mentally exhausting. The work was repetitive and dispiriting, involving steady concentration and manual dexterity; meanwhile, the danger from the machines' slashing cutter knives and from the very air, saturated with fine particles of tobacco dust, was constant.

In northern cities such as Detroit and Pittsburgh, few industrial jobs were open to black women, the vast majority of whom were forced to find employment as domestics or in steam laundries. In Chicago, post–World War I labor shortages provided some employment for black women in the packinghouses, though invariably in jobs disdained by even impoverished immigrant whites. Black women were assigned work as lard scrapers and intestine handlers. Even work in the casing department, where animal intestines were used to make sausage—"the nastiest, most evil, kind of work you could imagine," according to one woman—was sought by black women, so great was their desire to escape work as servants in white women's homes.[7]

During both world wars, some black women were able to break into the clerical and white-collar ranks, although in most cases only temporarily. During the World War I labor shortage, for example, the Chicago mail-order firm Montgomery Ward hired hundreds of black women as clerks and order processors, only to dismiss them at the end of the conflict. The

Pullman Company employed several hundred black women for service on its sleeping cars. The number of black women working as teachers and nurses also grew, reflecting the expanding black populations in the northern cities. In the South, however, it was common for ill-paid schoolteachers to have to supplement their income by working as domestics or seamstresses. Thus, on the whole, apart from the decline in agricultural work, black women's employment profile changed little in the century after Emancipation; into the 1960s, a large majority of employed black women still toiled as domestics and low-wage service workers.[8]

African American women did not acquiesce in their plight. Rising levels of education throughout the postmigration period attested to their determination to escape poverty and victimization. Women played important roles in blacks' efforts to improve their lives through labor organization, both as the wives, sisters, daughters, and companions of male workers and in their own right. The Ladies' Auxiliaries of the Brotherhood of Sleeping Car Porters (BSCP), for example, played a crucial role in that union's eventual success in bringing the Pullman Car Company to the bargaining table. Porters' wives, daughters, and sisters organized meetings, collected dues, raised funds, and walked picket lines, often serving as surrogates for their husbands, fathers, and brothers threatened by dismissal and blacklisting for union activity. Indeed, auxiliary leaders such as Rosina Tucker challenged the gendered ideology of A. Philip Randolph and other BSCP leaders that would relegate women to domestic roles, even as they provided critical support in the union's struggle. Black women, declared the wife of a BSCP officer in 1938, had to fight both for their ill-paid and victimized sister workers and for the creation of a truly interracial labor movement. "If there ever was a race that needed organization," declared Hazel Smith, "it is the Negro. . . . Only solidarity can save the black and white workers."[9]

CIO organizers also found African American women to be strong union supporters. In the Chicago packinghouses, activists such as Marian Simmons, Ercell Allen, and Katie Mae Washington were impatient with their white coworkers who felt that union affairs should be left to the menfolk. "They still seemed to think," complained Simmons, "that the men were looking out for their best interests." Single and living among other young activists in a boardinghouse, Washington quickly got "powerfully involved in the union" during World War II after moving to the Windy City from Mississippi.[10] The building of a strong union in the late 1930s and during World War II among North Carolina tobacco workers relied heavily on women in the stemming sheds and in the black community. In June 1943, for example, it was African American women who launched a decisive sit-down strike in the large R. J. Reynolds plant in Winston-Salem,

North Carolina. "Every worker should be in a union," declared strike leader Geneva McClendon in a subsequent interview. "I knew about unions from reading newspapers. . . . I figured the CIO was a good union."[11]

Domestic and personal service work, in contrast, did not often lend itself to assertive organization, despite the fact that few black women liked working in white people's homes. Low wages, long hours of washing, scrubbing, and cleaning, and frequent personal affronts characterized domestics' work lives in the postbellum South. To be sure, some employers were kindly and considerate, but the very disparity of wealth and power that put black women to heavy labor in white homes served as a reminder of slavery. Nor did movement north in the Great Migration bring significant change. Surveys conducted in Philadelphia in the early 1930s found that domestics sometimes worked ninety hours a week for wages as low as 15 cents an hour. Depression conditions encouraged employers to exploit desperate black women. "There are so many people out of work," observed a Pittsburgh woman, "that I am sure I can find a girl for $6.00 a week."[12]

In the 1930s and 1940s, films and radio shows often portrayed black domestic workers in idealized fashion. Characters such as "Mammy," played by Hattie McDaniel in Gone with the Wind, and "Rochester," played by Eddie Anderson on the Jack Benny Program, appeared as respected members of white employers' families. Their spunkiness, sagacity, and common sense contrasted with the white stars' ineptitude and pretensions; viewers and listeners were encouraged to applaud their insouciance and down-to-earth wisdom. In reality, however, domestic workers' female employers often treated them harshly, and the culture of white males encouraged sexual exploitation. Chiseling on wage payments was commonplace, with employers attempting to substitute leftover food and cast-off clothing for agreed-upon monetary wages. Employers expected household servants to be available at short notice, whatever their own families' needs. Observed one octogenarian domestic worker from South Carolina in 1937, "when dey pays you dat little bit of money, dey wants every bit [of] your time."[13]

Despite their disadvantages, even domestic workers found ways to resist employers' demands. Although collective action was difficult, on occasion, women in urban areas banded together to protest ill treatment and to demand higher wages and an end to demeaning treatment. In 1881, for example, domestic workers formed the Washerwomen's Association of Atlanta. Backed by local black churches, the association eventually involved more than three thousand women who demanded higher pay for their arduous work. An alarmed white newspaper warned, "Not only washerwomen, but the cooks, house servants and nurses are [also] asking for an increase."[14] The arrests of strike leaders and other repressive actions, however, quickly squelched this protest, although in general, southern domestics were able to thwart employers' efforts to censor or control their leisure activities and to resist the demand that they "live in" at the employer's residence.

There were scattered efforts to develop domestic workers unions. In some northern cities, labor organizations, in collaboration with social welfare groups such as the Urban League and the Young Women's Christian Association, recruited domestics in an effort to establish standardized pay rates, hours of employment, and work schedules that factored in the needs of the women's own families. In mid-1930s, the AFL Building Service Union's Domestic Workers Local 149 in New York City represented about a thousand women, black and white; in Baltimore, a similar CIO organization attempted, with little success, to establish work and pay standards. Such efforts stood little chance of success in view of the fragmented character of the domestic labor market and the disparity of wealth and power that confronted domestic workers. More effective were informal networks of women who relied on church affiliation and neighborhood and kin relationships to arrive at common notions of fairness with regard to payment and job expectations. These women supported one another through informal boycotts of abusive employers, tacit agreement over wage rates, and resistance to the often imperious expectations of the white families for whom they toiled.

For African American women, the post–World War II decades were a frustrating and discouraging time. On the one hand, experiences during the war had encouraged the hope that expanding job opportunities might offer a route out of the domestic service trap. Although the drastic shrinkage in agricultural employment created rural joblessness, it also promised to free black women from a different kind of dead-end labor. Moreover, the movement North, along with belated efforts by southern white politicians to increase funding for black schools in an effort to forestall threatened integration, resulted in the expansion of blacks' educational opportunities, which young African American women were particularly active in exploiting. Indeed, by the early 1970s, black women had reached parity with their white age cohorts with respect to years of schooling.

But both traditional patterns of discrimination and the shifting contours of northern employment limited black women's opportunities. As late as the mid-1960s, a majority of employed African American women still toiled in the domestic and heavy labor sectors of the economy. Thus, this increasingly well-educated and ambitious generation of workers who had proved the falsity of racial stereotypes during World War II was still trapped in an essentially nineteenth-century conception of race and gender roles. As was the case with their black brothers, husbands, and companions, changes in the political and legal structures would be required to open the doors to more remunerative and productive employment.

Discrimination and Public Policy, 1945–1964

By the mid-1960s, manpower and employment experts were describing an interlocking series of crises in the northern cities that had once seemed to promise so much. De facto segregation in urban housing markets, abetted by the discriminatory policies of federal loan guarantee programs, sharply limited the ability of black workers to compete for jobs on the suburban periphery. Underfunded and overcrowded inner-city schools disadvantaged black youngsters in job markets at a time when competition for entry-level positions was mounting. Although thousands of African American men who had gained good-paying and union-protected jobs in the 1940s had been able to hold on to them, by the late 1950s, employment prospects for the rising generation of young blacks looked increasingly bleak as northern-based industries began closing inner-city plants and moving operations to suburban, greenfield, and southern locations, far from the centers of black population.

Chicago's black community was typical of those in urban America, showing a sharp division between older workers in relatively secure and well-paying industrial jobs, on the one hand, and younger individuals unable to find work or locked into dead-end jobs, on the other. "Negro income earners at the lower end of the scale," declared the authors of one detailed study in 1968, "are virtually an urban peasantry, living at a subsistence income, and clearly out of the main stream of the economy. . . . [They] appear to be locked in poverty in the midst of a wealthy city."[15] The situation in Cleveland, Detroit, Pittsburgh, and other magnet cities differed only in the details.

Moreover, tenacious patterns of discrimination retained their force in postwar labor markets. Even in the automobile and steel industries, where most workers were represented by progressive labor unions, job-seeking blacks often encountered blatant prejudice and discrimination. "When we moved into the South," reported a General Motors manager in 1957, "we agreed to abide by local custom and not hire Negroes for production work."[16] Nor was discrimination confined to Dixie. Black workers in Detroit, Chicago, Cleveland, and other northern cities regularly experienced rejection and discrimination. According to the conventional wisdom to which corporate employers still clung, black men were suited only for heavy manual labor or janitorial work and black women for domestic and service occupations. Skilled welders and experienced machine operators of both sexes were told that the only jobs available were as custodians. Blacks responding to want ads saw inexperienced whites hired while they were turned away. An Urban League study of employment patterns in the heavily industrialized (and unionized) state of Ohio at the height of the Korean War found few black workers in many of the state's largest industrial facilities. In a Cleveland Chevrolet plant, for example, only 120 of 2,000 workers were "nonwhite." At National Cash Register's large Dayton facility, only 140 of 10,000 workers were black, none of them production workers. In Cincinnati, the Radio Corporation of America employed only 2 blacks among its 1,500 workers.[17] Even in industries in which African Americans had gained a foothold, the news was often not good in the shifting post–World War II economy. Thus, the shipbuilding industry collapsed, taking with it as many as 200,000 jobs held by African Americans during its heyday and marking a bitterly ironic final chapter in their protracted fight against employer and union discrimination. In steel, pulp and paper, coal mining, and other "old" industries, technological innovation eliminated thousands of entry-level and unskilled jobs, with African Americans taking the heaviest hits.

Hard-core union discrimination was particularly notorious in the construction industry. Building trades unions, which represented a large majority of workers in heavy construction, remained citadels of white privilege. Into the early 1970s, African American representation in the elite craft unions was minuscule. In 1967, for example, the electrical workers, ironworkers, sheet metal workers, and plumbers unions each reported that blacks accounted for less than 2 percent of their membership. Most building trades locals had no black members at all.[18] Antidiscrimination measures and public criticism pressured these unions into adopting paper plans to recruit black members, but the results were almost uniformly disappointing. Civil rights groups and other critics charged that the building trades unions continued to rely on arcane testing and educational standards, cumbersome bureaucratic procedures, and hostile treatment of black applicants to keep the unions virtually lily-white.

Even in the industrial sector, where unions such as the UAW and the steelworkers had actively recruited black members in the 1930s and 1940s and enjoyed a reputation for racial enlightenment, African Americans' entry into the skilled trades and other desirable job categories was slow and limited. In the UAW, for example, as of 1960, blacks constituted a tiny 2 percent of the union's 150,000 craft workers. The whites who dominated the auto union's Skilled Trades Department successfully used delay, obfuscation, and harassment of black applicants to defy UAW leaders' frequent—but punchless—calls for reform.[19] In steel, as well as in auto and other industrial sectors, the seniority provisions of union contracts often had the effect of confining black members to job categories in the hot, heavy, and dangerous departments into which they had initially been relegated by discriminatory employers.

Even when they enjoyed more equal treatment or won legal battles to open up job categories, circumstances conspired against African American workers. In the late 1950s and early 1960s, meatpacking, a stronghold of black unionism in the large midwestern cities, underwent a drastic structural transformation. In response to dramatic changes in transportation, refrigeration, and packaging, meatpackers began abandoning their old inner-city facilities and moving operations back into rural feedlots. By 1964, the great Chicago stockyards had closed down entirely, and in these years, the industry's labor force was reduced by almost one-quarter. Almost forty thousand packinghouse workers, a disproportionate number of them African American, lost their jobs as production shifted to rural locations in Kansas, the Dakotas, Iowa, and Nebraska.[20] At the same time, just as black railroaders finally began to benefit from court decisions to open up jobs and progression lines in the elite operating trades, competitive challenges from the booming airlines and motor trucking companies begin to shrink the rail labor force.

Still, changes in public policy and in the legal environment in the two decades after the end of World War II offered an increasingly diverse, if not always effective, array of legislative and legal weapons to black workers in their struggle against job discrimination. On both the federal and the state and local levels, as well as in the federal courts, governmental bodies explicitly affirmed that job discrimination was a legitimate target of public policy and that public authorities had both the legal and the ethical obligation to intervene in private labor markets to combat it. Although a coalition of Republicans and southern Democrats prevented Congress from passing a law to create a permanent (and more potent) Fair Employment Practice Committee (FEPC) to continue and expand the work of that wartime agency, action by the executive branch, independent agencies such as the National Labor Relations Board (NLRB), and the federal courts expressed official disapproval of job discrimination and created mechanisms to expand job opportunities for minorities. In addition, in this twenty-year period, almost half the states and a number of the nation's largest cities created statutory antidiscrimination agencies charged with advancing equal employment opportunities.

The most ambitious of the state initiatives was the Ives-Quinn Act, passed by the New York State legislature in 1945. This legislation created the Commission on Human Rights (CHR), which by 1960 had a budget of over $1 million and employed an eighty-member professional staff. In other states, however, comparable agencies were typically grossly underfunded and undermanned, leading critics to charge that these bodies were mere window dressing, designed more to appease minority groups than to effect significant change in employment opportunities. Even New York's CHR, which enjoyed some success in opening up clerical and white-collar employment in hotels, banks, insurance companies, department stores, and other financial and service sectors, could only nibble at the edges of employment discrimination.

Whether as sharecroppers, tenants, or, more rarely, landowners, cotton-growing African American farmers relied on family labor, as these turn-of-the-century Floridians attest. (Florida State Library and Archives)

Ginning day in an early twentieth-century north Florida community. Only now would croppers learn the payout for their yearlong labor. (Florida State Library and Archives)

Railroad grading in Florida in the 1880s. (Florida State Library and Archives)

Use of African American convict laborers was commonplace in the early twentieth-century Sou
(Wisconsin State Historical Society, image 27946)

On the Jacksonville docks, 1912. Black longshoremen, many of them union members, worked he South's Gulf and Atlantic ports. (Florida State Library and Archives)

Unionized black carpenters (above) and bricklayers, Jacksonville, 1899. They pursued respectability and economic security, despite the national unions' racial discrimination. (Library of Congress LC-USZ62-35753 and LC-USZ62-35754)

Through the first half of the twentieth century, sleeping-car porters transcended demeaning treatment to build a strong and influential union. (Museum of History and Industry, Seattle)

(Above) Officers of the Railway Men's International Benevolent Industrial Association, c. 1
Excluded from the whites-only railroad brotherhoods, black railroaders tried to build their
organizations. (New York Public Library Digital Collection) (Below) A. Philip Randolph (ce
bottom row) worked tirelessly with black rairoaders to build unions. Here he appears w
delegation of locomotive firemen in Washington in 1939. (Library of Congress LC-US:
97544)

In the absence of other job opportunities, domestic service was the lot of many African American women, North and South. Tallahassee, Florida, 1901. (Florida State Library and Archives)

Stripping tobacco leaves was one of the few industrial occupations available to African Ame女
women. Richmond, Virginia, 1899. (Library of Congress LC-USZ62-69316)

(Above) Black women did find work in the World War I–era Chicago meatpacking industry, but not in the genteel conditions suggested by this 1919 photograph. (New York Public Library Schomburg Collection) (Below) Black men, North and South, worked in the foundries, where injury and lung disease were common. Birmingham, Alabama, 1950. (Library of Congress HAER ALA-37-BIRM,45-)

(Above) For generations, African Americans were virtually excluded from employment i southern textile industry. The Mechanical Department in a Cannon Mills plant in Kanna North Carolina, in 1928 was no exception. (Southern Labor Archives, Special Collection Archives, Georgia State University) (Below) Sporadic, low-wage agricultural labor was t of countless African American men and women in the South. These Memphis residents a ing trucked off to nearby Arkansas for work in the cotton fields (1938). (New York Pub brary Digital Collection)

The slaughterhouses of Chicago and other midwestern cities provided jobs for thousands of blacks during the Great Migration and afterward. (Wisconsin Historical Society, image 26120)

African American picket captains at Ford's River Rouge plant, 1941. Winning the allegian
black workers was one of the greatest challenges of the fledgling United Automobile Wor
(Walter P. Reuther Library, Wayne State University)

During World War II, white workers' resistance to employment gains by African Americans flared into violence. Here, the first black motorman in Philadelphia, Thomas Allen, is escorted by police (1944). (Library of Congress LC-USZ62-35354)

Roy Wilkins (1901–1981), executive secretary of the NAACP from 1955 to 1976, the Reverend Martin Luther King Jr. (1929–1968), and A. Philip Randolph (1889–1979) in 1957. (Library of Congress LC-USZ62-126523)

he postwar period, black workers found both good-paying union jobs and explosive racial
ions in inner-city plants such as Chrysler's antiquated Hamtramck, Michigan, facility (June
2). (Walter P. Reuther Library, Wayne State University)

As early as the mid-1950s, recession and unemployment had eroded black workers' gains. Detroit, May 1956. (Walter P. Reuther Library, Wayne State University)

the spring of 1968, Memphis sani-
tion workers insisted on recogni-
n of their human worth in the
ike that brought Dr. King to that
y. (Photograph by Richard Cop-
; Walter P. Reuther Library, Wayne
ate University. Used with permis-
n of Richard Copley.)

1977, AFSCME organizer Leamon Hood (center) and striking Atlanta sanitation workers
und public authorities unresponsive to their efforts to link labor rights and civil rights. (Photo-
aph by Cecil Layne; private collection of Leamon Hood)

The 1968 Ocean Hill–Brownsville teachers' strike split New York City's black-labor coaliti
(Photograph by Hans Weissenstein; Robert F. Wagner Labor Archives, New York Univers
United Federation of Teachers Photographs Collection)

W president Walter Reuther and SCLC leader Ralph Abernathy join local activist Mary Moul-
e in support of Charleston's striking hospital workers on May 11, 1969. (National Union of
ospital and Health Care Employees, 1199 SEIU Archives, Kheel Center, Cornell University)

These Detroit mail carriers were among thousands of African American participants in the massive postal workers' walkout of March 1970. (Walter P. Reuther Library, Wayne State University)

In the pulp and paper industry, African American workers used the union's annual convention to carry on their struggle to end segregation and gain greater job opportunities. (PACE-USWA; courtesy of Tim Minchin)

Title VII of the 1964 Civil Rights Act played a key role in opening up textile jobs for southern blacks. (*Textile Industries*, November 1968; courtesy of Tim Minchin)

State and local statutes relied on individual complaints to trigger official investigations. These statutes required the enforcement bodies they established to attempt to resolve disputes between job applicants and employers through mediation and compromise. The filing of individual complaints of discrimination usually entailed lengthy and expensive legal or quasi-legal proceedings that, even when successful from the job seeker's perspective, typically resulted only in modest restitution.

Even in New York, results were disappointing. There, the CHR had certain powers to launch its own investigations, use individual cases to document patterns of discrimination, and pressure employers to stop discriminating and even to seek out minority applicants, but both the coverage and the implementation of the antidiscrimination law were sporadic at best. Nevertheless, in New York, the CHR's efforts helped to double black employment in retail sales, financial establishments, and public utilities during the 1950s, and a similar body created by the city of Philadelphia boasted similar results. But in other states and municipalities, antidiscrimination agencies were not as well funded and were armed with weaker legal weapons; as a result, gains in black employment in states such as Michigan, Connecticut, and Pennsylvania (outside of Philadelphia) were modest at best.[21] Declared two contemporary students in a 1964 study, "the FEP [fair employment practices] laws in effect in most Northern and Western states and in several major Northern cities have up to now resulted in only a very modest and spotty decrease in discriminatory employment practices." NAACP labor secretary Herbert Hill, a fierce advocate of aggressive civil rights measures, was more categorical: state and city agencies were "ineffectual agents of social change," he insisted, as he called for potent federal legislation.[22]

Certainly, if discrimination in employment was to be eliminated, action by state and local governments was inadequate. As of the early 1960s, none of the southern states had adopted fair-employment measures, and in fact, they each demonstrated strident hostility toward any civil rights claims on the part of their largely disfranchised African American citizens. Meanwhile, despite the power of the conservative coalition in Congress, action on the part of the federal government was more promising. All the postwar presidents, along with various agencies of the federal government, acknowledged the need for federal leadership in this area. For example, in 1946, President Harry Truman appointed a prestigious special committee to survey and make recommendations on civil rights. Its report, issued in the fall of 1947 as a book titled *To Secure These Rights,* called for the breaking down of racial barriers in education, housing, voting, and military service, and it recommended the creation of a permanent FEPC. The next year, Truman issued an executive order ending segregation in the armed forces. Truman also advanced an ambitious civil rights legislative agenda, although it fell victim to the hostility of southern Democrats and their Republican allies in Congress.

The administration of Republican Dwight D. Eisenhower (1953–1961) continued the pattern of federal support for civil rights, although the president warned repeatedly of the dangers of precipitous change. In 1954, the Supreme Court, led by Eisenhower-appointed Chief Justice Earl Warren, issued its monumental *Brown v. Board of Education of Topeka* decision, outlawing segregation in the nation's public schools. Although Eisenhower often expressed ambivalence about the decision itself and about other efforts to change the country's racial practices and policies, he used federalized National Guard troops in 1957 to protect African American children in Little Rock, Arkansas, from violent white resistance to the desegregation of a high school there. Moreover, it was during the Eisenhower years—though primarily through the efforts of the Democratic congressional majority—that the Civil Rights Acts of 1957 and 1960 were passed, the first general civil rights laws enacted since the end of Reconstruction.

In the area of job discrimination, Eisenhower took some small, tentative steps. Though rejecting the notion of a permanent FEPC, which the president characterized as a "Federally compulsory thing," he did appoint a Government Contract Committee (GCC), which Vice President Richard Nixon chaired. Its charge was to identify and remedy racial discrimination in federal government employment and among private contractors that did business with the federal government, using quiet persuasion and low-key appeals to contractors to end discriminatory hiring and job assignment practices. Impatient black advocates charged, with justification, that the Civil Rights Acts and the activities of the GCC were largely ineffectual in promoting change. All these measures relied on private—and expensive—litigation and on fact-finding and conflict resolution as remedies for discrimination in education, voting, law enforcement, and employment, making them more symbolic gestures than substantive reforms.

Initially, the John F. Kennedy administration (1961–1963), though rhetorically bolder in its identification with civil rights, followed a cautious course. With the House and Senate evenly divided between Republicans and Democrats, and with the GOP–southern Democratic alliance as potent as ever, Kennedy believed that any strong civil rights measures were certain to derail his entire legislative program. Only after civil rights activism in the South and the violent response to it exposed the naked repression and discrimination inflicted on Americans of color did Kennedy put forth major civil rights legislation. In the meantime, however, he established the President's Committee on Equal Employment Opportunity (PCEEO), to be chaired by Vice President Lyndon Johnson. Among other things, Executive Order 10925, which established this body, required that contractors doing business with the federal government "take affirmative action to ensure that applicants are employed, and that employees are treated during employment, without regard to their race, creed, color, or national origin."[23]

Though seemingly stronger than Eisenhower's GCC, the PCEEO, like its predecessor, largely confined its activities to documenting employment patterns and urging contractors to comply with equal employment guidelines. With a small staff and a limited budget, the PCEEO was vulnerable to the charge by increasingly vocal civil rights groups that it represented just another exercise in tokenism. The committee did encourage large federal contractors to establish "Plans for Progress," which were voluntary—and unenforceable—agreements to increase minority recruitment and upgrading. Although some defense contractors actually began to hire more African Americans and to recruit blacks for white-collar work, most employers simply ignored the PCEEO. Especially in the South, few contractors even bothered to submit a Plan for Progress. Indeed, observed *Business Week* magazine—ordinarily no friend of federal intervention in private business—the "Plans for Progress were . . . largely meaningless."[24]

Another key limitation of these administrative measures, as well as state and local antidiscrimination statutes, was that racial discrimination by unions was virtually impossible to address. Thus, black workers and their allies took some satisfaction from the fact that even as the various presidential administrations sought ways to address job discrimination without incurring unacceptable political damage, the federal courts and key governmental agencies were moving haltingly against union discrimination. As early as 1944, in *Steele v. Louisville & Nashville Railroad Company, Brotherhood of Locomotive Firemen and Enginemen, et al.,* the Supreme Court had ruled that a union operating under the terms of the Railway Labor Act—in this case, the whites-only Brotherhood of Locomotive Firemen and Enginemen (BLFE)—had a duty to represent fairly the interests of all workers in its bargaining unit. This applied, said the Court, even to black firemen, who were ineligible for actual membership in the union.

This ruling provided little immediate relief to black railroaders, since it required expensive, time-consuming litigation and was applicable only to the particular complainants in the case. In subsequent rulings, however, the federal courts sporadically began to follow the trail of logic that was implicit, but not applied, in the *Steele* decision. How could a union operating under the cover of federal legislation fairly represent the interests of all workers in a given bargaining unit if some of those workers were barred from participating in the union's deliberations? How effectively could a union such as the BLFE *represent* workers who had no voice in framing its bargaining positions and no standing to influence the union's administration of the resulting contract? For some legal scholars and friends of equal employment opportunity, implicit in *Steele* and related cases was the power of the courts to require that unions using the services of the Railway Labor Act's Mediation Board or the National Labor Relations Act's NLRB admit African Americans as equal members. Indeed, as early as 1945, the NLRB had ruled, following *Steele,* that it could not make its services available to unions that discriminated on racial grounds. The effect of this ruling, however, was blunted by two considerations: first, the railroad and building trades unions, which were most guilty of such discrimination, characteristically did not use the board's services in gaining union recognition, and second, the board itself had declared that the establishment of segregated locals did not violate fair representation requirements. Still, by the early 1960s, although case law and subsequent NLRB rulings had not definitively challenged union discrimination and segregation per se, the potential existed for an expansive conception of federal power to require unions to discard their racist membership requirements.[25]

Red Scare, Black Workers, 1945–1950

Throughout the first postwar decades, the relationship between organized labor and African American workers was complex and contentious. The upheavals of the 1930s and 1940s resulted in a vast increase in the number of black workers enrolled in unions and brought racial issues to the fore in American unions as never before. But precisely because questions involving African American workers, civil rights, and the labor movement were becoming central, friction and conflict became increasingly prominent. During these years, organized labor emerged as a key political and legislative ally of the burgeoning civil rights movement as it sought federal action to outlaw segregation and discrimination in schools, housing, and the political process. Even so, critics charged that the mainstream labor movement's anticommunist obsession caused it to abandon and even to sabotage efforts to sustain interracial union activism in the South, which had the potential to transform the country's political landscape. Moreover, despite organized labor's real achievements in collective bargaining—achievements that benefited thousands of black workers along with their white counterparts—the labor movement remained open to the charge that it was insensitive and unresponsive to the claims of black workers. Indeed, this criticism was leveled most tellingly by black trade unionists, including A. Philip Randolph.

In the immediate aftermath of the war, leaders of the embattled labor movement initially gave relatively little attention to racial issues. With the bitter experience of union defeat in the wake of World War I constantly in mind, AFL president William Green, CIO chief Philip Murray, and the leaders of such war-expanded unions as the United Automobile Workers, the United Steelworkers, the International Brotherhood of Teamsters, and the unions in electrical manufacturing, meatpacking, and metalworking had to negotiate the rough transition from all-out war production to the uncertainties of a peacetime economy. Fear of a return to Depression-era levels of unemployment haunted them. From the fall of 1945 through the next year, a massive strike wave dominated public attention as unionists sought wage gains to compensate for wage restraints during the war. In November 1946, the election of the first Republican-controlled Congress since 1931 heightened unionists' anxiety, especially since Republican leaders and their southern Democratic allies resolved to chasten organized labor and to reverse the pro-union legislation of the 1930s.

Of all the postwar issues affecting the labor movement, none was more contentious than the growing controversy over the role of communists and their allies in American unions. And in this case, African American workers figured significantly. During most of the war years, the United States had been allied with the Soviet Union in the common struggle against Nazi Germany. American communists, along with many people who, though not actual members of the Communist Party, looked to the Soviet Union for leadership in the antifascist struggle, had strongly supported the U.S. war effort. Nowhere was their commitment to the Allied cause more evident than in the unions, most of them CIO affiliated, in which they played a significant leadership role. In unions such as the United Cannery, Agricultural, Packing, and Allied Workers of America (UCAPAWA); the United Electrical Workers; the International Longshoremen's and Warehousemen's Union; the International Union of Mine, Mill, and Smelter Workers (IUMMSW); and the National Maritime Union, communists and those closely allied with them had played a major role in union building and were prominently represented in leadership positions. In the CIO more generally, communists and their allies occupied strategic positions in national headquarters and in many of the state and local bodies. The industries whose workers these unions represented were at the center of the wartime economy, producing and transporting materiel essential to the war effort. Throughout the period of U.S. belligerency (1941–1945), communists had eagerly embraced the no-strike pledge made in 1942 by the AFL and the CIO and had consistently supported the efforts of government officials and employers to maximize production and downplay workers' grievances. Certainly, even those pro-Soviet unions with large African American memberships had discouraged any hint of job actions to combat workplace discrimination.

The presence of communists in American unions had always been a contentious issue. Since the founding of the Communist Party of the United States in 1919, their ideological and political opponents had charged, with considerable justification, that communists' primary loyalty was to the Soviet Union and that they placed its interests above those of the workers they presumed to speak for. The speed with which American communists shifted ground on international issues in response to abrupt changes in Soviet foreign policy and the ardor with which communists embraced the call for workers' sacrifice during the war led many trade unionists and politicians to regard them and their allies as an alien presence in the labor movement and in American society in general. So long as the war against Nazi Germany raged, these contentious matters could be laid aside in the interest of attaining a common goal. But with the end of the war, and with the United States and the USSR increasingly at odds over the character and details of the postwar world order, the presence of communists in labor organizations at the heart of the American economy became a matter of heated public controversy.

Virtually from the beginning of the communist movement in the United States, communists had highlighted the victimization and exploitation of African Americans. Making a special effort to recruit blacks into the Communist Party, they supported black activists in their fight against segregation and discrimination in the workplace and in the community. In the 1930s, communists embraced the CIO in its efforts to organize workers in the mass production industries, often proving to be particularly effective and courageous organizers in their eagerness to reach out to African American workers. Although relatively few blacks actually joined the Communist Party, communists' commitment to interracial unionism and community activism gave them credibility among African Americans, especially since their rhetorical support for racial equality was backed up with hard and sometimes dangerous work in the factories, fields, and neighborhoods and on the picket lines. In the stockyards, auto plants, mines, and mills; among field hands in the segregated South and on the factory farms of California; on the merchant ships and loading docks; and in the canneries and tobacco factories, communists demonstrated a sturdy and vigorous commitment to interracial labor activism, usually under the banner of the CIO.

Indeed, during this period, some of the most extensive and effective examples of interracial unionism occurred in CIO unions with a communist-oriented leadership. In northern Alabama, Memphis, Winston-Salem, and elsewhere, CIO affiliates such as the IUMMSW and UCAPAWA worked hard to gain the support of poorly paid black workers whose arduous jobs often placed them in strategic locations in the production processes in the mills, smelters, and agricultural processing and tobacco factories. Organizers for these unions combated racial division and sought to build genuinely interracial organizations, invariably in the face of fierce opposition by employers and local white elites.

Union leaders hoped that by stressing the common economic interests of black and white workers they could overcome the racial antagonisms that were rarely absent in the Jim Crow South of the 1940s. And they enjoyed considerable success, with the UCAPAWA winning bargaining rights among twelve thousand tobacco workers in a hotly contested NLRB election in Winston-Salem in December 1943, and the IUMMSW building several locals embracing more than five thousand men in and around the industrial town of Bessemer, just north of Birmingham. In Memphis as well, during and just after World War II, the UCAPAWA and several smaller communist-oriented affiliates, such as the CIO's United Furniture Workers, used effective appeals to African American workers to build successful local unions and to stir black political activism.

Sustaining a genuinely interracial union presence was difficult, however. In contrast to most political groups of the 1930s and 1940s, the Communist Party consistently and prominently focused its members' attention on matters of racial injustice and civil rights. Organizers and functionaries of communist-influenced unions, both white and black, characteristically evinced a genuine respect for the tenacious culture of endurance and mutuality that African Americans in southern industrial towns had developed in resistance to the prevailing system of Jim Crow. They encouraged union members to join local NAACP chapters and spearheaded demands for voting rights and improved public services for black citizens. This close identification with African Americans, both in the workplace and in the community, laid the UCAPAWA, the IUMMSW, and other communist-oriented unions open to attack from rival AFL unions, public officials, and employers. Although union representatives constantly stressed the relationship between racial division and low wages and poor working conditions, many white workers regarded these unions as "nigger-loving" organizations. IUMMSW leaders, declared one disgruntled white member of an Alabama local, were "trying . . . to change our way of living—the segregation policy that we have been raised up under in the South."[26]

The success of these outposts of militant biracial unionism, along with the large-scale organizing gains on the part of more orthodox AFL and CIO unions in the shipyards, aircraft factories, iron mines, and textile mills of the wartime South, encouraged laborite hopes. A permanent breakthrough seemed possible. Indeed, for many labor partisans, the South held the key to labor's continued vitality, and to some, black workers held the key to success in Dixie.

The labor movement that emerged from World War II was both powerful and vulnerable. With a combined AFL and CIO membership of around thirteen million, organized labor now represented over 30 percent of the nonagricultural workforce, a record high. In the central industrial-transport-mining-construction blue-collar core of the economy, unions enrolled about 75 percent of the workers. Still, repeated efforts by business groups and conservative politicians to turn back the tide of union growth and to hamstring the postwar labor movement posed serious threats to organized labor's recently achieved position. Increasingly vocal business re-sistance to union power, along with conservative victories in the 1946 elections, highlighted the fragility of labor's new influence. "I think there is no question," declared one business executive, "but that if labor is permit-ted to consolidate its power . . . we shall find ourselves in a position in which labor is stronger than the government . . . and is able to dictate to it."[27] If the labor movement was to realize its potential and withstand the antiunion crusade—a crusade in which southern Democrats were sure to play a central role—it would have to expand its promising presence in the southern states dramatically.

After the war, leaders of both the AFL and, especially, the CIO believed that a concerted campaign to organize Dixie's workers was essential to the labor movement's long-range success. Industrially, organizing southern plants and mills would complete the resurgence of organized labor. A pow-erful union presence in the South's oil refineries, cotton textile mills, food processing plants, and loading docks and terminals would boost the stan-dards of southern workers and remove the South as a source of low-wage competition for workers and their unions in Michigan, Pennsylvania, and New England.

Equally important were the political possibilities that union expansion in the South offered. Labor activists had no doubt that successful work site organization would lead directly to working-class political mobiliza-tion that could undermine the power of the conservative Democrats who dominated the region's public life and key congressional committees. Of key importance to this agenda was the enfranchisement of African Americans, who represented a huge, untapped reservoir of progressive voters in the southern states. And since the overwhelming majority of the South's black population consisted of working people, biracial union or-ganizing and the forging of a progressive political presence in Dixie were inextricably intertwined.

Indeed, as the war ended, recent developments encouraged liberals in both the North and the South. Not only had the war brought large-scale industry—and substantial union membership—to Dixie; in addition, African Americans, spurred by a 1944 Supreme Court ruling that invali-dated the "white primary" and by blacks' participation in the labor move-ment and in NLRB elections, began registering to vote in record numbers. In the 1940s, the southern black electorate doubled to nearly 900,000, and for the first time in the twentieth century, blacks were being elected to local offices in parts of the upper South.[28] Moreover, owing to labor support and the enlarged black electorate, a number of relatively liberal white politi-cians were elected to state and federal office in the late 1940s. The emer-gence of southern politicians who welcomed labor support and quietly accepted or encouraged the expansion of the black electorate betokened bright promise for a rapidly industrializing South. Governors Ellis Arnall in Georgia and Jim Folsom in Alabama; senators such as Lister Hill of Alabama, Florida's Claude Pepper, and North Carolina's Frank Graham; and labor-backed congressmen such as Estes Kefauver in Tennessee, Henderson L. Lanham in Georgia, and and Albert Rains in Alabama brought fresh hope, as did the emergence of an expanding black electorate in larger southern cities. With both the AFL and the CIO planning postwar organizing drives in Dixie, progressive-minded southerners saw the immediate postwar period, in the retrospective words of one, as "a kind of lovely moment . . . when everything seemed to be working."[29]

In 1946, both the AFL and the CIO launched organizing drives in the South. The AFL effort was a relatively low-key affair as the older labor federation attempted to exploit its long-term, if modest, presence in the South and expand into the region's growing industrial sector. Although AFL organizers almost never challenged the South's racial order, by no means did they ignore black workers, nor were black workers unresponsive to AFL appeals. Control of the building trades and local transport in southern cities and control of the larger ports made the AFL's unsentimental and functional version of trade unionism seem like the only practical route to union representation for many black workers. As of 1946, about 10 percent of the AFL's seven million members were African American, about 60 percent of them in the South.[30]

Even the AFL's toleration of segregation in some of its affiliates did not necessarily turn away black workers. Separate locals in the International Longshoremen's Association, for example, provided leadership opportunities for black unionists that integrated locals, which were certain to be dominated by whites, could not. At the same time, AFL leaders realized that black workers resented second-class status, and they increasingly highlighted the federation's support for civil rights legislation and the biracial character of its annual conventions and organizing campaigns. Despite devoting considerable money and resources to its southern organizing campaign, however, the AFL's southern organizing campaign added only about ninety thousand new members in the late 1940s, probably less than 10 percent of them African American.[31]

The CIO's southern effort was more dramatically publicized and more generously funded. With an initial war chest of $1 million and employing two hundred organizers, the CIO's southern organizing campaign was launched in the spring of 1946. Dubbed "Operation Dixie," the southern drive had the trappings of a frontal assault on the South. "Like a champion fighter," declared a United Steelworkers' official, "we can't rest but must continue to bore ahead [and] ORGANIZE THE SOUTH!" The CIO News called the massive effort a "Holy Crusade" to bring the benefits of organization to exploited southern workers.[32]

From the start, however, the CIO suffered from myriad problems. The enormity of the task quickly absorbed the initial million-dollar outlay, and organizers often found that even workers sympathetic to their cause were reluctant to pay the initiation fees and the dues that were supposed to replenish the campaign's coffers and provide ongoing funding. Fierce resistance on the part of southern employers and public officials, along with the generally conservative postwar political environment, made the going slow. Early setbacks sapped organizers' confidence. A crushing defeat at a large North Carolina textile mill in October 1946 provided a stark warning that organizing Dixie would be frustrating and protracted.

In planning its foray into the South, CIO leaders from president Philip Murray on down had stressed the importance of cracking the huge southern cotton textile industry, which employed about half a million workers in hundreds of factories stretching along the southern piedmont from southern Virginia into northern Alabama. Victory in textiles, the thinking went, would pave the way to eventual victory in furniture making, food processing, oil refining, and other secondary industries. But unlike the northern-based auto, rubber, steel, and electrical appliances industries in which the CIO had built successful unions in the 1930s and during the war, the textile industry was highly decentralized, even fragmented. The southern textile industry consisted of hundreds of small companies, with even the relatively large Cannon enterprises accounting for only about 5 percent of the South's production of cotton goods. Organizing these many separate employers one by one, in the face of sharp hostility and without the kind of public support that had bolstered union growth between 1933 and 1945, soon proved to be a hopeless task. By the end of 1946, Operation Dixie was in retreat, never to recover the optimism and élan with which it had been launched.

From the start, some in the CIO had questioned the "textiles-first" strategy. In particular, those active in communist-oriented unions such as the IUMMSW, the Food, Tobacco, Agricultural, and Allied Workers of America (FTA; formerly known as the UCAPAWA, renamed in 1946), and the large United Electrical Workers had questioned whether concentration on the virtually lily-white textile labor force would yield results. FTA president Donald Henderson and others who had enjoyed success in building interracial unions among mine and smelter workers, food processing workers, furniture workers, and other sectors with large numbers of African Americans argued that the CIO should exploit the strength they had been developing among black workers and expand from the base they had established. After all, they argued, success in Winston-Salem, northern Alabama, Memphis, and elsewhere had proved that dedicated organizers who linked labor rights and civil rights could tap into the militancy of black workers and the vibrant networks of community support that sustained them to defeat even obdurate employers. In these places, vigorous local unions were having an impact both in the workplace and in the political arena. Why expend the CIO's limited resources in a frontal assault on the fragmented textile industry, whose almost exclusively white and rural-based labor force had shown only sporadic interest in the union appeal and whose votes had so often sustained some of the South's most reactionary and racist politicians, such as Georgia's Eugene Talmadge and Mississippi's Theodore Bilbo?

This perspective, of course, placed race at the heart of the debate over southern strategy. Top CIO leaders, including president Murray, director of organization Allan S. Haywood, and southern campaign director Van Bittner, rejected this approach. Although they supported civil rights and were eager to bring the gospel of unionism to both black and white workers, they believed that the race issue was too explosive to be foregrounded in the effort to expand organization in the South. "We are not mentioning the color of people" in our campaign, declared Bittner. Continued agitation on racial questions, he told FTA president Henderson, "is hurting our drive." Although one of the ultimate goals of the CIO's southern effort was liberalization of the South's politics and its racial order, the campaign had to concentrate on bread-and-butter issues, leaving the racial and political education of southern whites until after they had been safely brought into the union fold. From the start, CIO leaders stressed that the southern drive was "to be purely an organizational campaign," with "no extra curricular activities—no politics . . . no FEPC."[33]

Henderson and others active in the CIO's dozen or so pro-Soviet affiliates hinted that something other than a sober assessment of organizing prospects was at work in the formulation of CIO strategy. Bittner and his assistant director, Textile Workers vice president George Baldanzi (who succeeded Bittner after his death in 1949), were vociferous anticommunists. Men and women with connections to pro-Soviet affiliates were systematically weeded out in the selection of organizers dispatched to the South. As cold war antagonisms between the United States and the USSR deepened, the always incipient division between the CIO's communists and their allies, on the one hand, and its broad array of anticommunists, on the other, began to widen. In 1946, for example, staunch anticommunist Walter P. Reuther won the presidency of the massive UAW in a bitter battle against the communist-supported incumbent, while communists and anticommunists fought—sometimes literally—for control of UAW offices and local unions. And at the CIO's October 1946 convention in Atlantic City, anticommunists rammed through a resolution attacking communist influence in the organization.

With business interests and right-wing politicians stridently attacking the CIO as a veritable agent of Moscow, noncommunist CIO leaders increasingly sought to counter such charges by isolating and attacking the organization's pro-Soviet faction. And since communists were so closely identified with the cause of civil rights and with militant interracialism in both the workplaces and communities of the South, it was only a short step to regard outspoken advocacy of civil rights and black workers' interests as evidence of dangerous pro-communist sympathies. Hence, Henderson and other pro-Soviet CIO unionists believed that their colleagues had succumbed to the prevailing anticommunist hysteria and, in forging ahead with the flawed textiles-first strategy, were squandering the labor movement's only realistic chance to put the CIO at the forefront of the transformation of southern industrial and political life.

Murray, Bittner, and other mainstream CIO leaders, however, pointed out that for all the claims of their pro-Soviet colleagues, the FTA, the IUMMSW, and other small communist-oriented affiliates had organized only a small number of workers, black or white. Moreover, unions such as the FTA's Winston-Salem Local 22 were not so much interracial as black dominated. The growing number of white workers in the Winston-Salem factories deplored the FTA's ardent identification with black workers, its flouting of southern racial mores in the union's social activities, and its stridently pro-Soviet pronouncements on questions of foreign policy. The CIO, Murray and Bittner insisted, remained a stalwart supporter of civil rights legislation and an energetic champion of black workers' interests. But flagrant transgression of white workers' sensibilities could only increase racial division, thus benefiting employers and their reactionary political allies.

Moreover, events in Alabama, Tennessee, and North Carolina were intimately connected to the larger domestic and international political context. The ritualistic praise for Stalinist Russia emanating from pro-Soviet affiliates, along with Communist Party leaders' insistence that local unionists adopt resolutions of support for every twist and turn of Soviet foreign policy, fatally contrasted with their enlightened stand on racial issues. In 1948, matters came to a head on the political front. Because communist CIO members and their allies were loyal to the Communist Party line, as handed down in Moscow and transmitted through party headquarters in New York, they supported the third-party candidacy of communist-backed Henry Wallace in the 1948 presidential election. Convinced that support for Wallace threatened to throw the election to Republican Thomas E. Dewey, CIO leaders regarded the defection of fellow CIO members to Wallace as an act of outright political betrayal. Thus, reasoned CIO leaders, far from spearheading union growth in the South, the FTA, the IUMMSW, and the other pro-Soviet affiliates were sabotaging organized labor's liberal political agenda and undermining the CIO's admittedly more moderate, but ultimately more realistic, efforts to change the industrial and racial contours of the South.

By 1949, the conflict between the CIO's mainstream unionists and its pro-Soviet affiliates had become so intense that CIO leaders began moves to expel the FTA, the IUMMSW, the United Electrical Workers, and eight other allegedly pro-communist affiliates on the grounds that for years they had consistently followed policies that were, in effect, dictated by the Communist Party of the United States and, ultimately, by the Soviets. As part of this campaign, the CIO moved to supplant these organizations, aided by a key provision of the Taft-Hartley Act, passed in June 1947, that in effect banned communists from holding union office. The CIO created a rival electrical workers union, for example, to challenge United Electrical Workers locals, mostly in the Northeast and Midwest. The United Steelworkers and the UAW moved to take over the locals of pro-Soviet CIO affiliates in die casting, farm equipment manufacture, and other metal trades. And in the South, the United Steelworkers launched a campaign to drive the IUMMSW from Alabama's iron mines and smelters and to replace its locals there. In Winston-Salem, FTA Local 22 tried to fight off challenges by both the AFL and the CIO while combating an employer-led effort to eliminate any union presence among its labor force.

In Alabama, the United Steelworkers defeated the IUMMSW in a bitter and sometimes bloody contest for representation rights among iron ore and smelter workers, with the five thousand workers divided almost evenly, largely along racial lines. And in March 1950, Local 22 lost a deeply divisive four-way struggle (involving itself, a CIO challenger, an AFL rival, and a company-sponsored appeal for a "no-union" vote) to retain bargaining rights. In both these instances, workers divided sharply along racial lines, with black workers overwhelmingly supporting the IUMMSW and the FTA, in acknowledgment of these unions' long-standing and vigorous support for black workers' rights on and off the job. In both cases, opponents stressed the pro-Soviet orientation of the two communist-led organizations, which had the not-so-subtle effect of linking the ardent advocacy of racial justice with subversion and disloyalty. Although the CIO disavowed racist support and attempted to distinguish its principled criticism of its former affiliates' embrace of the Soviet Union from cruder forms of Red-baiting, it benefited from the votes of illiberal and even racist elements, especially in its successful Alabama campaign. In the end, the mainstream labor movement faced intractable dilemmas in the South. Its most racially progressive unions were those that cleaved most closely to the Communist Party line, with its mixture of progressive rhetoric and uncritical support for Stalinist repression. At the same time, its public identification with civil rights activism and racial integration alienated many white workers, including those among its southern membership.

African American Workers and the Labor Movement, 1950–1965

The labor movement's failure in the postwar South cast a long shadow. Unable to mobilize a coalition of white and black workers that a thriving southern labor movement might have built, both the AFL and the CIO (and, after their merger in 1955, the AFL-CIO) struggled against the odds to sustain a progressive presence in the South. On the one hand, organized labor's well-publicized support for antidiscrimination court rulings and legislative measures alienated thousands of white workers. On the other hand, the perceived need for circumspection and caution in supporting blacks' mounting demands for equality strained relations with civil rights advocates, the most progressive social force in postwar Dixie. Throughout the 1950s and into the 1960s, solid phalanxes of conservative Democratic congressmen and senators from the South, many of them elected and re-elected without challenge, thwarted organized labor's liberal political agenda. Meanwhile, state after state adopted so-called right-to-work laws, which had the effect of hamstringing union organizing, especially among the South's low-wage and minority workers.

As an assertive civil rights movement emerged in the South in the 1950s, both the AFL and the CIO, along with most of their affiliated unions, openly endorsed its goals. The CIO, for example, filed an amicus curiae brief in the landmark *Brown v. Board of Education* case in 1954, which outlawed segregation in the public schools. Lobbyists from the newly merged AFL-CIO played major roles in shaping and gaining passage of the Civil Rights Acts of 1957, 1960, 1964, and 1965. Unions such as the Teamsters, UAW, Amalgamated Clothing Workers, and Packinghouse Workers supported the southern civil rights campaigns associated with Dr. Martin Luther King Jr. with convention resolutions, financial aid, and political pressure. In the mid-1960s, the UAW dispatched staff members to assist in the dangerous task of voter registration in Mississippi and other Deep South states. At the massive August 1963 March on Washington, which brought 200,000 Americans of all ethnic and racial backgrounds to the nation's capital in support of civil rights legislation, organizers estimated that at least one-fifth of those present represented labor unions. UAW president Walter Reuther, whose union helped finance the march, was one of the featured speakers, and it was veteran trade unionist A. Philip Randolph himself who introduced the eloquent Dr. King as he strode to the platform to deliver his "I have a dream" speech.

But organized labor paid a price for its identification with the civil rights movement. In the South, thousands of white workers, many of them union members, joined the anti-integration White Citizens Councils and denounced national union leaders such as Reuther and AFL-CIO president

George Meany for their support of civil rights. In Alabama, one influential state labor leader, in accepting appointment to a biracial commission ostensibly created to calm racial tensions, declared, "We will fight at every turn if the Negro race seeks to mongrelize the white race." Throughout the Deep South, in the tense and violent days of the late 1950s and early 1960s, southern trade unionists were prominent in the Ku Klux Klan and the White Citizens Councils. They openly used local union halls for Klan and Citizens Council meetings. In cities such as Birmingham, Montgomery, Atlanta, Memphis, and New Orleans, white union members began movements to disaffiliate their local unions from civil rights–supporting national unions (and thus from the AFL-CIO). There was even a movement to establish a "Southern Federation of Labor," a whites-only labor organization designed to supplant the AFL-CIO and recruit workers "interested in maintaining the cherished ideals of our Southland." In August 1956, members of the carpenters union in Montgomery, Alabama, erected a gallows downtown from which an effigy representing the NAACP was hanged. It bore a sign reading "Built by Organized Labor."[34]

Throughout the heyday of civil rights activism in the South—roughly 1954 to 1968—both national and southern labor loyalists fought this tide of racist working-class activism. In Mississippi, for example, state AFL-CIO head Claude Ramsay battled constantly, against heavy odds, to stem defections from the state's small labor movement and to counteract the influence of the Klan, the Citizens Councils, and racist politicians on union members. In Alabama, his counterpart Barney Weeks likewise fought racist sentiment within the labor movement, arranging for integrated facilities at statewide labor conferences and quietly upholding national AFL-CIO stands on civil rights issues. In seeking to deflect antiblack sentiment among rank-and-file workers and local unionists, Weeks hammered home the adverse effects that black subordination had on white workers' wages and living standards. "We gave them heavy doses of economics in which we showed how the best way . . . to keep the wages of the whites down [was] to keep blacks a little lower," he declared.[35]

National AFL-CIO leaders venturing south likewise stressed common economic interests in attempting to hold together their southern memberships. For over two decades, CIO (and later AFL-CIO) southern political director Daniel Powell worked to reconcile white workers to the labor movement's pro–civil rights agenda by stressing the economic advantages of a strong biracial labor movement. Southern labor activists and visiting leaders of northern-based unions soft-pedaled race issues, hammering home the message that the subordination of blacks translated into lower wages for whites. But throughout the 1950s and early 1960s, as both civil rights protests and violent white reaction mounted, southern labor adherents found themselves and their movement increasingly fighting defensive battles rather than aggressively advancing labor's agenda or joining forthrightly with African Americans in their brave struggle for human rights. Stunning defeats of racially progressive southern politicians in the 1950 elections set a pattern that prevailed for the next fifteen years. "Lots of laboring people with whom I talked," reported a disappointed North Carolina liberal after a disastrous primary defeat in 1950, "told me that they had much rather work for lower wages than to have their children going to school with Negroes."[36]

Attacked by southern white workers for its pro–civil rights stand, organized labor also came under criticism from civil rights advocates, both within and outside the labor movement. Black activists charged that most unions, whatever their verbal support for civil rights legislation, chronically ignored or shortchanged African American workers. They pointed to the building trades unions, which systematically excluded black applicants from training and apprenticeship programs. They criticized industrial unions such as the UAW and United Steelworkers for failing to upgrade and advance their large black memberships in deference to white members who were determined to keep highly skilled jobs for themselves. They called attention to the caution and inertia of even those unions and union leaders who enjoyed public reputations for racial progressivism. In the late 1950s and early 1960s, for example, NAACP labor secretary Herbert Hill repeatedly called attention to the inadequacies of ostensibly liberal unions such as the International Ladies' Garment Workers' Union (ILGWU), the United Steelworkers, and the UAW. In widely circulated publications and in congressional testimony, Hill charged that the New York–based ILGWU, which, from its inception in 1900, had projected a racially liberal image, was in fact guilty of systematic discrimination against its large black and Puerto Rican membership. He also charged that in southern steelworkers locals, "Negro workers are permanently locked in menial and unskilled job classifications," while "white workers with less seniority are promoted."[37] Likewise, the UAW came under sharp scrutiny as critics pointed to the lack of black representation in the industry's skilled trades and in the union's leadership structure.

Even seemingly neutral features of standard union contracts, such as seniority provisions, worked against black workers' interests, argued black activists and their allies. In itself, the inclusion of strict seniority provisions governing layoffs, job assignments, and opportunities for promotion and upgrading was a major achievement of the industrial unions. Without strong seniority clauses in union contracts, employers would be free to play favorites, punish dissident workers, and pit worker against worker in these crucial matters of workplace governance. But typically, in unions such as the United Steelworkers, detailed seniority provisions were the responsibility of local bargaining committees, which, reflecting the majority status of white workers, often advanced seniority clauses that effectively confined black workers to the hot, heavy, and dangerous jobs and preserved promotion opportunities for white workers. Even in northern plants, admitted one local president, although contracts ensured that "limitations on the promotion of white workers have been largely wiped out," seniority provisions imposed "a definite ceiling . . . on job opportunities for the majority of our negro workers."[38] Throughout the postwar period, national union leaders struggled to square seniority rights with black workers' legitimate demand that the union recognize the inequity of earlier contractual arrangements that had confined blacks to a narrow range of low-skilled jobs. Especially after passage of the Civil Rights Act of 1964, with its prohibition against workplace discrimination, issues of seniority, transfer rights, promotion, and protection against layoffs proved deeply contentious, always threatening to undermine the interracial solidarity that industrial unions proclaimed.

Black workers repeatedly protested against discrimination in the building trades and on the railroads and against the de facto discrimination tolerated by leaders such as Reuther and long-term ILGWU president David Dubinsky. In 1950, a group of black activists met in Chicago to initiate a black workers' support organization that would work within the House of Labor to highlight African American grievances against unions in both the AFL and the CIO and otherwise promote the hiring, recruitment, and defense of black workers. Throughout the five years of its existence (1951–1956), the National Negro Labor Council (NNLC), as it was eventually called, incurred the hostility of the official labor leadership. Many of its activists were associated with suspect unions, including several that had been ejected from the CIO in 1949 and 1950 because of their communist orientation, and even those in noncommunist unions were from dissident or radical-leaning locals. For example, the man chosen to head the NNLC, William R. Hood, was an officer in the UAW's huge Local 600, which represented the eighty thousand members at the fabled River Rouge Ford facility and was famous—or infamous—for its defiance of UAW president Reuther. Indeed, Local 600's African American activists, who had played a crucial role in the union's victory over Ford in 1941 (see chapter 4), remained an outpost of communist influence in the UAW into the 1950s, long after Reuther had purged pro-Soviet staff members and union officers. Another prominent figure in the Detroit-area NNLC chapter was Coleman Young, an organizer for the United Public Workers, one of the unions purged from the CIO. Young was a sharp-tongued critic of Reuther and would one day be the mayor of Detroit.

Throughout the early 1950s, the NNLC kept up a drumbeat of criticism of the mainstream labor movement. It challenged unions to expand the organization of black workers, particularly in the South; to promote

African Americans to meaningful leadership positions within the unions; and to eliminate discrimination within the unions themselves. In response to charges that it constituted a "dual union"—that is, a rival to unions affiliated with the AFL and the CIO—Hood insisted that the NNLC sought only to prod organized labor to live up to its antidiscrimination rhetoric and to bring the labor movement into the forefront of the civil rights movement. Local NNLC organizations joined black workers on picket lines, exposed discriminatory practices on the railroads, challenged corporations to adopt nondiscriminatory hiring practices as they opened new plants in the South, and kept up a barrage of criticism of established unions' lethargy and evasion in racial matters. Its strident criticism of a labor movement already under attack in the South for being *too* concerned with the interests of black workers and its connections with discredited pro-Soviet elements ensured that few in the AFL or CIO would welcome association with the NNLC or mourn its disbandment in 1956 in the face of government harassment.

Mainstream labor leaders might dismiss the NNLC as being tainted by communism, but they found it hard to ignore the criticisms of the NAACP. From the mid-1930s onward, the association had worked closely with progressive elements in the labor movement, particularly those in the CIO. Organized labor's support for a permanent FEPC, its postwar efforts in behalf of civil rights legislation, and its participation in liberal politics meshed with the NAACP agenda. As late as 1957, the civil rights organization had honored AFL-CIO president George Meany for his antidiscrimination efforts. But labor secretary Hill, executive secretary Roy Wilkins, and other association leaders grew increasingly impatient with the AFL-CIO and its slowness in addressing racial discrimination. In 1957, for example, the labor federation admitted two railroad unions as affiliates, the Brotherhood of Locomotive Firemen and Enginemen and the Brotherhood of Railroad Trainmen, despite their whites-only membership policies. Widely publicized NAACP reports authored by Hill and issued in 1958 and 1961 documented anew the exclusionary practices and policies of the building trades unions and the failure of organized labor to address the structural problems in the economy that were associated with massive unemployment among younger black workers. "Today," claimed Hill in a January 1961 report, "five years after the AFL-CIO merger, the national labor organization has failed to eliminate the broad pattern of racial discrimination and segregation in many important affiliated unions. . . . Efforts to eliminate discriminatory practices . . . have been piecemeal and inadequate."[39]

Even more disturbing were the sharp criticisms of the venerable head of the Brotherhood of Sleeping Car Porters, A. Philip Randolph. Randolph's anticommunist credentials were indisputable, as was his commitment to the labor movement as the linchpin in the struggle for racial justice. But as black workers grew more outspoken in their criticism of the labor movement, and as the urban crisis facing African Americans intensified, Randolph, always vigorous in his efforts to prod fellow labor leaders, stepped up his in-house critique of the AFL-CIO.

The clash between a labor establishment whose concern for racial justice was tempered by the racial demographics of union membership and the practicalities of the American workplace, on the one hand, and frustrated black activists, on the other, came to a head in 1959 at the AFL-CIO's annual convention. Randolph, along with other BSCP delegates, introduced a series of resolutions demanding that the federation leadership take immediate action to compel affiliates to end discrimination and segregation. These resolutions came as no surprise; for almost a quarter century, Randolph had risen at such gatherings to urge the elimination of discrimination in the House of Labor—and with some success, since organized labor had moved from the AFL's diffident and defensive position of the 1920s and 1930s to forthright advocacy of civil rights and outspoken condemnation of segregation and discrimination. Moreover, Randolph regarded AFL-CIO president Meany, who was presiding during the protracted debate over these resolutions, as a good-faith friend of racial justice. But as far as Randolph and his convention allies were concerned, the time for high-sounding resolutions and promises of change had passed; it was time for prompt and effective action. It was time for "racially segregated local unions [to] be liquidated and eliminated."[40]

As leader of an organization with dozens of affiliated unions, Meany faced a dilemma when it came to matters of racial discrimination, as Randolph well knew. The AFL-CIO's only power over its affiliates was that of expulsion. Meany believed that it would be self-defeating to use this ultimate weapon in the case of the relatively few remaining lily-white affiliates, because once they were expelled, the AFL-CIO would have no further leverage. Meany believed that he had been successful in persuading, shaming, and cajoling affiliates into dropping the color bar, opening up apprenticing programs, and reaching out to recruit black workers. Moreover, some black delegates at the convention opposed Randolph's call for the "liquidation" of segregated locals, since these blacks-only locals provided their only opportunity to gain positions of leadership. In response to Randolph's motion, Meany invoked union autonomy and union democracy: what right, he challenged, did he, or Randolph, have to override the wishes of black workers who wanted to keep the union they had had for so many years?

Randolph rejected this position. Segregation was wrong, period. It did not matter that some black workers favored separate black locals, just as it did not matter that some workers might favor a corrupt or a communist leader. The AFL, the CIO, and the AFL-CIO had expelled unions guilty of corruption and communist orientation, regardless of the wishes of those unions' membership. It was time to apply the same standard to segregation. "I don't believe," Randolph declared, "that the members of a union have a right to maintain a Jim Crow local." Over the years, Meany and Randolph had publicly debated these issues on many occasions. Now, however, in an uncharacteristic loss of composure, the burly AFL-CIO president bridled at Randolph's insistent demands. Meany flared, "I am for the democratic rights of the Negro members" who want to retain their segregated locals. Perhaps momentarily forgetting the seventy-year-old Randolph's iconic status as the champion of black workers for over forty years, Meany snarled, "Who the hell appointed you as the guardian of all the Negroes in America?"[41]

Meany's blunt language was a public-relations disaster. African Americans in and out of the labor movement were appalled that Randolph, who combined a gentlemanly demeanor with his fierce insistence on racial equality, had been addressed in such a fashion. "Randolph speaks for millions of colored people throughout the nation in and out of his union," one liberal newspaper observed, while the *Baltimore Afro-American* newspaper termed Meany's outburst "shocking and distasteful." Randolph himself was more perplexed than offended. "I know George didn't mean it," Randolph said, according to veteran *New York Times* labor reporter A. H. Raskin. "When he thinks it over, he'll regret it." He told another reporter that he still regarded Meany as an ally in the fight against discrimination and that Meany's language was merely part of the rough-and-ready give-and-take characteristic of labor movement discourse.[42]

But in fact, for the next several years, Randolph's high-profile critiques of his fellow laborites repeatedly brought him into conflict with the AFL-CIO hierarchy. In May 1960, as the civil rights movement was entering a particularly activist and confrontational stage in the South, the BSCP leader helped launch a new organization, the Negro American Labor Council (NALC), designed to intensify the pressure on organized labor and to bring black labor activists more forcefully into the civil rights movement. Elected president of the NALC, Randolph sounded the clarion: "We reject 'tokenism,' that thin veneer of acceptance masquerading as democracy . . . [that] history has placed upon the Negro and [believe that] the Negro alone [has] the basic responsibility to complete the uncompleted civil war revolution through keeping the fires of freedom burning in the civil rights movement." NALC founders pledged to fight against segregation; discrimination in hiring, job training, and promotion; and the lack of black representation in labor organizations and to work with groups such as the NAACP to bring public pressure to bear on the AFL-CIO. When Randolph attempted to present a detailed critique of specific unions' racial practices and policies at the AFL-CIO Executive Council meeting the next year, Meany and his cohorts lashed out at the veteran activist, accusing him of having "gotten close to those militant groups." At an October 1961 meeting of the council, Randolph was formally censured on the grounds that his criticisms of the AFL-CIO were responsible for "the gap that has developed between organized labor and the Negro community." For his part, Randolph dismissed the AFL-CIO's defense of its racial record as "innocuous, sterile and barren" and shrugged off the censure, challenging the labor movement to rediscover the militant activism that had built the unions in the 1930s and to align itself more directly with the Freedom Riders, student activists, and protest marchers who were fighting for racial justice in the South, even as timid labor leaders combined verbal support with practical inertia.[43]

For some of the younger militants in the NALC, the AFL-CIO Executive Council's rebuke of Randolph revealed the emptiness and hypocrisy of the labor establishment's racial attitudes and policies. "Where was David Dubinsky, where was Walter Reuther? . . . Where were all those liberals" on the Executive Council? asked one outraged activist. Clearly, declared NALC treasurer Richard Parrish, the censure of Randolph "was a show of power to demonstrate to Negro union members that they represent nothing when it comes to setting policies in the labor movement even though they pay dues."[44] Martin Luther King Jr. called the censure "shocking and deplorable," while James Hoffa, president of the teamsters union, which the AFL-CIO had expelled in 1957, termed it "a gross injustice to a labor leader who has done more than anyone in the labor movement" to advance the cause of civil rights.[45]

Over the next eighteen months, Meany pulled back from his angry dismissal of NAACP and NALC criticism, acknowledging that organized labor needed to address the concerns of black workers, even if, in his view, the public airing of its shortcomings risked strengthening the labor movement's corporate and segregationist enemies. At its December 1961 convention, the AFL-CIO unanimously adopted a strong civil rights resolution, and early the next year, Meany accepted Randolph's invitation to address an NALC gathering at which he acknowledged the council's good intentions and the legitimacy of black workers' impatience. Indeed, Randolph's reconciliation with Meany prompted some of the more extreme NALC activists to turn on him, employing language far more insulting than any emanating from the AFL-CIO Executive Council. Thus, declared NALC militant James Hougton, Randolph's efforts to come to terms with Meany exposed him as "the greatest Uncle Tom in the American labor movement." By 1964, Randolph concluded that the NALC had been captured by extremists, and he resigned from its presidency.[46]

It was never Randolph's intention to undermine the labor movement, which he continued to regard as a crucial element in the effort to achieve racial justice and to create a more equitable society. Moreover, despite his critique of the AFL-CIO's response to continuing segregation and discrimi-

nation within the House of Labor, Randolph broadly agreed with organized labor's economic program. Along with Meany, Reuther, and the rest
of his fellow union presidents, he considered expansionary fiscal measures,
tax relief for lower-income families, more generous public provisions for
the jobless and disadvantaged, and New Deal–like public works projects as
being key to achieving the full employment that would lift African Americans
and other minorities out of unemployment and poverty.

Public opinion polls and election results during these years indicated
that the mass of African Americans, workers and others alike, shared
Randolph's view of the labor movement as a flawed but essential ally. In
the late 1950s, a series of congressional hearings revealed disturbing patterns of corruption and abuse of members' rights in the teamsters union
and other labor organizations. Opinion polls showed declining trust in organized labor and growing hostility toward labor leaders. Yet throughout
this period, African Americans bucked the general trend, registering consistently higher levels of support for organized labor than the general population or even white blue-collar workers. Blacks were more inclined to join
unions and were more consistent supporters of union representation, as
evidenced in NLRB elections, than were their white counterparts. As of the
early 1960s, blacks constituted about 11 percent of the general population
but about 15 percent of union members. Black voters regularly showed
higher levels of support for labor-endorsed political candidates than did
whites or even white union members.

Particularly telling was the behavior of black voters in a series of referenda held in the 1950s in states such as Ohio, Oklahoma, and California
on so-called right-to-work measures. The Taft-Hartley Act of 1947 permitted states to outlaw "union security"—that is, the ability of a union to bargain with an employer for contractual provisions that required all workers
in a given bargaining unit to become dues-paying members of the union or
pay an equivalent fee. Under federal labor law, all workers in a bargaining
unit, union members or not, were covered by the terms of collective bargaining agreements. Unionists held that without such security provisions,
"free riders" would reap the benefits of union protection, including wage
increases and access to grievance procedures, without bearing the costs of
negotiating and administering the contract. By 1960, at least eight southern states, where restrictions on black suffrage prevailed, had prohibited
union security provisions, led by Florida, which had outlawed the so-called
union shop in a statewide referendum in 1944, even before passage of Taft-
Hartley.

Corporate and agricultural interests and other proponents of right-to-
work laws hoped to capitalize on organized labor's declining public image
in the 1950s by sponsoring referenda in major industrial states. By the
1950s, it was clear that the right-to-work movement had been successful in

discouraging unionization in the South, partly because these laws made it difficult for unions to collect the dues needed to carry out their ordinary functions, and partly because they sent a message—often explicitly articulated in southern states' promotional brochures—to workers and employers that the state government was hostile to organized labor. Hence, in 1958, when the National Right to Work Committee sought passage of a right-to-work amendment to the state constitution in heavily industrialized and unionized Ohio, the labor movement mobilized in a massive effort to defeat the measure. In view of criticism by the NAACP and others about the inadequacy of organized labor's antidiscrimination efforts, AFL-CIO political operatives were initially doubtful about the voting proclivities of African Americans in the Buckeye State. Yet when the votes were counted and the right-to-work measure went down to a narrow defeat, they discovered that African Americans had voted overwhelmingly for labor's position, with fully 85 percent of black voters opposing the measure. Likewise, the narrow defeat of an Oklahoma initiative in 1964 could be attributed to the black electorate's support for labor's position. At the 1961 AFL-CIO convention, King urged the labor movement to intensify its support for black voting rights in the South. Blacks, he declared, "will vote liberal and [with] labor because they need the same liberal legislation labor needs."[47]

Throughout the heyday of the civil rights movement, relationships between organized labor and African Americans were complex and often difficult. White workers constituted the great majority of the membership and leadership of most unions, as well as that of the AFL-CIO overall. Blacks constituted about 15 percent of union members and, apart from the declining BSCP, held few leadership positions. The dramatic events and images of the civil rights era—the eloquent speeches of Dr. King, the dignity and heroism of black citizens seeking basic human rights, the assaults on peaceful demonstrators, the water hoses and snarling police dogs, the murders of civil rights workers black and white—helped create support for change in the nation's racial order among all kinds of citizens. Hence, the backing of voting rights, public accommodations laws, and an end to mandated segregation, as expressed in convention resolutions, financial contributions, and political action, aroused little controversy and much support among rank-and-file workers, at least outside the South. Public opinion polls showed that blue-collar workers were sympathetic to the cause of racial justice as advanced by the mainstream civil rights movement, as were others outside the South. And many union activists ventured south to participate in the struggle, some paying with their lives.

Still, the implications of racial change in the world of work were more contentious. Would the entry of large numbers of black workers in the building trades, for example, create labor surpluses and thus jeopardize the standards that construction unions had struggled to achieve? Would black access to skilled positions come at the expense of white workers who had had no personal role in past discrimination? The labor movement's constant exposure to racial issues, Meany and other white labor leaders believed, both denigrated organized labor's real achievements in promoting workplace equality and deflected attention from labor's demand for the expansionary economic policies that could provide jobs for white and black workers alike. Through the 1950s and into the 1960s, for all the controversy surrounding the steps the labor movement took, or failed to take, with respect to racial justice in the House of Labor, unionists continued to be strong supporters of civil rights in general. As President Kennedy's omnibus civil rights bill wound its way through Congress in 1963 and 1964, spokespeople for black workers and union leaders alike paid particular attention to what the final version of the law would say about matters of job access and employment discrimination.

6

AFFIRMATIVE ACTION AND
LABOR ACTION

The passage of pioneering civil rights legislation in the mid-1960s held great promise. In particular, the Civil Rights Act of 1964 outlawed discrimination on the basis of race in employment, thus inscribing into law a fundamental public commitment that black activists and their allies had been urging for decades. It soon became apparent, however, that the law's seemingly simple prohibition of racial discrimination was neither self-defining nor self-enforcing. Would the new law's reliance on individual litigation by those claiming discrimination blunt its impact? In carrying out the law's mandate to improve the economic situation of African Americans, was the newly created Equal Employment Opportunity Commission (EEOC) permitted—or perhaps even obligated—to consider the crippling effects of generations of prior discrimination? Would the new law lead to compensatory treatment of African American workers and thus compromise the hard-won seniority provisions of collective bargaining contracts? Even as black workers, civil rights organizations, employers, and labor unionists wrestled with these issues, the effects of sweeping reform of the country's immigration laws began a long-term process of ethnic diversification, which in turn both expanded federal antidiscrimination efforts and complicated their application to African Americans, the Civil Rights Act's initial target.

The struggle over equal employment opportunities and affirmative action did not take place in a vacuum. Throughout the 1960s and 1970s, African American workers sought through union activism to achieve material improvements and to end racist treatment in the workplace, often linking their struggles to the goals of the civil rights movement. Black workers were crucial to the expansion of union membership in public employment, the one notable exception to organized labor's numerical decline in these years. Dramatic strikes of African American sanitation, hospital, and other public workers invoked the liberationist language of the civil rights movement and brought thousands of low-wage service and public workers into the AFL-CIO.

African American workers' picket-line activism dovetailed with the goals and aspirations of the civil rights movement and, at least initially, reinforced the labor-black political coalition that undergirded the liberal domestic policies of the Lyndon Johnson administration. In addresses to labor audiences, Dr. Martin Luther King Jr. repeatedly emphasized the need for black-labor collaboration. In 1965, A. Philip Randolph's close associate Bayard Rustin authored an influential magazine article arguing the need to move "From Protest to Politics." Rustin linked the successful struggles of the civil rights movement to the ongoing battle for social and economic justice. Organized labor, with its expanded minority membership, he insisted, was a critical element in the effort to begin "refashioning our political economy."[1] By the late 1970s, however, a combination of public hostility, mounting fiscal and economic problems, and the resistance of employers—private enterprises and public authorities alike—stymied this black-led labor resurgence and inaugurated a renewed period of laborite retreat that brought new dilemmas to the race-labor nexus.

The Realm of Law

From 1964 to the early 1980s, the passage and early implementation of the nation's first federal statutory prohibition of job discrimination produced significant positive results for African American workers. Title VI of the 1964 Civil Rights Act gave statutory sanction to efforts to eliminate discrimination in firms doing business with the government. Even more promising was Title VII, which created the five-member EEOC to oversee equal employment opportunity generally. Although the language of the law itself and of the congressional debate surrounding its passage reflected a narrow, individual-rights conception of workplace equality, the staff of the EEOC, U.S. Department of Justice lawyers, and representatives of the U.S. Department of Labor's Office of Federal Contract Compliance (OFCC), aided by sympathetic federal courts, seized on ambiguities in the law's language to expand definitions of workplace equality and promote remedial action to address the effects of past discrimination. Administrative rulings in 1969 and 1970 broadened the OFCC's mandate. Amendments in 1972 to the Civil Rights Act likewise expanded the EEOC's power to monitor hiring and promotion practices, which it used to foster racial balance and "affirmative action" in recruitment, job progression, and promotion. Throughout the late 1960s and 1970s, black workers, civil rights groups, African American lawyers, and officials of both the EEOC and the OFCC won court orders and negotiated "consent decrees"—plans agreed to by employers facing punitive court judgments—that opened up a broad range of industrial employment to black workers.

Critics quickly reacted, charging that EEOC functionaries, Department of Justice and OFCC officials, and federal judges were twisting the plain language of the Civil Rights Act far beyond its simple prohibition of future discrimination. Defenders of these assertive measures, however, pointed to the 1964 law's preamble, which declared that one of its key purposes was improvement of the economic opportunities available to African Americans. Without attacking the effects of past discrimination, they argued, those charged with implementing the new law would be unable to fulfill its mandate. Failure to actively encourage the recruitment, retention, and promotion of minority workers, they held, would sanction the lowly status of African American workers and turn the promise of the new law into just another example of toothless tokenism.

Whatever the disagreements among scholars, lawyers, and politicians, African American workers had no doubt about the justice of the government's position. Their day-to-day experience told them that aptitude tests, educational qualifications, and seniority lists were often unrelated to job content, functioning primarily to perpetuate discriminatory hiring and promotion policies. Thus, in 1971, black workers applauded when the U.S. Supreme Court ruled in a landmark case, *Griggs v. Duke Power*, that the company's standardized preemployment tests were unrelated to work content and had a "disparate impact" on black applicants. Likewise, EEOC and OFCC exposure of the role that seniority provisions played in sustaining the racial status quo in the country's workplaces jibed with the long experience of black workers and fostered hopes of redress.

Around the country, but especially in the South, African American workers eagerly turned to the courts under the aegis of Titles VI and VII, aided and encouraged by the EEOC and Justice Department lawyers. The Civil Rights Act permitted complainants to seek legal redress in the form of class-action suits. It also permitted the EEOC to join these suits as "friends of the court" (amicus curiae) and to provide technical legal assistance. Moreover, the act permitted the Department of Justice to identify patterns of discrimination in a particular company or industry and to file charges without having to rely on individual complainants to inaugurate action. Title VI of the Civil Rights Act also strengthened the federal government's long-term program of attacking racial discrimination in firms doing business with the government. Along with Executive Order 11246, issued by President Johnson in September 1965, this section of the act beefed up the federal government's ability to compel firms to end discriminatory practices and, eventually, develop affirmative action plans. Thus, by the late 1960s, federal authorities in the Justice Department, the EEOC, and the OFCC were working in concert in a broad attack on racial and gender discrimination.

Class-action suits filed by ordinary workers played a key role in opening the doors of employment for black workers. In workplaces as disparate as southern textile mills, New York City newsrooms, telephone company offices, and construction sites around the country, women and African Americans of both genders came together, often without formal organization, to claim their newly established rights. And in doing so, they quickly found that the logic of equal employment opportunity impelled them to seek remedial action as the only means of overcoming the crippling effects of long-term racial and gender discrimination. Thus, what came to be called "affirmative action," though not without precedent in pre-1964 racial discourse, grew directly out of the efforts of rank-and-file men and women to give substance to the rights and opportunities inscribed in the Civil Rights Act and in closely related executive orders.

The vast southern textile industry, by far the region's largest industrial employer, was a prime site for this legal action. With the help of the NAACP and other civic and legal aid organizations, African American workers filed suit after suit, charging racial discrimination in hiring, work assignments, and promotion policies. In addition to documenting the widespread existence of ongoing racial discrimination, these cases highlighted the futility of attempting to remedy current injustices without taking into account past patterns of discrimination.

In the case involving the largest number of black textile workers, *Sledge v. J. P. Stevens* (1970), a federal district court found the South's second largest textile employer guilty of systematic discrimination in its hiring practices. In addition, the litigants demonstrated that the Stevens company routinely shunted blacks into dead-end jobs, discouraged them from seeking promotions, and burdened them with extra, uncompensated work assignments. In *Sledge* and other cases, black women established clear patterns of discriminatory hiring. For instance, whereas white women accounted for up to 40 percent of the industry's southern labor force, until the mid-1960s, black women were all but excluded from textile jobs. In other cases in the South's tobacco, pulp and paper, and garment and textile industries, African American workers demonstrated similar widespread patterns of abuse, often revealing companies' encouragement of harassment and even physical violence by white workers against blacks who tried to enter upgraded or supervisory positions. Although critics charged that the EEOC was overstepping its authority and that Title VII was causing disruption and uncertainty in American industry, black workers were eloquent in welcoming the new dispensation. Thus declared one South Carolina litigant, "The Negroes . . . were not put in this world just to do the hard, common work. The Civil Rights Act gives us certain privileges and we would like to exercise these rights now."[2]

Largely as a result of this remarkable litigation, between the early 1960s and the early 1980s, black employment in southern textile mills grew dramatically, from around 5 percent of production workers to nearly

25 percent. The sheer numbers were impressive: in 1960, mills in three leading southern textile states employed about 8,500 black workers; by 1980, the figure stood at 76,600—a ninefold increase. The gains of black women were particularly notable. In the key textile state of South Carolina, for example, between 1960 and 1970 the number of African American women employed in the mills surged from a minuscule 240 to over 8,000. Although tight labor markets, the growth of textile production, and the loss of white labor to emerging industrial sectors in the South no doubt prodded employers to look to African Americans, it was equally clear that governmental pressure, in the form of EEOC hearings and a revitalized program of federal contract compliance in an industry heavily dependent on U.S. military contracts, played a critical role. The timing of black advancement, reported two academic investigators, indicated "that government activity played an important role in integrating textiles." Or, in the words of Corine Lytle Cannon, one of the first black women hired at the large Cannon Mills in North Carolina, "That was the whole thing. It would never have been if it had not been for the Civil Rights Act. It would still be just like it were."[3]

The southern pulp and paper industry was another major battleground in the 1960s and 1970s. Unlike their counterparts in textiles, paper manufacturers had always employed substantial numbers of black workers, but they were invariably relegated to "outside" work in the wood yard or to custodial or common labor jobs. Even when black workers were given more responsible or complex assignments, they were paid at common labor rates. Since the pulp and paper industry was a relatively high-wage sector undergoing sustained expansion in the South, both aggrieved black workers and civil rights organizations targeted it for litigation. Virtually from the day Title VII became operative, complaints from African American pulp and paper workers, often facilitated by the NAACP's Legal Defense Fund, flooded into EEOC offices. Through the 1970s and into the 1980s, federal courts found large corporations such as International Paper, Weyerhaeuser, Crown-Zellerbach, and Continental Can guilty of discrimination in hiring and job placement. Nor was the union, the United Paperworkers International Union (UPIU), blameless. Indeed, into the 1970s, the UPIU maintained separate, inferior local unions for black workers and used collective bargaining contracts to protect the status and wage rates of its white members at the expense of dues-paying blacks. Thus, black workers' legal actions often named their union as codefendant. In one key example, *United States v. Local 189*, a federal district court ruled in March 1968 that the seniority provisions of the existing collective bargaining contract that froze blacks in low-wage, dead-end jobs violated Title VII. The court forced the company and the union to change the seniority system and thus open the way for blacks to advance into more skilled and responsible positions. Afterward, federal authorities relied on this case in negotiating consent decrees with other firms. The most significant of these was the Jackson Memorandum of the summer of 1968, wherein the huge International Paper Company, whose mills dotted the South, along with the UPIU, agreed to implement sweeping changes in hiring, promotion, and wage policies.

Even with the support of federal authorities and favorable court rulings, black workers had to struggle to claim their industrial rights, as white workers clung to their historical advantages. Some employers saw the new order as a way to broaden the labor pool from which they could recruit workers and hire black workers at lower wages. Many managers and personnel directors, however, held on to the myths that black workers were more prone to absenteeism and were unsuited to jobs requiring skill and judgment, often ignoring their own in-house research when it contradicted these hoary assumptions. Moreover, employers resented the intrusion of public authorities into what most regarded as the virtually sacred managerial prerogatives of hiring and firing. Thus, black workers seeking entry into factory work or trying to move from laboring into skilled positions had to enlist the help of the EEOC and the courts, and then they had to battle hostility and sometimes even threats of physical injury at the hands of white coworkers and foremen.

In 1965, at the Crown-Zellerbach plant in Bogalusa, Louisiana, for example, black workers who were finally promoted into "white" lines of progression after enduring relentless harassment and intimidation found this notice pinned to their time cards: "You have been patronized by a Knight of the Ku Klux Klan." Even two decades later, after blacks had gained some entry into desirable jobs at Florida's St. Joe Paper Company, both the employer and many white workers collaborated in discouraging blacks from seeking advancement. The first African American at St. Joe to achieve a relatively high-wage job reported a consistent pattern of resistance and antagonism at the hands of fellow workers and managers alike. "It was hard, dangerous [work]," recalled R. C. Larry. "They ride you all the time. . . . They were making it hard for me because I was the first one, the first black that ever went on the paper machine."[4]

In addition to the paper and textile industries, federal authorities moved against some of the country's leading corporations, working closely with aggrieved black workers and job aspirants. In 1968, in a case launched by two black workers, a federal district court compelled Philip Morris, one of the country's largest tobacco companies, to provide advancement opportunities for African American workers beyond those it had instituted in 1966 in compliance with the Civil Rights Act. In the 1970s, EEOC exposure of racial and gender discrimination in the Bell Telephone system led to consent decrees that increased the employment of African Americans and, at least in theory, opened up new lines of progression to women and minorities. In 1974, nine of the country's largest steel manufacturers, along with the United Steelworkers of America, signed a consent decree, modifying traditional seniority practices and providing enhanced opportunities for minorities and women to move into higher-paying and more secure jobs. Some employers, though not acknowledging past discrimination, established plans of affirmative action through the collective bargaining process, without waiting for litigation.

Efforts of black plaintiffs, supported by the EEOC and other federal agents, to broaden the Civil Rights Act's antidiscrimination coverage often entailed "affirmative action," which could mean anything from informing African Americans that historically discriminatory companies were now in compliance with the Civil Rights Act to establishing numerical targets for the hiring and upgrading of black workers. Efforts to use the law's guarantee of future nondiscrimination to offset the crippling effects of past discrimination aroused sharp opposition. White workers defended contractual seniority rights, citing language in the Civil Rights Act that protected existing collective bargaining agreements. But since many such agreements had the effect of freezing blacks permanently into undesirable jobs, black litigants, the EEOC, and eventually the federal courts sought to temper seniority provisions with plans to facilitate the hiring and upgrading of African Americans. Unions, both to avoid charges of discrimination and out of a genuine commitment to racial advance, often helped devise these plans and pledged to cooperate with employers in implementing them.

In one notable example, the United Steelworkers agreed with a Louisiana employer, Kaiser Aluminum, to implement a program of preferential training and promotion of black workers that modified the seniority provisions of the collective bargaining contract. Doing so, both company and union officials agreed, was necessary to overcome decades of discriminatory treatment that had relegated black workers to only the lowest positions on the company's job ladder. But many white union members felt betrayed, and the consent decree entered into by steel companies and the United Steelworkers in 1974 triggered outrage among many white steelworkers, who had come to regard their privileged access to better-paying jobs in the mills as an inherent right. "I can't understand my union going along with such an agreement," protested one local leader from the Pittsburgh area.[5] In Louisiana, Brian Weber, a white union member, sued both Kaiser Aluminum and the United Steelworkers, charging that this agreement violated the Civil Rights Act by sanctioning reverse discrimination. Eventually, the Supreme Court in *Kaiser Aluminum & Chemical Corporation and United Steelworkers of America, AFL-CIO v. Brian F. Weber* (1978) validated the agreement on the grounds that no public authorities were involved and that the two parties had the right to take remedial steps to give substance to the Civil Rights Act's guarantee of equal opportunity. *Weber*, however, ignited a storm of protest. "Big Labor," declared one critic, "has . . . paired with Big Business, Big Government and the Big Left to deprive Brian Weber of equal opportunity." White workers and conservative journalists and lawyers challenged hiring and promotion arrangements that sought to achieve racial balance in the workplace. Employers decried what they regarded as bureaucratic governmental interference with personnel policies. Politicians and social commentators attacked affirmative action programs, whether mandated by the EEOC, ordered by the courts, or "voluntarily" entered into to avoid litigation. So-called affirmative action, they declared, was in reality "discrimination in reverse," and it violated the plain language of the Civil Rights Act. Declared Senator Orrin Hatch, a Republican from Utah, labor-management agreements to promote racial balance in hiring and promotion constituted "the most radical assault upon the principles of equal protection and of liberty since our Republic was founded." Added conservative writer Carl Cohen, "Reverse discrimination is not an invention or a hypothesis . . . it is a sociological and legal fact."[6]

The most controversial and bitterly contested debate over affirmative action took place in the construction industry. The heavy construction sector, which involved commercial structures, road building, and most public facilities, was heavily unionized, with organizations such as the United Brotherhood of Carpenters and Joiners, the International Brotherhood of Electrical Workers, the International Union of Operating Engineers, and other craft unions supplying about three-quarters of the workers. The mix of craft specialties on building sites varied from job to job and even from day to day, so contractors relied on the unions to supply the requisite number of trained craftsmen. Since their emergence in the late nineteenth century, the building trades unions had struggled, with considerable success, to establish favorable wage, benefits, and safety standards in an industry notable for its high accident rate and economic uncertainty. Building tradesmen justified their high hourly wages as partial compensation for the industry's notorious instability and its chronic unemployment.

The building trades unions' chief means of maintaining these standards was by limiting the numbers of apprentices and hence the supply of workers. Restriction of entry into the trades through union-controlled apprenticeship programs, they argued, was also necessary for reasons of occupational safety and sound construction practices. Because they worked in diverse environments and with fellow workers who were often strangers to them, building tradesmen believed that only a common, union-oriented program of training and certification could provide the confidence and stability workers needed for self-protection and for efficient operations. Unions such as the plumbers, ironworkers, and electrical workers jealously guarded the doors of entry, the allocation of slots in apprenticing programs, and the seniority lists that governed job referrals. Thus, it was common for local unions to give preferential treatment to relatives and friends of current members and to favor applicants of particular ethnic groups or religious backgrounds.

From their inception in the late nineteenth and early twentieth centuries, the major building trades unions had used racial exclusion to restrict entry into their trades to white men, thus imposing an early form of de facto affirmative action in behalf of whites. These unions barred blacks from apprenticeship programs, struck or boycotted construction sites where nonunion workers were employed, and secured the passage and enforcement of state and municipal licensing ordinances that required the employment of union (i.e., white) workers. The federal Davis-Bacon Act of 1931, which required contractors to pay union-established wages in federally funded projects, had been inspired at least in part by a determination to eliminate competition from lower-wage minority workers. Thus, it is not surprising that in 1960, only 1.5 percent of electricians, 3.3 percent of plumbers, and 4.4 percent of carpenters were African American. Only among laborers were black workers in the building trades significantly represented, constituting almost 26 percent of that group.[7] "Today," declared one critic in 1968, "there are fewer Negro plumbers or electricians than Negro Ph.D.s." Added an Urban League official, "Exclusion in the craft unions is so complete that segregation would be a step forward."[8]

Jobs in the building trades were as desirable as they were visible. Wage rates were high, and the fact that the trades required formal training and apprenticeships gave them a unique prestige among blue-collar workers. Erecting a convention center or building an interstate highway contrasted sharply with repetitive machine tending or a demeaning service-sector job. For many, toiling at a skilled trade among burly fellow construction workers in open view epitomized a rare and valued combination of manly skill, strength, and autonomy. If federal programs of equal employment opportunity and strict contract compliance were to have real meaning, many black workers and civil rights advocates insisted, they had to target the contractors and building trades unions that controlled this lucrative and prestigious work.

Since much construction work, especially in urban areas, was visible to the public, the virtually all-white composition of the workforce was a constant reminder in both northern and southern cities of a racial hierarchy that shut blacks out of skilled jobs and relegated them, at best, to common labor. Before the advent of the modern civil rights movement, African Americans could do little more than decry the massive discrimination that characterized construction. But as blacks became increasingly assertive after World War II, the anomaly of a lily-white labor force building the roadways, commercial establishments, and public facilities in the nation's urban centers—where a growing number of African Americans were migrating—triggered increasingly strident protest. In the 1960s, demands for the recruitment and employment of black workers, especially on projects involving public funds, escalated. Well before the passage of the Civil Rights Act, the NAACP and other local organizations around the country picketed job sites, often employing tactics designed to attract the media and dramatize the restrictive actions of the building trades unions.

Moreover, African Americans who sought entry into construction work found that they had some unlikely allies in the business community and in the Republican Party. During the war-fed economic boom of the 1960s, inflationary pressures were strong. Contractors identified union work rules and restrictive apprenticing requirements as key factors in rising construction costs. An attack on the building trades unions' discriminatory recruitment practices, some economists argued, would bring an influx of new minority workers, which in turn would force wages down, eliminate objectionable work rules and jurisdictional bottlenecks, and permit a more flexible use of labor. Thus, doing the right thing in terms of civil rights would reap the dual benefit of reducing labor costs and undermining the building trades unions. In the words of a longtime critic of organized labor, "The civil rights issue may well provide a means of solving some construction problems. . . . Minority groups are the best potential sources of . . . craftsmen. . . . I look on the civil rights problem not only as one that must be solved for its own sake . . . but also as a means of helping to alleviate the shortage of construction craftsmen." One national business magazine was more direct: in October 1969, referring to the fact that protests against discrimination in urban construction projects were often timed for the beginning of the workweek, *Fortune* headlined that "Black Mondays Are Good for US."[9]

The struggle to integrate the building trades was long and contentious. Militant blacks picketed construction sites, confronted union apologists, and filed dozens of lawsuits. Rank-and-file white workers responded by attacking protesters, boycotting projects when contractors hired nonunion workers to meet EEOC requirements, and exerting their considerable political influence in local governments to protect existing practices. Building trades union leaders reacted ambivalently. On the one hand, they saw attacks on their hiring halls and seniority lists as merely the latest effort by employers to cripple their unions. They accused their critics of using inflammatory racial issues as an excuse to lower wages and impose dangerous work practices. Thus, shortly after passage of the Civil Rights Act, Peter T. Schoemann, president of the plumbers union, provocatively denounced "spoon feeding or coddling or giving special breaks to anybody because of the color of their skin."[10]

On the other hand, the building trades unions *were* vulnerable. Beginning in the late 1960s, one of the most dramatic effects of the civil rights movement was the election of African American mayors and city council members in some of the country's largest cities. Clearly, building tradesmen would have to at least make gestures of compliance with the Civil Rights Act and appear to be cooperating with public authorities by opening construction jobs to blacks. Declared Schoemann in 1968, "it is absolutely imperative that we institute affirmative action programs." Yes, he told his overwhelmingly white membership, it would not be the lawyers, federal bureaucrats, and corporate executives who would pay the price for integration of the building trades; rather, the blue-collar white worker "will be threatened economically by the rise of the Negro multitudes." But, he counseled, if his union and the other building trades failed to adopt some form of outreach and training, they would invite more drastic and threatening federal and corporate action later on. "The way to take the castor oil," he advised, "is to take it in a big dose now."[11]

Controversy over affirmative action in the construction industry came to a head in the late 1960s and early 1970s. Through the mid- to late 1960s, the sometimes raucous confrontations between civil rights adherents and white building tradesmen in virtually every large American city often shared headlines with violent racial upheavals in places such as Los Angeles, Newark, Detroit, Chicago, and Washington, D.C. During the Johnson administration (1963–1969), federal authorities, motivated by both a desire to improve conditions among black urban dwellers and a hope that employment gains would help deflate these bitter outbursts, developed numerical targets for the hiring of minority workers in federally funded projects in various cities. In the late 1960s, the situation in Philadelphia emerged as a kind of test case for this sort of affirmative action. With a population that was about 30 percent African American, the Pennsylvania metropolis was experiencing a downtown building boom. Over half a billion dollars in federal funds was slated to pour in for the construction of a hospital, a new U.S. Mint, and buildings at the University of Pennsylvania. The heavily unionized local building trades anticipated years of steady, high-wage employment. But civil rights activists were determined to gain a share of this largess for African American workers, who, they pointed out, were almost completely absent from the building trades unions. The ironworkers local, for example, included only 12 African Americans among its 850 members, while only 3 of the plumbers union's 500 members were black. Large locals of sheet metal workers, elevator installers, and stonemasons had no minority members at all.[12]

Officials in the new Nixon administration (1969–1974) saw the situation in Philadelphia as an opportunity to advance key racial, economic, and political objectives. Assistant Secretary of Labor Arthur Fletcher, a long-term critic of the restrictive practices of the building trades unions, revised a plan initially outlined by the Johnson administration under which Philadelphia's OFCC would establish numerical targets for the recruitment of black and other minority workers. Over a five-year period, according to what became known as the Philadelphia Plan, minority participation would rise in yearly increments from its current abysmally low level to about 20 percent. Contractors and unions were to file detailed reports on their efforts to recruit minorities and had to satisfy Department of Labor and OFCC officials that they were making "good-faith" efforts to expand minority representation. When queried as to whether the plan's goals constituted hiring quotas, which were presumably prohibited by the Civil Rights Act, Secretary of Labor George Shultz responded that a quota system for black workers already existed in the Philadelphia construction industry. "We found a quota system" in place, he told reporters. "It was there. It was zero."[13]

Richard Nixon's campaign for the presidency in 1968 had not been notable for its concern with civil rights. But the president believed that Republicans could appeal effectively to business-oriented blacks. As the assistant secretary of labor responsible for employment standards, Fletcher had long been an advocate of black capitalism and of market-driven solutions to blacks' economic problems. Moreover, both he and Shultz, along with Nixon's other economic advisers, were convinced that a critical component of the rising inflation of the late 1960s was a combination of the construction boom, significantly fueled by federal funds, and restrictions in the labor supply imposed by the building trades unions. Recruitment of minority workers would, they believed, increase the pool of building tradesmen and thus help moderate the unions' wage demands. Finally, Nixon's political strategists believed that programs such as the Philadelphia Plan could not help but drive a wedge between two of the Democratic Party's core constituencies—organized labor and African Americans. As Nixon aide John Ehrlichman later recalled, "the unions hated the whole thing [the Philadelphia Plan]. Before long, the AFL-CIO and the NAACP were locked in combat . . . and the Nixon Administration was located in the sweet and reasonable middle."[14]

It was true that most trade unionists bridled at the Philadelphia Plan and similar programs devised for other cities. "We are 100 percent opposed to a quota system, whether it be called the Philadelphia plan or whatever," one union leader declared. AFL-CIO president George Meany, whose career had begun in the plumbers union, was outspoken in his condemnation. As a high-ranking union leader, Meany had consistently supported civil rights legislation and regarded labor's alliance with African American voters a key component of the liberal-labor coalition. But he believed that it was a mistake to focus on the racial policies of the building trades unions.

The key to black economic advance, he argued, was economic growth. The energies of civil rights supporters should be directed toward expansionary fiscal policies and legislation to boost employment and income among working people of all racial groups. Whereas the fight for lower interest rates, more generous Social Security and unemployment benefits, and a higher minimum wage united working people, the imposition of hiring quotas pitted white and black workers against each other and weakened the labor movement. Moreover, he argued, the labor movement generally, and even the much-maligned building trades unions, exhibited a greater degree of racial integration and had done more to benefit black workers and their families than any other American institution. One saw few black faces in the corporate offices, the banks, the newspapers, and the television stations, he noted. "But we in the Building Trades are singled out as 'the last bastion of discrimination.'" Nixon and his henchmen, Meany charged, "are trying to make a whipping boy out of the Building Trades."[15]

The Philadelphia Plan and other affirmative action programs in the construction industry triggered a sharp backlash among rank-and-file white workers and members of Congress. Senator Everett Dirksen, the Minority Leader, told Nixon, "I myself will not be able to support you on this ill-conceived scheme." Indeed, the president would soon find that, among lawmakers, the plan was "about as popular as a crab in a whorehouse."[16] Construction workers in Pittsburgh, Chicago, and elsewhere confronted administration officials with angry mass demonstrations and pledges of painful political retaliation. Nonetheless, in February 1970, Shultz issued an order that required all businesses holding federal contracts to adopt affirmative action plans, with a view to achieving a racial balance in the workplace similar to that in the surrounding community. At the stroke of a pen, more than a quarter million businesses, employing twenty million workers, were, at least in theory, required to file detailed hiring goals and indicate how they were going to be achieved.

Shultz's Order No. 4 brought to the fore another issue as well. In 1965, Congress had replaced the 1924 National Origins Immigration Act with a radically different measure eliminating ethnic and racial categories in the admission of immigrants. Throughout the postwar period, immigration from Europe had stagnated, and discriminatory quotas had kept the number of newcomers from Asia small. The end of quotas and restrictions on Asians, along with a booming U.S. job market and intense population pressures in Mexico and other Latin American countries, encouraged a new wave of immigrants. In the 1970s and 1980s, the number of legal immigrants from Asia and Latin America soared. In the 1970s, for example, 1.6 million people of Asian origin came to the United States, followed by an additional 1.75 million in the 1980s. In that decade, legal Mexican immigrants totaled 1.66 million. Whereas the 1965 act had envisioned a yearly total of about 330,000 immigrants, by 1982, the annual average had swollen to almost 600,000, the overwhelming majority from Asia and Latin America.[17]

This influx, along with the relatively high birthrate among newcomers, began to change the basic demographic profile of the American people. Thus, Shultz's Order No. 4, along with other Title VI and Title VII enforcement measures, now routinely included people of Hispanic, Asian, and other ethnic descent as being among those entitled to antidiscrimination protection—and thus to affirmative action treatment. It was hard to oppose the broadening of antidiscrimination mandates, but in doing so, federal officials inadvertently deflected attention from African Americans—the group the Civil Rights Act of 1964 had explicitly targeted for help. Although both Hispanics and Asians had suffered historically from discrimination and exclusion, none had been slaves, and none had endured the full range of Jim Crow restrictions. Certainly, new entrants from Mexico, Korea, China, and other non-Western countries had neither themselves nor as part of an ethnic cohort suffered from systematic, legalized racial oppression, as had virtually all African Americans. Moreover, evidence suggested that, despite the Civil Rights Acts, prejudice against blacks remained far stronger than that directed against other racial and ethnic minorities.[18]

In part because the Immigration Act of 1965 made desirable job skills the determining factor in establishing the eligibility of those seeking entry, the educational and economic profiles of post-1965 immigrants were relatively high. In particular, evidence accumulated that a large proportion of people migrating to the United States from Asia after 1965 brought substantial financial and educational resources with them. Thus, affirmative action programs initially designed to assist African Americans often benefited new immigrants who had neither participated in the decades of social protest that led to the civil rights legislation nor suffered the variety and intensity of discrimination that generations of African Americans had. In fact, the sweeping new affirmative action regulations introduced during the Nixon administration sometimes helped those who had little need for special consideration. Through the 1970s and into the 1980s, the very term "affirmative action" became anathema to many Americans, who equated it with special, unmerited privileges. Meanwhile, Americans' hostility toward such "preferential" treatment in educational admissions and employment was concentrated on its application to African Americans; they showed little concern when men and women of Asian or Latin American descent were the beneficiaries.[19]

Actual application of Order No. 4's bold affirmative action mandates was spotty and inconsistent. Responding to white backlash to the Philadelphia Plan and eager to cultivate white building tradesmen, who were considered leading supporters of Nixon's Vietnam War policies, the Department of Labor and the OFCC backed away from its stern mandates. Instead, throughout the mid-1970s, federal officials encouraged the development of so-called hometown plans in various large cities, schemes by which local political leaders, unionists, and contractors would establish minority employment goals, which were loosely monitored by the OFCC. Almost universally, the hometown plans resulted in little progress in minority hiring and soon came under harsh attack by civil rights forces.

As for the broader implications of Order No. 4, neither the Department of Labor nor the OFCC possessed adequate financial or manpower resources to monitor the quarter million federal contractors it covered. Indeed, the order's combination of sweeping and seemingly hard-and-fast affirmative action requirements, on the one hand, and weak to nonexistent enforcement, on the other, tended to discredit the very concept of affirmative action as being both too intrusive and too ineffectual. Thus, in 1976, NAACP labor secretary Herbert Hill, contrasting Order No. 4's broad assertions with the OFCC's uncertain implementation, called the agency (renamed the Office of Federal Contract Compliance Programs in 1975) "functionally useless" as an agent of black progress in employment.[20]

Still, in the decade and a half after passage of the Civil Rights Act, African American workers made some important gains. Even in the building trades, despite the foot-dragging and outright hostility of construction unions, blacks made progress. Between 1970 and 1974, for example, almost half the new members of the building trades unions were African Americans and members of other minority groups. For all their resistance, the AFL-CIO's construction unions trained more black workers in their apprenticeship programs than were trained in a variety of job-training schemes devised for the nonunion construction sector. The desegregation of the textile industry, advances in the pulp and paper industry, and opportunities won through court rulings and consent decrees in other fields changed the "color of work" in the United States. Through the 1970s, the average earnings of black workers, measured as a percentage of white workers' wages, grew dramatically. By the mid-1970s, the yearly earnings of black males working full time were almost 75 percent of those of white workers, sharply up from the 60 percent of the early 1960s. For black women, the gains were even sharper, rising from 68 percent in 1964 to 90 percent a decade later.[21]

Were these gains the basis for a new, egalitarian economic dispensation for African Americans? Could the political coalition of blacks and organized labor, as envisaged by Randolph and Rustin, surmount job site conflicts and provide the basis for liberal advance? Much depended on the general performance of the economy, for a sharp downturn could mean a return to the old theme of "last hired, first fired" and roll back these hard-won achievements. In addition, sustained economic advance for African Americans depended on the political climate. Governmental support for black litigants under Title VII and federal sponsorship of affirmative action had been crucial, but these methods had also aroused intense popular and political opposition. An economic downturn and the election of critics of the aggressive pursuit of workplace equality and of affirmative action would no doubt test the stability and permanency of black workers' gains.

Civil Rights and Labor Struggles, 1963–1981

In the last third of the twentieth century (and into the twenty-first), the U.S. labor movement fell on hard times. Early in this period, however, signs of renewed labor activism abounded. Through the late 1960s and into the early 1970s, workers exhibited a degree of strike activity not seen since the end of World War II. And while union membership in the private sector continued to stagnate, organization among public employees surged. African American workers played key roles in these developments, as black sanitation, janitorial, and hospital workers filled the ranks of revitalized public employee unions, which in turn brought issues of social and economic equity into the forefront of the struggle for civil rights.

However, as African American politicians rose to power in major cities and faced mounting fiscal crises, they often found themselves combating the very unions they had once seen as allies in the civil rights struggle. The defeat of a sanitation workers strike in Atlanta in 1977, when African American mayor Maynard Jackson fired hundreds of poorly paid black trash collectors, set the tone for the new antiunion dispensation. The federal government's crushing of a strike by more than eleven thousand air traffic controllers in 1981 sent a message to employers everywhere that attacks on organized labor were the order of the day. For the next quarter century, a reeling labor movement struggled to find ways to recoup its sagging fortunes and to energize liberal-labor political action. During this time of trial, African Americans remained among the most union-minded of American workers, although critics complained that even a reformed labor movement was failing to acknowledge the centrality of their role in labor's political and organizational life.

Although overshadowed by racial, environmental, feminist, and antiwar protests, labor militancy was alive and well in the 1960s and early 1970s. A decade-long strike wave began in 1966. In 1970, more than 5,700 strikes entailed the loss of over 66 million workdays. Almost three dozen of these walkouts involved at least 10,000 workers each, the largest number of such strikes since the Korean War. During 1970, one-sixth of the nation's 14 million union members—including 200,000 postal workers, whose summer walkout defied the federal government—were on strike at one time or another. Major walkouts—some of them erupting over the objections of established union leaders—punctuated the first half of the 1970s.[22]

Public employees were at the heart of this activism. Until the 1960s, few of the men and women who worked for municipal, state, or federal governments had belonged to unions. In many political jurisdictions, union membership was illegal. But beginning in the late 1950s and gathering force through the next decade, public employees, led by teachers, sanitation workers, and hospital and social service employees, flocked into unions such as the American Federation of Teachers (AFT), the American Federation of State, County, and Municipal Employees (AFSCME), and Hospital Workers Local 1199. The National Education Association (NEA), hitherto a bland professional organization, became a militant labor union, enrolling over a million members. In all, between 1955 and 1973, membership in public employee unions expanded from around 400,000 to over 4 million. During this period, a booming economy, growth in the number of public workers, inflationary pressures, and a growing sense of entitlement among public employees (traditionally regarded as humble "public servants") combined to fuel this activism. In response to the rising political and economic power of public employees, thirty-seven states passed laws acknowledging the right of state and municipal workers to organize and bargain collectively. In January 1962, President John F. Kennedy issued Executive Order 10988, legitimating—indeed, seemingly encouraging—the unionization of federal employees.

African Americans were at the center of much of this activism. Since at least the 1940s, blacks' representation in public employment had been proportionately greater than that of whites. Moreover, the federal War on Poverty of the mid-1960s both expanded federal payrolls and funded increased employment of state and local workers. Blacks were heavily represented among poorly paid (and often disdainfully treated) general labor, sanitation, and nonprofessional hospital staffs. Through the 1960s, the rising tide of the civil rights movement, with its mass mobilization, its invocation of human rights, and its righteous indignation over exclusion and mistreatment, swept up thousands of African Americans who toiled in low-wage and ill-appreciated work. It was a short step from demanding equal rights in schools, restaurants, and voting booths to demanding higher wages, improved working conditions, and fair treatment from the politicians and administrators who ran hospitals, oversaw garbage collection, and managed other public services in the nation's states and cities.

In linking civil rights to labor activism, black workers had an eloquent advocate in Dr. Martin Luther King Jr. After passage of the Civil Rights Acts of 1964 and 1965, King increasingly turned his attention to questions of economic inequality, and the Southern Christian Leadership Conference

(SCLC), which he headed, inaugurated a Poor People's Campaign at the end of 1967. From the time of the Montgomery bus boycott of 1955–1956, which had launched his career as the public tribune of the civil rights movement, King had worked closely with labor activists. Although the AFL-CIO did not formally endorse the August 28, 1963, March on Washington, many affiliated unions had done so, and some estimates held that at least a quarter of the 250,000 people who gathered at the Lincoln Memorial to hear King's "I have a dream" speech were trade unionists. Unions such as the United Automobile Workers (UAW), the United Packinghouse Workers, and the AFT helped fund SCLC activities and provided both money and manpower for voter registration drives and civil rights marches in the South. For King and his colleagues in the SCLC, the civil rights movement would not be complete without an attack on the economic inequality that afflicted both whites and blacks and that, in their view, compromised the nation's democratic pretensions. Despite the complicity of some unions in workplace discrimination, King believed that organized labor could be a potent force for social justice and an ally in the effort to bring civil rights into the economic realm. Indeed, in 1961, King had reminded delegates to the AFL-CIO national convention that "Negroes are almost entirely a working people" and had declared that "our needs are identical with labor's needs. . . . any crisis which lacerates you [is] a crisis in which we bleed."[23]

After 1965, King began shifting attention to problems of housing, employment, and economic development in the northern cities, but it was in the South that some of the most dramatic examples of the fusion of civil rights and labor rights emerged. In a number of cities, African American sanitation workers and hospital employees rebelled against poverty-level wages and demeaning treatment at the hands of white managers and supervisors, using the vehicle of trade unionism to give voice to their racially inflected grievances. In Bakersfield, California, St. Petersburg, Florida, Atlanta, Georgia, and other cities, sanitation workers formed unions and struck in protest over low wages, unsafe working conditions, and chronic maltreatment. During the second half of the 1960s, the number of sanitation workers on strike each year averaged almost eleven thousand, and the number of strikes more than doubled compared with the number occurring earlier in the decade. Although most of these strikes were illegal, the fact that most sanitation workers in these cities were African American quickly transformed these labor disputes into civil rights crusades. In the November 1966 St. Petersburg walkout, for example, the city's African American community quickly rallied to the strikers' defense when the city manager threatened to fire 350 sanitation workers. This was not merely a labor dispute, declared civil rights leaders, and the state NAACP director vowed to "get the total [black] community behind the garbage men." In the end, city officials backed down, rescinding the order to fire the strikers and instituting more equitable personnel policies, although still refusing to recognize the union.[24]

In the winter and spring of 1968, the connection between civil rights and labor activism reached a peak in the Memphis, Tennessee, sanitation workers strike. The walkout began on February 13 when thirteen hundred black sanitation workers struck. In one sense, their demands were quintessential labor demands—better pay, improved working conditions, greater job security. However, the immediate trigger for the strike was an incident that starkly illustrated the racial injustices that lay at the heart of the city's management of garbage collection. For decades, black workers had been relegated only to the most arduous and insecure jobs in the sanitation department. The city avoided the expense of buying safer and more sanitary equipment by requiring that the garbage men transfer household refuse into leaky leather buckets, lug the buckets to the antiquated trucks, and dump the contents in. Recalled one worker, "You carried those tubs on your head and shoulders. Most of the tubs were leakin' and that stuff was fallin' all over you."[25] For this work, sanitation men received wages so low that many qualified for federal food stamps and other welfare benefits. Moreover, on rainy days—of which Memphis had many—black workers were sent home without pay while white workers remained "on the clock."

It was the tragic result of this practice that triggered the initial walkout. Early in February, two black sanitation workers sought shelter during a rainstorm in one of the old garbage trucks, and they were crushed to death when the truck's powerful compactor malfunctioned. Their deaths drove home the discrimination and ill treatment that characterized the labor policies of the Memphis Public Works Department. For several years, local activists had been attempting, with little success, to build an AFSCME local among the sanitation workers, but the men's deaths, along with the city's failure to accept responsibility for employing defective equipment, galvanized the sanitation workers and triggered the February 13 walkout.

By 1968, the heyday of the civil rights movement was past. The Freedom Rides of the early 1960s, the marches and demonstrations against segregation, and the pathbreaking federal legislation of 1964 and 1965 had begun a veritable revolution in the South. But the plight of the sanitation workers served as a reminder that formal, legal equality would remain an abstraction without decent pay and safe working conditions. Leaders of the strike, which quickly brought national AFSCME leaders into the city, appealed to Memphis's substantial black middle-class and professional communities for support. Stressing the connection between work and citizenship, the striking workers adopted as their rallying cry, replicated on hundreds of posters and placards, the slogan "I *am* a man." For their part, city officials refused to meet with strikers' representatives and blamed outside agitators for inflaming the workers.

As the strike wore on, national AFSCME leaders Jerry Wurf and William Lucy appealed to Memphis's local unions and to national labor organizations for financial and moral support. With few exceptions, they found the local labor council (dominated by the building trades unions, which had few black members) unresponsive and even dismissive. AFSCME, which was in the midst of a massive growth in membership, ultimately contributed more than $500,000 to sustain the Memphis strikers. AFL-CIO president George Meany kicked in $25,000, telling Wurf that he was with the embattled AFSCME Local 1733 "money, marbles, and chalk" and urging the federation's affiliates to assist as well.[26] Other unions such as the UAW, United Steelworkers, and Communications Workers made donations. Dr. Martin Luther King Jr.'s decision to go to Memphis in support of the strikers ensured that the strike would receive national attention.

Indeed, the actual conduct of the strike, which lasted until April, took on the character of a civil rights demonstration rather than a labor-management dispute. At various times, unionists occupied the city council's chambers to protest Mayor Henry Loeb's refusal to meet with worker representatives, enlisted the support of the city's black clergy and civil rights organizations to mount mass marches through downtown, and called on national civil rights supporters to publicize and advance their cause. On March 18, King addressed a mass meeting at the Memphis Mason Temple, explicitly linking the sanitation workers' struggle to the ongoing southern freedom struggle. Echoing the prevailing notion of appropriate gender roles, King linked the workers' low wages and lowly status with black southerners' quest for recognition of their manhood. "We are tired of our men being emasculated so that our wives and daughters have to go out and work in the white lady's kitchen," he declared. And he warned the strikers not to "let anybody tell you to go back on the job and paternalistically say, 'Now, you are my men, and I'm going to do the right thing for you.'"[27]

King pledged to return to Memphis to lead a protest march and to otherwise buoy the labor–civil rights coalition that was forming in support of the strike. He did so twice, first on March 28, and then again on April 3. The March 28 demonstration, however, erupted into mayhem, with militant young blacks challenging King's nonviolent approach and breaking from the marchers' ranks to smash windows and confront battle-ready police. Declared one dissident, "We've got to do some *fighting*. Not marching—fighting!"[28] Memphis's overwhelmingly white police force was only too ready to respond in kind, clubbing and macing marchers indiscriminately. Though shaken by the violence, in which one young African American was killed and scores were beaten, King returned to the city to lead another march, scheduled for April 5, but this one would be organized and controlled directly by his trusted lieutenants. On the evening of the fourth, as he stood on the balcony outside his room at the Lorraine Motel, King was shot to death by a gunman, identified as James Earl Ray.

Insofar as national attention was concerned, the successful conclusion of the strike was an anticlimax. King's tragic death spurred negotiations. After ten days of acrimonious talks orchestrated by a veteran federal labor expert sent to Memphis by President Lyndon Johnson, the two sides came to an uneasy agreement. On April 16, sanitation workers ratified a settlement that included the city's formal recognition of Local 1733, a modest pay increase, and the city's pledge to continue discussing in good faith such matters as sick leave, overtime, pensions, and other issues. Provisions permitting workers to have their union dues automatically deducted by a credit union ensured that the AFSCME local would have the financial and organizational strength to establish itself firmly and go on to organize other low-wage city and school board employees.

A number of other sanitation workers strikes were, like the Memphis strike, deeply enmeshed in the civil rights movement. The same was true in the organization of low-wage hospital workers in New York, Charleston, Baltimore, and elsewhere. Spearheading innovative attempts to organize nurse's aides, cafeteria and maintenance workers, orderlies, and other hospital service workers was a unique labor organization, Hospital Workers Local 1199, headquartered in New York City. With its origins in the heady labor radicalism of the 1930s, this union was nominally a local of the Retail, Wholesale, and Department Store Workers Union, a small CIO (and, after 1955, AFL-CIO) affiliate. In the 1950s, however, the union began branching out from its initial clientele of pharmacists and other drugstore workers to recruit hospital employees. The vast majority of those doing the housekeeping, maintenance, and medical support work in New York City's hospitals were African Americans and other people of color. Local 1199 officers and organizers, imbued with egalitarian zeal, reached out to civil rights organizations and community groups, developing innovative cultural programs that celebrated ethnic diversity and the contributions of African Americans, Puerto Ricans, and other minorities. Union president Leon Davis declared, "The fight of the hospital workers is symbolic of all the problems of the minority groups in the city." Another leader went further, asserting the connection between labor activism in New York and the black freedom struggle in the South. "Really and truthfully," recalled Doris Turner, "they were one [struggle], just being waged on different fronts, different places."[29] By the mid-1960s, Local 1199 had organized thousands of low-wage New York hospital workers and had established itself as a living embodiment of the race-labor nexus.

In 1969, Local 1199 leaders, eager to expand, took the message of race-based union activism into the South. In Charleston, South Carolina, the grievances of the overwhelmingly black nonprofessional staff of the Medical College Hospital of the University of South Carolina had been festering for years. The Magnolia City's white elites boasted of racial harmony, pointing to cordial relations between civic leaders and Charleston's well-established black middle and professional class. But in the hospitals, hundreds of black women toiled as aides, cafeteria workers, and maintenance and janitorial staff for poverty-level wages. Medical College Hospital employed no black nurses or doctors. White workers, no matter how young and inexperienced, barked orders at black coworkers, no matter how skilled or proficient, and generally treated them with disdain. Formal job descriptions, promotion ladders, and rules governing workplace discipline and rewards were nonexistent, breeding insecurity and frustration. Beginning in 1967, groups of workers began holding clandestine meetings with a view to discussing their grievances with hospital managers. Initially, the dissident workers were not seeking union representation, but the hospital administration's unwillingness to even meet with workers impelled rank-and-file leader Mary Moultrie, a nurse's aide, to contact Local 1199. Committed to the proposition that labor rights and civil rights were fundamentally connected, and eager to expand from their New York base, Local 1199 leaders agreed to assist the Charleston workers. They dispatched a staff representative to the city and chartered the Medical College Hospital group as Hospital Workers Local 1199B.

Through the early months of 1969, hospital administrator Dr. William McCord refused to meet with workers' representatives. On March 18, after a particularly frustrating effort to air their concerns, one hundred Medical College Hospital workers engaged in a short protest in the hospital's auditorium. McCord responded by firing twelve activists, including Moultrie. On March 20, in response, some three hundred workers went out on strike, demanding recognition of the union and reinstatement of their twelve colleagues. McCord refused to acknowledge these demands, stating only that he was "not about to turn a 25 million dollar complex over to a bunch of people who don't have a grammar school education."[30]

The strike lasted for over three months. From the outset, Local 1199B activists and national union organizers portrayed the strike as a civil rights struggle. The unique dynamics of the black community in Charleston, however, made this effort difficult. Many of the city's three hundred black clergymen, though committed to improved conditions for African Americans, identified closely with white business and governmental elites and regarded the sometimes raucous actions of the hospital workers and their supporters as detrimental to the gradual progress they believed they were making. A group of pro-union clergymen emerged, however, and invited representatives of the SCLC to Charleston to mobilize the black community in the

AFFIRMATIVE ACTION AND LABOR ACTION 197

strikers' behalf. National labor organizations competed with one another to make financial contributions, and New York schoolchildren and college students sent donations. On Mother's Day, SCLC chair Ralph Abernathy, Coretta Scott King, Local 1199 president Leon Davis, and UAW president Walter Reuther, along with six northern congressmen, led a march and rally that drew ten thousand supporters.

Jailed local activists were eloquent in connecting this labor struggle to the fight for racial justice. The union, said one worker, was "like an oak tree in a petrified forest." It was time, she insisted, to "decide now or forget forever the hope of becoming a real American citizen." One of the original twelve fired nurse's aides vowed to a reporter that even though she, her husband, and their two young daughters were faced with eviction for nonpayment of rent, "I won't go back until they realize black people are entitled to have a union too."[31]

In the end, the strike's settlement in June was a mixed bag. Union negotiators backed off from the demand for union recognition, agreeing to the establishment of a new, presumably authoritative grievance procedure in which workers were entitled to "outside" (i.e., union) representation. The state legislature increased the hospital's budget, permitting a modest wage increase. Negotiators hammered out a compromise by which the hospital administration would cooperate with a credit union to have union members' dues deducted from their paychecks, presumably providing Local 1199B with a stable financial footing, which in turn would enable it to press for formal recognition at a future date. National union leaders, well aware that the settlement was less than optimal, nonetheless hoped that it would lead to subsequent improvements. Workers celebrated the end of the strike, agreeing with influential Charleston clergyman Henry Grant—whose sympathy for the strikers had been coupled with skepticism about the goals and tactics of Local 1199B—that the settlement was "more than a compromise. . . . It was a victory."[32]

As things turned out, however, Local 1199B did not have the staying power necessary for long-term success. Almost immediately, hospital administrators reneged on key parts of the agreement. By now, however, the national union was pursuing organizing prospects in a number of other locales and provided little ongoing support. Gradually, Local 1199B lost membership and was in no position to confront a management that felt free to ignore the leaderless organization. Within a year, the union had disbanded and returned its charter to New York City.

Yet in a larger sense, the Charleston strike was successful in advancing the human rights agenda shared by union activists and civil rights adherents. In the city itself, it exposed the poverty and racism that lurked beneath the public facade of racial harmony. In the wake of the strike, black voter registration mushroomed, and black representation on the city commission and in its legislative delegation grew accordingly. More generally, declared a key African American strike supporter, "The important thing was a changing of . . . blacks' attitudes—that you are not helpless. . . . You are somebody."[33]

For Hospital Workers Local 1199, the Charleston experience provided important lessons that its organizers used in subsequent campaigns. Union publicists produced a film documenting the Charleston struggle, *I Am Somebody*, in which ordinary workers spoke eloquently about what that struggle meant to them. Within weeks of the Charleston settlement, Local 1199 had established unions in several other cities, using *I Am Somebody* as an effective organizing tool. Its most notable campaign took place in Baltimore later in 1969, where the union waged a lengthy strike involving hundreds of African American hospital support and maintenance workers at Johns Hopkins University Hospital. Once again, the union enlisted the SCLC and Mrs. King, this time to help mobilize the East Baltimore black community in behalf of the ill-treated workers. The hospital workers' slogan "Union Power, Soul Power" resonated convincingly in the Maryland city and helped provide the impetus for an overwhelming union election victory and the creation of a stable and effective local union there.[34]

Although those urging a melding of union and civil rights struggles enjoyed some notable successes, race relations within the labor movement often continued to be abrasive and sometimes destructive. The unique atmosphere of the 1960s, with dissident activists challenging all established institutions and long-term leaders, permeated the labor movement as well. Critics of the AFL-CIO's lethargy in purging the labor movement of racial segregation and discrimination became more vociferous. However, even labor organizations with records of racial progressivism found themselves under attack. Two episodes, one involving the UAW and the other the rapidly expanding AFT, illustrated the often abrasive confrontations between black militants and established leaders, even those with strong civil rights credentials.

Throughout the postwar period, the UAW, under the leadership of Walter Reuther, enjoyed a strong reputation as a dynamic and progressive force, not only with respect to the contracts it won for its own members but in the broader community as well. UAW leaders had consistently backed civil rights legislation and had contributed manpower and money to the southern civil rights movement. At the August 1963 March on Washington, the UAW had provided important logistical and financial support, and Reuther had been among the speakers preceding King at the Lincoln Memorial. In the South, the international union compelled its locals to desegregate, often in the face of the militant racism of white members. The UAW's contracts with the major automakers and automotive industry suppliers brought high wages, medical insurance, pension rights, and other significant benefits to its members, who in the late 1960s included about 300,000 black workers, about half of them working in Detroit-area plants.

But there was a less admirable side to the UAW as well. African American workers were overwhelmingly concentrated in the lowest job grades. The union's Skilled Trades Department, from which Reuther himself had come, remained virtually lily-white. Skilled white autoworkers proved to be even more effective than the notorious building trades in freezing blacks out of apprentice programs and desirable, high-wage jobs. For all his public dynamism and advocacy of racial justice, Reuther, critics charged, was dilatory and ineffectual in his efforts to end racial discrimination in the union itself. Reuther's highly publicized support for civil rights in the South, one black activist claimed, "had not fooled black workers" in Detroit. In commenting on the UAW president's participation in the Charleston hospital strike, Charles Denby declared that Reuther was "always glad to integrate anything—outside of his own union."[35]

Throughout the late 1960s and into the 1970s, discontent among young black autoworkers threatened to tear the UAW apart, especially in its Detroit heartland. In 1967, the Motor City had exploded in violence as African Americans, outraged at police brutality in the city's black wards, took to the streets. After several nights of torching, looting, and lethal police retaliation, thirty-four people were dead and large sections of the central city burned. President Johnson dispatched forty-seven hundred federal troops to restore order.

Racial tensions infested the large inner-city auto plants as well. The economic boom stimulated by the Vietnam War increased the auto workforce, with General Motors, Ford, and especially Chrysler hiring thousands of black workers, many of them young men who combined the toughness of life in the city's black ghettos with the expectations born of the civil rights movement. Bridling at the casual racial slurs of white supervisors and coworkers, often assigned to work with antiquated and malfunctioning equipment in decaying inner-city plants, and rebelling against the frantic pace of the work, young black workers rejected the hierarchies of power and authority that had traditionally ruled the auto plants. Through the late 1960s, dozens of incidents, often involving violence and sometimes firearms, broke out as angry young workers confronted hectoring foremen, disdainful coworkers, and aging union officers.[36]

Nor was this in-plant conflict confined to individual fights and protests. In many of the Detroit-area plants, as well as some in Chicago and other northern cities, young black workers formed embryonic workplace groups, with a cadre of black radicals providing an ideological and organizational framework. Student radicals at Wayne State University and shop floor activists in the plants helped create workers councils, the largest and most active of which emerged at the large Dodge Main plant, which employed thirty thousand workers. The Dodge group adopted the name Dodge Revolutionary Union Movement (DRUM), and similar bodies arose in other area factories. In 1968, these various groups came together in the League of Revolutionary Black Workers (LRBW), whose leaders linked the conditions faced by black autoworkers not only to the struggles of southern blacks in the United States but also to the plight of people of color throughout the world who were rebelling against capitalism and colonialism. Declared one sympathetic observer, the league might very well serve as the "vanguard for the social revolution."[37]

In Detroit, these militant blacks attacked the auto companies and the city's corporate elites. But they reserved much of their disdain and bitterness for "their" union, the UAW, which union shop contracts required them to join. They charged that union leaders, content with high wages and fat fringe benefits, paid little attention to the chaos and mayhem that festered in the increasingly inhospitable and dangerous auto plants. The white-dominated UAW leadership ignored black workers' demands for an end to racist language and demeaning treatment. Grievance officers trivialized the complaints of black workers and greeted protests with their own racist language. Indeed, asserted LRBW activists, though the fabled autoworkers union may have been the solution to workers' problems in the past, it had now become an integral part of the problem. "I finally got the news," went the words of a song coined by an LRBW member, "how my dues was bein' used."[38]

UAW veterans responded in kind. The new cohort of black workers, they believed, failed to appreciate the struggles and sacrifices made by the older generation to build the union and wrest good contracts from the powerful auto companies. Young dissidents spouting dime-store Marxist rhetoric weakened the union and sowed anarchy in the plants. When DRUM and other local organizations pulled unauthorized wildcat strikes to protest the union's lack of responsiveness to black workers' grievances, UAW staff members led the way in smashing the picket lines. When LRBW-backed candidates seemed poised to win election to some local union offices, the UAW mobilized the normally quiescent retiree vote to defeat them. The LRBW, declared UAW secretary-treasurer Emil Mazey, himself a radical labor organizer of 1940s vintage, consisted of a "handful of fanatics who are nothing but black fascists, using the same tactics of coercion and intimidation that Hitler . . . used." The irony of yesterday's radicals and civil rights advocates breaking dissident picket lines and exchanging harsh epithets with young militant black workers was not lost on Reuther's corporate and political critics.[39]

In the end, the briefly vibrant revolutionary union movement faded. Although the discontent and complaints of rank-and-file black workers were real enough, only a handful of the dissidents were in fact committed revolutionaries. Many of the young blacks entering the plants in the late 1960s had no intention of spending their working lives in the auto factories; turnover among this cohort was high, making it impossible for DRUM and the other plant organizations to maintain continuity. Whereas some old-line leaders dismissed black workers' concerns, others saw the LRBW as a warning that the UAW had to put its own race-relations house in order. UAW leaders appointed more black staff members and supported the election of "responsible" black officers in the inner-city plants. Reuther's death in a plane crash in May 1970 removed the most visible symbol of the UAW's racial dilemmas. The winding down of the Vietnam War, the return of hard times to the auto industry in the mid-1970s, and the general cooling of the dissident passions of the 1960s put an end to this outbreak of raw racial antagonism in the UAW. Underlying problems of blacks' lack of access to skilled jobs and tensions between whites and blacks in the plants and union halls remained, even as the UAW leadership attempted to sustain the union's identification with progressive approaches to the country's ongoing racial problems.

A situation in New York City involving its large and powerful teachers union, the United Federation of Teachers (UFT), proved even more divisive than developments in Detroit. The AFT, of which the UFT was the largest and most influential component, was at the forefront of the surge in public employee unionism in the 1960s. In 1968, the UFT represented more than fifty-seven thousand teachers and related professionals in the city's public school system. Under the leadership of Albert Shanker, a former junior high school teacher, it had grown from a group of impotent and often antagonistic local teachers groups into one of the city's most influential and visible labor organizations.

Both the UFT and the AFT were faithful allies of the civil rights movement. In 1963, the New York teachers union had sent a large contingent to the March on Washington, and both it and the national union had supported the civil rights legislation of the 1960s. Since the Supreme Court's *Brown v. Board of Education* decision in 1954, the AFT had pressed for racial integration of the schools, even at the risk of alienating white members and potential members in the South. In 1965, the AFT donated generously to the SCLC's southern voter registration efforts, and Shanker worked closely with labor-oriented African American leaders such as Bayard Rustin and A. Philip Randolph on a variety of labor and civil rights initiatives.

But the controversy that erupted in the Ocean Hill–Brownsville section of Brooklyn in 1968 pitted labor, in the form of Shanker's UFT, and elements of the civil rights movement in a bitter confrontation. Frustrated in efforts to achieve meaningful integration of the city's vast public school system, African American educational activists, supported by sympathetic white civic leaders and foundation donors, promoted a plan to decentralize governance of the schools by devolving decision making from the remote central bureaucracy to local citizen-elected boards of education. In 1967, Ocean Hill–Brownsville, an impoverished, largely minority section of Brooklyn, became one of the districts chosen for a pilot decentralization project. The UFT initially supported the general concept of decentralization, although its leaders insisted that all personnel matters—including the firing and reassignment of teachers—remain lodged with the city's central educational administration and that the existing master contract between the UFT and the school board remain in force.

The board elected by the voters of Ocean Hill–Brownsville in the fall of 1967 chose former assistant principal Rhody McCoy as the district's administrator. This choice reflected the board's determination to rebuild the schools in a way that would foster black pride and black autonomy. In May 1968, the board dismissed thirteen teachers and five school principals. Since the regulations governing this experiment in community control were unclear with regard to the status of teachers terminated or reassigned by the local board, its action appeared to violate the basic provisions of the city's collective bargaining contract with the UFT. "From the point of view of the union," declared Sandra Feldman, the UFT's field representative in the district and a long-term civil rights activist, "it was a totally basic issue." The terminated teachers and principals had been dismissed with no semblance of due process. "The union," Feldman believed, "had no choice" but to call a citywide strike when the fall term began to force the reinstatement of its members.[40]

There were myriad complications and confusions in this escalating conflict between two seemingly liberal positions: democratic direction of children's education through popularly elected representatives versus basic rights of due process as contained in virtually every union contract. Complicating this fissure in the liberal coalition was the emergence of a revived black nationalism, energized by both the victories of the civil rights movement and the fierceness of white resistance to it. Angry voices urging "black power" challenged the established, integrationist civil rights leadership and infused the debate over community control of the schools.

In New York, this conflict raged throughout the fall of 1968. Teachers defied court orders and staged three separate walkouts. Huge protest rallies besieged Mayor John V. Lindsay. By now, Shanker and others in the UFT had become hostile to the very concept of community control, and critics charged that they sabotaged several promising compromises to achieve the larger objective of scuttling the whole program. In Ocean Hill–Brownsville itself, parents confronted striking teachers, who in turn accosted colleagues who dared to cross the picket lines. Ugly racial and religious rhetoric surfaced, with some community-control advocates depicting the UFT as a

Jewish-run cabal determined to maintain the subordination of people of color. For his part, Shanker ignored that many of the teachers recruited by the community board were in fact Jewish and fixed on the utterances of a handful of extremists in an effort to discredit the whole concept of local board control.

Influential members of the city's vibrant liberal-labor community backed Shanker and the UFT, arguing that although decentralization of school governance might well improve the educational experiences of black children, the union was right in insisting on the contractual rights of its members. In itself, declared A. Philip Randolph and other black labor leaders, decentralization was more promise than panacea. The union had no choice but to insist on a "framework that includes due process" and ample funding for the experiment. Initially, the potent New York City labor movement also backed Shanker and the UFT. As strike followed strike and one proposed settlement after another failed, however, unions with large minority memberships, notably Hospital Workers Local 1199 and the large AFSCME District Council 37, broke ranks to denounce the strikes and demand a settlement that preserved community control. Indeed, one Local 1199 leader threatened that if the UFT and the mainstream labor movement continued on their course, "those of us who are black and Puerto Ricans and Hispanic will set up our own labor movement."[41]

When the strikes finally ground to a halt in November, the UFT gained most of its objectives. The Ocean Hill–Brownsville board's authority was eliminated, and a state-appointed administrator took over control of the district. The teachers whose termination had triggered the original dispute were reinstated. Subsequently, after heavy UFT lobbying, the New York State legislature passed a law that sharply limited the city's ability to decentralize school governance and specifically protected teachers' rights with respect to dismissal and transfer. In subsequent years, the UFT went on to organize extensively among the school system's paraprofessionals and teacher's aides, many of whom were African American and Puerto Rican, seemingly suffering no ill effects from the protracted and racially charged Ocean Hill–Brownsville strike.

Even so, the rawness of the conflict between the predominantly Jewish leadership of the UFT, on the one hand, and militant elements in the African American community, on the other, had long-range effects. For decades, New York's Jews and African Americans had shared a common cause in the liberal-labor coalition that dominated the city's politics. The bitter strike fractured this long-standing alliance and pushed many "outer-borough" Jews (i.e., those living in Brooklyn, Queens, and Staten Island) and white ethnics to the right. Through the next decade and beyond, public opinion polls and voting patterns revealed increased racial polarization in a city that had once been a beacon of interracial activism. An affair such as the Ocean Hill–Brownsville strike, which highlighted the difficulty of accommodating both contractual union rights and claims of black autonomy. exposed the vulnerability of the labor–civil rights alliance in the very heartland of liberal politics, New York City.[42]

These labor and civil rights struggles of the late 1960s and early 1970s—sometimes exposing fissures in the liberal coalition, sometimes providing opportunities for common action—occurred during a period of economic growth and low unemployment. But during the mid-1970s, the U.S. economy showed signs of faltering. As noted by historian Aaron Brenner, during the 1970s, the country drifted from "unprecedented prosperity and confidence to . . . long-term stagnation and doubt."[43] Declining productivity, intensified international competition, mounting public debt associated with the war in Vietnam and increased public expenditures, and growing resentment against taxes brought an end to the ambitious social experiments that had flourished in the 1960s. As early as 1973, one leading commentator was warning about "The Fiscal Crisis of the State,"[44] wherein the pledges made by public authorities in the turbulent 1960s to rebellious minorities were running headlong into the political-economic system's inability to generate the surpluses necessary to fund social programs aimed at improving their conditions. As a result, expansive public programs that seemed to provide something for everyone now gave way to the politics of scarcity, as rival groups struggled to claim shares of dwindling public resources. Nowhere was this process more apparent than in the nation's older cities, where for the first time African Americans were gaining top political positions even as the wherewithal with which to address festering urban problems was shrinking.

In Atlanta in 1977, a confrontation between sanitation workers and African American mayor Maynard Jackson powerfully and poignantly illustrated the racial and labor implications of the new politics of scarcity. In 1973, when Jackson was elected as the city's first black mayor, he enjoyed enthusiastic labor support, including that of AFSCME, which represented Atlanta's sanitation workers. These workers believed that the election of a beneficiary of the civil rights struggle, a pioneering black businessman-politician, would enable them at last to improve their poverty-level wages. Ratcheting inflation had eroded their already slender pay packets, and workers' impatience mounted during protracted contract negotiations with city authorities. In the summer of 1976, Jackson averted a threatened strike with a small temporary pay hike. A one-day wildcat strike in January 1977 further demonstrated the workers' discontent.

But this situation was different from that prevailing in the sanitation strikes of the 1960s. The theme of maltreatment of humble black men by arrogant white managers and politicians no longer shaped the public discourse. The issue was wages, not manhood or civil rights. Moreover,

Jackson was immensely popular with Atlanta's black majority, which seemed largely immune to appeals that had mobilized the black community in behalf of victimized sanitation workers in earlier strikes. As the first African American mayor of a large southern city and one of the first in the country, Jackson fell under particularly close scrutiny from the overwhelmingly white banking and business leaders who dominated the city's economy. As a successful attorney and businessman, he believed that the confidence and support of these powerful men were crucial to his effort to expand economic opportunities for African Americans. He worked successfully with the city's power elite, for example, in the massive expansion of Atlanta's international airport, insisting that minority workers be given access to the many construction and airport service jobs being created. Faced with severe budgetary limitations, however, Jackson was determined to demonstrate that black political power was compatible with fiscal responsibility. Sanitation workers, he believed, would have to wait until general economic growth provided budgetary surpluses to fund their admittedly overdue wage increases. To be sure, Jackson acknowledged, "the employees need a pay increase," but he quickly added, "we don't have [the money]." To which union leader Leamon Hood responded, "Every time someone has to bite the bullet, it's always us."[45]

By 1977, sanitation strikes had become a familiar feature of urban life, nowhere more so than in the South. Although city officials deplored the strikes and often threatened mass firings, they recognized the workers' rootedness in the black community and usually found other ways of dealing with the strikers. Certainly, such had been the case in the earlier strikes in St. Petersburg and Memphis and in a 1970 walkout in Atlanta. But Jackson believed that he was up against the wall. Granting wage increases, he believed, would fatally unbalance the city's budget and break faith with the bankers and business leaders he relied on to invest in economic development and thus generate jobs. So when the sanitation workers walked off their jobs on March 28, 1977, Jackson was ready for them. He depicted the strike as an arrogant grab for power orchestrated by AFSCME's national officers in Washington. If he caved in to the union's "outlandish" demands, he insisted, he would discredit the whole notion of responsible black political leadership in the South.[46]

The mayor acted quickly, issuing an ultimatum: those workers not reporting for work on April 1 would be terminated. As might be expected, the business community applauded, but the city's African Americans supported the mayor as well. When the firings took effect on April 1, hundreds of black Atlantans showed up to apply for those jobs. The city's black elite, the local branches of both the NAACP and the Urban League, the president of the SCLC, and most of the city's prominent black religious leaders endorsed the mayor's tough stance. On April 4, the ninth anniversary of his son's murder, Martin Luther King Sr. proclaimed his support for Jackson's course, adding that in view of the union's irresponsible behavior, he had every right to "fire the hell out of them."[47]

AFSCME sought to rally public opinion. It publicized the economic plight of the sanitation workers, depicting them as humble, hardworking, long-suffering public servants. The union sought to discredit the mayor, charging him with hypocrisy and double-dealing. At a nationally televised baseball game, strikers displayed a large banner declaring, "Maynard's Word Is Garbage." Some local ministers and civil rights advocates came to the union's defense and tried to depict the strike as a civil rights issue, linking the Atlanta struggle to those in Memphis and Selma. But Jackson rejected the comparison. His economic policies, he insisted, were bringing jobs to black Atlanta. Failure to balance the city's budget would alienate those with the power to continue to underwrite the city's resurgence. It was not "liberal to make a predominantly black city financially unsound," he stated. Repeatedly, the mayor rejected compromises that involved rehiring the striking workers. On April 29, AFSCME admitted defeat, and strikers were allowed to reapply individually for their old jobs, hoping to be taken back as vacancies arose and at lower wages than they had been making when they walked out.[48]

Clearly, much had changed between Memphis in 1968 and Atlanta in 1977. Impoverished and victimized black workers had become greedy saboteurs of economic progress. Labor struggles were now just that: disagreements about wages, budgets, and business confidence. They were not about manhood, respect, and human rights. Black economic progress could not be won on the picket line or in street marches; it was to be gained by balancing budgets, brokering deals, and reassuring the white power structure that with black political power came a willingness to face down unions, whatever their racial composition. Even the rhetoric of conflict was different. No soaring tribune of human rights, Jackson nonetheless had a gift for pithy phrases. Clearly indicating his fiscal priorities and driving home the necessity of resisting the strikers' demands, he vowed, "Before I take the city into a deficit financial position, elephants will roost in trees."[49]

The Atlanta strike proved to be a bellwether. Throughout the late 1970s and into the next decade, cities around the country were faced with the same dilemmas—namely, the volatile combination of militant public employee unions and straitened fiscal resources. Public reaction against union demands was embodied in the passage of California's Proposition 13, a ballot initiative endorsed by voters in June 1978 that sharply curtailed the state's ability to tax and thus to support public services. Moreover, politicians around the country found that head-on conflict with public employee unions could be popular among voters. Whereas a decade earlier taxpayers had often sympathized with underpaid teachers, police, and sanitation workers, increasingly they saw public workers as disruptive, greedy, and irresponsible. In some cases, elected officials baited unions into risky strike actions, a tactic that allowed them to portray themselves as stern guardians of the public purse. Capping this reaction against union militancy was the action of the new Republican administration of President Ronald Reagan, which, in the summer of 1981, summarily fired more than eleven thousand striking air traffic controllers, barred them from employment by the federal government, and recruited an entirely new workforce to control air traffic.

Reagan's action had important consequences. Private employers felt emboldened to use the hitherto risky tactic of striker replacement, and throughout the 1980s and 1990s, they did so repeatedly, humbling some of the nation's strongest unions and all but eliminating the strike as an offensive tactic. The crushing of the Professional Air Traffic Controllers Organization (PATCO) strike was also rooted in the immediate past, building on the reaction against public workers exhibited by Jackson and other political leaders, many of them men and women with otherwise strong liberal credentials. Observes historian Joseph A. McCartin, "in the late 1970s, firing strikers became normalized as a legitimate managerial tactic . . . long before PATCO," and "onetime labor allies—like Maynard Jackson—played a critical role in this legitimizing process."[50]

7

BACK TO THE FUTURE

Even as thousands of black workers filed complaints of discrimination with the Equal Employment Opportunity Commission (EEOC) and began legal action against employers, the economic and social forces that had so powerfully affected black workers in the 1950s and 1960s accelerated, posing still greater challenges to new cohorts, especially in the northern cities. In the 1980s and 1990s, industrial employment at first stagnated and then began to shrink, both proportionately and absolutely. In many cases, this downturn affected industries such as textiles just as African Americans were finally gaining a foothold. From the "creative destruction" of the American industrial regime emerged an increasingly information- and service-based economy that dramatically transformed the country's employment mix. Whole new categories of jobs in data processing, communications, and financial, legal, and information services often required specialized credentials, even as entry-level blue-collar work disappeared. At the same time, what celebrants of the new economy called the "Great American Job Machine" was generating millions of new low-wage and benefits-poor service-sector jobs.

In both cases, many African Americans, especially young black men, found themselves ill equipped to compete in the rapidly changing job market. De facto segregation, poor inner-city schools, and crime-ridden neighborhoods made it difficult for young blacks to qualify for new high-tech jobs. In the 1980s and 1990s, conditions in the great American cities deteriorated as joblessness, high dropout rates, single-parent households, and decaying social and public services trapped thousands in a cycle of despair and criminality. Meanwhile, the influx of Hispanic, Caribbean, and Asian immigrants brought competition with native-born blacks at both ends of the emerging job spectrum.

Throughout the 1990s and into the new century, debate raged among activists, social scientists, and public commentators about the character and dimensions of the social pathologies that afflicted the urban ghettos. Some observers stressed the continuance of racial discrimination and the impact of structural economic forces in disadvantaging young blacks in the rapidly changing economy. Others pointed to misguided welfare policies, a black leadership trapped in the rhetoric of the past, and the resultant welfare dependency and criminality. Regardless of the methodological, political, or ideological perspectives brought to the debate, however, virtually all agreed that access to stable and remunerative employment was critical if African Americans were to participate fully in the twenty-first century's economic order.

The 1980s and 1990s were decades of tribulation for organized labor as well. One of the great ironies of this period was that the labor movement, which had for decades regarded race and gender issues as distractions in its efforts to advance the interests of its core white male constituency, now increasingly identified itself as a champion of interracial solidarity and cultural diversity. As employment in the traditional areas of labor's strength—construction, transport, mining, and manufacturing—shrank, a declining labor movement struggled to find new recruits in the expanding service and governmental fields, sectors in which women and minority workers were disproportionately represented. Organizers often found that, despite labor's checkered historical record, black workers were more receptive to the union appeal than were their white counterparts. And politically, African Americans overwhelmingly remained the most reliable bloc of voters for liberal and labor-endorsed candidates and in state referenda on labor issues. A leadership revolt in the AFL-CIO in 1995 propelled a slate of reform-minded unionists to the top positions in the labor federation. These men and women pledged initiatives that would center on the recruitment of people of color and on cooperation with women's rights activists and progressive racial and ethnic civic organizations. After a decade of unprecedented activity by the national labor federation, however, it remained uncertain whether the embattled labor movement was actually committed to such a program and not merely going through the motions. Indeed, the dismay of black activists was heightened in the summer of 2005 with the departure of a group of high-profile unions from the AFL-CIO and the creation of a new initiative, the Change to Win (CTW) coalition. Ostensibly designed to revitalize the labor movement's organizing efforts, plans for CTW threatened to undo some of the recent gains in black representation in the AFL-CIO's leadership structure and triggered angry accusations of bad faith from some of the country's leading black union activists.

Affirmative Action, the Latter Stages

Although Title VII and pressure by the Office of Federal Contract Compliance Programs (OFCCP) had a measurably positive impact on black employment, in many cases, consent decrees and other settlements proved less beneficial than they initially appeared. The decree entered into in 1974 involving the EEOC, major steel producers, and United Steelworkers was a case in point. In the decades before its promulgation, activist black workers, supported by civil rights groups, had kept up a drumfire of criticism and exposure in the form of public protests and lawsuits against the steel companies' job placement and promotion policies and against their own union's complicity in limiting opportunities for black workers in the mills. But the EEOC-facilitated negotiations leading to the decree ignored dissident blacks and their supporters, involving only representatives of the companies, the union, and the government. Critics charged that those involved in the negotiations were more concerned with protecting the company and the union from legal action than with achieving equity for those workers whose activism had forced the issue. Moreover, the union's national leaders largely regarded the complaints of black workers as distracting annoyances, while in the hundreds of local unions, officers regularly refused to assist black workers' efforts to understand the complex agreement and thus claim the opportunities it might offer. Indeed, local officers often encouraged or even participated in "backlash" protests by white workers, who claimed that their black coworkers were now gaining unfair advantages.

The consent decree itself proved to be an uncertain instrument for black advancement. Although it modified seniority provisions and thus presented opportunities for black workers to bid for better jobs in previously "white" departments, it also included complicated qualifications and special exceptions designed to make the decree "color blind" in its implementation. As a result, African Americans often found that white workers ended up benefiting more from its provisions than they did. Moreover, although the terms of the decree in effect acknowledged that black workers had been victims of discrimination and provided monetary compensation for some 34,500 of them, the actual payments were small (averaging about $300), and to claim them, workers had to agree not to sue the company or the union for past discrimination.[1]

Likewise, the consent decrees signed by the Bell System in the 1970s led to mixed results at best for the women and minorities whose activism had led to them. These agreements were ostensibly aimed at opening up jobs and lines of progression for black and female telephone workers. In fact, however, they relegated newly hired black and other minority women to the corporation's most tedious dead-end jobs, while white males used the decrees' gender blindness to claim jobs that were formerly women's preserve and thus leave themselves well positioned as the company introduced a wide range of labor-saving technology. According to one veteran employee, of the new jobs now available to women, many of them African American, "more than 75 percent . . . require women to remain seated at video terminals where they key in data at company-established productivity rates. . . . Computerized work measurements and strict supervision combine frequently with racism and sexism to form a virtual hell for most of these women."[2]

Even under the best of circumstances, neither the EEOC nor the OFCCP had sufficient resources to address the thousands of complaints that African Americans, women, and other minorities brought before them. In mid-1975, for example, the EEOC reported a backlog of more than 125,000 cases, some of them dating back to 1968. Congress granted increased powers to the beleaguered agency in 1972, giving it additional responsibilities but failing to provide the additional resources needed to meet them. Turnover among EEOC staff was high, leading to charges of administrative incompetence and ineffectiveness. Nor was the record of the OFCCP any more impressive. Although it engineered important agreements with the airlines to improve employment for minorities and women, all too often, contract compliance staggered under the dual burden of the high expectations engendered by Order No. 4 and the lack of adequate personnel and resources. Increasingly, the OFCCP relied on questionable promises of voluntary compliance on the part of well-heeled corporations staffed with astute lawyers whose job it was to protect their companies from damaging lawsuits and to limit the scope of change in hiring and promotion policies. The OFCCP devoted much of its effort to opening up construction work to African Americans, but a 1979 study by the General Accounting Office found that "ineffective enforcement and inadequate monitoring . . . [had] resulted in minorities making little progress."[3]

In the 1980s, both economic developments and political changes further blunted efforts to improve black workers' status and opportunities. Vigorous enforcement of Title VII; challenges to traditional patterns of hiring, promotion, and job placement; and programs of affirmative action—however defined—had always been controversial. With Republican Ronald Reagan's election in 1980, sharp critics of affirmative action and related programs gained power. Key figures in the new administration, including the assistant attorney general for civil rights and the chair of the EEOC, believed that the 1964 law mandated only *future* equality of employment opportunity and specifically prohibited compensation for past practices. Assistant Attorney General William Bradford Reynolds quickly became the administration's key spokesman in these matters, consistently denying that the government was empowered to consider the effects of previous mistreatment or to promote solutions that involved any recognition of prior racial disparities in employment.

Reynolds insisted that neither the Civil Rights Act of 1964 nor any subsequent amendments permitted the invocation of numerical targets, quotas, or other forms of racially inflected devices. At the same time, Reagan administration officials promoted the work of legal experts and social scientists whose widely reported studies argued that affirmative action and other compensatory initiatives actually diminished employment opportunities for ordinary black workers while unfairly benefiting educated and well-connected men and women of color. In particular, they pointed to the deleterious effects of the 1971 *Griggs* decision, which called aptitude and other prehire and promotion-related standardized tests into question. After *Griggs,* some critics of affirmative action held, companies were unwilling to risk being subjected to expensive and time-consuming legal action to defend these tests, which were in fact valid and accurate predictors of successful job performance. Thus, employers either resigned themselves to hiring underqualified applicants, thus compromising productivity and competitiveness, or moved their operations to areas where few African Americans resided. Concluded one 1992 study, preferential hiring and promotion policies were responsible for a 4 percent decrease in the gross national product annually. In 1987, federal judge Richard Posner pointed to the fallout from *Griggs* as being partially responsible for the shortage of entry-level jobs in the inner cities. To avoid the appearance of racial discrimination, he declared, "when deciding where to locate a new plant or where to expand an existing one, a firm will be attracted . . . to areas that have only small percentages of blacks in their labor pools."[4]

Through the 1980s and into the 1990s, bitter debate raged over these issues. Civil rights advocates, often citing detailed scholarly research, attacked both the change in policy and the research findings that purported to show the negative effects of vigorous and imaginative enforcement of civil rights law. They pointed to the positive role of affirmative action in opening up broad employment sectors to women, African Americans, and other people of color. Thus, in 1985, when President Reagan seemed poised to issue an executive order that would have ended all federally supported affirmative action efforts, a wide variety of feminist, civil rights, labor, and ethnic action groups went on the attack. "If President Reagan signs the proposed executive order," declared one civil rights attorney, "it would be the most anti–civil rights step taken by a President since Woodrow Wilson issued orders requiring . . . segregation . . . in Federal Government buildings."[5]

In addition, Reagan and Attorney General Edwin Meese found that the attack on affirmative action and the push for a narrow reading of the 1964 Civil Rights Act did not necessarily resonate well in corporate America or among state and local governments, even those under Republican control. Corporate employers were finding that a racially and sexually diverse workforce paid dividends in public relations and in marketing. State and local governments used programs of preferential hiring and promotion to recruit African Americans as police, firefighters, and other municipal employees who dealt directly with the public in increasingly black inner cities. Corporate executives and Republican mayors and governors joined civil rights advocates in rejecting Reagan's position and in urging the president not to issue the anticipated order. Republican mayor William Hudnut of Indianapolis spoke for many when he declared that a "lot of progress has been made with affirmative action goals. . . . it's a great mistake . . . to ask us to dismantle the program."[6] The Business Roundtable, a coalition of some of the country's largest and most powerful corporations, declared that affirmative action programs had "served American society, workers, and government contractors well for the past 20 years" and opposed the drastic shift in policy.[7]

In the end, Reagan backed off and did not issue the order. However, both he and his successor, George H. W. Bush, pursued the attack on affirmative action in the courts and in the political arena. With job insecurity increasing in a changing economy and with wages stagnating, the resentment of working-class white men over the perceived favoritism for women, blacks, and other minorities sharpened. Reagan's and Bush's use of the scare word "quotas" to characterize all affirmative action initiatives encouraged the white backlash against policies and programs that had earlier enjoyed widespread support or at least acquiescence. The successful reelection campaign of North Carolina's Republican senator Jesse Helms in 1990 illustrated the political potency of attacks on affirmative action. "You needed that job and you were the best qualified, but they had to give it to a minority because of a racial quota. Is that really fair?" asked the voice-over as a television advertisement showed a frustrated white man with a rejection letter.[8]

The competing claims of racial balance and traditional notions of individual rights led to highly charged confrontations, particularly in connection with public employment. In Detroit, for example, a budget crunch in the 1970s compelled large-scale layoffs in a police department that for decades had been an instrument of white power and had earned a notorious reputation for racist behavior. After the city became majority black in the 1950s and 1960s, African American political leaders launched an aggressive affirmative action program, arguing with considerable justification that the police force's reputation made the hiring and promotion of African American officers imperative in the tense and troubled city. Indeed, by 1980, the city's population was 70 percent African American; meanwhile, affirmative action and targeted recruitment among minorities boosted the proportion of black officers from less than 20 percent in 1974 to more than 33 percent four years later. African American officers also benefited from favorable retention and promotion policies, an important consideration during a period of budgetary constraint. White officers protested and undertook protracted legal action in an effort to derail the city's affirmative action program, using the language of fairness and professional competence to counteract the claims of racial equity and civic necessity that affirmative action advocates advanced. In Detroit, as in many other communities, both sides invoked the language of individual rights and social equity; in none of them did there seem to be a simple formula or an unambiguous right and wrong.[9]

Ambiguity and confusion reigned in the case of the building trades as well. On the one hand, through the 1970s, a variety of government-sponsored initiatives enjoyed some success in opening up apprenticeships and union membership to African Americans. During the period 1970 to 1974, for example, the building trades unions reported a decline in the number of white members, while over 40 percent of new members were members of minorities, mostly African American. The Department of Labor also reported modest success in working with the unions to increase the number of black apprentices in its Apprenticeship Outreach Program. On the other hand, it soon became clear that the recruitment of African Americans into the building trades would not provide the large number of jobs necessary to substantially remedy the overall employment problems of urban black communities or the costs of large-scale construction projects.

Whether because of the construction unions' historical inhospitableness to minority membership, the opening up of a broader range of alternative opportunities for black men with high school diplomas, or other factors, union leaders were not entirely disingenuous when they told affirmative action monitors that they were having trouble reaching their numerical targets for minority recruitment. And even as debates over affirmative action in construction raged, contractors associations, led by large national concerns such as Brown and Root, waged a direct attack on the building trades unions, driving them out of many local markets and, within a decade, shrinking union representation in large-scale construction from 80 percent to less than 20 percent. Although nonunion and antiunion builders had initially pointed to the unions' restrictive racial practices as part of their justification for seeking to end the union presence in heavy construction, through the 1990s and into the twenty-first century, union work sites were actually less racially segregated than their nonunion counterparts. Indeed, union-sponsored apprentice programs were compiling a better record of race and gender representation than were nonunion employers.[10]

Both the Reagan and the Bush administrations would have liked to end affirmative action, thus terminating these dilemmas. But neither president could muster sufficient support in Congress for legislative attacks on affirmative action. Both, however could and did use their appointments to federal agencies such as EEOC and especially to the federal courts to narrow the scope and erode the influence of affirmative action. As a result, by the late 1980s, reflecting the influence of Reagan appointees Sandra Day O'Connor, Anthony Kennedy, and Antonin Scalia, the Supreme Court moved in case after case to constrain affirmative action, protect the individual rights of nonminority workers, and require women and minority plaintiffs to offer tangible proof of overt individual discrimination. This trend was visible as early as 1984 when, in *Firefighters Local Union #1784 v. Stotts,* the Court ruled in favor of three white Memphis firefighters protesting a layoff policy that sought to sustain a degree of racial balance that had been achieved through the preferential hiring of blacks in a city whose population was 40 percent African American. More important, though, was the Court's ruling in *Ward's Cove Packing Company v. Atonio,* decided in 1989. Legal experts agreed that this case had the effect of overturning *Griggs* and calling into question the whole practice of considering numerical representation of minorities in an employer's labor force. After *Ward's Cove,* those charging racial or gender discrimination could not point to low percentages of female or black workers as evidence of discrimination; rather, they had to demonstrate specific acts and specific evidences of *intent* to discriminate. *Ward's Cove,* declared the American Civil Liberties Union, was an "outrage" that "reversed two decades of precedent" and "effectively read Title VII off the books."[11] But for Reaganites, the Supreme Court was finally returning to the original language and intent of the Civil Rights Act and had lodged the problem of discrimination in employment exactly where it should have remained—with an individual employer and an individual worker. As Reagan's EEOC chair, conservative African American jurist Clarence Thomas had repeatedly attacked affirmative action, and Bush's appointment of Thomas to the Supreme Court indicated that this trend would continue into the foreseeable future.

Black Workers in a Changing Economy

Through the end of the twentieth century and into the new millennium, a rapidly changing global economy posed new challenges even as it offered new opportunities for some African American workers. Many of the gains made as a result of Title VII and related antidiscrimination efforts eroded as U.S. manufacturing declined, and along with it a generation of nonskilled jobs that had paid relatively high wages to entry-level workers. At the same time, the weakening of attitudinal and institutional racism in the nation's schools and workplaces lowered barriers that had once limited the employment opportunities of men and women whose education and abilities equipped them to compete in the emerging economy. The result was a widening income and earnings gap within the African American population itself, along with growing physical and spatial separation between an emerging black middle class and an inner-city "underclass." The relationship among deindustrialization, public welfare and antidiscrimination policies, and the social pathologies that afflicted urban black populations generated myriad academic studies and fierce partisan controversy, but few effective remedies.

In the 1960s and 1970s, African American workers made substantial gains. At the beginning of this period, the average black worker earned about 57 percent of what white workers earned; in 1976, the figure stood at 73 percent. The reasons for the gains during this period differed from those that accounted for the last period of sustained improvement—1940 to 1955. At that time, the mass migration of blacks from low-income farms and domestic service occupations to northern industrial labor, along with the expanded black presence in public employment and their increasing representation in the labor movement, drove black wages upward, as did dramatic improvements in blacks' educational levels. By the 1960s, however, stagnating industrial employment in the North and the slowing of black migration from the South all but eliminated the earlier industrial and regional premiums.

Beginning in the late 1960s, the greatest relative gains in the earnings of African Americans occurred in the South. By the late 1970s, economists and statisticians had concluded that the rise of black employment in southern industry accounted for the bulk of the recent income gain. Clearly, the opening of the textile industry and the upgrading of black employment in pulp and paper, tobacco, and other southern-based sectors played a critical role in improving the relative position of African Americans, with Title VII, federal contract compliance efforts, and affirmative action programs also contributing significantly to their gains. Even in places where there were no formal EEOC or OFCCP proceedings, the threat of legal action and pressure from national corporate officials on local southern branches to obey the law and avoid litigation could open up employment opportunities to African Americans. For example, in one Mississippi town that had not experienced any Title VI or Title VII litigation, black employment expanded significantly in the 1970s and 1980s. "I wouldn't have my present job," declared one resident, "if it weren't for that law."[12]

The other factor associated with these improvements was the dismantling of racial barriers that had limited the opportunities, and thus the earnings, of relatively well-educated black Americans. Whereas black lawyers, doctors, teachers, and other professionals had been all but frozen out of mainstream employment opportunities prior to the civil rights upheavals of the 1950s and 1960s, it became increasingly possible for suitably credentialed African Americans to move at least partially up the corporate ladder, to compete for positions in academia, and to succeed in interracial work environments. Thus, before 1950, blacks were represented in the professional, managerial, and white-collar occupations at only half the rate of whites, but by the late 1970s, the proportion had increased to three-quarters.[13] During that same period, the proportion of nonwhites holding clerical and other white-collar jobs quadrupled, while the number of those working in low-wage domestic service and agricultural labor fell off sharply. By the mid-1970s, African American women had achieved near income parity with their white sisters, and in the mid-1980s, college-educated black couples were outpacing their white counterparts in terms of annual income.[14] Affirmative action programs benefited black professionals as employers that once shunned African Americans now embraced workforce diversity as a positive value and feared legal action if the normal recruitment process did not yield a sufficient number of qualified black (or female) applicants.

In the 1990s, controversy over job entitlements receded, although affirmative action remained a live issue in the area of college admissions. By the 1990s, many large employers had internalized some form of affirmative action and were continuing their efforts to identify, recruit, and sometimes train women and minorities for jobs previously unavailable to them. Public authorities on the state and local levels continued to seek qualified blacks, especially for law enforcement and public safety positions. Certainly, anyone visiting a southern shopping center or a northern office pool in the 1980s and 1990s would immediately see a degree of racial and gender diversity that had been unthinkable a generation earlier. Moreover, by the mid-1990s, many African Americans who may have been hired initially through affirmative action programs had accumulated sufficient seniority to be protected from the "last hired, first fired" trap.[15]

At the same time, however, accelerating economic forces had a powerful effect on the black American working class. The precipitous decline of U.S. manufacturing and the continuing shift of the nation's employment profile toward the high-tech and service sectors held ominous implications, especially for African American men and boys. The very industries that had been the focal point of job discrimination controversies in the 1960s and 1970s experienced a sharp decline that accelerated in the 1980s and 1990s. The case of textiles was particularly poignant. For nearly a century, black workers had been barred from all but the most menial work in the mills that provided the South with the bulk of its manufacturing employment. A breakthrough in textiles, declared the president of the North Carolina NAACP in 1967, was crucial because "the textile industry will continue for a long, long time. . . . It will be here for a long, long time and it will be a major industry."[16] But by the early 1980s, the industry was reeling from the effects of international competition from both foreign manufacturers and American concerns that moved their operations to low-wage sites abroad. Between 1980 and 1994, one authoritative study reported, the U.S. textile and garment industries lost over half a million jobs. The 1993 adoption of the North American Free Trade Agreement, which facilitated the importation of manufactured goods such as textiles and garments, sent a clear signal that this trend would continue into the foreseeable future. Declared one union official, "The government is saying 'We don't want this labor-intensive industry here.' We're being told, 'You guys are done.'"[17] Thus, no sooner had African Americans begun to build an industrial presence in the South than the region's mainstay industry collapsed, taking with it the jobs of thousands of black workers.

Steel provided another example. Decades-long agitation by black workers relegated to the least desirable jobs had at last begun to break down the racial division of labor. In the Pittsburgh area, for example, in the aftermath of the 1974 consent decree, black workers slowly gained greater entry into the skilled, supervisory, and white-collar departments. But, as with textiles, the 1980s brought a devastating decline to what had once been America's flagship industry. In city after city, U.S. Steel, Bethlehem Steel, and other corporations shut down furnaces and fabricating plants, laying off thousands of steelworkers. Between 1982 and 1987, steel companies eliminated more than 100,000 union-wage jobs. Almost overnight, reported historian John Hinshaw, "Once vibrant blue-collar cities, former mill towns evolved into ghettoes for the poor, the elderly, and minorities." Between 1979 and 1985, one major producer, Inland Steel, eliminated more than 10,000 jobs in its northern Indiana plants; by the spring of 2002, only 6,000 workers remained. Employment at U.S. Steel fell by 68 percent between its peak in 1959 and 1984. By the end of the century, only about 4,000 production-related jobs remained in that once-massive corporation. Layoffs hit African American steelworkers with particular force, since the ancient open-hearth furnaces and other antiquated facilities that employed disproportionate numbers of veteran black workers were the first to be scuttled. Declared Ruth Needleman, a close observer and chronicler of the life and work in the mills of northern Indiana, "The impact of plant closings, new technology, foreign imports, and restructuring on the Calumet Region [i.e., the area around Gary, Indiana], and especially on the African American communities, has been devastating."[18]

Deindustrialization accelerated in the 1990s and early twenty-first century. In 2005, the Bureau of Labor Statistics reported that since 1990, total manufacturing employment in the United States had declined by more than 20 percent. Between 1998 and 2004, more than three million manufacturing jobs disappeared. African Americans were particularly hard hit. In 1979, about 24 percent of black workers were employed in manufacturing; in 2004, the figure stood at only 10.6 percent—a falloff of 56 percent.[19]

Even in the automobile industry, a relatively stable source of black industrial employment, the proportion of production jobs held by African Americans showed an irregular downward trend between 1979 and 2004. The total number of jobs began a sharp decline in the late 1990s, and new job creation in the industry was migrating rapidly to exurban and rural areas with few resident African Americans.[20] In a trend dating back to the 1950s, both established automakers and new entrants into the U.S. market increasingly located new plants in areas remote from centers of urban— and hence African American—population. This tendency was particularly noticeable among foreign-affiliated producers such as Nissan and Toyota, which, through the 1980s and 1990s, chose to place their facilities in southern and midwestern sites without significant black populations. Thus, as of 2004, foreign-affiliated automakers employed more than sixty-three thousand workers, only a tiny percentage of them African American.[21]

The deindustrialization of the great American heartland hit young African American men with particular force. In the early years of the new century, rates of unemployment for inner-city black men in the sixteen to twenty-five age group soared to over 50 percent. Indeed, official statistics understated the problem because they did not include those who were no longer seeking work or those who were incarcerated. Whereas historically, African American men had been employed at higher rates than their white counterparts, detailed investigations now found that large numbers of black men of prime working age had dropped out of the labor market entirely.

The decline of manufacturing jobs, especially in the inner cities, helped intensify inner-city poverty and the social problems associated with it. High levels of unemployment were associated with a sharp rise in out-of-wedlock births and a growing proportion of single-parent, female-headed households. Drug trafficking and other forms of criminal activity flourished, providing sources of income that were otherwise lacking and contributing to the soaring levels of black male enmeshment in the criminal justice system. "Especially in the country's inner cities," observed the *New York Times* in March 2006, "finishing high school is the exception, legal work is scarcer than ever and prison is almost routine." One study found that in 2000, on a given day, more African American male high school dropouts in their late twenties were in prison than were employed. By every significant indicator, reported one academic investigator, these "young black men were falling farther back." Declared Harvard University researcher Gary Orfield, "'We're pumping out boys with no honest [employment] alternative, and of course their neighborhoods offer many other [illegal] alternatives.'"[22]

Even as the inner cities festered, however, other African Americans were moving into the mainstream. The easing of the color line in the late twentieth century led to dramatic increases in professional and white-collar employment. In the forty years since passage of the Civil Rights Act of 1964, for example, the percentage of black men with college degrees quadrupled, and the number of black professionals exploded—as of 2004, seventy-eight thousand black men held engineering degrees, an increase of one-third since 1994. Higher incomes and relaxation of overt housing discrimination underlay the movement of middle-class African Americans into suburban areas, leaving behind the traditional black ghetto, which all too often became an island of despair and social pathology. The same newspaper reports that chronicled the growth in out-of-wedlock births and urban poverty also noted that "black families where men are in the home earn median incomes that approach those of white families."[23]

The plight of the inner-city black working class triggered sharp disagreement among scholars and activists even as it receded to the margins of mainstream political discourse. Among the most prominent delineators of inner-city problems was sociologist-economist William Julius Wilson, whose several books focusing on Chicago provided a coherent frame of reference for considering the relationships among racism, structural economic forces, and the problems facing urban blacks. In *The Declining Significance of Race* (1980), *The Truly Disadvantaged: The Inner City, the Underclass, and Public Policy* (1987), and *When Work Disappears: The World of the New Urban Poor* (1996), Wilson argued that as overt racial discrimination in employment, housing, and education diminished, the traditional African American urban community began to fragment. As opportunities expanded for blacks, those with stable white-collar and professional occupations were moving, as their white counterparts had done in the past, into the suburbs of large cities such as Chicago. Coterminously, the long-term leaching of manufacturing enterprises out of the urban centers to exurban and greenfield sites and, increasingly, out of the country altogether eliminated the relatively well-paying entry-level jobs that had enabled an earlier generation to establish stable families and move into the economic and educational mainstream. "Many of today's problems in the inner-city ghetto neighborhoods—crime, family dissolution, welfare [dependency], low levels of social organization . . .—are fundamentally a consequence of the disappearance of work," Wilson concluded, even before the sharp downturn in manufacturing employment starting in the late 1990s.[24]

Wilson acknowledged that racial prejudice still remained a factor in blacks' economic difficulties. Yet, he held, the difficulties encountered by young urban black men in turn-of-the-century job markets often had less to do with racial prejudice than with employers' distaste for what they saw as the violent and irresponsible behavior of troubled inner-city residents. Indeed, Wilson found that black inner-city employers were even more likely than their white counterparts to "express . . . negative views of the job-related traits of inner-city blacks." The combination of chronic unemployment, street crime, and a decaying physical environment, explained the black president of a Chicago business college, "creates such bizarre kinds of behavior that it breeds a different set of values," rendering many inner-city black males simply uncompetitive in the job market.[25]

Wilson's analysis was challenged from both the Right and the Left.

Conservative African American commentators—notably Thomas Sowell and John McWhorter, along with scholars Stephan and Abigail Thernstrom—endorsed the view that racial prejudice was playing a diminishing role in the competition for jobs. The fact that so many African Americans had taken advantage of the new dispensation in race relations created by the 1960s civil rights legislation belied the idea that black workers were still victims of an unjust social and economic order. Indeed, the outdated rhetoric of aging civil rights leaders, who continued to define black workers' problems as problems of rights rather than of opportunities, misled inner-city dwellers. Moreover, they believed, the affirmative action programs of the 1960s and 1970s had actually distorted job markets, providing unneeded benefits to the well educated, forcing employers to hire underqualified workers, and having the unintended but very real consequence of inducing employers to locate away from centers of black population.

In two widely discussed books, *Losing the Race: Self-Sabotage in Black America* (2000) and *Winning the Race: Beyond the Crisis in Black America* (2006), McWhorter accused liberal elites and hidebound civil rights activists of encouraging young blacks to disdain hard work, family values, and individual responsibility. Rejecting Wilson's disappearance-of-work thesis, McWhorter declared, "Our problems . . . have not been the eclipse of the manufacturing economy, overly ambitious middle-class blacks [deserting the ghettos], drugs 'coming in,' structural racism, or any of the things commonly adduced." McWhorter blamed public policies that, in effect, promoted single parenthood, bred welfare dependency, and encouraged an unwillingness to conform to standard workplace expectations of comportment and demeanor. Urban black culture encouraged notions of "therapeutic alienation," according to McWhorter, which fed antisocial behavior and combined a sense of entitlement with hostility toward authority figures—most notably, would-be employers.[26]

To some commentators, however, a focus on the personal deficiencies of inner-city job seekers was a classic case of "blaming the victim." They pointed out that, despite the real gains of the civil rights era, hard-core racial prejudice was alive and well. Even during the relatively quiescent 1990s, the EEOC heard innumerable complaints from black workers who had been turned away in favor of less-qualified whites. Substantial disparities in pay and income between white and black workers of identical experience and education persisted. Journalist Richard Rothstein summarized detailed case studies that showed that employers were three times more likely to choose whites over blacks and to offer higher wages to whites even when applicants of both races presented identical qualifications. One recent study, he wrote in 2004, "found that whites' applications were more successful than blacks' even when the whites had criminal records and the otherwise identical blacks did not."[27]

Economists William A. Darity Jr. and Samuel L. Myers Jr., in a comprehensive survey of diverse economic indicators, found in 1998 that reports of black economic progress often rested on questionable statistical assumptions and data categories. For all but the very top echelon of African American income earners, progress in gaining parity with whites had come to a halt as soon as the early 1980s. To be sure, the disappearance of manufacturing jobs played a role, but the scarcity of well-paying entry-level jobs simply increased the effects of ongoing job discrimination. "To put it bluntly," they declared, "discrimination in a comprehensive sense lies at the core of matters, not just at the point of employment but throughout . . . American society [which] is quite distant from attaining a pure equal opportunity environment."[28]

By the first decade of the twenty-first century, what was most remarkable about the economic crisis of the urban black working class was not the sharply conflicting views about its causes and manifestations but rather its relative absence from political discourse. Neither candidate in the 2004 presidential election, for example, made more than passing allusions to the economic and social plight of the inner cities. Neither captured the atmosphere of despair and social catastrophe that pervaded many urban communities. Bromides about individual responsibility, reliance on "faith-based" charities, and praise for the beneficial effects of private enterprise substituted for coherent policies to address the jobs crisis. In June 2005, a foundation-supported commission consisting of academics, community leaders, and politicians began delving into the problems of inner-city youth, but its meetings received little attention in the press. To be sure, major national newspapers periodically addressed the growing pathologies afflicting urban blacks. In March 2006, the *New York Times* reported that "black men . . . face a far more dire situation than is portrayed by common employment and education statistics." A *Washington Post* series launched in the summer of 2006 used polling data and interviews to survey what one participant described as "beyond a crisis. . . . It is a catastrophe."[29]

But for many Americans, black and white, awareness of the state of the inner cities is filtered through widely circulated cultural images. Television police shows such as *NYPD Blue, Homicide: Life on the Streets,* and *The Wire* always included positive African Americans characters, but they tended to focus on the urban, mostly black, underworld of criminality, casual violence, and sexual license. Rap music and the sartorial fashions associated with it glorify the violent, misogynistic underside of urban black life. Observed the *Washington Post,* "A long, lucrative stream of music videos and movies extol the 'thug life.' . . . Rapper 50 Cent has built his chart-busting, multimedia career on his being shot nine times and left for dead during his days as a drug dealer in Queens. Similarly, rapper, actor and pitchman Snoop Dogg has written music referring to his gang-life past, and his playful public persona as a would-be pimp, to fame."[30]

Black Workers and the Labor Movement, 1980–2005

In the post-1980 period, the crisis of the black inner city coincided with hard times for the U.S. labor movement. In the 1980s and 1990s, union membership fell off sharply, particularly in the private sector. In a dramatically changing economy characterized by intensified international competition, industrial decline, and hostile public labor policies, African Americans continued to be among the most union-minded workers, even as black union members were disproportionately affected by plant closures, union-busting campaigns, and migrating jobs. Union reformers stressed the crucial role of blacks, other people of color, and women in their efforts to rebuild and revitalize the labor movement. In the first years of the new century, however, sharp disagreements surfaced among labor activists over how to use black workers' union-mindedness to reverse labor's decline. At the same time, the influx of large numbers of immigrant workers raised troubling and divisive questions about their role in the economy generally, their place in the labor movement, and their relationship to native African American workers.

In the years surrounding the beginning of the twenty-first century, America's labor leaders took steps to identify organized labor more closely with the distinctive aspirations of workers of color. Constituency groups within the House of Labor, most notably the Coalition of Black Trade Unionists (CBTU), asserted the perspectives of women and people of color within the House of Labor itself. Some unions, notably the Service Employees International Union (SEIU), conducted innovative organizing campaigns that targeted blacks and other workers of color. In the 1980s and 1990s, the balance of numbers, and of power, in the labor federation shifted decisively from the old industrial, transport, and construction unions to organizations such as the SEIU and the American Federation of State, County, and Municipal Employees (AFSCME), which represented service and governmental employees, many of them African American. In 1995, the election of a reform-minded slate of officers in the AFL-CIO's first contested election since 1894 expanded the number of African Americans on its governing board.[31]

Yet a decade later, labor's crisis seemed, if anything, more desperate, triggering calls for a drastic structural overhaul of the entire House of Labor. In July 2005, five large unions representing 40 percent of the national labor federation's membership, several with large African American contingents, pulled out of the AFL-CIO to form a new national center of labor activism, the Change to Win (CTW) coalition. Black activists urged both sides to recognize the distinctive problems that African American workers faced and the unique opportunities for progressive revival that they offered. But, black unionists charged, despite rhetorical paeans to diversity, neither CTW nor the established AFL-CIO leadership was addressing the problems and possibilities that black workers embodied.

The decline of organized labor at the end of the twentieth century was precipitous. As late as 1980, more than 25 percent of American workers had belonged to unions. In 2005, the figure stood at about 12.5 percent, and less than 8 percent of the workers in private (as opposed to governmental) employment were enrolled in unions. Although African American workers continued to belong to unions at higher rates than their white, Hispanic, and Asian coworkers, there was a sharp drop-off in the number of black unionists. For example, the Bureau of Labor Statistics reported that by 2004, U.S. unions had lost 300,000 members, a vastly disproportionate number of them African American. Although black workers constituted only 13 percent of union membership, fully 55 percent of the union jobs lost had been held by African Americans, 70 percent of them women.[32] In 1983, almost 32 percent of all black workers were union represented; by 2004, that figure had fallen by almost half.[33]

Explanations for this free fall abounded. Analysts cited the decline in employment in industrial and extractive (i.e., mining) enterprises, the failures of labor leadership, aggressive union-busting on the part of private employers, the impact of global markets, and antiunion governmental policies. Indeed, some adherents of "free-market" economic policies hailed the decline in union membership and influence as salutary, since, in the words of two economists, over the past century, "labor unions have reduced U.S. output by . . . trillions of dollars."[34] Of course, union loyalists rejected this sort of analysis, arguing that the decline in union strength was a key factor in the three-decades-long stagnation in wages, the increase in the American workweek, and the growing gap between the affluent minority and working people of all ethnic and racial groups. Declared Secretary of Labor Robert Reich in the midst of the 1990s stock market boom, "a major shift from . . . paychecks to dividends and capital gains" was taking place in the new economy. "Things," he added, "are simply out of whack."[35]

By the mid-1990s, both organized labor's incumbent leaders and their challengers within the labor movement agreed, at least on paper, that African American workers and voters were at the core of hopes for a liberal-labor revival. Both sets of candidates pledged to increase African American representation in the AFL-CIO's governing bodies and on the organizing and administrative staff. Both vowed to step up efforts to expand organization in the service sector of the economy, where black workers were concentrated. Both invoked the spirits of Martin Luther King Jr. and

A. Philip Randolph—who had died in 1979 at age ninety—to emphasize the common aspirations and values of African American citizens and organized labor. "Our alliance is . . . needed today perhaps more than ever before," declared AFL-CIO secretary-treasurer Tom Donahue.[36]

In October 1995, a dissident slate of officers led by SEIU president John Sweeney emerged victorious at the AFL-CIO convention. The delegates also approved changes that expanded the federation's governing body, the Executive Council, and significantly increased the number of women and minorities serving on it. Sweeney's background as head of the expanding SEIU created expectations that the new AFL-CIO leadership would be particularly active in reaching out to women, African Americans, and low-wage workers of all descriptions.

During Sweeney's tenure, the SEIU had launched a "Justice for Janitors" campaign aimed at organizing custodial workers, especially those employed in the downtown office complexes of large cities. Working closely with rank-and-file workers, organizers combined the traditional strike with innovative tactics and well-crafted appeals to gain public sympathy for these low-wage workers, most of whom were African American and Hispanic. In Denver, Los Angeles, Boston, Houston, and other cities, the union won recognition and achieved important contract benefits. Other successful SEIU campaigns targeted hospital workers, home-care workers, and nursing home employees, bringing a sense of crusading activism to the project of bringing large numbers of African Americans and other people of color into the House of Labor. The SEIU's successes engendered hope that the Sweeney regime might revitalize the AFL-CIO and that marginalized low-wage minority workers might become the spearhead of a broad resurgence. In 2002, one enthusiastic academic supporter declared, "The SEIU and the janitors are opening a new path for American democracy comparable to that achieved by the early CIO and the Civil Rights movement of the 1950s and 1960s."[37]

Translating the SEIU's successes into a more general advance for the labor movement proved elusive, however. Nor did the increased representation of black unionists on the AFL-CIO Executive Council work wonders, especially since there were no black leaders among the large unions that dominated the decision-making apparatus. Noted new member Clayola Brown, the African American vice president of the textile and garment workers union and national president of the A. Philip Randolph Institute, "I sit on the AFL-CIO Council. Those boys don't ask me anything."[38]

Troubled, too, were the AFL-CIO's relations with "constituent" groups, notably the CBTU. In 1965, in response to the rise of black militancy both in the labor movement and in society at large, the AFL-CIO had created the A. Philip Randolph Institute and named Randolph's long-term associate Bayard Rustin as its director. The Randolph Institute was to be an in-house body, financed largely by the AFL-CIO and its constituent unions. Its central aims were to make organized labor a part of the African American community by establishing local chapters throughout the country and working with local unionists and other liberal activists to highlight the economic issues that Rustin believed the civil rights movement must address after the achievement of voting rights. Chapters of the institute would mobilize voters and press for full employment policies, increased support for impoverished inner-city schools, and urban housing initiatives. The institute would be a visible presence of the black-labor political coalition on which hope for liberal domestic policies rested.[39]

Being directly connected to the AFL-CIO and largely dependent on it for funding, the Randolph Institute did not provide a forum for dissident black activists who highlighted the limitations of the labor movement's racial policies and programs. "The Randolph Institute," declared Rustin, "does not see itself as an adversary to the labor movement."[40] Through the remainder of the century and into the next one, the institute helped mobilize African American voters, who soon became the Democratic Party's most reliable supporters. Indeed, as divisive issues such as affirmative action and "law and order" became more important in the 1970s and 1980s, black support for labor-endorsed candidates far outstripped that of union members overall and of the white working class generally. In the 1960 presidential election, Republican Richard Nixon had captured about 60 percent of the black vote, but with the passage of civil rights laws in the 1960s—and particularly the 1965 Voting Rights Act—African Americans regularly rewarded the Democrats with massive majorities, often approaching 90 percent, in a vastly expanded black electorate. Rustin's hope for a potent black-labor-liberal alliance was thus only partially realized, as increasing numbers of white workers, including union members, turned to candidates such as Alabama governor George Wallace, Richard Nixon, and eventually Ronald Reagan to protest what many perceived as excessive black militancy, rising crime rates, and unfair affirmative action initiatives. Strains in the labor-black political alliance were particularly evident in cities such as Detroit, Chicago, Baltimore, Milwaukee, and Philadelphia, as racial antagonisms affected law enforcement, housing, and municipal services, and industrial decline in these places pitted worker against worker in a competition for jobs and public resources.

For their part, African American laborites continued to believe that a more militant and outspoken organization of black workers within the House of Labor was needed. The CBTU was the answer to that felt need. In the fall of 1972, for the first time in its history, the AFL-CIO refused to endorse either major-party presidential candidate—neither incumbent Republican Richard Nixon nor Democratic nominee Senator George McGovern of South Dakota. Although McGovern had a strong pro-labor voting record in the Senate and had long been one of the leading liberal voices in Congress, AFL-CIO president George Meany deplored his vocal opposition to the war in Vietnam. A rigid anticommunist, Meany believed that a bizarre coalition of naive peace-mongers, countercultural zealots, and dangerous radicals was taking over the machinery of the Democratic Party. Certainly, changes in the party's delegate selection process and in its institutional operations were designed to limit the influence of traditional power brokers such as Meany and to increase the weight of racial minorities, feminists, young people, and other hitherto marginal groups. For African Americans, however, Meany's refusal to endorse McGovern— which, in effect, meant a kind of tacit, backhanded endorsement of Nixon, whose name was anathema to laborites—courted disaster. In a hastily called gathering, some twelve hundred African American labor activists met in Chicago in September 1972. Led by five of the country's most prominent black labor leaders, the convention denounced the AFL-CIO's "neutrality" declaration and went on to form a permanent body, the CBTU.

The following spring, delegates adopted a formal constitution and chose AFSCME secretary-treasurer William Lucy as the CBTU's president. Lucy and his fellow officers issued a founding statement that invoked the concerns that had earlier animated the Negro American Labor Council (NALC) and the defunct National Negro Labor Council (NNLC). The labor movement, they insisted, "must reflect greater participation of black trade unionists at every level." Organizing and mobilizing black workers in behalf of the liberal-labor agenda, they believed, was crucial: "We are convinced that the responsibility to . . . harness and use the expertise and power of this vast political resource rests with black trade unionists." Affirming their fealty to the AFL-CIO, they avoided direct attacks on the labor federation but insisted that "it is our challenge to make the labor movement more relevant to the needs and aspirations of black and poor workers." "Black union officials," they declared, must "become full partners in the leadership and decision-making of the American labor movement."[41]

Throughout the latter years of the twentieth century and beyond, CBTU members worked hard to expand black influence within the labor movement and to broaden organized labor's base. As president, Lucy emerged as the country's most prominent African American labor leader, narrowly losing a 1981 bid to become president of AFSCME, which in the 1980s became one of the AFL-CIO's largest and most dynamic affiliates. In the mid-1990s, the CBTU played an active role in the successful effort to broaden the AFL-CIO Executive Council, including the appointment of more women and people of color to the council and to staff positions in the federation and in its affiliated unions. From its inception, the CBTU stressed the role of women in the labor movement and reached out to other minorities, helping to sponsor and support other constituency organizations such as the Coalition of Labor Union Women, the Labor Council for Latin American Advancement, and the Asian Pacific American Labor Alliance. The CBTU was particularly active in establishing connections with labor and human rights organizations elsewhere, most notably in South Africa and Latin America, sometimes in implicit disagreement with the AFL-CIO's anticommunist position in foreign affairs.

Although the CBTU's idiom was less strident than that of the NNLC or the NALC, relations between it and the AFL-CIO were always edgy. Although the CBTU received funding from the AFL-CIO and from constituent unions, it was insistent in projecting itself as the legitimate voice of black labor. Its annual convention served as a wide-ranging forum for discussion of the problems of the labor movement. In the mid-2000s, differences between the CBTU and both the AFL-CIO and the CTW dissidents held significant implications for the CBTU and for black workers generally. The CBTU had always been active politically, regarding itself as a key element in mobilizing the African American vote. Thus, in the 2000 elections, CBTU supporters, with funding from the AFL-CIO's political war chest, did effective work in bringing out the black vote. In Florida, for example, state representative and CBTU activist Anthony Hill advanced a remarkably successful labor-black campaign, dubbed "Arrive with Five" (i.e., each voter was encouraged to show up at the polls with five additional voters), that helped elect a Democratic U.S. senator and came within a disputed eyelash of carrying Florida (and, as it turned out, the entire election) for Democrat Al Gore.

In 2004, however, AFL-CIO political operatives decided not to fund constituency groups such as the CBTU. In a complex and often acrimonious debate, reflecting in part the changes in election funding mandated by passage of the McCain-Feingold Act in 2002, Lucy and other leaders of constituency organizations charged that they were being frozen out of voter mobilization projects, despite their proven track record. CBTU activists believed that the AFL-CIO's new political program wasted vast sums of money going after disaffected white male voters while starving groups such as itself that had already been successful in generating high percentages of pro-labor voters. "Some 'constituent groups,'" charged CBTU council member Nat LaCour in an ironic reference to this mistaken strategy, "got over $100 million and their vote went down. If the CBTU and the [Randolph Institute] had that kind of money, we'd have gotten 100 percent of the vote," instead of the 89 percent support that black voters had demonstrated for Democratic presidential candidate Senator John Kerry.[42]

The subsequent debate in 2004–2005 over proposals to restructure the AFL-CIO also drew the fire of black unionists. Charging that under incumbent AFL-CIO president John Sweeney the federation had neglected organizing in favor of increasingly futile political action, SEIU head Andy

Stern proposed a drastic restructuring of the federation. The number of separate affiliated unions would be severely reduced, with a handful of mega-unions emerging. The AFL-CIO Executive Council's fifty-four members would be downsized to a streamlined body of sixteen. The AFL-CIO's central staff would be sharply reduced, with the financial savings returned to the newly restructured and consolidated affiliated unions to be spent in massive campaigns to organize the unorganized. When Stern and his supporters in several other unions, notably the teamsters, the food and commercial workers, the laborers, and the newly amalgamated union of garment, hotel, and service workers, found themselves stymied, they announced their secession from the AFL-CIO and the creation of a new labor center, the CTW coalition.

African American activists responded sharply, albeit ambivalently, to these developments. Among the seceding organizations was the SEIU, which was carrying out innovative programs of organizing low-skilled black and other minority workers. But Lucy and others stressed that plans to change the governing structure of the AFL-CIO would mean the loss of black and other minority representation on the Executive Council, which a generation of black unionists had struggled to attain. Moreover, AFSCME, whose leaders denounced the CTW initiative, remained in the AFL-CIO and provided a base for Lucy as the CBTU's highly visible and highly respected leader. One version of Stern's plans for a revamped labor federation would have all but eliminated funding for the constituent organizations, including, of course, the CBTU. Declared Bill Fletcher, a veteran black labor activist and former aide to AFL-CIO president Sweeney, "From my visits around the country, I have found that local activists feel both alienated from and scared of this debate. They feel that it is not about them and does not include them. I would go further and say that for union members of color, this is especially the case."[43]

It was an article of faith among many African American activists, and many white supporters as well, that blacks and other people of color represented the only real hope of reviving and revitalizing a labor movement that had been in decline for a quarter century. "Our opponents in business and on the political Right," declared Fletcher, "wish our annihilation. They are not talking about simply the reduction of [organized labor's] . . . numbers or power, but our total elimination."[44] Black workers, with their disproportionate propensity to belong to unions, their massive presence in the rapidly expanding service sector of the economy, and their vigorous political action that regularly turned out overwhelming majorities for liberal candidates, were at the forefront of the struggle to resist the tide of reaction. In the opinion of one close observer, "Blacks confront an environment in which elements of both white male-dominated labor camps [i.e., CTW and the AFL-CIO incumbents] appear to believe that minority constituency representation, and empowerment of largely black and brown big city labor councils, is something the New AFL-CIO can do without." "We are," Lucy insisted, "the most loyal segment of the trade union vote and the Democratic Party vote, yet our voices are not at the center of the discussion about . . . reforms." As the debate over structural change in the AFL-CIO escalated through the first half of 2005, Lucy insisted, "We need to raise the question: How will minority influence be enhanced?" But by the time of the CTW secession in July, there was no clear answer.[45]

Overlapping these structural and organizational issues was the problem of immigration and its relationship both to the labor movement generally and to the concerns of black workers in particular. Through the early 2000s, the large influx of workers from Mexico and Central America, both legal and undocumented, continued unabated. The sense that the country's borders were too porous and that the government had no effective control over this vast demographic development grew, especially after the terrorist attacks of September 11, 2001. On one level, the public debate over immigration was about the security of the borders, with those who feared a decisive undermining of Anglo-American culture and institutions pitted against those who saw large-scale immigration as a healthy and positive infusion of diversity and vigor that filled pressing needs for low-skilled labor.

In the House of Labor, fierce debate raged among scholars, trade unionists, and ordinary citizens over the impact of large-scale immigration on wages and opportunities for native American workers. Some studies seemed to indicate that the influx of low-skilled and poorly educated Hispanic immigrants jeopardized the employment prospects of America's most vulnerable native workers, particularly African Americans. Other studies, while acknowledging a marginal impact among urban black high school dropouts, pointed to the overall benefits that a vigorous and productive immigrant workforce was bringing to American society overall. In general, most African Americans active in the labor movement opposed the imposition of harsh penalties on illegal immigrants and favored legislative proposals that would facilitate undocumented immigrants' transition from illegal to legal status. Although these views sometimes put them in apparent opposition to the views of most African Americans, as reflected in public opinion polls, leaders such as Lucy, Hill, and many others believed that organized labor should welcome workers of all description while expanding efforts to organize them and to provide educational and other public services that would raise their standards and reduce the competitive aspects of immigration. Black unionists frequently invoked the notion of "black and brown" to suggest the advantages of an alliance among all people of color in an effort to build a stronger labor movement and to further progressive political agendas. Proponents of this approach pointed, for example, to the success of the Los Angeles labor movement in building black-brown coalitions and in electing in 2005 a strongly pro-labor mayor, Antonio Villaraigosa.

Yet tensions between Hispanic and African American workers and voters were very real. To some, it was alarming that the great majority of Hispanic people, when asked in polls about their ethnic identity, chose "white." Other polls showed that levels of attitudinal antiblack prejudice were higher among Hispanics and Asians in the United States than among white respondents. African Americans—products of the highly individuated sense of social identity of the dominant culture—often expressed resentment and hostility toward Asians and Hispanics who relied on closed networks of family members and old-country friends and neighbors to control certain categories of jobs and to promote group-oriented entrepreneurial activities. Although labor activists of all racial and ethnic backgrounds might ritualistically invoke the rhetoric of solidarity and mutuality, the United States has a long historical record of transforming once-despised and ethnically "other" immigrants into fellow whites—and always at the expense of African Americans, the perennial "other." Scholar George Yancey made the point succinctly: "the informal rejection of African Americans, rather than a tendency by the majority to oppress all minority groups in a roughly equal manner, is the linchpin to the American contemporary racial hierarchy."[46]

The questions raised by the debate over immigration are only the latest evidence of the ambiguities and ironies that have characterized the story of African American workers and their relationship to the broader working class and to the labor movement. Indeed, the very terms "black" and "white" are deeply problematic. Neither is a biological category. Both are and always have been social constructs, although the content of these constructs has undergone constant change and redefinition. As legal scholar Ian Haney-Lopez observed, voices of both the Right and the Left call for an end to racial categorization, the former in rejection of special legislative or judicial treatment, the latter in the cause of human solidarity. It is ironic, perhaps even tragic, that those who most ardently hope for African Americans' full integration into American life seem compelled to use the language of separation. "Negro and White, Unite and Fight" went the slogan of progressive CIO unionists in the 1930s and 1940s—at once celebrating interracial cooperation and endorsing the separation of the working class into two essential categories.[47]

By many measures, African American workers have made remarkable gains in modern America, both in their legal status and in their tangible achievements. In 1857, Justice Roger Taney declared that "the black man has no rights which a white man is bound to respect." For a century thereafter, African Americans struggled first to attain legal equality and then to make it practically, as well as theoretically, real. The federal civil rights laws of the 1950s and 1960s finally gave substance to the Civil War–era grant of citizenship under the Fourteenth Amendment. In the realm of employment rights, the Fair Employment Practice Committee, state equal employment laws, presidential initiatives, and Titles VI and VII of the Civil Rights Act of 1964 removed legal sanction from employment discrimination. For two decades, affirmative action helped change the "color of work" in the United States. Even after the heyday of legal progress had passed, employers that felt no compunction about penalizing workers for their union sympathies solemnly intoned their commitment to equal employment opportunity insofar as race was concerned. Indeed, at least on a rhetorical level, the term "equal opportunity employer," once an oxymoron, had become a cliché.

More tangibly, African Americans' movement in the first half of the twentieth century out of the low-wage, agricultural South was the basis for substantial gains in relative income. Civil rights laws and affirmative action programs spurred greater progress in the 1960s and 1970s. It is true that these gains in income have been volatile. Moreover, even as black income rose, the wealth of black families remained a minor fraction of whites' wealth, owing in large part to the powerful effects of ongoing housing discrimination. Still, the vast expansion of the black middle class, the surge into the professions, and the visibility of blacks in public life, entertainment, and sports constituted a sea change from the world of the early 1960s.

Yet there have been ironies as well. Black access to good jobs in industries such as textiles, railroads, steel, and a host of others was no sooner achieved than those sectors began to decline. For the past two generations, the northern cities, once regarded as a "land of hope," have become a dead end for young black males. The end of legal sanction for segregation and discrimination has helped propel those with access to resources and educational opportunities out of once-thriving black neighborhoods and into a deracinated suburban world, leaving behind troubled cities and fragmented communities. Rising incomes and broadened opportunities for some coexist with poverty and despair for many. Whereas during the heyday of Jim Crow, black unemployment rates were characteristically lower than those of whites, for the past fifty years, black joblessness has far exceeded that of whites. Whereas before the civil rights revolution, the participation of African American males in the labor force regularly surpassed that of their white cohorts, today, the relationship is sharply reversed. Statistics on longevity, criminal incarceration, poverty rates, and a host of other social indicators vividly reveal the limits of the economic advancement of the black working class.

Ironies also abound with respect to the relationship between black workers and the labor movement. Certainly, today's diversity-celebrating and affirmative action–supporting AFL-CIO is a far cry from the racist and immigrant-bashing labor movement of a century ago. Indeed, it is precisely among people of color, along with women, that the hope of future revival is lodged. Into the new century, African American workers were more likely than any other discrete racial or ethnic cohort to join unions, and African American voters continued to be the most loyal and cohesive element in the liberal-labor political coalition. Yet recent efforts to reform and revitalize the national labor movement have drawn sharp criticism from black activists, who charge that both the current AFL-CIO leadership and their challengers in the CTW coalition have been marginalizing African Americans. Declared labor activist Dwight Kirk, "it is more than ironic that a decade after Black trade unionists successfully thrust color and gender into labor's last major leadership 'makeover' they and their allies are now on the defensive, fighting to protect past diversity gains from the knives of some new 'reformers.'"[48]

A hundred years ago, W. E. B. DuBois declared that "the problem of the Twentieth Century is the problem of the color-line." It took the mainstream U.S. labor movement almost a century to acknowledge the pertinence of that remark. "We're the only ones that can save the labor movement," proclaimed one veteran African American activist in a debate over the most recent proposals to achieve laborite resurgence through structural reform.[49] Whether multiracial labor revival is possible in the political economy of globalized production, continuing domestic political frustration, and ongoing immigration is the problem of the twenty-first century.

NOTES

Introduction

1. Risa Lauren Goluboff, "'Let Economic Equality Take Care of Itself': The NAACP, Labor Litigation, and the Making of Civil Rights in the 1940s," *UCLA Law Review* 52, no. 5 (June 2005): 1393–1486, has helped me understand the reasons for my youthful obtuseness.

2. There is an extensive historical literature on African American workers and their relationship to white workers and to the labor movement. Readers can follow historiographical debates on the broad theme of race and labor in a number of spirited essays. See, for example, Herbert Hill, "Race, Ethnicity and Organized Labor: The Opposition to Affirmative Action," *New Politics,* n.s., 1, no. 2 (Winter 1987): 31–82, and the ensuing discussion in ibid., 1, no. 3 (Summer 1987): 22–71; Herbert Hill, "The Problem of Race in American Labor History," *Reviews in American History* 24, no. 2 (June 1996): 189–208; Herbert Hill, "Myth-Making as Labor History: Herbert Gutman and the United Mine Workers of America," *International Journal of Politics, Culture and Society* 2, no. 2 (Winter 1988): 132–200; Gunther Peck, "White Slavery and Whiteness: A Transnational View of the Sources of Working-Class Radicalism and Racism," *Labor: Studies in Working-Class History of the Americas* 1, no. 2 (Summer 2004): 41–63; Eric Arnesen, "Following the Color Line of Labor: Black Workers and the Labor Movement before 1930," *Radical History Review* 55 (Winter 1993): 53–87; Eric Arnesen, "Up from Exclusion: Black and White Workers, Race, and the State of Labor History," *Reviews in American History* 26, no. 1 (March 1998): 146–74; Eric Arnesen, "Whiteness and Historians' Imagination," *International Labor and Working-Class History* 60 (Fall 2001): 3–32, and Responses and Arnesen Reply, 33–92; Eric Arnesen, "Passion and Politics: Race and the Writing of Working-Class History," *Journal of the Historical Society* 6, no. 3 (September 2006): 323–56; Alex Lichtenstein, "Racial Conflict and Racial Solidarity in the Alabama Coal Strike of 1894: New Evidence for the Gutman-Hill Debate," *Labor History* 36, no. 1 (Winter 1995): 63–76; Bruce Nelson, "Working-Class Agency and Racial Inequality," *International Review of Social History* 41, part 3 (1996): 407–20; Stanford M. Lyman, "The 'Chinese Question' and American Labor Historians," *New Politics* 7, no. 4 (Winter 2000): 113–48; Michael Goldfield, "Was There a Golden Age of the CIO? Race, Solidarity, and Union Growth during the 1930s and 1940s," in *Trade Union Politics: American Unions and Economic Change, 1960s–1990s,* ed. Glenn Perusek

and Kent Worcester (Atlantic Highlands, N.J.: Humanities Press, 1995), 78–110; Michael Goldfield, "Race and the CIO: The Possibilities for Racial Egalitarianism during the 1930s and 1940s," *International Labor and Working-Class History* 44 (Fall 1993): 1–32.

3. See, for example, Noel Ignatiev, *How the Irish Became White* (New York: Routledge, 1995); Thomas A. Guglielmo, *White on Arrival: Italians, Race, Color, and Power in Chicago, 1890–1945* (New York: Oxford University Press, 2003); David R. Roediger, *The Wages of Whiteness: Race and the Making of the American Working Class*, rev. ed. (London: Verso, 1999); David R. Roediger, *Working toward Whiteness—How America's Immigrants Became White: The Strange Journey from Ellis Island to the Suburbs* (New York: Basic Books, 2005). For critical commentary, see Arnesen, "Whiteness and Historians' Imagination"; and Peter Kolchin, "Whiteness Studies: The New History of Race in America," *Journal of American History* 89, no. 1 (June 2002): 154–73. See also Evelyn Nakano Glenn, *Unequal Freedom: How Race and Gender Shaped American Citizenship and Labor* (Cambridge, Mass.: Harvard University Press, 2002).

4. George Yancey, *Who Is White? Latinos, Asians, and the New Black/Nonblack Divide*, paperback ed. (Boulder, Colo.: Lynne Rienner, 2004).

5. See Najia Aarim-Heriot, *Chinese Immigrants, African Americans, and Racial Anxiety in the United States, 1848–82* (Urbana and Chicago: University of Illinois Press, 2003); Andrew Gyory, *Closing the Gate: Race, Politics, and the Chinese Exclusion Act* (Chapel Hill: University of North Carolina Press, 1998); Erika Lee, *At America's Gates: Chinese Immigration during the Exclusion Era, 1882–1943* (Chapel Hill: University of North Carolina Press, 2003).

6. Matt Garcia, *A World of Its Own: Race, Labor, and Citrus in the Making of Greater Los Angeles, 1900–1970* (Chapel Hill: University of North Carolina Press, 2001); Zaragosa Vargas, *Labor Rights Are Civil Rights: Mexican American Workers in Twentieth-Century America* (Princeton, N.J.: Princeton University Press, 2005); Emilio Zamora, *The World of the Mexican Worker in Texas* (College Station: Texas A&M University Press, 1993); Neil Foley, *The White Scourge: Mexicans, Blacks, and Poor Whites in Texas Cotton Culture* (Berkeley: University of California Press, 1997). See also Charles Montgomery, *The Spanish Redemption: Heritage, Power, and Loss on New Mexico's Upper Rio Grande* (Berkeley: University of California Press, 2002).

7. John D. Skrentny, *The Minority Rights Revolution* (Cambridge, Mass.: Belknap Press of Harvard University Press, 2002), 344–45; Toni Morrison quoted in Stephen Steinberg, "Immigration, African Americans, and Race Discourse," in *Race and Labor Matters in the New U.S. Economy*, ed. Manning Marable, Immanuel Ness, and Joseph Wilson (Lanham, Md.: Rowman and Littlefield, 2006), 175.

8. The classic modern critique of organized labor as an economic and political actor is Mancur Olson, *The Logic of Collective Action: Public Goods and the Theory of Groups* (Cambridge, Mass.: Harvard University Press, 1965). For more recent econometric perspectives that see unions as enemies of productivity, progress, and social equity, see Morgan O. Reynolds, "Labor Unions," in Library of Economics and Liberty, *The Concise Encyclopedia of Economics*, n.d., http://www.econlib.org/LIBRARY/Enc/LaborUnions.html (accessed July 20, 2006); and Richard Vedder and Lowell Gallaway, "The Economic Effects of Labor Unions Revis-

ited," *Journal of Labor Research* 23, no. 1 (Winter 2002): 105–30. Price Fishback, *Soft Coal, Hard Choices: The Economic Welfare of Bituminous Coal Miners, 1890–1930* (New York: Oxford University Press, 1992), challenges mainstream labor historiography from an econometric perspective. The most relevant market-celebrating studies of the history of race and labor are David E. Bernstein, *Only One Place of Redress: African Americans, Labor Regulations, and the Courts from Reconstruction to the New Deal* (Durham, N.C.: Duke University Press, 2001); and Paul D. Moreno, *Black Americans and Organized Labor: A New History* (Baton Rouge: Louisiana State University Press, 2006). For a detailed discussion of these books and the issues they raise, see Robert H. Zieger, "Race and Labor in the Twentieth Century" (a review of David E. Bernstein, *Only One Place of Redress: African Americans, Labor Regulations, and the Courts from Reconstruction to the New Deal*), *Reviews in American History* 29, no. 4 (December 2001): 567–72; and Robert H. Zieger, "How Unions Hurt African American Workers: A View from the Right," *Labor History* (forthcoming), available at http://www.clas.ufl.edu/users/rzieger/reviews.htm#Moreno (accessed September 12, 2006).

9. In addition to the sources cited in note 2, above, see Nancy MacLean, "Achieving the Promise of the Civil Rights Act: Herbert Hill and the NAACP's Fight for Jobs and Justice," 13–19; Nelson Lichtenstein, "Herbert Hill in History and Contention," 25–31; and Alex Lichtenstein, "Herbert Hill and the 'Negro Question,'" 33–39, all in *Labor: Studies in Working-Class History of the Americas* 3, no. 2 (2006); Bruce Nelson, "'CIO Meant One Thing for the Whites and Another Thing for Us': Steelworkers and Civil Rights, 1936–1974," in *Southern Labor in Transition, 1940–1995*, ed. Robert H. Zieger (Knoxville: University of Tennessee Press, 1997), 113–45; Bruce Nelson, *Divided We Stand: American Workers and the Struggle for Black Equality* (Princeton, N.J.: Princeton University Press, 2001); William B. Gould, *Black Workers in White Unions: Job Discrimination in the United States* (Ithaca, N.Y.: Cornell University Press, 1977); Michael Goldfield, *The Color of Politics: Race and the Mainsprings of American Politics* (New York: New Press, 1997); and Roediger, *Working toward Whiteness.*

10. The phrase is Lizabeth Cohen's in *Making a New Deal: Industrial Workers in Chicago, 1919–1939* (Cambridge: Cambridge University Press, 1990).

11. For troubled reflections on this theme, see David Roediger, "What If Labor Were Not White and Male? Recentering Working-Class History and Reconstructing Debate on Unions and Race," *International Labor and Working-Class History* 51 (Spring 1997): 72–95.

12. Malcolm Gladwell, "The Risk Pool," *New Yorker*, August 28, 2006, 35.

13. Clayton Sinyai, *Schools of Democracy: A Political History of the American Labor Movement* (Ithaca, N.Y.: ILR Press, 2006), 2–3.

1. The First Fruits of Freedom

1. Quoted in Eric Foner, *Politics and Ideology in the Age of the Civil War* (New York: Oxford University Press, 1980), 98.

2. Quoted in Thavolia Glymph, "Freedpeople and Ex-Masters: Shaping a New Order in the Postbellum South, 1865–1868," in *Essays on the Postbellum Southern Economy*, ed. Thavolia Glymph and John J. Kushma (College Station: Texas A&M University Press, 1985), 59; Donald G. Nieman, *To Set the Law in Motion:*

The Freedmen's Bureau and the Legal Rights of Blacks, 1865–1868 (Millwood, N.Y.: KTO Press, 1979), 40.

3. Quoted in Heather Cox Richardson, *The Death of Reconstruction: Race, Labor, and Politics in the Post–Civil War North, 1865–1901* (Cambridge, Mass.: Harvard University Press, 2001), 6.

4. Ibid., 36, 34.

5. Foner, *Politics and Ideology,* 101. See also Ira Berlin, Steven Hahn, Steven F. Miller, Joseph P. Reidy, and Leslie S. Rowland, "The Terrain of Freedom: The Struggle over the Meaning of Free Labor in the U.S. South," *History Workshop* 22 (Autumn 1986): 108–30.

6. Quoted in Julie Saville, *The Work of Reconstruction: From Slave to Wage Laborer in South Carolina, 1860–1870* (Cambridge: Cambridge University Press, 1994), 95.

7. Quoted in John Cox and La Wanda Cox, "General O. O. Howard and the 'Misrepresented Bureau,'" *Journal of Southern History* 19 (1953): 452.

8. Quoted in Eric Foner, *Reconstruction: America's Unfinished Revolution, 1863–1877* (New York: Harper and Row, 1988), 164.

9. Quoted in Foner, *Politics and Ideology,* 120.

10. Arna Bontemps, "A Summer Tragedy," in *Black Voices: An Anthology of Afro-American Literature,* ed. Abraham Chapman (New York: New American Library, Mentor Books, 1968), 93.

11. Thomas Jackson Woofter, *Negro Migration: Changes in Rural Organization and Population of the Cotton Belt* (New York: W. D. Gray, 1920), 88.

12. Quoted in Edward L. Ayers, *The Promise of the New South: Life after Reconstruction* (New York: Oxford University Press, 1992), 210.

13. W. E. B. DuBois, *The Negro Artisan* (1902), quoted in Roger L. Ransom and Richard Sutch, *One Kind of Freedom: The Economic Consequences of Emancipation,* paperback ed. (Cambridge: Cambridge University Press, 1977), 34–35.

14. Quoted in Henry M. McKiven Jr., *Iron and Steel: Class, Race, and Community in Birmingham, Alabama 1875–1920* (Chapel Hill: University of North Carolina Press, 1995), 47.

15. Quoted ibid., 30.

16. Quoted in Sterling D. Spero and Abram L. Harris, *The Black Worker: The Negro and the Labor Movement* (New York: Columbia University Press, 1931; reprint, New York: Atheneum, 1972), 349.

17. Quoted in Melton Alonza McLaurin, *Paternalism and Protest: Southern Cotton Mill Workers and Organized Labor, 1875–1905* (Westport, Conn.: Greenwood, 1971), 64, 63.

18. Quoted in Foner, *Politics and Ideology,* 78.

19. Quoted in David Roediger, *The Wages of Whiteness: Race and the Making of the American Working Class,* rev. ed. (London: Verso, 1999), 58.

20. Quoted in Bernard Mandel, *Labor: Free and Slave—Workingmen and the Anti-Slavery Movement in the United States* (New York: Associated Authors, 1955), 120–21.

21. Quoted in Harry V. Jaffa, *A New Birth of Freedom: Abraham Lincoln and the Coming of the Civil War* (Lanham, Md.: Rowman and Littlefield, 2000), 276.

22. Quoted in Mandel, *Labor: Free and Slave,* 73, 70.

23. Phillips quoted in Richard Hofstadter, *The American Political Tradition and the Men Who Made It* (1948; reprint, New York: Vintage Books, 1974), 205.

24. Quoted in David Montgomery, *Beyond Equality: Labor and the Radical Republicans, 1862–1872* (New York: Knopf, 1967), 179–80.

25. Steward and Marx quoted in Sumner Eliot Matison, "The Labor Movement and the Negro during Reconstruction," *Journal of Negro History* 33, no. 4 (October 1948): 441–42, 444.

26. Quoted in Sidney H. Kessler, "The Organization of Negroes in the Knights of Labor," *Journal of Negro History* 37, no. 3 (July 1952): 249.

27. Quoted in Philip A. Taft, *The A. F. of L. in the Time of Gompers* (New York: Harper and Brothers, 1957), 303.

28. Quoted ibid., 308.

29. Quoted ibid., 312.

30. Quoted in Philip S. Foner, *Organized Labor and the Black Worker, 1619–1973* (New York: International Publishers, 1974), 79.

31. Quoted ibid.

32. Ibid.

33. Quoted in Jeffrey Gould, "The Strike of 1887: Louisiana Sugar War," *Southern Exposure* 12 (November–December 1984): 48.

34. Caffery and Pugh quoted ibid., 51, 53.

35. Quoted in Eric Foner, *Nothing but Freedom: Emancipation and Its Legacy* (Baton Rouge: Louisiana State University Press, 1983), 88.

36. Quoted ibid., 90.

37. Quoted ibid., 93.

38. Quoted ibid., 103.

39. Quoted in Daniel Letwin, *The Challenge of Interracial Unionism: Alabama Coal Miners, 1878–1921* (Chapel Hill: University of North Carolina Press, 1998), 75, 79.

40. Ibid., 93.

41. Ibid., 92–93.

42. Quoted in Eric Arnesen, *Waterfront Workers of New Orleans: Race, Class, and Politics, 1863–1923* (Urbana and Chicago: University of Illinois Press, Illini Books, 1994), 93–94.

43. Quoted ibid., 140.

44. Quoted ibid., 155.

45. Quoted ibid.

46. Paul Ortiz, *Emancipation Betrayed: The Hidden History of Black Organizing and White Violence in Florida from Reconstruction to the Bloody Election of 1920* (Berkeley and Los Angeles: University of California Press, 2005), 46–53; quote on 49.

47. C. Vann Woodward, *Origins of the New South, 1877–1913*, paperback ed. (1951; Baton Rouge: Louisiana State University Press, 1970), 229.

2. Into the New Century

1. David M. Oshinsky, *"Worse Than Slavery": Parchman Farm and the Ordeal of Jim Crow Justice* (New York: Free Press, 1996), 34.

2. Ibid., 55.

3. Alex Lichtenstein, *Twice the Work of Free Labor: The Political Economy of Convict Labor in the New South* (London: Verso, 1996), 42.

4. Ibid., 81.

5. Matthew J. Mancini, *One Dies, Get Another: Convict Leasing in the American South, 1866–1928* (Columbia: University of South Carolina Press, 1996), 162.

6. Figures are from C. Vann Woodward, *Origins of the New South, 1877–1913*, paperback ed. (1951; Baton Rouge: Louisiana State University Press, 1970), 214.

7. Oshinsky, *"WorseThan Slavery,"* 55.

8. Ibid., 135–55.

9. Lichtenstein, *Twice the Work of Free Labor,* 164–65.

10. Ibid., 165.

11. Gilbert Osofsky, *Harlem: The Making of a Ghetto* (New York: Harper and Row, 1966), 18.

12. W. E. B. DuBois, *The Black North in 1901: A Social Study* (1901; reprint, New York: Arno Press, 1969), 22.

13. Quoted in David M. Katzman, *Before the Ghetto: Black Detroit in the Nineteenth Century* (Urbana: University of Illinois Press, 1973), 121–22.

14. Quoted in Arnold Shankman, *Ambivalent Friends: Afro-Americans View the Immigrant* (Westport, Conn.: Greenwood, 1982), 158.

15. David A. Gerber, *Black Ohio and the Color Line, 1860–1915* (Urbana: University of Illinois Press, 1976), ch. 11.

16. Niles Carpenter, *Nationality, Color, and Economic Opportunity in the City of Buffalo* (1927; reprint, Westport, Conn.: Negro University Press, 1970), 155.

17. Shankman, *Ambivalent Friends,* 150.

18. Quoted in Brian Kelly, "Sentinels for New South Industry: Booker T. Washington, Industrial Accommodation and Black Workers in the Jim Crow South," *Labor History* 44, no. 3 (August 2003): 346.

19. Rick Halpern, *Down on the Killing Floor: Black and White Workers in Chicago's Packinghouses, 1904–54* (Urbana and Chicago: University of Illinois Press, 1997), 39.

20. Quotes from Eric Arnesen, "Specter of the Black Strikebreaker: Race, Employment, and Labor Activism in the Industrial Era," *Labor History* 44, no. 3 (August 2003): 323, 328–29.

21. W. E. B. DuBois, *The Philadelphia Negro: A Social Study* (1899; reprint, New York: Benjamin Blom, 1967), 127.

22. Ibid., 134.

23. Quoted in Kelly, "Sentinels for New South Industry," 345.

24. Excerpts from "News Accounts of the 1910 Convention of the AFL in St. Louis, November 19, 1910," in *The Samuel Gompers Papers,* vol. 8, *Progress and Reaction in the Age of Reform, 1909–13,* ed. Stuart Kaufman (Urbana: University of Illinois Press, 2001), 137.

25. Bernard Mandel, "Samuel Gompers and the Negro Workers, 1886–1914," *Journal of Negro History* 40, no. 1 (January 1955): 41.

26. Excerpt from "News Account of an Address [by Samuel Gompers] in Mobile, May 18, 1895," in *Samuel Gompers Papers,* vol. 4, *A National Labor Movement Takes Shape, 1895–98,* ed. Stuart Kaufman (Urbana: University of Illinois Press, 1992), 26.

27. John H. M. Laslett, "Samuel Gompers and the Rise of American Business Unionism," in *Labor Leaders in America,* ed. Melvyn Dubofsky and Warren Van Tine (Urbana and Chicago: University of Illinois Press, 1987), 76.

28. Organizer Will Winn quoted in Mandel, "Samuel Gompers and the Negro Workers," 47; Gompers remarks ibid., 48–49.

29. Quoted in Mandel, "Samuel Gompers and the Negro Workers," 48, 46.

30. As cited in David Levering Lewis, *W. E. B. Du Bois: Biography of a Race, 1868–1919* (New York: Henry Holt, 1993), 222, n. 24.

31. See the splendid article by Eric Arnesen, "'Like Banquo's Ghost, It Will Not Go Down': The Race Question and the American Railroad Brotherhoods, 1880–1920," *American Historical Review* 99, no. 5 (December 1994): 1601–33.

32. Quoted in Sterling D. Spero and Abram L. Harris, *The Black Worker: The Negro and the Labor Movement* (New York: Columbia University Press, 1931; reprint, New York: Atheneum, 1972), 66.

33. Quoted in David E. Bernstein, *Only One Place of Redress: African Americans, Labor Regulations, and the Courts from Reconstruction to the New Deal* (Durham, N.C.: Duke University Press, 2001), 34, 134, n. 26.

34. Quoted in Jacqueline Jones, *American Work: Four Centuries of Black and White Labor* (New York: Norton, 1998), 326.

35. Quoted in Andrew Gyory, *Closing the Gate: Race, Politics, and the Chinese Exclusion Act* (Chapel Hill: University of North Carolina Press, 1998), 41; emphasis added.

36. Quoted in Laslett, "Samuel Gompers," 76–77.

37. Gyory, *Closing the Gate,* 287, n. 4.

38. Gompers pamphlet quoted in Erika Lee, *At America's Gates: Chinese Immigration during the Exclusion Era, 1882–1943* (Chapel Hill: University of North Carolina Press, 2003), 26.

39. Quotations ibid., 64–68.

40. Quoted in Arnesen, "'Like Banquo's Ghost,'" 1617.

41. W. C. Pearce quoted in Herbert G. Gutman, "The Negro and the United Mine Workers of America," in *The Negro and the American Labor Movement,* ed. Julius Jacobson (Garden City, N.Y.: Anchor Books, 1968), 51.

42. Quoted in Ronald L. Lewis, "Job Control and Race Relations in Coal Fields, 1870–1920," *Journal of Ethnic Studies* 12, no. 4 (Winter 1985): 48.

3. Great War, Great Migration

1. Stewart E. Tolnay and E. M. Beck, "Rethinking the Role of Racial Violence in the Great Migration," in *Black Exodus: The Great Migration from the American South,* ed. Alferdteen Harrison (Jackson: University Press of Mississippi, 1991), 22.

2. James R. Grossman, *Land of Hope: Chicago, Black Southerners, and the Great Migration* (Chicago: University of Chicago Press, 1989), 183.

3. Peter Gottlieb, *Making Their Own Way: Southern Blacks' Migration to Pittsburgh, 1916–30* (Urbana and Chicago: University of Illinois Press, 1987), 92.

4. George Edmund Haynes, *Negro New-Comers in Detroit, Michigan: A Challenge to Christian Statesmanship—A Preliminary Survey* (New York: Home Missions Council, 1918; reprint, 1969), 8–9; Darlene Clark Hine, "Black Migration to

the Urban Midwest: The Gender Dimension, 1915–1945," in *The Great Migration in Historical Perspective: New Dimensions of Race, Class, and Gender*, ed. Joe William Trotter Jr. (Bloomington and Indianapolis: Indiana University Press, 1991), 128.

5. A. C. Powell quoted in Eric Arnesen, *Black Protest and the Great Migration: A Brief History with Documents* (Boston: Bedford; New York: St. Martin's, 2003), 11.

6. Letter from Memphis, April 23, 1917, in "Letters of Negro Migrants of 1916–1918" (collected under the direction of Emmett J. Scott), *Journal of Negro History* 4, no. 3 (July 1919): 337; letter from New Orleans, May 20, 1917, in "More Letters of Negro Migrants of 1916–1918"(collected under the direction of Emmett J. Scott), *Journal of Negro History* 4, no. 4 (October 1919): 442.

7. James R. Grossman, "Black Labor Is the Best Labor: Southern White Reactions to the Great Migration," in *Black Exodus: The Great Migration from the American South*, ed. Alferdteen Harrison (Jackson: University Press of Mississippi, 1991), 55, 52, 53.

8. Arnesen, *Black Protest*, 17; Neil A. Wynn, *From Progressivism to Prosperity: World War I and American Society* (New York: Holmes and Meier, 1986), 114, 183.

9. Quoted in Joanne J. Meyerowitz, *Women Adrift: Independent Wage Earners in Chicago, 1880–1930* (Chicago: University of Chicago Press, 1988), 36.

10. George E. Haynes, *The Negro at Work during the World War and during Reconstruction: Statistics, Problems, and Policies Relating to the Greater Inclusion of Negro Wage Earners in American Industry and Agriculture* (Washington, D.C.: Government Printing Office, 1921), 127.

11. Hine, "Black Migration to the Urban Midwest," 139.

12. "Two Schools—One North, One South," *Chicago Defender*, April 17, 1917.

13. Figures are from Dale L. Hiestand, *Economic Growth and Employment Opportunities for Minorities* (New York: Columbia University Press, 1964), 7–9.

14. Quoted in Kenneth Kusmer, *A Ghetto Takes Shape: Black Cleveland, 1870–1930* (Urbana: University of Illinois Press, 1976), 190–91.

15. Sterling D. Spero and Abram L. Harris, *The Black Worker: The Negro and the Labor Movement* (New York: Columbia University Press, 1931; reprint, New York: Atheneum, 1972), 181.

16. Ibid., 467.

17. Eric Arnesen, "'Like Banquo's Ghost, It Will Not Go Down': The Race Question and the American Railroad Brotherhoods, 1880–1920," *American Historical Review* 99, no. 5 (December 1994): 1617.

18. Quotes from Philip S. Foner, *Organized Labor and the Black Worker, 1619–1973* (New York: International Publishers, 1974), 135, 133.

19. Ibid., 137; William B. Wilson to John H. Walker, Springfield, Ill., July 10, 1917, in *Black Workers in the Era of the Great Migration, 1916–1929* (University Publications of America microfilm, 1985), reel 14.

20. Quoted in Eric Arnesen, *Brotherhoods of Color: Black Railroad Workers and the Struggle for Equality* (Cambridge, Mass.: Harvard University Press, 2001), 71.

21. Quoted in Foner, *Organized Labor and the Black Worker*, 142.

22. Philip A. Taft, *The A. F. of L. in the Time of Gompers* (New York: Harper and Brothers, 1957), 316.

23. Eugene Kinckle Jones and Fred Moore to Samuel Gompers, June 6, 1918, in *The Black Worker: A Documentary History from Colonial Times to the Present,* vol. 5, *The Black Worker from 1900 to 1919,* ed. Philip S. Foner and Ronald L. Lewis (Philadelphia: Temple University Press, 1983), 421.

24. Report of Committee on Organization, 1918 convention, ibid, 422.

25. Quotes from Foner, *Organized Labor and the Black* Worker, 140; Eric Arnesen, "Following the Color Line of Labor: Black Workers and the Labor Movement before 1930," *Radical History Review* 55 (Winter 1993): 75.

26. Taft, *The A. F. of L. in the Time of Gompers,* 316.

27. Quotes in Foner, *Organized Labor and the Black Worker,* 143, 145.

28. Quoted in William M. Tuttle Jr., *Race Riot: Chicago in the Red Summer of 1919* (New York: Atheneum, 1970), 125–26.

29. Ibid., 120.

30. Ibid., 136.

31. Grossman, *Land of Hope,* 212, 213.

32. Walter White quoted in David Brody, *The Butcher Workmen: A Study of Unionization* (Cambridge, Mass.: Harvard University Press, 1964), 86.

33. Quotes in William H. Harris, *Keeping the Faith: A. Philip Randolph, Milton P. Webster, and the Brotherhood of Sleeping Car Porters, 1925–1937* (Urbana: University of Illinois Press, 1977), 20, 21.

34. [Ira Reid], *Negro Membership in American Labor Unions, by the Department of Research and Investigations of the National Urban League* (1930; reprint, New York: Negro Universities Press, 1969), 123.

35. Spero and Harris, *The Black Worker,* 121.

36. Ibid., 123.

37. Ibid., 311.

38. Ibid., 313.

39. Melinda Chateauvert, *Marching Together: Women of the Brotherhood of Sleeping Car Porters* (Urbana and Chicago: University of Illinois Press, 1998), 23.

40. Harris, *Keeping the Faith,* 30.

41. Ibid., 31.

42. Quoted in David Levering Lewis, *W. E. B. Du Bois: The Fight for Equality and the American Century, 1919–1963* (New York: Henry Holt, 2000), 309.

43. Telegram from Gov. John Lind to William B. Wilson, July 7, 1917, and Congressman John T. Watkins to William B. Wilson, July 14, 1917, in *Black Workers in the Era of the Great Migration,* reel 13.

44. Quoted in William J. Breen, "Sectional Influences on National Policy: The South, the Labor Department, and the Wartime Labor Mobilization, 1917–1918," in *The South Is Another Land: Essays on the Twentieth-Century South,* ed. Bruce Clayton and John A. Salmond (Westport, Conn.: Greenwood, 1987), 78.

45. Ibid.

46. Wilson to John Lind, July 16, 1917, in *Black Workers in the Era of the Great Migration,* reel 14.

47. Dillard quoted in Breen, "Sectional Influences on National Policy," 72; Division of Negro Economics, U.S. Department of Labor, *Negro Migration in 1916–17,* with an introduction by J. H. Dillard (1919; reprint, New York: Negro Universities Press, 1969), 9–13.

48. Division of Negro Economics, *Negro Migration,* 34.

244 NOTES TO PAGES 96–104

49. Inspector's Report on Visit to Pittsburgh, August 12–13, 1920; Eugene Kinckle Jones, Executive Secretary, National Urban League, to William B. Wilson, September 18, 1919; and draft article by Haynes for the *Detroit Compass,* c. June 25, 1920, all in *Black Workers in the Era of the Great Migration,* reel 12.

50. Haynes, *The Negro at Work during the World War and during Reconstruction,* 21, 26–31; Haynes to William B. Wilson, July 8, 1919, *Great Migration,* reel 14.

51. Quoted in Arnesen, *Brotherhoods of Color,* 49.

52. Ibid., 72.

53. Quoted in Joseph A. McCartin, *Labor's Great War: The Struggle for Industrial Democracy and the Origins of Modern American Labor Relations, 1912–1921* (Chapel Hill: University of North Carolina Press, 1997), 153.

54. Quoted ibid., 153.

55. Quoted ibid., 155.

56. Haynes, *The Negro at Work,* 29; Haynes to William B. Wilson, July 8, 1919, in *Black Workers in the Era of the Great Migration,* reel 14.

57. A complicated piece of legislation, the 1924 Immigration Act specified that the quotas established would be based on the 1890 census. However, 1890 would be the base year only until an expert commission of demographers and statisticians could develop an authoritative way of determining the actual ethnic and racial composition of the American population. Under the law, the 1920 census would replace that of 1890 as the basis for quotas in 1927—a change seemingly (and actually) benefiting the countries of eastern, central, and southern Europe. Meanwhile, the task of developing a coherent method of determining national origins proved to be impossible, with the commission's report consisting of a hodgepodge of theories, speculations, enumerations, and assumptions. In this lengthy process, two themes remained constant: the effort to sharply reduce the overall *number* of immigrants, and the virtual exclusion of nonwhite would-be immigrants. See Mae M. Ngai, "The Architecture of Race in American Immigration Law: A Reexamination of the Immigration Act of 1924," *Journal of American History* 86, no. 1 (June 1999): 67–92.

58. Quoted in Otis L. Graham Jr., *Unguarded Gates: A History of America's Immigration Crisis* (Lanham, Md.: Rowman and Littlefield, 2004), 47.

59. Quoted in Lawrence H. Fuchs, "The Reactions of Black Americans to Immigration," in *Immigration Reconsidered: History, Sociology, Politics,* ed. Virginia Yans-McLaughlin (New York: Oxford University Press, 1990), 296.

60. Quoted in David J. Hellwig, "Black Leaders and United States Immigration Policy, 1917–1929," *Journal of Negro History* 66, no. 2 (Summer 1981): 120.

61. Quoted in David E. Bernstein, *Only One Place of Redress: African Americans, Labor Regulations, and the Courts from Reconstruction to the New Deal* (Durham, N.C.: Duke University Press, 2001), 58.

62. Quoted in Eric Arnesen, "Specter of the Black Strikebreaker: Race, Employment, and Labor Activism in the Industrial Era," *Labor History* 44, no. 3 (August 2003): 324.

63. Quoted in Bernstein, *Only One Place of Redress,* 56.

64. Thomas N. Maloney and Warren C. Whatley, "Making the Effort: The Contours of Racial Discrimination in Detroit's Labor Markets, 1920–1940," *Journal of Economic History* 55, no. 1 (September 1995): 472.

4. Race and Labor in Depression and War

1. The organization was first called the Committee on Industrial Organization, which sought to function as a ginger group within the AFL. In 1938, renamed the Congress of Industrial Organizations, the CIO officially became what it had already been in fact: a separate organization.

2. Harvard Sitkoff, *A New Deal for Blacks: The Emergence of Civil Rights as a National Issue,* vol. 1, *The Depression Decade* (New York: Oxford University Press, 1978), 36.

3. Quoted ibid., 39, 35.

4. Raymond Wolters, *Negroes and the Great Depression: The Problem of Economic Recovery* (1970; reprint, Westport, Conn.: Greenwood, 1978), 312.

5. Jerold S. Auerbach, "Southern Tenant Farmers: Socialist Critics of the New Deal," *Labor History* 7, no. 1 (Winter 1966): 6.

6. Donald H. Grubbs, *Cry from the Cotton: The Southern Tenant Farmers' Union and the New Deal* (Chapel Hill: University of North Carolina Press, 1971), 69.

7. Auerbach, "Southern Tenant Farmers," 16.

8. Horace Cayton and George S. Mitchell, *Black Workers and the New Unions* (Chapel Hill: University of North Carolina Press, 1939), 323.

9. Quotes in Robert H. Zieger, *The CIO: 1935–1955* (Chapel Hill: University of North Carolina Press, 1995), 85, 84.

10. Journalist George Schuyler quoted in Cayton and Mitchell, *Black Workers and the New Unions,* 209–10.

11. Bruce Nelson, "Organized Labor and the Struggle for Black Equality in Mobile during World War II," *Journal of American History* 80, no. 3 (December 1993): 954.

12. Quoted in Robert H. Zieger and Gilbert J. Gall, *American Workers, American Unions: The Twentieth Century,* 3d ed. (Baltimore: Johns Hopkins University Press, 2002), 93–94.

13. Rick Halpern, *Down on the Killing Floor: Black and White Workers in Chicago's Packinghouses, 1904–54* (Urbana and Chicago: University of Illinois Press, 1997), 96–97.

14. Nelson, "Organized Labor and the Struggle for Black Equality," 953; Robert Korstad and Nelson Lichtenstein, "Opportunities Found and Lost: Labor, Radicals, and the Early Civil Rights Movement," *Journal of American History* 75, no. 3 (December 1988): 787.

15. Paul Street, "The 'Best Union Members': Class, Race, Culture, and Black Worker Militancy in Chicago's Stockyards during the 1930s," *Journal of American Ethnic History* 20, no. 1 (Fall 2000): 27.

16. Quoted ibid., 19.

17. Quoted in Halpern, *Down on the Killing Floor,* 109.

18. Quoted in Street, "The 'Best Union Members,'" 19.

19. Quoted in Halpern, *Down on the Killing Floor,* 153.

20. August Meier and Elliott Rudwick, *Black Detroit and the Rise of the UAW* (New York: Oxford University Press, 1979), 7.

21. Ibid., 13.

22. Ibid., 5.

23. Ibid., 36.

24. Ibid., 84.

25. Ibid., 84, 85.

26. Ibid., 102.

27. Quoted ibid., 106.

28. The figures in this paragraph are rough estimates, based on William H. Harris, *The Harder We Run: Black Workers since the Civil War* (New York: Oxford University Press, 1982), 122, and Zieger, *The CIO,* 152–53.

29. Quoted in Zieger and Gall, *American Workers, American Unions,* 123.

30. Quoted in Andrew Edmund Kersten, *Race, Jobs, and the War: The FEPC in the Midwest, 1941–1946* (Urbana and Chicago: University of Illinois Press, 2000), 17–18.

31. Eric Arnesen, *Brotherhoods of Color: Black Railroad Workers and the Struggle for Equality* (Cambridge, Mass.: Harvard University Press, 2001), 191.

32. Wolters, *Negroes and the Great Depression,* 185–86.

33. NWLB Case No. 771, June 5, 1943, in *Termination Report of the National War Labor Board: Industrial Disputes and Wage Stabilization in Wartime,* vol. 2, appendix G (Washington, D.C.: Government Printing Office, 1946), 339–40.

34. Arnesen, *Brotherhoods of Color,* 206–9.

35. Ibid., 202.

36. Allan M. Winkler, "The Philadelphia Transit Strike of 1944," *Journal of American History* 59, no. 1 (June 1972): 78.

37. Nelson, "Organized Labor and the Struggle for Black Equality," 952.

38. Quoted in John Barnard, *American Vanguard: The United Auto Workers during the Reuther Years, 1935–1970* (Detroit: Wayne State University Press, 2004), 195.

39. Quoted in Winkler, "The Philadelphia Transit Strike," 89.

40. Alex Lichtenstein, "Exclusion, Fair Employment, or Interracial Unionism: Race Relations in Florida's Shipyards during World War II," in *Labor in the Modern South,* ed. Glen T. Eskew (Athens: University of Georgia Press, 2001), 135.

41. Quoted in Meier and Rudwick, *Black Detroit and the Rise of the UAW,* 170–71.

42. Quotes in Zieger, *The CIO,* 157, 156.

43. Accurate figures on the racial composition of AFL and CIO unions during the 1940s are notoriously difficult to establish. By the end of the war, there were probably about one million black members of AFL and CIO unions, about two-thirds of them in the former.

44. Quoted in Marshall F. Stevenson Jr., "'It Will Take More Than Official Pronouncement': The American Federation of Labor and the Black Worker, 1935–1955" (paper presented at the 81st annual meeting of the Association for the Study of Afro-American Life and History, Charleston, S.C., October 4, 1996).

45. Philip S. Foner, *Organized Labor and the Black Worker, 1619–1973* (New York: International Publishers, 1974), 251.

46. Green and Myrdal quoted ibid., 252.

47. Bruce Nelson, "Class and Race in the Crescent City: The ILWU, from San Francisco to New Orleans," in *The CIO's Left-Led Unions,* ed. Steve Rosswurm (New Brunswick, N.J.: Rutgers University Press, 1992), 41.

48. Harold M. Baron and Bennett Hymer, "The Negro Worker in the Chicago

Labor Market," in *The Negro and the American Labor Movement,* ed. Julius Jacobson (New York: Doubleday/Anchor, 1968), 241.

5. Race and Labor in the Postwar World

1. Arthur M. Ross, "The Negro in the American Economy," in *Employment, Race, and Poverty,* ed. Arthur M. Ross and Herbert Hill (New York: Harcourt, Brace and World, 1967), 17–18.

2. William Julius Wilson, *The Declining Significance of Race: Blacks and Changing American Institutions,* 2d ed. (Chicago: University of Chicago Press, 1980), 103; Thomas J. Sugrue, *The Origins of the Urban Crisis: Race and Inequality in Postwar Detroit* (Princeton, N.J.: Princeton University Press, 1996), 112.

3. Ross, "The Negro in the American Economy," 33.

4. Thomas J. Sugrue, "'Forget about Your Inalienable Right to Work': Deindustrialization and Its Discontents at Ford, 1950–1953," *International Labor and Working-Class History* 48 (Fall 1995): 115; Harold M. Baron and Bennett Hymer, "The Negro Worker in the Chicago Labor Market," in *The Negro and the American Labor Movement,* ed. Julius Jacobson (New York: Doubleday/Anchor, 1968), 275.

5. Quoted in Ira Katznelson, *When Affirmative Action Was White: An Untold History of Racial Inequality in Twentieth-Century America* (New York: Norton, 2005), 59–60.

6. Quoted in Jacqueline Jones, *Labor of Love, Labor of Sorrow: Black Women, Work, and the Family from Slavery to the Present* (New York: Basic Books, 1985), 237.

7. Rick Halpern, *Down on the Killing Floor: Black and White Workers in Chicago's Packinghouses, 1904–54* (Urbana and Chicago: University of Illinois Press, 1997), 83.

8. Bette Woody, *Black Women in the Workplace: Impacts of Structural Change in the Economy* (Westport, Conn.: Greenwood, 1992), 50; Jones, *Labor of Love,* 260–62.

9. Quoted in Melinda Chateauvert, *Marching Together: Women of the Brotherhood of Sleeping Car Porters* (Urbana and Chicago: University of Illinois Press, 1998), 74–75.

10. Quotes in Halpern, *Down on the Killing Floor,* 176, 174.

11. Quoted in Robert Rodgers Korstad, *Civil Rights Unionism: Tobacco Workers and the Struggle for Democracy in the Mid-Twentieth Century South* (Chapel Hill: University of North Carolina Press, 2003), 21.

12. Quoted in Jones, *Labor of Love,* 207.

13. Ibid.

14. Ibid., 148.

15. Baron and Hymer, "The Negro Worker," 246.

16. Quoted in Nelson Lichtenstein, *The Most Dangerous Man in Detroit: Walter Reuther and the Fate of American Labor* (New York: Basic Books, 1995), 373.

17. Bruce Nelson, *Divided We Stand: American Workers and the Struggle for Black Equality* (Princeton, N.J.: Princeton University Press, 2001), 216–17.

18. William B. Gould, *Black Workers in White Unions: Job Discrimination in the United States* (Ithaca, N.Y.: Cornell University Press, 1977), 282.

19. Lichtenstein, *Reuther,* 374.

20. Halpern, *Down on the Killing Floor,* 247.

21. Paul H. Norgren, "Fair Employment Practice Laws—Experience, Effects, Prospects," in *Employment, Race, and Poverty,* ed. Arthur M. Ross and Herbert Hill (New York: Harcourt, Brace and World, 1967), 546–47.

22. Quotes in Hugh Davis Graham, *The Civil Rights Era: Origins and Development of National Policy, 1960–1972* (New York: Oxford University Press, 1990), 118, 119.

23. Terry H. Anderson, *The Pursuit of Fairness: A History of Affirmative Action* (New York: Oxford University Press, 2004), 60.

24. Ibid., 65.

25. In 1964, the NLRB finally ruled that "the failure to represent black workers fairly in a unit was an unfair labor practice" that could be remedied by the board through the federal courts (thus relieving the complainant of litigation expenses). See Gould, *Black Workers in White Unions,* 37.

26. Harvey A. Levenstein, *Communism, Anticommunism, and the CIO* (Westport, Conn.: Greenwood, 1981), 332; Robert H. Zieger, *The CIO, 1935–1955* (Chapel Hill: University of North Carolina Press, 1995), 282.

27. Quoted in Elizabeth A. Fones-Wolf, *Selling Free Enterprise: The Business Assault on Labor and Liberalism, 1945–1960* (Urbana and Chicago: University of Illinois Press, 1994), 22.

28. Steven F. Lawson, *Black Ballots: Voting Rights in the South, 1944–1969* (New York: Columbia University Press, 1976), 134; Robert Korstad and Nelson Lichtenstein, "Opportunities Found and Lost: Labor, Radicals, and the Early Civil Rights Movement," *Journal of American History* 75, no. 3 (December 1988): 793.

29. Quoted in Robert H. Zieger, "A Venture into Unplowed Fields: Daniel Powell and CIO Political Action in the Postwar South," in *Labor in the Modern South,* ed. Glenn T. Eskew (Athens: University of Georgia Press, 2001), 159.

30. Marshall F. Stevenson Jr., "'It Will Take More Than Official Pronouncement': The American Federation of Labor and the Black Worker, 1935–1955" (paper presented at the 81st annual meeting of the Association for the Study of Afro-American Life and History, Charleston, S.C., October 4, 1996).

31. Ibid.

32. Zieger, *The CIO,* 233.

33. Ibid.

34. Robert J. Norrell, "Labor Trouble: George Wallace and Union Politics in Alabama," in *Organized Labor in the Twentieth-Century South,* ed. Robert H. Zieger (Knoxville: University of Tennessee Press, 1991), 251–55.

35. Ibid., 260.

36. Quoted in Zieger, "A Venture into Unplowed Fields," 173.

37. Bruce Nelson, "'CIO Meant One Thing for the Whites and Another Thing for Us': Steelworkers and Civil Rights, 1936–1974," in *Southern Labor in Transition, 1940–1995,* ed. Robert H. Zieger (Knoxville: University of Tennessee Press, 1997), 115.

38. Quoted ibid.

39. Quoted in Philip S. Foner, *Organized Labor and the Black Worker* (New York: International Publishers, 1973), 331.

40. Quoted in Jervis Anderson, *A. Philip Randolph: A Biographical Portrait* (New York: Harvest Books, 1973), 301.
41. Ibid., 302.
42. Ibid., 303–4.
43. Foner, *Organized Labor and the Black Worker*, 333–36.
44. Ibid., 336.
45. Quotes in Anderson, *A. Philip Randolph*, 308.
46. Ibid., 309.
47. Gilbert J. Gall, *The Politics of Right to Work: The Labor Federations as Special Interests, 1943–1979* (Westport, Conn.: Greenwood, 1988), 143.

6. Affirmative Action and Labor Action

1. Bayard Rustin, "From Protest to Politics: The Future of the Civil Rights Movement," *Commentary*, February 1965; John D'Emilio, *Lost Prophet: The Life and Times of Bayard Rustin* (New York: Free Press, 2003), 398–403.
2. Timothy J. Minchin, *Hiring the Black Worker: The Racial Integration of the Southern Textile Industry, 1960–1980* (Chapel Hill: University of North Carolina Press, 1999), 57.
3. Ibid., 53; James J. Heckman and Brook S. Payner, "Determining the Impact of Federal Antidiscrimination Policy on the Economic Status of Blacks: A Study of South Carolina," *American Economic Review* 79, no.1 (March 1989): 144, 146, 171.
4. Timothy J. Minchin, *The Color of Work: The Struggle for Civil Rights in the Southern Paper Industry, 1945–1980* (Chapel Hill: University of North Carolina Press, 2001), 166, 202.
5. Quoted in John Hinshaw, *Steel and Steelworkers: Race and Class in Twentieth-Century Pittsburgh* (Albany: State University of New York Press, 2002), 217.
6. Quoted in Nancy MacLean, *Freedom Is Not Enough: The Opening of the American Workplace* (Cambridge, Mass.: Harvard University Press, 2006), 254–55.
7. Marc Linder, *Wars of Attrition: Vietnam, the Business Roundtable, and the Decline of Construction Unions* (Iowa City: Fanpihua Press, 1999), 244, table.
8. Quoted in MacLean, *Freedom Is Not Enough*, 90–91.
9. Herbert Northrup, *Fortune*, quoted in Linder, *Wars of Attrition*, 250–51.
10. Ibid., 248–49.
11. Ibid., 249.
12. Terry H. Anderson, *The Pursuit of Fairness: A History of Affirmative Action* (New York: Oxford University Press, 2004), 115–16.
13. Quoted ibid., 118.
14. Quoted ibid., 120.
15. Meany quoted ibid.
16. Dirksen quoted ibid., 121.
17. Hugh Davis Graham, *Collision Course: The Strange Convergence of Affirmative Action and Immigration Policy in America* (New York: Oxford University Press, 2002), 97–100.
18. John D. Skrentny, *The Minority Rights Revolution* (Cambridge, Mass.: Belknap Press of Harvard University Press, 2002), 343–44.
19. Ibid.

20. Hill quoted in Robert J. Weiss, *"We Want Jobs": A History of Affirmative Action* (New York: Garland, 1997), 190. See also Judith Stein, "Affirmative Action and the Conservative Agenda: President Richard M. Nixon's Philadelphia Plan of 1969," in *Labor in the Modern South,* ed. Glenn T. Eskew (Athens: University of Georgia Press, 2001), 182–206.

21. Graham, *Collision Course,* 25.

22. Aaron Brenner, "Rank-and-File Rebellion, 1966–1975" (PhD diss., Columbia University, 1996), 41.

23. Quoted in Joseph C. Goulden, *Jerry Wurf: Labor's Last Angry Man* (New York: Atheneum, 1982), 172.

24. Quotations in Joseph A. McCartin, "'Fire the Hell Out of Them': Sanitation Workers' Struggles and the Normalization of the Striker Replacement Strategy in the 1970s," *Labor: Studies in the Working-Class History of the Americas* 2, no. 3 (Fall 2005): 72, 73.

25. Quoted in Steve Estes, "Strike toward Freedom: The Politics of Paternalism in Memphis and Charleston," n.d. (c. 1999–2000), www.citadel.edu/civilrights/papers/estes.pdf (accessed July 21, 2006).

26. Goulden, *Jerry Wurf,* 177.

27. Quoted in Estes, "Strike toward Freedom."

28. Ibid.

29. Leon Fink and Brian Greenberg, *Upheaval in the Quiet Zone: A History of Hospital Workers' Union Local 1199* (Urbana and Chicago: University of Illinois Press, 1989), 113.

30. Quoted ibid., 137.

31. Ibid., 144, 145.

32. Ibid., 155.

33. William Saunders quoted in Stephen O'Neill, "The Struggle for Black Equality Comes to Charleston: The Hospital Strike of 1969," *Proceedings of the South Carolina Historical Association* (1986): 90.

34. Gregg L. Michel, "'Union Power, Soul Power': Unionizing Johns Hopkins University Hospital, 1959–1974," *Labor History* 38, no. 1 (Winter 1996–1997): 28–66.

35. Quoted in Robert H. Zieger and Gilbert J. Gall, *American Workers, American Unions: The Twentieth Century,* 3d ed. (Baltimore: Johns Hopkins University Press, 2002), 227.

36. Heather Ann Thompson, *Whose Detroit? Politics, Labor, and Race in a Modern American City* (Ithaca, N.Y.: Cornell University Press, 2001), 48–70.

37. Peter B. Levy, *The New Left and Labor in the 1960s* (Urbana and Chicago: University of Illinois Press, 1994), 77.

38. Dan Georgakas, *Detroit, I Do Mind Dying: A Study in Urban Revolution* (New York: St. Martin's, 1975).

39. Mazey quoted in Zieger and Gall, *American Workers, American Unions,* 227.

40. Quoted in Levy, *The New Left,* 79.

41. Quotes ibid., 81; Joshua Freeman, *Working-Class New York: Life and Labor since World War II* (New York: Free Press, 2000), 225.

42. Jerald E. Podair, *The Strike That Changed New York: Blacks, Whites, and the Ocean Hill–Brownsville Crisis* (New Haven, Conn.: Yale University Press, 2002).

43. Brenner, "Rank-and-File Rebellion," 29.

44. See James R. O'Connor, *The Fiscal Crisis of the State* (New York: St. Martin's, 1973).

45. Quoted in McCartin, "'Fire the Hell Out of Them,'" 84.

46. Ibid., 85.

47. Ibid., 68.

48. Ibid., 84–86.

49. Ibid., 84.

50. Ibid., 71.

7. Back to the Future

1. Dennis C. Dickerson, *Out of the Crucible: Black Steelworkers in Western Pennsylvania, 1875–1980* (Albany: State University of New York Press, 1986), 244–45; Ruth Needleman, *Black Freedom Fighters in Steel: The Struggle for Democratic Unionism* (Ithaca, N.Y.: Cornell University Press, 2003), 205–8.

2. Venus Green, *Race on the Line: Gender, Labor, and Technology in the Bell System, 1880–1980* (Durham, N.C.: Duke University Press, 2001), 241.

3. Quoted in Robert J. Weiss, *"We Want Jobs": A History of Affirmative Action* (New York: Garland, 1997), 189.

4. Raymond Wolters, *Right Turn: William Bradford Reynolds, the Reagan Administration, and Black Civil Rights* (New Brunswick, N.J.: Transaction Publishers, 1996), 171 (productivity), 184 (Posner quote).

5. Quoted in Nancy MacLean, *Freedom Is Not Enough: The Opening of the American Workplace* (Cambridge, Mass.: Harvard University Press, 2006), 306.

6. Terry H. Anderson, *The Pursuit of Fairness: A History of Affirmative Action* (New York: Oxford University Press, 2004), 186.

7. Quoted in MacLean, *Freedom Is Not Enough,* 310.

8. Quoted in Anderson, *Pursuit of Fairness,* 206–7.

9. Dennis A. Deslippe, "'Do Whites Have Rights?': White Detroit Policemen and Reverse Discrimination Protests in the 1970s," *Journal of American History* 91, no. 3 (December 2004): 932–60.

10. See the state studies reported at http://www.buildingtrades.org/training/studies.html (accessed July 14, 2006).

11. Quoted in Anderson, *Pursuit of Fairness,* 204.

12. John J. Donohue III and James Heckman, "Continuous versus Episodic Change: The Impact of Civil Rights Policy on the Economic Status of Blacks," *Journal of Economic Literature* 29, no. 4 (December 1991): 1603–43; Jonathan S. Leonard, "The Impact of Affirmative Action Regulation and Equal Employment Law on Black Employment," *Journal of Economic Perspectives* 4, no. 4 (Fall 1990): 47–63. The quote is in Frederick M. Wirt, *We Ain't What We Was: Civil Rights in the New South* (Durham, N.C.: Duke University Press, 1997), 178.

13. Wolters, *Right Turn,* 179.

14. Weiss, *"We Want Jobs,"* 196; Wolters, *Right Turn,* 187.

15. Anderson, *Pursuit of Fairness,* 181.

16. Kelly Alexander quoted in Timothy J. Minchin, *Hiring the Black Worker: The Racial Integration of the Southern Textile Industry, 1960–1980* (Chapel Hill: University of North Carolina Press, 1999), 270.

17. Quoted in Robert H. Zieger, "From Primordial Folk to Redundant Workers: Southern Textile Workers and Social Observers, 1920–1990," in *Southern Labor in Transition, 1940–1995,* ed. Robert H. Zieger (Knoxville: University of Tennessee Press, 1997), 289.

18. John Hinshaw, *Steel and Steelworkers: Race and Class in Twentieth-Century Pittsburgh* (Albany: State University of New York Press, 2002), 243; Needleman, *Black Freedom Fighters,* 211.

19. U.S. Department of Commerce, Office of Aerospace and Automotive Industries, "U.S. Automotive Industry Employment Trends," March 30, 2005, http://www.ita.doc.gov/td/auto/domestic/staffreports/Jobloss.pdf (accessed July 13, 2006); "DNC Ad Says Bush Lost Manufacturing Jobs," August 11, 2004, http://www.factcheck.org/article234.html (accessed July 15, 2006).

20. John Schmitt and Ben Zipperer, "The Decline in African-American Representation in Unions and Auto Manufacturing, 1979–2004" (briefing paper, Center for Economic and Policy Research, Washington, D.C., January 2006), http://www.cepr.net/publications/african_americans_manufacturing_2006_01.pdf (accessed July 15, 2006).

21. Wolters, *Right Turn,* 184; Department of Commerce, "U.S. Automotive Industry Employment Trends."

22. Quotes in Eric Eckholm, "Plight Deepens for Black Men, Studies Warn," *New York Times,* March 20, 2006.

23. "At the Corner of Progress and Peril," *Washington Post,* June 2, 2006.

24. William Julius Wilson, *When Work Disappears: The World of the New Urban Poor* (New York: Knopf, 1996), xiii.

25. Ibid., 130–31.

26. John McWhorter, "Defined by Defiance," *Chicago Sun-Times,* January 22, 2006.

27. Richard Rothstein, "Must Schools Fail?" *New York Review of Books,* December 2, 2004.

28. William A. Darity Jr. and Samuel L. Myers Jr., *Persistent Disparity: Race and Economic Inequality in the United States since 1945* (Cheltenham, UK, and Northampton, Mass.: Edward Elgar, 1998), 51.

29. Eckholm, "Plight Deepens for Black Men"; Gail Christopher in "At the Corner of Progress and Peril."

30. "At the Corner of Progress and Peril."

31. More precisely, the only contested election in the AFL's history as a separate organization (1886–1955) took place in 1894; until 1995, there had never been a contest for the AFL-CIO presidency.

32. Dwight Kirk, "Laboring over Organized Labor," April 4, 2005, Pacific News Service, http://news.pacificnews.org/news/view_article.html?article_id=dcb6 30eab89ab9fc4b167cdc61525168 (accessed July 19, 2006).

33. Schmitt and Zipperer, "The Decline in African-American Representation."

34. Richard Vedder and Lowell Gallaway, "The Economic Effects of Labor Unions Revisited," *Journal of Labor Research* 23, no. 1 (January 1, 2002): 1 http://infotrac.galegroup.com.lp.hscl.ufl.edu/itw/infomark/285/406/1681153w18/purl=rcl_GBFM_0_A83452882&dyn=5!xrn_9_0_A83452882?sw_aep=gain40375 (accessed February 17, 2007).

35. Quoted in Tom Donahue, "The Black-Labor Alliance," June 30, 1995, http://www.aflcio.org/mediacenter/prsptm/sp06301995a.cfm (accessed July 20, 2006).

36. Ibid.

37. Gerald F. Friedman, "Justice for Janitors and the Rebirth of the American Labor Movement," October 24, 2002, http://www.fguide.org/Bulletin/janitors.htm (accessed August 1, 2006).

38. Quoted in Stan Goff, "Back to Gary—Report from the CBTU Convention," July 8, 2005, http://stangoff.com/?p=160 (accessed July 10, 2006).

39. Bayard Rustin, "From Protest to Politics: The Future of the Civil Rights Movement," *Commentary,* February 1965; John D'Emilio, *Lost Prophet: The Life and Times of Bayard Rustin* (New York: Free Press, 2003), 398–403.

40. Quoted in D'Emilio, *Lost Prophet,* 434.

41. Quoted in Philip S. Foner, *Organized Labor and the Black Worker, 1619–1973* (New York: International Publishers, 1974), 435.

42. Quoted in Goff, "Back to Gary."

43. Quoted in "Black Labor's Voice amidst the Madness," *Black Commentator,* May 19, 2005, http://www.blackcommentator.com/139/139_cover_cbtu.html (accessed February 17, 2007).

44. Ibid.

45. Ibid.; "No 'Labor Reform' without Blacks," *Black Commentator,* March 3, 2005, http://www.blackcommentator.com/128/128_cover_labor.html (accessed July 15, 2006).

46. George Yancey, *Who Is White? Latinos, Asians, and the New Black/Nonblack Divide* (Boulder, Colo.: Lynne Rienner, 2003), 154. See also Roger Waldinger and Michael I. Lichter, *How the Other Half Works: Immigration and the Social Organization of Labor* (Berkeley and Los Angeles: University of California Press, 2003), 205–17. For a more optimistic view of the future of black-brown labor activism, see Ruth Milkman, *L.A. Story: Immigrant Workers and the Future of the U.S. Labor Movement* (New York: Russell Sage Foundation, 2006).

47. Ian Haney-López, *White by Law: The Legal Construction of Race* (New York: New York University Press, 1996); Thomas A. Guglielmo, *White on Arrival: Italians, Race, Color, and Power in Chicago, 1890–1945* (Oxford: Oxford University Press, 2003), 137–42.

48. Dwight Kirk, "Laboring over Organized Labor," April 4, 2005, http://news.pacificnews.org/news/view_article.html?article_id=dcb630eab89ab9fc4b167cdc61525168 (accessed June 22, 2006).

49. Henry Nicholas of AFSCME quoted in Goff, "Back to Gary."

BIBLIOGRAPHICAL ESSAY

The historical literature on African American workers and on the racial policies and practices of the U.S. labor movement is vast and growing. For discussions of some of the major trends in this scholarship, key interpretive controversies, and overviews of the field, see note 2 in the introduction. Readers can also find reviews of a number of recent books at http://www.clas.ufl.edu/users/rzieger/reviews.htm (accessed December 16, 2006).

There are several valuable general histories of race and labor. Particularly useful for both its broad sweep and its detailed examination of organized labor's record on race is Philip S. Foner, *Organized Labor and the Black Worker, 1619–1973* (New York: International Publishers, 1974). William H. Harris, *The Harder We Run: Black Workers since the Civil War* (New York: Oxford University Press, 1982), provides a brisk overview, and two books by Jacqueline Jones, *Labor of Love, Labor of Sorrow: Black Women, Work, and the Family from Slavery to the Present* (New York: Basic Books, 1985) and *American Work: Four Centuries of Black and White Labor* (New York: Norton, 1998), offer a wealth of information, as well as sharp commentary. Philip S. Foner and Ronald L. Lewis, eds., *The Black Worker: A Documentary History from Colonial Times to the Present*, 8 vols. (Philadelphia: Temple University Press, 1978–), is a rich collection of documentary material. Sterling D. Spero and Abram L. Harris, *The Black Worker: The Negro and the Labor Movement* (New York: Columbia University Press, 1931; reprint, New York: Atheneum, 1972), remains useful, as does John Bracey, August Meier, and Eliott Rudwick, eds., *Black Workers and Organized Labor* (Belmont, Calif.: Wadsworth, 1970). Recent overviews of twentieth-century labor history that highlight the roles of black workers include Nelson Lichtenstein, *State of the Union: A Century of American Labor* (Princeton, N.J.: Princeton University Press, 2002), and Robert H. Zieger and Gilbert J. Gall, *American Workers, American Unions: The Twentieth Century*, 3d ed. (Baltimore: Johns Hopkins University Press, 2002). David E. Bernstein, *Only One Place of Redress: African Americans, Labor Regulations, and the Courts from Reconstruction to the New Deal* (Durham, N.C.: Duke University Press, 2001), and Paul D. Moreno, *Black Americans and Organized*

Labor: A New History (Baton Rouge: Louisiana State University Press, 2006), are sharply critical of organized labor from a libertarian perspective. Two books by David Roediger, *The Wages of Whiteness: Race and the Making of the American Working Class*, rev. ed. (New York: Verso, 1999), and *Working toward Whiteness: How America's Immigrants Became White—The Strange Journey from Ellis Island to the Suburbs* (New York: Basic Books, 2005), advance controversial perspectives on the racial dynamics of America's working class. Philip S. Foner, *History of the Labor Movement in the United States*, 6 vols. (New York: International Publishers, 1947–1982), combines Marxist orthodoxy with compendious coverage of and special interest in the roles of African American working people.

Biographical studies are relatively few, although A. Philip Randolph has been the subject of a number of illuminating works. Notable are Jervis Anderson, *A. Philip Randolph: A Biographical Portrait* (New York: Harvest Books, 1973); William H. Harris, *Keeping the Faith: A. Philip Randolph, Milton P. Webster, and the Brotherhood of Sleeping Car Porters, 1925–1937* (Urbana: University of Illinois Press, 1977); Beth Tomkins Bates, *Pullman Porters and the Rise of Protest Politics in Black America, 1925–1945* (Chapel Hill: University of North Carolina Press, 2001); Paula F. Pfeffer, *A. Philip Randolph, Pioneer of the Civil Rights Movement* (Baton Rouge: Louisiana State University Press, 2000); and Leon Fink, "A Voice for the People: A. Philip Randolph and the Cult of Leadership," in Leon Fink, *Progressive Intellectuals and the Dilemmas of Democratic Commitment* (Cambridge, Mass.: Harvard University Press, 1997), 184–213. David Levering Lewis's outstanding biography of W. E. B. DuBois contains much material on DuBois's difficult relationship with labor and radical movements, as well as on his pioneering investigations of black workers' conditions and prospects. See David Levering Lewis, *W. E. B. Du Bois: Biography of a Race* (New York: Henry Holt, 1993), and *W. E. B. Du Bois: The Fight for Equality and the American Century, 1919–1963* (New York: Henry Holt, 2000). Nelson Lichtenstein, *The Most Dangerous Man in Detroit: Walter Reuther and the Fate of American Labor* (New York: Basic Books, 1995), stresses the racial dilemmas of labor-liberalism in the post–World War II period, while Michael K. Honey, *Going Down Jericho Road: The Memphis Strike, Martin Luther King's Last Campaign* (New York: Norton, 2007), explores the troubled relationship between the labor and civil rights movements. Memoirs of African American labor activists offer vivid accounts of hardship and activism. See especially Nate Shaw, *All God's Dangers—The Life of Nate Shaw*, comp. Theodore Rosengarten (New York: Knopf, 1974); Nell Irvin Panter, *The Narrative of Hosea Hudson: His Life as a Negro Communist in the South* (Cambridge, Mass.: Harvard University Press, 1979); and Charles Denby, *Indignant Heart: A Black Worker's Journal* (Boston: South End Press, 1978).

Much of the scholarship treating the post-Emancipation experiences of African Americans quite appropriately focuses on the rural South. Steven Hahn, *A Nation under Our Feet: Black Political Struggles in the Rural South from Slavery to the Great Migration* (Cambridge, Mass.: Belknap Press of Harvard University Press, 2003), is an outstanding contribution. C. Vann Woodward's classic study, *Origins of the New South, 1877–1913* (Baton Rouge: Louisiana State University Press, 1951), remains essential. It can be supplemented with Edward L. Ayers, *The*

Promise of the New South: Life after Reconstruction (New York: Oxford University Press, 1992). Eric Foner, *Reconstruction: America's Unfinished Revolution, 1863–1877* (New York: Harper and Row, 1988; Perennial Classics edition, 2002), pays close attention to the economics of the postwar era, while Heather Cox Richardson, *The Death of Reconstruction: Race, Labor, and Politics in the Post–Civil War North, 1865–1901* (Cambridge, Mass.: Harvard University Press, 2001), traces the retreat from egalitarianism in the Gilded Age.

The intricacies and dilemmas of the late-nineteenth-century southern cotton culture and the role of African Americans in it can be followed in a number of outstanding studies. See especially Gerald David Jaynes, *Branches without Roots: Genesis of the Black Working Class in the American South, 1862–1882* (New York: Oxford University Press, 1986); Roger L. Ransom and Richard Sutch, *One Kind of Freedom: The Economic Consequences of Emancipation,* paperback ed. (Cambridge: Cambridge University Press, 1977); Jonathan M. Wiener, *Social Origins of the New South: Alabama, 1860–1885* (Baton Rouge: Louisiana State University Press, 1978); and Robert Higgs, *Competition and Coercion: Blacks in the American Economy, 1865–1914* (Cambridge: Cambridge University Press, 1977). Also useful is William Cohen, *At Freedom's Edge: Black Mobility and the Southern White Quest for Racial Control, 1861–1915* (Baton Rouge: Louisiana State University Press, 1991). Alex Lichtenstein, "Proletarians or Peasants? Sharecroppers and the Politics of Protest in the Rural South, 1880–1940," *Plantation Society in the Americas* 5, nos. 2 and 3 (Fall 1998): 297–331, is an insightful analysis. See also Scott P. Marler, "Fables of Reconstruction: Reconstruction of the Fables," *Journal of the Historical Society* 4, no. 1 (Winter 2004): 113–37, and Jane Dailey, "Land, Labor, and Politics across the Post-Emancipation South," *Labor History* 44, no. 4 (November 2003): 509–22.

Literature on the working lives of African Americans in other postbellum agricultural sectors is less extensive. On struggles in the rice-growing regions of South Carolina and Georgia, see Julie Saville, *The Work of Reconstruction: From Slave to Wage Laborer in South Carolina, 1860–1870* (Cambridge: Cambridge University Press, 1994); Eric Foner, *Nothing but Freedom: Emancipation and Its Legacy* (Baton Rouge: Louisiana State University Press, 1983); and John Scott Strickland, "'No More Mud Work': The Struggle for the Control of Labor and Production in Low Country South Carolina, 1863–1880," in *The Southern Enigma: Essays on Race, Class, and Folk Culture,* ed. Walter J. Fraser Jr. and Winfred B. Moore Jr. (Westport, Conn.: Greenwood, 1983), 43–62. The turbulent struggle for control of work life in Louisiana sugar production is examined in John C. Rodrigue, *Reconstruction in the Cane Fields: From Slavery to Free Labor in Louisiana's Sugar Parishes, 1862–1880* (Baton Rouge: Louisiana State University Press, 2001); Rebecca Scott, "Fault Lines, Color Lines, and Party Lines: Race, Labor, and Collective Action in Louisiana and Cuba, 1862–1912," in *Beyond Slavery: Explorations of Race, Labor, and Citizenship in Postemancipation Societies,* ed. Frederick Cooper, Thomas C. Holt, and Rebecca J. Scott (Chapel Hill: University of North Carolina Press, 2000), 61–106; and Jeffrey Gould, "The Strike of 1887: Louisiana Sugar War," *Southern Exposure* 12 (November–December 1984): 45–55. Jeffrey R. Kerr-Ritchie, *Freedpeople in the Tobacco South: Virginia, 1860–*

1900 (Chapel Hill: University of North Carolina Press, 1999), and Jane Dailey, *Before Jim Crow: The Politics of Race in Postemancipation Virginia* (Chapel Hill: University of North Carolina Press, 2000), are valuable for conditions in the upper South.

A number of recent publications address the role of black workers in mining, manufacturing, and construction work. The harsh but sometimes surprisingly biracial world of coal mining is illuminated in Daniel Letwin, *The Challenge of Interracial Unionism: Alabama Coal Miners, 1878–1921* (Chapel Hill: University of North Carolina Press, 1998); Brian Kelly, *Race, Class, and Power in the Alabama Coalfields, 1908–21* (Urbana and Chicago: University of Illinois Press, 2001); and Ronald L. Lewis, "Job Control and Race Relations in Coal Fields, 1870–1920," *Journal of Ethnic Studies* 12 (1986): 35–64. Herbert G. Gutman's influential article "The Negro and the United Mine Workers of America: The Career and Letters of Richard L. Davis and Something of Their Meaning: 1890–1900," in Herbert G. Gutman, *Work, Culture, and Society in Industrializing America: Essays in American Working-Class and Social History* (New York: Vintage Books, 1977), 121–208, stresses the interracial potential of the fledgling United Mine Workers of America, as does Alex Lichtenstein's "Racial Conflict and Racial Solidarity in the Alabama Coal Strike of 1894: New Evidence for the Gutman-Hill Debate," *Labor History* 36, no. 1 (Winter 1995): 63–76. Eric Arnesen, *Waterfront Workers of New Orleans: Race, Class, and Politics, 1863–1923* (Urbana and Chicago: University of Illinois Press, Illini Books, 1994), also examines patterns of cooperation and conflict among dockworkers of both races during this period.

In contrast, Henry M. McKiven Jr., *Iron and Steel: Class, Race, and Community in Birmingham, Alabama 1875–1920* (Chapel Hill: University of North Carolina Press, 1995), emphasizes the exploitation of black workers by both employers and white craft unionists. Melton Alonza McLaurin, *Paternalism and Protest: Southern Cotton Mill Workers and Organized Labor, 1875–1905* (Westport, Conn.: Greenwood, 1971), documents white workers' hostility toward black labor in this expanding sector. Peter J. Rachleff, *Black Labor in Richmond, 1865–1900* (Philadelphia: Temple University Press, 1984; Illini Books ed., 1989), focuses on black self-actualization and political protest in a study of Richmond's black working class.

With reference to the racial agendas of organized labor, the first two volumes of Philip Foner's vast undertaking cited earlier must be consulted; see *From Colonial Times to the Founding of the American Federation of Labor* (1947) and *From the Founding of the A. F. of L. to the Emergence of American Imperialism* (1955). Philip A. Taft, *The A. F. of L. in the Time of Gompers* (New York: Harpers, 1957), presents the AFL's perspective. David Montgomery, *Beyond Equality: Labor and the Radical Republicans, 1862–1872* (New York: Knopf, 1967), explores the fluid world of race and labor reform in the Civil War era, while Sumner Eliot Matison, "The Labor Movement and the Negro during Reconstruction," *Journal of Negro History* 33, no. 4 (October 1948): 426–68, provides a succinct overview. On the Knights of Labor, see especially Melton Alonza McLaurin, *The Knights of Labor in the South* (Westport, Conn.: Greenwood, 1978); Sidney H. Kessler, "The Organization of Negroes in the Knights of Labor," *Journal of Negro History* 37, no. 3 (July 1952): 248–76; Leon Fink, "'Irrespective of Party, Color or Social Standing': The Knights of Labor and Opposition Politics in Richmond, Virginia," *Labor History* 19, no. 3 (Summer 1978): 325–49; and Kenneth Kann, "The Knights of Labor and the Southern Black Worker," *Labor History* 18, no. 1 (Winter 1977): 49–70.

Bernard Mandel, "Samuel Gompers and the Negro Workers, 1886–1914," *Journal of Negro History* 40, no. 1 (January 1955): 34–60, remains valuable. A splendid article by Eric Arnesen, "'Like Banquo's Ghost, It Will Not Go Down': The Race Question and the American Railroad Brotherhoods, 1880–1920," *American Historical Review* 99, no. 5 (December 1994): 1601–33, breaks new ground in treating the racial policies and attitudes in the labor movement. Alexander Saxton explores organized labor's hostility toward Asian workers in two books: *The Indispensable Enemy: Labor and the Anti-Chinese Movement in California* (Berkeley and Los Angeles: University of California Press, 1971), and *The Rise and Fall of the White Republic: Class Politics and Mass Culture in Nineteenth-Century America* (London: Verso, 1990). Andrew Gyory, *Closing the Gate: Race, Politics, and the Chinese Exclusion Act* (Chapel Hill: University of North Carolina Press, 1998), finds white workers' response to Asian immigration more complex. Stanford M. Lyman, "The 'Chinese Question' and American Labor Historians," *New Politics* 7, no. 4 (Winter 2000): 113–48, is a sharp critique of Gyory's book. See also the exchange between Lyman and Gyory: Andrew Gyory, "A Reply to Stanford Lyman," *New Politics* 8, no. 1 (Summer 2000); and Stanford M. Lyman, "Engels Was Right! Organized Labor's Opposition to Chinese in the U.S.," *New Politics* 8, no. 1 (Summer 2000), available at http://www.wpunj.edu/newpol/issue29/lyman29. htm (accessed December 27, 2006).

The best book on the subject of postbellum unfree labor is Alex Lichtenstein, *Twice the Work of Free Labor: The Political Economy of Convict Labor in the New South* (London: Verso, 1996). Matthew J. Mancini, *One Dies, Get Another: Convict Leasing in the American South, 1866–1928* (Columbia: University of South Carolina Press, 1996), and David M. Oshinsky, *"Worse Than Slavery": Parchman Farm and the Ordeal of Jim Crow Justice* (New York: Free Press, 1996), are also excellent. Tera W. Hunter, *To 'Joy My Freedom: Southern Black Women's Lives and Labor after the Civil War* (Cambridge, Mass.: Harvard University Press, 1997), examines the lives of female domestic workers. W. E. B. DuBois, *The Philadelphia Negro: A Social Study* (1899; reprint, New York: Benjamin Blom, 1967), and W. E. B. DuBois, *The Black North in 1901: A Social Study* (1901; reprint, New York: Arno Press, 1969), are vivid contemporary studies of the emerging northern black working class. Important material on black workers and workplace tensions can be found in David M. Katzman, *Before the Ghetto: Black Detroit in the Nineteenth Century* (Urbana: University of Illinois Press, 1973); Gilbert Osofsky, *Harlem: The Making of a Ghetto* (New York: Harper and Row, 1966); and David A. Gerber, *Black Ohio and the Color Line, 1860–1915* (Urbana: University of Illinois Press, 1976). Warren C. Whatley, "African-American Strikebreaking from the Civil War to the New Deal," *Social Science History* 17, no. 4 (Winter 1993): 525–58, and Eric Arnesen, "Specter of the Black Strikebreaker: Race, Employment, and Labor Activism in the Industrial Era," *Labor History* 44, no. 3 (August 2003): 319–37, treat a controversial subject. Brian Kelly, "Beyond the 'Talented Tenth': Black Elites, Black Workers, and the Limits of Accommodation in Industrial Birmingham, 1900–1921," in *Time Longer Than Rope: A Century of African American Activism, 1850–1950,* ed. Charles M. Payne and Adam Green (New York: New York University Press, 2003), 276–301, and Brian Kelly, "Sentinels for New South Industry: Booker T. Washington, Industrial Accommodation and Black Workers in the Jim Crow South," *Labor History* 44, no. 3 (August 2003): 337–58, treat relations between black elites and black workers. African American attitudes toward immigration are dealt with in Arnold Shankman, *Ambivalent Friends: Afro-Americans View the Immigrant* (Westport, Conn.: Greenwood, 1982), and David J. Hellwig, "Black Leaders and United States Immigration Policy, 1917–1929," *Journal of Negro History* 66, no. 2 (Summer 1981): 110–27.

A number of important books deal with the African American experience in particular industries. Meatpacking has been particularly well covered. See Rick Halpern, *Down on the Killing Floor: Black and White Workers in Chicago's Packinghouses, 1904–54* (Urbana: University of Illinois Press, 1997); Roger Horowitz, *Negro and White, Unite and Fight! A Social History of Meatpacking, 1930–1990* (Urbana: University of Illinois Press, 1997); and James R. Barrett, *Work and Community in the Jungle: Chicago's Packinghouse Workers, 1894–1922* (Urbana: University of Illinois Press, 1987). Eric Arnesen, *Brotherhoods of Color: Black Railroad Workers and the Struggle for Equality* (Cambridge, Mass.: Harvard University Press, 2001), is outstanding. The complex and changing relationship of black workers to the textile industry in the twentieth century is dealt with in Mary Frederickson, "Four Decades of Change: Black Workers in Southern Textiles, 1941–1981," in *Workers' Struggles, Past and Present: A "Radical America" Reader,* ed. James Green (Philadelphia: Temple University Press, 1983), 62–82, and Bryant Simon, *A Fabric of Defeat: The Politics of South Carolina Millhands, 1910–1948* (Chapel Hill: University of North Carolina Press, 1998). Ronald L. Lewis, *Black Coal Miners in America: Race, Class, and Community Conflict, 1780–1980* (Lexington: University Press of Kentucky, 1987), treats a critical sector. William P. Jones, *The Tribe of Black Ulysses: African American Lumber Workers in the Jim Crow South* (Urbana and Chicago: University of Illinois Press, 2005), is an imaginative study. Herbert R. Northrup published a number of monographs on the employment of black workers in a variety of basic industrial and transportation fields. See Northrup and others, *Negro Employment in Basic Industry: A Study of Racial Policies in Six Industries* (Philadelphia: Industrial Research Unit, Wharton School of Finance and Commerce, University of Pennsylvania, 1970), as well as other volumes by Northrup on automobiles, steel, maritime, longshore, garments, tobacco, and other industries. There is no adequate study of blacks in the building trades, but see Marc Linder, *Wars of Attrition: Vietnam, the Business Roundtable, and the Decline of Construction Unions* (Iowa City: Fanpihua Press, 1999), and William B. Gould, *Black Workers in White Unions: Job Discrimination in the United States* (Ithaca, N.Y.: Cornell University Press, 1977).

The Great Migration of the 1910s and 1920s is ably examined in James Grossman, *Land of Hope: Chicago, Black Southerners, and the Great Migration* (Chicago: University of Chicago Press, 1989); Peter Gottlieb, *Making Their Own*

Way: Southern Blacks' Migration to Pittsburgh, 1916–1930 (Urbana and Chicago: University of Illinois Press, 1987); Earl Lewis, *In Their Own Interests: Race, Class, and Power in Twentieth-Century Norfolk, Virginia* (Berkeley: University of California Press, 1991); and Carole Marks, *"Farewell, We're Good and Gone": The Great Black Migration* (Bloomington: Indiana University Press, 1989). On labor-related racial violence in the World War I era, see Elliott M. Rudwick, *Race Riot at East St. Louis, July 2, 1917* (Carbondale: Southern Illinois University Press, 1964); Malcolm McLaughlin, "Reconsidering the East St. Louis Race Riot of 1917," *International Review of Social History* 47 (2002): 187–212; William M. Tuttle Jr., *Race Riot: Chicago in the Red Summer of 1919* (New York: Atheneum, 1970); and Nan Elizabeth Woodruff, "The New Negro in the American Congo: World War I and the Elaine, Arkansas Massacre of 1919," in *Time Longer Than Rope: A Century of African American Activism, 1850–1950*, ed. Charles M. Payne and Adam Green (New York: New York University Press, 2003), 150–78. Studies of African American workers in the 1920s are few, but Theodore Kornweibel Jr., "An Economic Profile of Black Life in the Twenties," *Journal of Black Studies* 6, no. 4 (June 1976): 307–20, and Theodore Kornweibel Jr., *No Crystal Stair: Black Life and the "Messenger," 1917–1928* (Westport, Conn.: Greenwood, 1975), are useful. See also William Wayne Giffin, *African Americans and the Color Line in Ohio, 1915–1930* (Columbus: Ohio State University Press, 2005); Joe William Trotter Jr., *Black Milwaukee: The Making of an Industrial Proletariat, 1915–45* (Urbana and Chicago: University of Illinois Press, 1985); and Thomas N. Maloney and Warren C. Whatley, "Making the Effort: The Contours of Racial Discrimination in Detroit's Labor Markets, 1920–1940," *Journal of Economic History* 55, no. 1 (September 1995): 465–93.

The decade of the 1930s is well served. Harvard Sitkoff, *A New Deal for Blacks: The Emergence of Civil Rights as a National Issue*, vol. 1, *The Depression Decade* (New York: Oxford University Press, 1978), and Raymond Wolters, *Negroes and the Great Depression: The Problem of Economic Recovery* (1970; reprint, Westport, Conn.: Greenwood, 1978), provide excellent overviews. Robert H. Zieger, *The CIO, 1935–1955* (Chapel Hill: University of North Carolina Press, 1995), places racial issues in the context of labor's advance in the 1930s and 1940s. Of particular interest is Horace Cayton and George S. Mitchell, *Black Workers and the New Unions* (Chapel Hill: University of North Carolina Press, 1939), which contains vivid interview material. Robin D. G. Kelley, *Hammer and Hoe: Alabama Communists during the Great Depression* (Chapel Hill: University of North Carolina Press, 1990), and Robert Rodgers Korstad, *Civil Rights Unionism: Tobacco Workers and the Struggle for Democracy in the Mid-Twentieth Century South* (Chapel Hill: University of North Carolina Press, 2003), highlight the role of communists in building interracial unions in the South. August Meier and Elliott Rudwick, *Black Detroit and the Rise of the UAW* (New York: Oxford University Press, 1979), treats a critical industry.

The literature on World War II is rich. There are two illuminating studies of the Fair Employment Practice Committee: Merl E. Reed, *Seedtime for the Modern Civil Rights Movement: The President's Committee on Fair Employment Practice, 1941–1946* (Baton Rouge: Louisiana State University Press, 1991), and Andrew

Edmund Kersten, *Race, Jobs, and the War: The FEPC in the Midwest, 1941–1946* (Urbana and Chicago: University of Illinois Press, 2000). See also William H. Harris, "Federal Intervention in Union Discrimination: FEPC and the West Coast Shipyards during World War II," *Labor History* 22, no. 3 (Summer 1981): 325–47, as well as the biographical studies of A. Philip Randolph cited earlier. Robert Korstad and Nelson Lichtenstein, "Opportunities Found and Lost: Labor, Radicals, and the Early Civil Rights Movement," *Journal of American History* 75, no. 3 (December 1988): 786–811, illuminates the relationship between wartime labor activism and growing black political development. Bruce Nelson, "Organized Labor and the Struggle for Black Equality in Mobile during World War II," *Journal of American History* 80, no. 3 (December 1993): 952–88, and Alex Lichtenstein, "Exclusion, Fair Employment, or Interracial Unionism: Race Relations in Florida's Shipyards during World War II," in *Labor in the Modern South*, ed. Glen T. Eskew (Athens: University of Georgia Press, 2001), 135–57, examine a key wartime industry. See also Karen Tucker Anderson, "Last Hired, First Fired: Black Women Workers during World War II," *Journal of American History* 69, no. 1 (June 1982): 82–97, and Allan M. Winkler, "The Philadelphia Transit Strike of 1944," *Journal of American History* 59, no. 1 (June 1972): 73–89. Robert C. Weaver, *Negro Labor: A National Problem* (New York: Harcourt, Brace, 1946), and Herbert Northrup, *Organized Labor and the Negro* (New York: Harper and Brothers, 1944), are important contemporary studies.

Risa Lauren Goluboff, "'Let Economic Equality Take Care of Itself': The NAACP, Labor Litigation, and the Making of Civil Rights in the 1940s," *UCLA Law Review* 52, no. 5 (June 2005): 1393–1486, is a detailed analysis of the retreat from wartime concern with workplace rights. Bette Woody, *Black Women in the Workplace: Impacts of Structural Change in the Economy* (Westport, Conn.: Greenwood, 1992), has good material on the postwar period. Michael Honey, *Southern Labor and Black Civil Rights: Organizing Memphis Workers* (Urbana and Chicago: University of Illinois Press, 1993), stresses the negative effects of anticommunism on southern union development, as does Korstad's *Civil Rights Unionism*, cited earlier. See also Rick Halpern, "The CIO and the Limits of Labor-Based Civil Rights Activism: The Case of Louisiana's Sugar Workers, 1947–1966," in *Southern Labor in Transition*, ed. Robert H. Zieger (Knoxville: University of Tennessee Press, 1997), 86–112, and Horace Huntley, "The Red Scare and Black Workers in Alabama: The International Union of Mine, Mill, and Smelter Workers, 1945–53," in *Labor Divided: Race and Ethnicity in United States Labor Struggles, 1835–1960*, ed. Robert Asher and Charles Stephenson (Albany: State University of New York Press, 1990), 129–45. Harvey Levenstein, *Communism, Anti-Communism, and the CIO* (Westport, Conn.: Greenwood, 1981), and Jeff Woods, *Black Struggle, Red Scare: Segregation and Anti-Communism in the South, 1948–1968* (Baton Rouge: Louisiana State University Press, 2004), are also useful.

Thomas J. Sugrue, *The Origins of the Urban Crisis: Race and Inequality in Postwar Detroit* (Princeton, N.J.: Princeton University Press, 1996); Kenneth D. Durr, *Behind the Backlash: White Working-Class Politics in Baltimore, 1940–1980* (Chapel Hill: University of North Carolina Press, 2003); and Robert O. Self, *American Babylon: Race and the Struggle for Postwar Oakland* (Princeton, N.J.:

Princeton University Press, 2003), deal with racial tensions in urban settings. Thomas J. Sugrue, "'Forget about Your Inalienable Right to Work': Deindustrialization and Its Discontents at Ford, 1950–1953," *International Labor and Working-Class History* 48 (Fall 1995): 112–30, and Harold M. Baron and Bennett Hymer, "The Negro Worker in the Chicago Labor Market," in *The Negro and the American Labor Movement*, ed. Julius Jacobson (New York: Doubleday/Anchor, 1968), 232–85, are good on the racial implications of early postwar deindustrialization.

Bruce Nelson, *Divided We Stand: American Workers and the Struggle for Black Equality* (Princeton, N.J.: Princeton University Press, 2001); Bruce Nelson, "'CIO Meant One Thing for the Whites and Another Thing for Us': Steelworkers and Civil Rights, 1936–1974," in *Southern Labor in Transition, 1940–1995*, ed. Robert H. Zieger (Knoxville: University of Tennessee Press, 1997), 113–45; and Robert J. Norrell, "Caste in Steel: Jim Crow Careers in Birmingham, Alabama," *Journal of American History* 73, no. 3 (December 1986): 669–94, are critical of the racial policies of the steelworkers union. But see Judith Stein, "Southern Workers in National Unions: Birmingham Steelworkers, 1936–1951," in *Organized Labor in the Twentieth-Century South*, ed. Robert H. Zieger (Knoxville: University of Tennessee Press, 1993), 183–222, and especially Judith Stein, *Running Steel, Running America: Race, Economic Policy, and the Decline of Liberalism* (Chapel Hill: University of North Carolina Press, 1998), for the political economy of race relations in what used to be America's bellwether industry. Kevin Boyle, "'There Are No Union Sorrows That the Union Can't Heal': The Struggle for Racial Equality in the United Automobile Workers, 1940–1960," *Labor History* 36, no. 1 (Winter 1995): 5–23, explores the racial dilemmas of this progressive union. Kevin Boyle, "The Kiss: Racial and Gender Conflict in a 1950s Automobile Factory," *Journal of American History* 84, no. 2 (September 1997): 496–523, presents an unusually imaginative and revealing insight into the racial dynamics of the decade.

Affirmative action has generated an impressive literature. For a good overview, see Terry H. Anderson, *The Pursuit of Fairness: A History of Affirmative Action* (New York: Oxford University Press, 2004). Robert J. Weiss, *"We Want Jobs": A History of Affirmative Action* (New York: Garland, 1997), is insightful, and Nancy MacLean, *Freedom Is Not Enough: The Opening of the American Workplace* (Cambridge, Mass.: Harvard University Press, 2006), is particularly strong on gender issues. Hugh Davis Graham, *The Civil Rights Era: Origins and Development of National Policy, 1960–1972* (New York: Oxford University Press, 1990); Paul Moreno, *From Direct Action to Affirmative Action: Fair Employment Law and Policy in America, 1933–1972* (Baton Rouge: Louisiana State University Press, 1997); and John D. Skrentny, *The Minority Rights Revolution* (Cambridge, Mass.: Belknap Press of Harvard University Press, 2002), are strong on the legislative and judicial aspects of civil rights and affirmative action. Ira Katznelson, *When Affirmative Action Was White: An Untold History of Racial Inequality in Twentieth-Century America* (New York: Norton, 2005), is challenging, as is Raymond Wolters, *Right Turn: William Bradford Reynolds, the Reagan Administration, and Black Civil Rights* (New Brunswick, N.J.: Transaction Publishers, 1996), albeit from a sharply different direction. The Philadelphia Plan is treated in Judith Stein,

"Affirmative Action and the Conservative Agenda: President Richard M. Nixon's Philadelphia Plan of 1969," in *Labor in the Modern South*, ed. Glenn T. Eskew (Athens: University of Georgia Press, 2001), 182–206, and Thomas J. Sugrue, "Affirmative Action from Below: Civil Rights, the Building Trades, and the Politics of Racial Equality in the Urban North, 1945–1969," *Journal of American History* 91, no. 1 (June 2004): 145–73. Dennis A. Deslippe, "'Do Whites Have Rights?' White Detroit Policemen and Reverse Discrimination Protests in the 1970s," *Journal of American History* 91, no. 3 (December 2004): 932–60, examines the complexities of race-based public employment.

Two outstanding books by Timothy J. Minchin, *The Color of Work: The Struggle for Civil Rights in the Southern Paper Industry, 1945–1980* (Chapel Hill: University of North Carolina Press, 2001), and *Hiring the Black Worker: The Racial Integration of the Southern Textile Industry, 1960–1980* (Chapel Hill: University of North Carolina Press, 1999), detail the combination of grassroots activism and legal maneuvering that brought desegregation to two major industries. John Hinshaw, *Steel and Steelworkers: Race and Class in Twentieth-Century Pittsburgh* (Albany: State University of New York Press, 2002); Dennis C. Dickerson, *Out of the Crucible: Black Steelworkers in Western Pennsylvania, 1875–1980* (Albany: State University of New York Press, 1986); and Ruth Needleman, *Black Freedom Fighters in Steel: The Struggle for Democratic Unionism* (Ithaca, N.Y.: Cornell University Press, 2003), highlight the limits of African American advance in the steel industry. Venus Green, *Race on the Line: Gender, Labor, and Technology in the Bell System, 1880–1980* (Durham, N.C.: Duke University Press, 2001), treats telephone work.

The relationship between immigration reform and affirmative action is traced in Hugh Davis Graham, *Collision Course: The Strange Convergence of Affirmative Action and Immigration Policy in America* (New York: Oxford University Press, 2002). Other important recent works dealing with relations between African Americans and the new immigrants include George Yancey, *Who Is White? Latinos, Asians, and the New Black/Nonblack Divide* (Boulder, Colo.: Lynne Rienner, 2003); Roger Waldinger and Michael I. Lichter, *How the Other Half Works: Immigration and the Social Organization of Labor* (Berkeley and Los Angeles: University of California Press, 2003); and Ruth Milkman, *L.A. Story: Immigrant Workers and the Future of the U.S. Labor Movement* (New York: Russell Sage Foundation, 2006). See also Otis L. Graham Jr., *Unguarded Gates: A History of America's Immigration Crisis* (Lanham, Md.: Rowman and Littlefield, 2004), for a provocative historical perspective on immigration and labor.

Two books by Michael Goldfield stress the role of race in organized labor's post–World War II retreat. See *The Decline of Organized Labor in the United States* (Chicago: University of Chicago Press, 1987), and *The Color of Politics: Race and the Mainsprings of American Politics* (New York: New Press, 1997). Bayard Rustin's classic argument for a black-labor coalition is found in his essay "From Protest to Politics: The Future of the Civil Rights Movement," *Commentary,* February 1965. Southern white working-class resistance to racial progress is examined in Alan Draper, *Conflict of Interests: Organized Labor and the Civil Rights Movement in the South, 1954–1968* (Ithaca, N.Y.: ILR Press, 1994); Robert J.

Norrell, "Labor Trouble: George Wallace and Union Politics in Alabama," in *Organized Labor in the Twentieth-Century South*, ed. Robert H. Zieger (Knoxville: University of Tennessee Press, 1991), 250–72; Robert S. McElvaine, "Claude Ramsay, Organized Labor, and the Civil Rights Movement in Mississippi, 1959–1966," in *Southern Workers and Their Unions, 1880–1975: Selected Papers*, ed. Merl E. Reed, Leslie S. Hough, and Gary M. Fink (Westport, Conn.: Greenwood, 1981), 110–42; Robert H. Zieger, "A Venture into Unplowed Fields: Daniel Powell and CIO Political Action in the Postwar South," in *Labor in the Modern South*, ed. Glenn T. Eskew (Athens: University of Georgia Press, 2001), 158–81; and Michelle Brattain, "Making Friends and Enemies: Textile Workers and Political Action in Post–World War II Georgia," *Journal of Southern History* 58, no. 1 (February 1997): 91–138.

Labor militancy in the civil rights era is analyzed in Aaron Brenner, "Rank-and-File Rebellion, 1966–1975" (PhD diss., Columbia University, 1996). The standard work on the Memphis sanitation workers strike is Joan Turner Beifuss, *At the River I Stand* (Memphis: St. Luke's Press, 1990), but see also Michael K. Honey, "Martin Luther King, Jr., the Crisis of the Black Working Class, and the Memphis Sanitation Strike," in *Southern Labor in Transition, 1940–1995*, ed. Robert H. Zieger (Knoxville: University of Tennessee Press, 1997), 146–75, and Steve Estes, "'I Am a Man!': Race, Masculinity, and the 1968 Memphis Sanitation Strike," *Labor History* 41, no. 2 (May 2000): 153–70. The Charleston hospital workers strike is ably chronicled in Leon Fink and Brian Greenberg, *Upheaval in the Quiet Zone: A History of Hospital Workers' Union Local 1199* (Urbana and Chicago: University of Illinois Press, 1989). See also Gregg L. Michel, "'Union Power, Soul Power': Unionizing Johns Hopkins University Hospital, 1959–1974," *Labor History* 38, no. 1 (Winter 1996–1997): 28–66. Joseph A. McCartin, "'Fire the Hell Out of Them': Sanitation Workers' Struggles and the Normalization of the Striker Replacement Strategy in the 1970s," *Labor: Studies in the Working-Class History of the Americas* 2, no. 3 (Fall 2005): 67–92, is an important article. On the overall trajectory of public workers' militancy, see Paul Johnson, *Success while Others Fail: Social Movement Unionism and the Public Workplace* (Ithaca, N.Y.: ILR Press, 1994).

The explosive workplace racial tensions in Detroit are conveyed in Heather Ann Thompson, *Whose Detroit? Politics, Labor, and Race in a Modern American City* (Ithaca, N.Y.: Cornell University Press, 2001), and Dan Georgakas, *Detroit, I Do Mind Dying: A Study in Urban Revolution* (New York: St. Martin's, 1975). The standard work on the Ocean Hill–Brownsville affair is Jerald E. Podair, *The Strike That Changed New York: Blacks, Whites, and the Ocean Hill–Brownsville Crisis* (New Haven, Conn.: Yale University Press, 2002), while Joshua Freeman, *Working-Class New York: Life and Labor since World War II* (New York: Free Press, 2000), illuminates the tensions within New York's liberal-labor community. Peter B. Levy, *The New Left and Labor in the 1960s* (Urbana and Chicago: University of Illinois Press, 1994), establishes the broader national context.

The urban crisis of the contemporary black working class is examined in the work of William Julius Wilson and Jon McWhorter, as cited in the notes to chapter 7. In addition, William A. Darity Jr. and Samuel L. Myers Jr., *Persistent Disparity:*

Race and Economic Inequality in the United States since 1945 (Cheltenham, UK, and Northampton, Mass.: Edward Elgar, 1998), is perceptive and compelling. Two important collections of papers place current race-labor issues in historical context. See Patrick L. Mason, ed., *African Americans, Labor, and Society: Organizing for a New Agenda* (Detroit: Wayne State University Press, 2001), and Manning Marable, Immanuel Ness, and Joseph Wilson, eds., *Race and Labor Matters in the New U.S. Economy* (Lanham, Md.: Rowman and Littlefield, 2006). Coverage of race-related labor issues and of organized labor in general in the daily media is sporadic at best. Several of the articles in Correspondents of the *New York Times, How Race Is Lived in America: Pulling Together, Pulling Apart* (New York: Times Books–Henry Holt, 2001), deal with the world of work. The newspaper articles and Web site material cited in chapter 7 suggest what is available to the student of the contemporary race-labor nexus. The Web site for the Coalition of Black Trade Unionists, http://www.cbtu.org/, is particularly useful.

INDEX

A. Philip Randolph Institute, 225–26, 228.
    See also Rustin, Bayard
Abbott, Robert, 117
Abernathy, Ralph, 197
affirmative action, 3, 152–53, 175–90,
    209–15, 216–17, 233. *See also* Civil
    Rights Act, 1964
African American workers
    agricultural, 9–10, 13–19, 30–36, 59, 74,
        108–9, 109–10, 124, 140, 142, 145.
        See also sharecroppers; Southern
        Tenant Farmers Union
    in automobile industry, 104, 113, 118–
        23, 134, 135, 141, 149, 166, 198–201,
        219. *See also* Dodge Revolutionary
        Union Movement; United Automobile
        Workers of America
    in building trades, 5, 62, 64, 70, 79, 85–
        86, 100, 102, 149, 182–85, 186–87,
        189, 214. *See also* building trades
        unions; Philadelphia Plan; *individual
        unions*
    in coal mining, 36–39, 46, 47, 54, 62, 69,
        110–11. *See also* United Mine Workers
        of America
    domestic, 19, 58, 59, 74, 104, 124, 142,
        144, 146–48
    general conditions and circumstances of,
        2, 9–10, 19–22, 104–5, 107–12, 139–
        47, 189–90, 208, 215–23, 232
    hospital, 195–98, 225
    in laundries, 98, 144
    in longshoring, 10, 19, 23, 36, 39–42, 57,
        61, 68, 81, 91, 129, 136
    in meatpacking, 71, 72, 73, 75, 81–85,
        115, 144, 145, 150

non-free labor, 43–51
    professional, 140–41, 145, 148, 217,
        219–20
    public workers, 54, 86, 124, 141, 175,
        191, 212, 213–14, 215. *See also*
        African American workers: sanitation
    pulp and paper, 129, 178, 179. *See also*
        Jackson Memorandum
    in railroads, 19, 23, 29, 54, 57, 60, 62–
        64, 70, 76, 78, 85, 86–88, 91, 93, 96–
        97, 102, 106–7, 127, 129–30, 130–31,
        135, 145, 153–54. *See also* railroads,
        unions; Randolph, A. Philip
    sanitation, 175, 190, 192–93, 193–95,
        204–6
    in shipbuilding, 124–25, 130–31, 132,
        133, 141
    in steel industry, 20–21, 23, 53, 71, 73,
        75, 79, 98, 115, 129, 218. *See also*
        *Kaiser Aluminum & Chemical
        Corporation and United Steelworkers
        of America, AFL-CIO v. Brian F. Weber*
    telephone, 55, 180–81, 210–11. *See also*
        Bell Telephone Company
    textile, 21–22, 178–80, 217–18. *See also*
        affirmative action; *Sledge v. J. P. Stevens*
    tobacco, 57, 129, 144, 145–46, 162, 178.
        See also Food, Tobacco, Agricultural,
        and Allied Workers
    white-collar, 54, 55, 75, 104, 144–45,
        150, 217–18, 218–19, 219–20
    women, 42, 55, 57, 73–74, 123, 124,
        139, 142–47, 210–11, 217
Agricultural Adjustment Act (1933), 108–9
Agricultural Adjustment Act (1937), 110
Agricultural Adjustment Administration, 109

Alabama Dry Dock and Shipbuilding Co., 132
Aliquippa, Pa., 132
Allen, Ercell, 145
Amalgamated Clothing Workers of America, 112, 164
Amalgamated Meat Cutters and Butcher Workmen, 81–85, 116, 117
American Federation of Labor (AFL), 61, 80, 86, 90, 108, 116, 124, 125, 134, 136–37, 155, 157–58, 164, 169
and African American workers, 28–29, 57, 60–69, 76, 78–81, 85–87, 98, 106, 124–25, 135–37, 167, 168
and Asian workers, 62, 64–65, 66, 69
and Congress of Industrial Organizations (CIO), 112, 113, 168
founding and early development, 27–28
legislative and political activities, 101, 102–3, 113, 139, 159
and Randolph, 89–91, 125–26
See also Gompers, Samuel; Green, William; Meany, George; individual unions
American Federation of Labor–Congress of Industrial Organizations (AFL-CIO), 164, 186, 189, 228
and affirmative action, 231
and African American workers, 168–72, 192, 198, 224–25, 225–26, 227, 229, 230–31
internal dissent in, 209, 223–24, 225–26
legislative and political activities, 165–66, 173, 226–27, 228, 230
See also Meany, George; Randolph, A. Philip
American Federation of State, County, and Municipal Employees (AFSCME), 191, 223, 227
and Atlanta sanitation workers' strike, 204–6
and Memphis sanitation workers' strike, 193–95
American Federation of Teachers, 191, 192, 198, 201–4
American Federationist, 62, 135
American Railroad Union, 29, 63
Anderson, Eddie, 146
Armour and Company, 116
Arnall, Ellis, 159
Arnesen, Eric, 2
Asians and Asian Americans, 2–4, 62, 187–88, 231. See also Chinese Exclusion Act; Chinese workers; Filipino workers; immigration; Japanese
Asian Pacific American Labor Alliance, 228

Atlanta, 36, 146–47, 195
sanitation workers' strike, 190, 204–6
automobile industry, 104, 113, 118–23, 134, 135, 141, 149, 166, 198–201, 219. See also United Automobile Workers of America

Bakersfield, Calif., 192
Baldanzi, George, 161
Baltimore, 53, 132, 147, 195, 198, 226
Baltimore Afro-American, 170
Bankhead-Jones Farm Tenancy Act, 110
Bay Area Council against Discrimination, 130
Beaufort, S.C., 34
Bedford, Robert, 84
Bell Telephone Company, 55, 180–81, 210–11
Bernstein, David, 5
Bessemer, Ala., 157
Bethlehem Steel Corporation, 218
Bilbo, Theodore, 161
Birmingham, Ala., 20–21, 36, 38, 98–99, 110–11, 195
Bittner, Van, 161, 162
"Black Codes," 11
Black Shirts, 107
Blackstone, Rev. William L., 110
Bogolusa, La., 180
Bontemps, Arna, 17
Boston, 52, 225
Bratton, I. H., 115
bricklayers union (Bricklayers, Masons and Plasterers' International Union), 91
Brotherhood of Locomotive Engineers, 66
Brotherhood of Locomotive Firemen and Enginemen, 102, 129–30, 131, 153–54. See also railroads, unions
Brotherhood of Railroad Trainmen, 97, 168
Brotherhood of Railway Carmen, 63–64
Brotherhood of Sleeping Car Porters (BSCP), 76, 101, 103, 126, 136, 145, 168, 170
origins and early development of, 89–91
See also railroads, unions; Randolph, A. Philip
Brotherhood of Sleeping Car Porters Ladies' Auxiliaries, 145
Brown, Clayola, 225
Brown, Joseph E., 47
Brown, Joseph M., 47
Brown and Root, Inc., 214
Brown v. Board of Education of Topeka, 152, 164, 201
Buffalo, 54, 135
Building Service Employees Domestic Workers Local, 147, 149

building trades unions
  African American workers and, 5, 62, 64, 70, 79, 85–86, 100, 102, 149, 182–85, 186–87, 189, 214
  decline of, 214
  history and character of, 182–84
  See also American Federation of Labor; Philadelphia Plan; individual unions
Bureau of Refugees, Freedmen, and Abandoned Lands. See Freedmen's Bureau
Bush, George H. W., and affirmative action, 213, 214
Business Roundtable, and affirmative action, 213
Business Week, 153
Butte, Mont., 132

Caffery, Donelson, 31–32
Cannon, Corine Lytle, 179
Cayton, Horace, 113, 118
chain gangs, 45, 48, 49–50, 50–51. See also convict leasing; New South
Chamberlain, Daniel H., 33
Change to Win coalition, 209, 223–24, 228–30
Charleston, S.C., 36, 39
  hospital workers' strike, 195–98, 199
  See also Hospital Workers Local 1199, 1199B
Chávez, César, 4
Chicago, 52, 53, 68, 71, 72, 73, 74, 75 81, 104, 107, 113, 142, 144, 148, 150, 187, 220, 226
  labor activity in, 81–85, 116–18, 185, 199
  racial violence in, 83–84, 96
Chicago, Burlington, and Quincy Railroad, 63
Chicago Defender, 71, 74, 93, 117, 118
Chicago Federation of Labor, 82, 84
Chinese Exclusion Act, 1882, 3, 64–65, 66
Chinese workers, 3, 22, 27, 28, 63, 64–65, 66, 67, 69, 77, 100
Chrysler Corporation, 118, 120, 199
Cincinnati, 149
Cincinnati Daily Gazette, 11
CIO News, 159
civil rights, 1, 125, 211–12, 213
  and immigration, 188
  and labor movement, 6, 90, 134–35, 138, 139, 154, 156, 157, 160–61, 163, 164–65, 165–66, 167, 176, 190–207, 225
  legislation, 9, 140, 150, 151, 152, 174
  See also Civil Rights Act (1964); Civil Rights Act (1965)
Civil Rights Act (1957), 152, 164

Civil Rights Act (1960), 152, 164
Civil Rights Act (1964), 6, 164, 167, 191, 209–11, 212, 219, 232
  and employment discrimination, 175–90
  Title VI, 6, 188, 217, 232
  Title VII, 6, 176, 177, 178, 188, 209–10, 211, 215, 217, 232
  See also Equal Employment Opportunities Commission
Civil Rights Act (1965), 191, 226
Cleveland, 53, 54, 73, 74, 148, 149
Coalition of Black Trade Unionists (CBTU), 223, 225–28, 228–30
Coalition of Labor Union Women, 228
Cohen, Carl, 182
Colored Farmers Alliance, 35
Combahee River, S.C., 33, 34
Commission on Human Rights (New York State), 150, 151
Communications Workers of America, 194
Communist Party of the United States, 117, 155–56, 162, 163
communists
  and African Americans, 156, 160–61, 163
  and labor movement, 116–18, 160–61, 162, 163
  See also International Union of Mine, Mill, and Smelter Workers
Congress of Industrial Organizations (CIO), 106, 114, 115–18, 131, 136–37, 157, 159–61
  and African American workers, 112–23, 124, 128–29, 133–35, 137, 145–47, 167, 168
  and American Federation of Labor (AFL), 113, 168
  and automobile industry, 118–23
  communist influence in, 155, 156, 161, 162, 169
  legislative and political activities, 113, 139, 159, 161–62, 164
  and meatpacking industry, 116–18
  and women workers, 145–46, 147
  in World War II, 124, 132, 133–35, 155
  See also Communist Party of the United States; communists; United Automobile Workers; United Packinghouse Workers
Continental Can Company, 179
contract labor, 65
convict leasing, 45–47, 48. See also chain gangs; debt peonage; New South; prison farms
Cooper River, S.C., 34
Cotton Men's Executive Council (New Orleans), 40

cotton production, 14, 15–19, 30, 34–36.
  See also sharecroppers; sharecropping
Crescent City, Fla., 89
Crisis, 115
Crown-Zellerbach Corporation, 179, 180

Danville, Va., 64
Darrity, William A., Jr., 222
Davis, Leon, 195, 197
Davis, Richard, 68, 69
Davis-Bacon Act, 1931, 102
Dayton, 149
De Priest, Oscar, 74
Dearborn, Mich., 121
debt peonage, 49. See also chain gangs;
  convict leasing; New South; prison
  farms
Declaration of Independence, 23
Declining Significance of Race, The, 220
deindustrialization, 218–19
Democratic Party
  and civil rights legislation, 150, 151, 152
  1930s, 128
  post–World War II, 158–59, 164, 226,
    228
  Reconstruction era, 31, 34, 40
  World War I era, 93
  See also Johnson, Lyndon; Kennedy, John
    F.; Roosevelt, Franklin D.; Truman,
    Harry
Denby, Charles, 199
Densmore, John, 93–94
Denver, 225
Detroit, 53, 54, 71, 74, 104, 107, 113, 118,
    122, 141, 142, 143, 148, 167, 213–14,
    226
  race-labor conflict in, 132–33, 134, 185,
    198–201
  See also United Automobile Workers of
    America
Dewey, Thomas E., 162
Dillard, James H., 94, 95
Dirksen, Everett, 187
Division of Negro Economics. See United
  States Department of Labor, Division
  of Negro Economics
Dodge Revolutionary Union Movement
  (DRUM), 200–201
Donahue, Tom, 225
"Double V" campaign, 125
Draft Riot (1863), 77
Dred Scott v. Sandford (1857), 22, 23
Dubinsky, David, 167, 171
DuBois, William Edward Burghardt, 20,
    52, 58–59, 233
  on race and labor, 62, 89, 91

East, Clay, 108, 109
East St. Louis, Ill., 77–78
Ehrlichman, John, 186
Eisenhower, Dwight, 152, 153
Equal Employment Opportunities Commis-
  sion (EEOC), 175, 176–77, 178, 180,
  184, 210, 211, 214–15, 216, 221. See
  also affirmative action; Civil Rights
  Act (1964)
Ethridge, Mark, 127
Executive Order 8802, 123, 126
Executive Order 9346, 127
Executive Order 10988, 191

Fair Employment Practice Committee
  (FEPC), 6, 123–24, 125–27, 130–32,
  133, 134, 150, 152, 168, 232
Fair Labor Standards Act, 128, 143
"fair representation" (judicial doctrine),
  130
Farm Security Administration, 110
Farmers Alliances, 35
Feldman, Sandra, 202
Felton, William Mack, 53
Fernandina, Fla., 42
Fifteenth Amendment, 2
Filipino workers, 101
Firefighters Local Union #1784 v. Stotts,
  215
Fitzpatrick, John, 82
Fletcher, Arthur, 185–86
Fletcher, Bill, 229
Flint, Mich., 118
Florida
  African American workers in, 42, 98
  convict labor in, 47, 48, 50
  passes Right to Work law, 172
Folsom, Jim, 159
Food, Tobacco, Agricultural, and Allied
  Workers, 160, 162, 163. See also
  African American Workers, tobacco;
  communists, and labor movement; R.
  J. Reynolds Tobacco Company; United
  Cannery, Agricultural, Packing, and
  Allied Workers
Ford, Henry, and African American
  workers, 118–20
Ford Motor Company, 120–21, 167
  and African American workers, 113,
  119–23, 199
  See also Ford, Henry
Fort, William, 46
Fortune, 184
Fourteenth Amendment, 2, 232
"Free Labor" ideology, 10–11, 14

Freedmen's Bureau, 11, 14
Freedom Riders, 171

Gainesville, Fla., 93
Galveston, 39
Gary, Ind., 73, 75, 104, 132, 218
General Motors Corporation, 7, 118, 120, 148, 149, 199
Gladwell, Malcolm, 7
Goldfield, Michael, 5
Gompers, Samuel, 27, 28, 89, 65, 66, 89, 103
    and African American workers, 28–29, 60–61, 63, 67, 78–81
Gone with the Wind (film), 146
Gore, Al, 228
Gould, William, 5
Government Contract Committee, 152, 153. See also affirmative action
Graham, Frank, 159
Grant, Henry, 197
Great Depression, 70, 75, 101, 104–5, 106, 107–12, 137
Great Migration (1914–1929), 70–75, 76, 77, 93–94, 95, 96, 104–5, 113, 140, 146
Great Northern Railroad, 93
Green, Lucille, 89
Green, William, 90, 135, 136, 154
Green Pond Rifle Club, 34
Greenville to Atlanta Railroad, 48
Griggs v. Duke Power, 177, 212

Hale, Ulysses, 98
Hampton, Wade, 34
Haney-López, Ian, 231
Harper's Weekly, 11
Harris, Abram, 108
Harris, Lillian, 53
Hatch, Orrin, 182
Haynes, George Edmund, 94–95, 95–96, 99. See also United States Depart-
    ment of Labor, Division of Negro Economics
Haywood, Allan S., 161
Helms, Jesse, 213
Henderson, Donald, 160, 161, 162
Hill, Anthony, 228, 230
Hill, Arnold, 85, 102, 108
Hill, Herbert, 5, 151, 166, 168, 189
Hill, Lister, 159
Hinshaw, John, 218
Hispanic workers, 2, 3, 187–88, 225. See
    also immigration; Mexicans
Hocking Valley, Ohio, 54
Hoffa, James, 171

Homicide (television show), 222
Hood, Leamon, 205
Hood, William R., 167
Hospital Workers Local 1199, 191, 195–98
Hospital Workers Local 1199B, 196–97
Hotel and Restaurant Workers union
    (Hotel and Restaurant Employees), 90
Houston, 225
Houston, Charles, 130
Howard, General O. O., 11, 14
Hudnut, Richard, 213

I Am Somebody (film), 198
immigration, 22, 53–54
    and affirmative action, 188
    African Americans and, 100–103, 114, 230–31
    and labor movement, 65–66, 101
    legislation, 100–102, 187–88
    See also Chinese Exclusion Act
Immigration Act, 1924, 100–101, 187
Improved and Benevolent Order of Elks, 85
Indianapolis, 213
Industrial Workers of the World (IWW), 68, 115
injunctions (in labor disputes), 100, 102–3
Inland Steel Corporation, 218
International Association of Machinists, 63, 86, 124–25, 136
International Brotherhood of Boilermakers,
    Iron Shipbuilders, Forgers and Helpers
    (IBB), 125, 130–31
International Brotherhood of Electrical
    Workers, 182
International Brotherhood of Teamsters,
    62, 68, 136–37, 154–55, 164
International Ladies' Garment Workers'
    Union (ILGWU), 112, 166
International Longshoremen's and Ware-
    housemen's Union (ILWU), CIO, 137, 155
International Longshoremen's Association,
    91, 136
International Paper Corporation, 180
International Union of Marine and
    Shipbuilding Workers of America, 133–34
International Union of Mine, Mill, and
    Smelter Workers, 98, 113, 155, 156, 157, 160, 162, 163
International Union of Operating Engi-
    neers, 182
ironworkers' union (International Associa-
    tion of Bridge, Structural and Orna-
    mental Iron Workers), 185
Ives-Quinn Act, 150

J. P. Stevens and Co., 178
Jack Benny Program (radio show), 146
Jackson, Maynard, 190 204–6, 207
Jackson Memorandum, 180
Jacksonville, Fla., 39, 42
Japanese, exclusion of, 100
Johns Hopkins University Hospital, 198
Johnson, Andrew, 12
Johnson, Henry, 117
Johnson, Lyndon, 185, 195
   and civil rights, 152–53, 176
Johnstone, J. W., 83
Joseph James, et al. v. Marinship Corporation, et al., 131
"Justice for Janitors," 225

Kaiser Aluminum, 181
Kaiser Aluminum & Chemical Corporation and United Steelworkers of America, AFL-CIO v. Brian F. Weber, 181–82
Kansas-Nebraska Act, 1854, 23
Kennedy, Anthony, 214
Kennedy, John F., 191
   and civil rights, 152–53, 174
Kerry, John, 228
Key West, 42
King, Coretta Scott, 197, 198
King, Martin Luther, Jr., 171, 198, 224
   and labor movement, 173, 176, 191–92
   and March on Washington (1963), 1, 164
   and Memphis sanitation strike, 193–95
   murder of, 195
King, Martin Luther, Sr., 206
Kirk, Dwight, 233
Knights of Labor (Noble Order of the Knights of Labor), 26–28, 65, 138
   and African American workers, 27, 31, 35, 36, 37–38, 68, 115
Korean War, 141, 148, 190
Ku Klux Klan, 98, 107, 165, 166, 180

Labor Council for Latin American Advancement, 228
labor unions
   conservative critique of, 5, 224
   general character and functions of, 4–7
   See also American Federation of Labor; American Federation of Labor–Congress of Industrial Organizations; Change to Win coalition; Congress of Industrial Organizations; *individual unions*
Laborers union (Laborers' International Union), 91
LaCour, Nat, 228
Lanham, Henderson L., 159

Larry, R. C., 180
League of Revolutionary Black Workers (LRBW), 200–201
Lewis, John L., 4, 112, 113, 120
Lincoln, Abraham, 11, 23–24
Lind, John, 93
Lindsay, John V., 202
Little Rock, 81, 152
Loeb, Henry, 194
Los Angeles, 185, 225
Losing the Race, 221
Louisiana Sugar Planters Association, 31
Louisville and Nashville Railroad, 130
Loury, Glenn, 3
Lucy, William, 194, 227, 228, 230

March, Herbert, 117
March on Washington (1941), 126
March on Washington (1963), 2, 164, 192, 198
Martin, Homer, 121
Marx, Karl, 25
Mays, Robert, 87
Mazey, Emil, 200
McAdoo, William, 97
McCain-Feingold Act (2002), 228
McCartin, Joseph A., 207
McClendon, Geneva, 146
McCord, William, 196
McCoy, Rhody, 202
McDaniel, Hattie, 146
McGovern, George, 226–27
McNeill, George, 40
McNutt, Paul, 127, 129
McWhorter, John, 221
Meany, George, 4, 164–65, 174, 194, 227
   and civil rights, 168, 169–71, 186–87
   clashes with Randolph, 169–70
   meatpacking industry, 71, 72, 73, 75, 81–85, 115, 144, 145, 150
Medical College Hospital (Charleston, S.C.), 195
Meese, Edwin, 212
Memphis, 97, 156, 160
   sanitation workers' strike, 193–95, 205, 206
   See also King, Martin Luther, Jr.
Memphis Public Works Department, 193
Messenger, 89
Mexican War, 3
Mexicans, 3, 22, 187–88
   workers, 63, 101
Middleton, Henry, 33
Miller, Kelly, 85
Milwaukee, 54, 74, 226
Mitchell, George, 113

Mitchell, H. L., 108–9
Mobile, Ala., 39, 132, 133, 137
Montgomery, Ala., 195
Montgomery Advertiser, 72
Montgomery Ward, 144
Moreno, Paul, 5
Morgan City, La., 31
Morrison, Toni, 4
Moultrie, Mary, 196
Murray, Philip, 4, 115, 134, 154, 162
Muscle Shoals, Ala., 93–94
Myers, Isaac, 25
Myers, Samuel L., Jr., 222
Myrdal, Gunnar, 136

National Alliance of Postal Employees
   (NAPE), 86
National Association for the Advancement
   of Colored People (NAACP), 5, 59,
   95, 126, 157, 178, 217
   and African American workers, 56, 108,
   125, 205
   and labor movement, 80, 84, 112–13,
   115, 120, 122, 128, 130, 138, 166,
   168, 173, 189, 192–93, 205
   Legal Defense Fund, 179
National Association of Letter Carriers, 86
National Association of Machinists, 28–29
National Association of Postal Employees,
   91
National Cash Register, 149
National Colored Labor Union (NCLU),
   25–26
National Education Association (NEA),
   191
National Industrial Recovery Act, and labor
   relations, 110–11, 116, 118, 120, 127,
   137
National Labor Relations Act, 112, 127–
   28, 143, 154
National Labor Relations Board, 124, 127–
   28, 129, 130, 150, 154, 158. *See also*
   "fair representation"
National Labor Union (NLU), 25–26, 28
National Maritime Union, CIO, 155
National Negro Labor Council (NNCL),
   167–68, 227, 228
National Right to Work Committee, 173
National Urban League, 94, 96, 102, 148–49
   and African American workers, 108, 147,
   183, 205
   and labor movement, 80
National War Labor Board (World War I),
   92–93, 97–99
National War Labor Board (World War II),
   124, 129

Naturalization Act of 1790, 2
Needleman, Ruth, 218
Negro American Labor Council, 170–71,
   227, 228
Nelson, Bruce, 5
New Deal, 7, 110–13, 126, 127–28, 137,
   143
New Orleans, 36, 39–42, 61, 137, 195
New Orleans Board of Trade, 41
New Orleans Central Trades and Labor
   Assembly, 40, 41
"New South," 20–21, 44, 46, 48, 49, 51
New York City, 52, 53, 54, 71, 74, 113,
   147, 195, 201–4
New York Times, 170
   reports on urban black conditions, 219,
   222
Newark, 185
Nissan Motor Co., 219
Nixon, Richard, 152, 185–87, 188–89, 226
Norfolk, Va., 56, 104
Norris-LaGuardia Act (1932), 102–3
North American Free Trade Agreement
   (NAFTA), 217–18
North Carolina Highway Commission, 50
no-strike pledge, WWII, 155
NYPD Blue (television show), 222

Ocean Hill–Brownsville, conflict, 201–4
O'Connor, Sandra Day, 214
Office of Federal Contract Compliance
   (OFCC), 176, 189, 209–10, 211, 216.
   See also affirmative action; Equal
   Employment Opportunities Commission
Office of Production Management, 127
"Operation Dixie," 159–61
Order No. 4, 187, 188, 189
Orfield, Gary, 219
Origins of the New South, 42
Owen, Chandler, 89

Packard Motor Car Co., 133
Packinghouse Workers Industrial Union, 117
Packinghouse Workers Organizing
   Committee, 117–18
Palmer, A. Mitchell, 89
Parchman prison farm, Mississippi, 48, 49,
   50. *See also* chain gangs; convict
   leasing; New South
Parrish, Richard, 171
Pennsylvania Railroad, 71
Pensacola, Fla., 39, 42
Pepper, Claude, 159
Philadelphia, 52, 54, 59, 68, 74, 81, 113,
   146, 151, 185–87, 188–89, 226
   transit strike in (1944), 133.

Philadelphia Negro, The, 58
Philadelphia Plan, 185–87, 188–89
Philadelphia Transportation Company, 133
Philip Morris Company, 180
Phillips, Wendell, 24
Phillips County, Ark., race-labor conflict in, 35–36
Pinto Island, Ala., 132
Pittsburgh, 71, 73, 74, 79, 104, 113, 142, 187
Pittsburgh Courier, 101
"Plans for Progress," 153
Poor People's Campaign, 192
Portland, Ore., 130
Posner, Richard, 212
Powderly, Terence V., 66
Powell, Daniel, 165
President's Committee on Equal Employment Opportunity, 152–53. *See also* affirmative action
prison farms, 48, 49, 50. *See also* convict leasing; New South
Professional Air Traffic Controllers (PATCO), 207
Proposition 13 (California referendum), 206
Puerto Rican workers, 166, 195
Pugh, Mary, 32
Pullman, George, 88
Pullman Porters and Maids Protective Association, 88
Pullman Sleeping Car Company, 54, 83, 87–89, 103, 145. *See also* Brotherhood of Sleeping Car Porters; Randolph, A. Philip

R. J. Reynolds Tobacco Company, 145–46
Radio Corporation of America, and African American workers, 149
Railroads
    and African American workers, 19, 20, 23, 29, 54, 57, 60, 62–64, 70, 71, 76, 78, 86–88, 91, 93, 96–97, 102, 106–7, 127, 129–30, 130–31, 135, 145, 153–54
    unions, 5, 29, 57, 60, 62–64, 70, 76, 78, 85, 86–87, 89–91, 97, 101, 102, 103, 106–7, 126, 135, 145, 168, 170
    See also Brotherhood of Sleeping Car Porters; *individual unions*
Railway Labor Act (1926), 102, 103, 129, 130, 153–54
    1934 amendments to, 127
Railway Men's International Benevolent and Industrial Association (RMIBIA), 87
Rains, Albert, 159

Ramsay, Claude, 165
Randolph, A. Philip, 126, 138, 145, 164, 176, 189, 225
    background and agenda, 75–76, 89–91, 103–4, 105
    and Fair Employment Practice Committee, 126–27
    and immigration, 101
    and labor legislation, 103–4, 128–29
    relations with labor movement, 125–26, 136, 137, 154, 168–71
    See also Brotherhood of Sleeping Car Porters; Fair Employment Practice Committee
Raskin, A. H., 170
Ray, James Earl, 195
Reagan, Ronald, 207, 211, 212, 213, 214, 215, 226
Reconstruction (post–Civil War), 1, 9, 10, 15, 44–45, 92, 124, 137
"Redeemers, " 31
Reich, Robert, 224
Republican Party
    1920s, 100
    post–World War II, 150, 151, 152, 155, 184, 211–12, 213
    Reconstruction era, 26, 31, 33
    See also Bush, George H. W.; Eisenhower, Dwight; Nixon, Richard; Reagan, Ronald
Retail, Wholesale, and Department Store Workers Union, 195
Reuther, Victor, 135
Reuther, Walter, 4, 7, 161, 164, 171, 172, 197, 198–99
    and African American workers, 134, 135, 167
    See also United Automobile Workers of America
Reynolds, William Bradford, 211–12
rice production, 14
    race-labor conflict in, 30, 32–34
Richmond, Va., 36
right-to-work laws, 164, 172–73
Roediger, David, 5
Roosevelt, Franklin D., 109, 110, 126, 128, 131
Rothstein, Richard, 221
Rustin, Bayard, 176, 189, 201, 225–26. *See also* A. Philip Randolph Institute

St. Joe Paper Company, 180
St. Petersburg, Fla., sanitation workers' strike, 192–93, 205
San Francisco, 67
Sargent, Frank, 66

Savannah, Ga., 39
Scalia, Antonin, 214
Schoemann, Peter T., 184, 185
seniority, 149, 166–67, 179
Service Employees International Union,
    223, 225
Shanker, Albert, 201
sharecroppers, 15–19, 109
sharecropping, 13, 15–19, 51
Shipyard Negro Organization for Victory,
    130
Shultz, George, 186, 187
Simmons, Marian, 145
Sinyai, Clayton, 7
Skrentny, John, 3, 4
Sledge v. J. P. Stevens, 178
Smith, Hazel, 145
Smith-Connally Act (1943), 133
"social equality," 36–37
Social Security Act, 143
South Africa, 228
South Carolina, 13–14, 71
    race-labor conflict in, 30, 31, 32–34
Southern Christian Leadership Conference
    (SCLC), 191–92, 196–97, 201, 205
"Southern Federation of Labor," 165
Southern Tenant Farmers Union (STFU),
    109–10
Soviet Union, 155, 156, 161
Sowell, Thomas, 221
Sparrows Point, Md., 132
Steel industry, 20–21, 23, 53, 71, 73, 75,
    79, 98, 115, 129, 218
Steele, Bester William, 130
*Steele v. Louisville & Nashville Railroad
    Company, Brotherhood of Locomotive
    Firemen and Enginemen, et al.,* 131,
    153–54
Stern, Andy, 228–29
Steward, Ira, 25
Stockyards Labor Council, 82, 83, 84
strikebreaking, 38, 39, 57–58, 69, 82, 83,
    103
strikes
    air traffic controllers, 207
    automobile workers, 120, 122
    coal miners, 38, 69
    cotton workers, 35–36
    "hate" strikes, World War II, 132–33
    hospital workers, 175, 195–98, 199
    longshoring, 39–42
    port workers, 42
    post–World War II, 155
    Pullman Sleeping Car Company, 83
    rice workers, 30, 32–34
    sanitation workers, 175, 190, 192–95, 204–6

shipyard workers, 132–33
steelworkers, 79
sugar workers, 30–32, 34
teachers, 201–4
transit workers, 133
Sugar production, 13, 14
    race-labor conflict in, 30–32, 34
Sunflower County, Miss., 49
Sweeney, John, 225, 228, 229
Swift and Co., 116
Swing, Raymond, 98

Taft, William Howard, 98, 99
Taft-Hartley Act, 163, 172
Talmadge, Eugene, 161
Taney, Roger B., 22, 231
tenant farmers. *See* sharecroppers; share-
    cropping
Tennessee Coal and Mining Company, 47
textile industry, 21–22, 160, 161, 178–80,
    217–18
Textile Workers Union of America, CIO,
    161
Thibodaux, La., 32
Thomas, Clarence, 215
Thomas, Norman, 109
Thomas, R. J., 134
Tillman, Ben, 83
To Secure These Rights (federal government
    report), 151–52
Tobacco production, 14
Townsend, Willard, 131
Toyota Motor Corp., 219
Trade Union Unity League, 117
Transport Workers Union, 133
Trevellick, Richard, 24
Truly Disadvantaged, The, 220
Truman, Harry, 151–52
Tucker, Rosina, 145
*Tunstall v. Brotherhood of Locomotive
    Firemen and Enginemen, et al.,* 131
Turner, Doris, 195

United Association of Journeymen and
    Apprentices of the Plumbing and Pipe
    Fitting Industry, 64, 184–85
United Automobile Workers (UAW-AFL),
    122
United Automobile Workers of America
    (UAW-CIO; UAW-AFL-CIO), 120–23,
    154–55, 161, 163, 198–99
    and African American Workers, 198–201,
    132–33, 134, 135, 149, 166, 167
    and civil rights, 1, 164, 192, 192, 198–99
    Skilled Trades Department, 149, 199
    See also Reuther, Walter

United Brotherhood of Carpenters and Joiners, 182
United Cannery, Agricultural, Packing, and Allied Workers, 155, 156, 157. *See also* communists, and labor movement; Food, Tobacco, Agricultural, and Allied Workers
United Electrical Workers, CIO, 155, 160, 163
United Federation of Teachers, 201, 202
United Furniture Workers, CIO, 157
United Mine Workers of America (UMW), 38–39, 57, 62, 67–68, 68–69, 91, 110–13
United Mine Workers of America Journal, 111
United Packinghouse Workers, 164, 192
United Paperworkers International Union, racial policies of, 179–80
United States Department of Agriculture, 50, 92, 94
United States Department of Commerce, 94
United States Department of Justice, 49, 133, 176–77
United States Department of Labor, 73, 92, 94, 131, 189
  Bureau of Labor Statistics, 224
  Division of Negro Economics, 77, 92, 94–95, 96, 99
  Women's Bureau, 144
United States Employment Service, 93, 96, 131
United States Mediation Board, 129, 130, 154. *See also Steele v. Louisville & Nashville Railroad Company, Brotherhood of Locomotive Firemen and Enginemen, et al.; Tunstall v. Brotherhood of Locomotive Firemen and Enginemen, et al.*
United States Post Office, 54, 86
United States Railroad Administration, 78, 87, 92, 96–97, 99–100. *See also* African American workers, in railroads; railroads, unions
United States Steel Corporation, 218
United States Supreme Court, 110
  civil rights cases, 59, 130, 152, 153, 158, 202, 214
  See also individual cases
United States v. Local 189, 179
United Steelworkers of America, 134, 154–55, 163, 166, 167, 181, 194

Van Wagoner, Murray D., 122

Vardaman, James K., 49
Vietnam War, 188–89, 199, 201, 204, 227
Villaraigosa, Antonio, 231
Villard, Oswald Garrison, 59

Wagner, Robert F., 128
Walker, C. J., 53
Wallace, George, 226
Wallace, Henry, 162
Walsh, Frank, 98, 99
Ward's Cove Packing Company v. Atonio, 215
Warren, Earl, 152
Washerwomen's Association of Atlanta, 146–47
Washington, Booker T., 29, 30, 56, 58, 59, 72
Washington, D.C., 96, 185
Washington, Katie Mae, 145
Washington Post, 222–23
Wayne State University, 199
Weber, Brian, 181–82
Webster, Milton, 138
Weeks, Barney, 165
Weyerhaeuser Corporation, 179
When Work Disappears, 220
White, George, 74
White, Walter, 122, 126, 128
White Citizens Councils, 164, 165
"Whiteness," scholarship relating to, 2
Whittier, John Greenleaf, 24
Who Is White? 2
Wilkins, Roy, 120, 168
Wilson, William B., 78, 93, 94, 95, 99
Wilson, William Julius, 220, 221
Wilson, Woodrow, 93, 212
Wilson Meats, 116
Winning the Race, 221
Winston-Salem, N.C., 145–46, 156, 157, 160–61, 162, 163
Wire, The (television show), 222
Women workers, African American, 42, 55, 57, 73–74, 123, 124, 139, 142–47, 210–11, 217
Woodward, C. Vann, 42
Wurf, Jerry, 194

Yancey, George, 2, 231
"Yankee Girl" (poem), 24
Young, Coleman, 167
Young Women's Christian Association, 147